Process, Form, and Substance

A Rhetoric for Advanced Writers

S·E·C·O·N·D E·D·I·T·I·O·N

Richard M. Coe

Simon Fraser University

Prentice Hall, *Englewood Cliffs, New Jersey 07632*

Library of Congress Cataloging-in-Publication Data

COE, RICHARD M.
  Process, form, and substance : a rhetoric for advanced writers /
Richard M. Coe.—2nd ed.
    p.   cm.
  ISBN   0-13-326604-4
  1. English language—Rhetoric.   I. Title.
PE1408.C5426 1990
808'.042—dc20   89-29676
                       CIP

Editorial/production supervision: F. Hubert
Cover design: Donna Wickes
Manufacturing buyer: Mary Ann Gloriande

 © 1990, 1981 by Prentice-Hall, Inc.
A Division of Simon & Schuster
Englewood Cliffs, New Jersey 07632

Previously published under the title
Form and Substance: An Advanced Rhetoric

Printed in the United States of America

10   9   8   7   6   5   4   3   2   1

ISBN   0-13-326604-4

Prentice-Hall International (UK) Limited, *London*
Prentice-Hall of Australia Pty. Limited, *Sydney*
Prentice-Hall Canada Inc., *Toronto*
Prentice-Hall Hispanoamericana, S.A., *Mexico*
Prentice-Hall of India Private Limited, *New Delhi*
Prentice-Hall of Japan, Inc., *Tokyo*
Simon & Schuster Asia Pte. Ltd., *Singapore*
Editora Prentice-Hall do Brasil, Ltda., *Rio de Janeiro*

To
Samuel P. Coe
my first and most important writing teacher

Kenneth Burke,
the great North American rhetorical theorist

and all the writing students
with whom I have learned
whatever I know about teaching writing

Contents

To the Instructor

Tнiс book is for students who already read and write well enough to survive at college or university, for good student writers who are trying to get better. Although I have been careful to keep the text readable, this is not a simplified presentation.

Minimally, *Process, Form, and Substance* is addressed to student writers who have college-level reading abilities and can already write 500-word essays well enough to get good grades in a college writing course. Though they still may make some sentence-level errors, they know most of the so-called "basics" and write clear, correct sentences and coherent paragraphs most of the time (at least when they are in control of the subject matter).

There is no shortage of textbooks, written at a tenth grade reading level, that explain the basics of the writing process and help students produce the quality of writing required at college or university. Because it assumes student writers who start with some degree of competence, *Process, Form, and Substance* can move from straightforward to more sophisticated processes, forms and writing techniques. It can cover material ordinary textbooks never reach.

While it is certainly possible to make generalizations about writing, each writer is an individual. Not all writers write the same way, and a strategy that is effective for some writers—or readers—may not work for others. I doubt if anyone will want to master all the heuristics and other techniques for getting started that are discussed in Chapter 2. But rather than imposing my own preferences, I leave it to individual instructors and students to make their own selections, to choose the ones that work for them. At any event, it is probably more important for students to grasp the concept of heuristics— and the possibility of inventing their own heuristics to serve their own special purposes—than to master any one standard heuristic.

The aim is for students to come to understand their own writing processes— and how to intervene in their own processes in order to improve the quality of both process and product. They should acquire techniques for dealing with process problems (e.g., procrastination). And they should come to understand how a weakness in their written product can be eliminated by changing the part of their writing process which produces it.

It is useful for student writers to understand writing as both a creative and a communicative process, as both psychological and social. To become sophisticated writers, prepared for the kinds of writing they will likely face beyond college, they should learn to deal with complex writing tasks and contexts (e.g., writing for multiple or hostile audiences). They should learn to write for widely divergent purposes, audiences and occasions. They should not only master academic discourse, but also learn to analyze the conventions of other discourses, to understand those conventions as applications of basic rhetorical principles.

Form and Process. Over the past twenty-five years, traditional formalist approaches to teaching composition have gradually been giving way to process approaches for the development of writing abilities. Because those who raised the banner of process did so in opposition to the inadequacies of traditional formal approaches, an unfortunate dichotomy was created. But any effective writing course should help students with their writing processes; and, one way or another, any effective writing course must help students deal with conventions and other formal structures.

Process, Form, and Substance is very much a process textbook, firmly committed to the assumption that the best way to improve someone's writing is to improve the process that produces it. Chapters 1 through 5 take a pure process approach. Even such topics as paragraphing, titles, openings, transitions, endings, and conventions are discussed not formally, but in terms of how they facilitate the reading process—hence in Chapter 4, where writing is discussed in specific relation to readers.

But there is no need to throw out the baby with the bathwater: writing is a *form*-ing process. If we understand form in relation to function and process, if we understand formal structures as they function in social and individual creative and communicative processes, there is no need to adopt an either/or, which-side-are-you-on mentality. We can understand standard rhetorical structures as prepared ways of responding, as a social memory of effective strategies for responding to certain types of writing tasks and situations. The formal structure of a particular piece of writing is in this sense like a fossil memory of the strategic process used to produce that text. And standard structures represent the time-tested social processes of a discourse community.

Chapters 6 through 9 of this book, therefore, discuss in both formal and rhetorical terms the basic structures that underlie most thinking and writing. These chapters cover the traditional modes of discourse (narration, description, explanation, and persuasion) and the traditional patterns of development (comparison/contrast, classification and division, definition, analogy, exemplification, process analysis, causal explanation, and logical progression). Most of this material will be familiar, but with a difference that matters, a difference that allows it to be integrated into a process approach. Rhetorical structures are treated not only as patterns for arranging material, but also as modes of inquiry, strategies for discovering and developing material. Thus the section on process analysis in Chapter 8 can help students develop more sophisticated insights when they are analyzing their own writing processes in Chapter 1.

In Chapter 10, the process and formal approaches come together. Instead of teaching particular special types of writing—there are, after all, so many, and the world is changing too quickly to allow us to predict accurately which our students will need five or ten years hence—this chapter is built around a heuristic for analyzing and teaching oneself any genre of writing. Much of the chapter is devoted to academic discourse (including the research paper) because that is the immediate concern of most student writers. But the conventional formal features of academic discourse are explained in terms of their social functions, in terms of how they serve the purposes of the academic discourse community. In addition to developing a deeper understanding of academic discourse, students learn to analyze the conventional structures of any discourse community as manifestations of that community's social and rhetorical processes.

In short, the core of this book is Chapters 2 through 5, which help students master that intertwined set of creative, cognitive, communicative, social languaging processes we call writing. Chapter 1 can help focus students' attention to take best individual advantage of the other chapters. Chapters 6 through 9 present tried and proven strategies for achieving basic writing purposes. Chapter 10 not only explains academic writing, it also offers students a strategy for teaching themselves whatever types of writing they may want or need to master.

There are, of course, many ways to use any textbook. When I teach from this book, I take students through the first half more or less in order, starting with either Chapter 1 or Chapter 2. I refer them to particular sections of Chapters 6–10 that are relevant to particular writing tasks. If they are analyzing their own writing processes in Chapter 1, I have them read the section on process analysis in Chapter 8. When they are learning to analyze audiences and deal with readability in Chapter 4, I have them read Chapter 9 and write persuasions (and because it is the appropriate heuristic for inventing arguments, I also review Aristotle's *topoi*, Chapter 2, pages 89–96). Because my belief is that, in the end, a successful teacher helps students get to where they do not need a teacher any more, I usually end my advanced course with Chapter 10, which teaches them how to teach themselves new genres.

Many writing textbooks and teachers organize according to the classical pattern, teaching invention, arrangement and style in that order. *Process, Form, and Substance* adapts easily to such an approach if one simply teaches the basic patterns of arrangement, Chapters 6–8, in conjunction with Chapter 3 (and keeps Chapter 9 paired with Chapter 4).

Alternatively, in a course based on patterns of development, one could work from Chapter 6 through to the end, referring to sections of the first five chapters as the processes they discuss become relevant to particular writing problems. Or one could use Chapter 1 to define goals and then move to whatever parts of the book are most relevant to those goals. Or one could start with Chapter 10, use it as a basis for investigating the particular types of writing, and then move to the parts of the book that are most relevant to producing those types of writing.

Tradition and the Individual Talent

Process, Form, and Substance is based on the most recent research and theory. It deals with writing as a learning process, as a cognitive process of thinking and feeling, as a communicative process, as a social process that takes place in discourse communities. Because it makes no sense to ignore centuries of accumulated insight, however, *Process, Form, and Substance* is also based on two venerable, intertwined traditions: humanism and rhetoric. Though the emphasis is practical, I believe it matters that students understand this book is just not one person's opinion, but also a distillation of a 2500-year tradition informed by contemporary research.

Epigraphs. For that reason, every chapter and section begins with epigraphs that represent both traditional and "state of the art" knowledge about writing. These epigraphs are, no doubt, the most difficult reading in the book. I tell students not to worry if, when they start to read a chapter, they cannot understand the epigraphs. But after we have finished with that chapter, I often go back to one of the epigraphs and ask students to explain how it relates to what they have learned; this serves both as a stimulation and as kind of test of how well the chapter has been understood.

Cross-references. This book contains significant new material as well as traditional material that may be unfamiliar. Since most readers will not be reading the entire book from beginning to end, they may run into concepts or terms that are unfamiliar even though explained elsewhere in the book. Consequently, I have included many cross-references, as well as an index. But students should not feel compelled to check every cross-reference. If they understand the particular passage, they will generally do better to ignore the cross-reference and get on with their reading.

Instructor's Manual. Both to guide students and instructors who might want to learn more about some particular concept or technique and, as with the epigraphs, to make some intellectual antecedents explicit, the first edition of this book contained a feature unusual in composition textbooks: suggestions for additional reading. For the second edition, these suggestions have been expanded and moved to an instructor's manual. In addition to references to textbooks that have especially useful treatments of particular topics and to key readings in both Classical and New Rhetoric, these suggestions now include a bit of background reading specifically for instructors. More important, for instructors new to a rhetorical process approach, the instructor's manual makes explicit underlying principles and framing assumptions. And, of course, it provides pedagogical materials and suggestions.

Entitlement

Those who used the first edition of this book will notice the title has been revised to include the word *process*. It is somewhat unusual, though hardly unprecedented, to change a title while producing a new edition. But this book was always about writing as a *process* that *forms substance*, always based on Aristotle's assertion that substance is created when matter is formed. Without the word *process*, the title was inaccurate. In both editions, Part I is pure process approach, Part II an attempt to find a place within process for a reconceived, rhetorical presentation of the strategies and insights embodied in traditional forms. One of the major themes of this book is that words matter because, by titling, they create emphasis, influence perceptions and interpretations. Thus it seems especially important to provide an accurate title.

Acknowledgments

I have been influenced by certain superior textbooks. In alphabetical order, the most significant are Ann Berthoff's *Forming/Thinking/Writing*, Edward Corbett's *Classical Rhetoric for the Modern Student*, Peter Elbow's *Writing Without Teachers* and *Writing With Power*, Ken Macrorie's *Telling Writing*, Martin and Ohmann's *The Logic and Rhetoric of Exposition*, Joseph Williams' *Style: 10 Lessons in Clarity and Grace*, and Young, Becker, and Pike's *Rhetoric: Discovery and Change*. These titles represent a wide span of approaches, and not all have not been "best sellers." But they are intelligent, innovative, and have been influential.

I also wish to thank the following people for reviewing the text in manuscript: Janet H. Carr (Northeastern University), Kevin Dungey (University of Maryland), John Hagman (Western Kentucky University), George E. Kennedy (Washington State University), Edward Klein (University of Notre Dame), Mary E. McGann (Rhode Island College), Jeannette P. Morgan (University of Houston), James E. Porter (Purdue University), Duane H Roen (University of Arizona), Mike Rose (University of California, Los Angeles), Hephzibah Roskelly (University of Massachusetts, Boston), Kathy Shaw (Modesto Junior College), Laurel Sutton (Oral Roberts University) and Richard Young (Carnegie-Mellon University). Many of them made very useful, supportive, and insightful suggestions. I also wish to thank Phil Miller, Nancy Perry, Frank Hubert, and Ann Knitel of Prentice-Hall for their faith, support, flexibility, and cheerful attention to the kinds of detail that matter.

I am grateful to Sheila Cano and Jeannie Kamins for permission to reproduce their artwork. I am also grateful for copyright permissions from the Association for the Study of Afro-American Life and History for Ossie Davis' words; from the Anti-Defamation League of B'nai B'rith for an image from the "Rumor Clinic"; from Viking-Penguin for facsimile manuscript pages from *Writers at Work: The Paris Review Interviews*, First, Second, and Third Series. Copyright 1957, 1958, 1963, 1967 by The Paris Review, Inc. Reprinted by permission of Viking-Penguin, a Division of Penguin Books, U.S.A., Inc.; from Harper & Row for an excerpt from Richard Wright's *Black Boy* (which begins on page 125 of this text), copyright 1945 by Richard Wright, copyright renewed 1973 by Ellen Wright; from the Institute for Social Journalism for Jon Bennett's "Who Wrote That Viewpoint"; from Oxford University Press for two paragraphs from Edward P.J. Corbett's *Classical Rhetoric for the Modern Student* and for a sample essay from Mina Shaughnessy's *Errors and Expectations*; from McGraw-Hill for an image from R.L. Gregory's *The Intelligent Eye*; and from the University of Illinois Press for a puzzle picture from the *American Journal of Psychology*.

Student Writing

This book could not have been written without the gracious permission of many students to use their writing as examples. Virtually without exception, these students can now write much better than the examples indicate, but they have allowed their earlier writing to be reproduced here so that other students might learn more easily. Reviews of the first edition of this textbook concurred that the student writing is among its greatest strengths; certainly it is this writing that concretizes the principles and processes *Process, Form, and Substance* attempts to teach. So I here acknowledge them, first and last.

Rick Coe

To the Student

I F you are using this book, you are probably already a pretty good writer. Not as good as you would like to be, not as good as you can be, but better than average. To grow as a writer, you must concentrate on overcoming your weaknesses, on learning what you do not yet know. But it is also important to keep firmly in mind that you do write better than the average person, probably also better than you yourself wrote not very long ago. This textbook is based on the most up-to-date theory and research, and also on a venerable 2500-year tradition of rhetoric and humanism. With its help, you will soon write both more successfully and more confidently than you already do.

A Process Approach. The most effective way to improve your writing is to improve the process by which you produce it. Your written products can become more satisfying and successful. And the process itself can become more fruitful and fulfilling.

If you were trying to help a friend with her tennis serve, you would not just tell her to read the relevant passage in the official rule book, take her to Wimbledon to show her how the pros serve, and then repeat over and over again, "No, no! Don't hit the ball into the net." Knowing the rules is useful, and watching the pros can be inspirational. But it would be more important to do a detailed analysis of how your friend actually serves. Perhaps you would videotape her serving and look at the video in slow motion. You would contrast that video with analyses of how expert tennis players serve. You would locate the cause of the problem—perhaps she is reaching too high—and suggest how she should change her process. You would give her exercises designed to adjust her reach and develop an effective serve. You would have her practice serving in real or simulated game situations. And during all this you would be careful to give encouragement as well as criticism. In short, to help her produce a better serve, you would work on improving the process that produces her serve.

If such a "process approach" makes sense for developing relatively simple physical abilities like serving a tennis ball, it makes even more sense for developing writing abilities. If you want to improve your writing, you want help with your writing process. It is not enough just to learn the conventions of good form, to examine models of expert writing, to write and have the results criticized. You need to look at the process that produces the written product, to pay attention to *how* successful writers produce effective writing.

By shifting your attention to writing as process, a process approach can develop your writing abilities more quickly—and without damaging your self-confidence.

Taken together, the first five chapters of this book constitute a comprehensive process approach to the development of writing abilities. These chapters discuss writing as a learning process, writing as a creative process, writing as a thinking process, writing as a communicative process, writing as a languaging process. For writing is not so much *a* process as a set of intertwined processes.

Because a process approach means paying attention to writing processes and how they can be improved to get better results, Chapter 1 focuses on the learning process. This chapter can help you examine your own writing process, define your strengths and weaknesses, and set specific goals. Thus it can help you make better use of the rest of the text.

Chapters 2 and 3 focus on writing as a creative process. Any creative process has two contradictory aspects: (1) encouraging inspiration, generating material and strategies; (2) finding focus, creating structure, and revising. Chapter 2 discusses creativity, getting started, and generating material. Chapter 3 focuses on the critical processes of organizing and revising, transforming what has been generated into well-structured, coherent writing. Chapter 3 also includes a discussion of collaborative writing and editing. Between them, these two chapters can help you guide your creative writing process.

Because writing is a communicative as well as a creative process, Chapter 4 focuses on writing for readers. It emphasizes the techniques by which writers make their writing coherent and accessible to readers. This chapter can help you produce readable prose. Then, in order to help you develop your style, Chapter 5 focuses on persona, voice, diction, and sentence structure.

A Forming Process.   Writing is a forming process. As you write, you shape your understandings; and you give them shapes your readers can grasp. There comes a point in the creative process when it is useful for writers to understand the structure of a contrast, definition, process analysis or causal explanation, to know the standard form for a term paper, research report, leaflet, business proposal, or whatever. Many standard structures represent tried and true strategies for achieving particular communicative goals.

Chapters 6–8 present the basic patterns of development that are also basic patterns of thought, important in most kinds of writing. These chapters also deal with issues like objectivity and problems like how to represent complex subjects without oversimplifying. Chapter 9 focuses on persuasive writing. Chapter 10 explains how to analyze any particular type of writing in order to learn it, and then illustrates that analytic process by applying it to academic discourse (especially term papers). After working through Chapter 10, you will have a much better understanding of the types of writing required at colleges and universities; you should also understand how you can teach yourself whatever type of writing you may want or need to do in the coming years.

Process, Form, and Substance begins with a focus on you and your learning process. It looks at writing as a creative process, a communicative process, a language process. It approaches writing as process, as structure, as strategy and finally as social process. Thus it ends with a focus on the communities of discourse, created by writing, within which writing works. None of these perspectives is the whole story; each can help you grow as writer. Each can help you see how to write more confidently and successfully, can help you make your writing more satisfying and fulfilling.

The Physical Process

A "bad back" or "stiff neck" is an occupational hazard for writers— more easily prevented than treated—and easily avoided by paying a little attention to the physical process of writing. Writing is often intense, and when our minds are intense most of us also tense our muscles. Writing is also sedentary, usually performed while sitting, and the human body is not well evolved for sitting hunched over a table, desk, or keyboard. A few simple precautions can save you a lot of pain and "down time."

1. Sit on a chair that helps you support your back and neck properly. The chair should be low enough so that your feet reach the floor easily; and you should be able to swing your knees easily out from under the table or desk. The ideal chair has a firm cushioned seat, slopes forward slightly, and swivels easily. (*Note*: kneeling chairs are designed to accomplish the same objective, albeit by a different strategy.)

2. Sit with the bottom of your spine pushed against the back of the chair, your feet flat on the floor or a short stool (not dangling). Check the relationship between your arms and the writing surface or keyboard. Your arms should reach straight from the elbows to the paper or keyboard, so a good writing table, desk, or keyboard is usually a few inches lower than your kitchen table.

3. Check also the relationship between your head and whatever you have to look at while writing—be that books, note cards, pieces of paper, or a computer screen. Your neck will be happier if you do not spend too much time looking too far down, up, or to the side. Computer screens should be at eye level. Papers or books you type from for extended periods should not lie flat on the table.

4. Take a break at least once an hour. Stand up, move around, shrug, and stretch.

Rick Coe

Process

C·H·A·P·T·E·R 1

Learning to Write

Put writing in your heart. . . . The scribe is released from manual tasks; it is he who commands.

ANCIENT EGYPTIAN

For the one point in which we have our greatest advantage over the brute creation is that we hold converse one with another and can reproduce our thought in words.

CICERO

People are animals that talk.

SASHA ALEXANDRA (AGE 3)

Of all those arts in which the wise excel,
Nature's chief masterpiece is writing well.

JOHN SHEFFIELD

Learn your ABC's, it is not enough, but learn them! . . . begin! You must know everything! You must take over the leadership!

BERTOLT BRECHT

THIS chapter is about learning to write better. It will help you assess your present writing abilities and define the tasks before you. It will provide both a platform from which you can grow and a basis for evaluating that growth later. This chapter will help you focus your attention so that you can take maximum advantage of the rest of the book— so that you can learn what you as an individual most need and want to learn about writing.

People learn better when they have specific goals and strategies instead of vague intentions like, "I want to learn to write better." People also learn better when they participate actively in their own learning processes, when they set their own goals and help monitor their own progress. By the time you have worked your way through this chapter, you will have:

1. Defined your own motives, strengths, weaknesses, and ambitions as a writer.
2. Analyzed your own writing process.
3. Determined the relationship between your writing process and present weaknesses.
4. Set writing goals and devised plans for achieving those goals.

Because both learning and writing begin with motivation, this chapter begins with a discussion of motives—both practical and humanistic, for you have much to gain by treating writing not as a technical skill but as a humanistic discipline. Next comes a section about how people write—because the best way to improve the quality of your written products is to improve the *process* which produces them. The last section will help you define individual goals for yourself—because you are more likely to achieve clearly defined goals.

Why Write?

For in the other powers which we possess . . . we are in no respect superior to other living creatures. . . . Through [language] we educate the ignorant and appraise the wise; for the power to speak well is taken as the surest index of a sound understanding, and true, just, and well-ordered discourse is the outward image of a good and faithful soul. With this faculty we both contend against others on matters which are open to dispute and seek light for ourselves on things which are unknown; for the same arguments which we use in persuading others when we speak in public, we employ also when we deliberate in our own thoughts. . . . None of the things which are done with intelligence take place without the help of speech.

ISOCRATES

Studies of experienced, effective writers show that they are highly and specifically motivated. They are trying to accomplish something, and they know that whether they succeed will depend to a significant extent on the quality of their writing.

If you are reading this book, you are probably about to put considerable effort into your writing. To get the most benefit from that effort, you should be clear about your motives. If you are not well motivated, if you mostly just go through the motions, much of the effort you put into a writing course will likely be largely wasted.

Where you should focus your effort depends in part on just what you want to accomplish with your writing. What kinds of writing are you likely to do in your life, both in your work and on other occasions? If you have chosen a profession, check what kinds of writing it involves. You may be surprised—a typical engineer spends two days of every five writing reports, proposals and other such documents. What kinds of writing are you likely to do beyond your work? And what indirect benefits might you gain through the discipline of becoming a better writer? In what ways might becoming a better writer help you become a better person?

Practical Motives

Writing began in ancient times as a way of keeping records—a kind of social memory—and soon developed into an important means of communication. In spite of telephones, computers, audio and video recorders, and other new technologies for recording and communicating information, there is now more writing than ever. The ability to write is now more important to more people than ever in human history.

The ability to write with some degree of competence is one of the qualities that generally distinguishes professionals from other workers. To get a professional job, you usually must write, if only an application letter and a resumé. To do the job, you ordinarily must write: records, reports, proposals, recommendations, instructions, memoranda, and letters of various sorts. And, of course, you usually have to write in university courses just to qualify for a professional job.

The technology of writing is changing. Word processors are replacing typewriters. Inexpensive photocopying, computer networking, and FAX transmission have changed our relationship to the written word. Word processors have changed even the process of writing, largely by making revision easier. Even the nature of authorship is changing, as collaborative writing becomes increasingly common and important. For all the changes, however, technological advances have made writing more common and more important than ever.

This importance follows from the nature of our society. In a modern, specialized, computer-based, industrial society like ours, the division of labor is complex and hierarchical. The people who make important decisions are often far from the decision points: their awareness of options and consequences usually depends on written reports and on recommendations from specialists and experts. To make their decisions known and to get them implemented, moreover, the decision makers usually depend on written instructions and guidelines. In a complex and centralized society, this kind of information flow is crucial.

Much of this information is communicated in writing because writing has certain advantages over other means of communication. Unlike a conversation, writing is easily preserved. Unlike a recording, writing is easily skimmed, scanned, edited, or updated. And because writing is so important, a person who can write effectively gains a significant degree of power and respect.

The power of the written word extends to areas beyond your job. As a consumer in an economy where manufacturers, suppliers, and even sources of credit may be hundreds or thousands of miles away from users, your ability to write an effective letter of complaint may be crucial to your getting what you paid for—or even a response. A letter to the editor, a local union leaflet, a grant proposal for a community project—there are many uses to which you can put your ability to write. As a citizen in a large democratic society, your ability to write persuasively can make the difference between your opinion having some impact or having none at all.

What are *your* practical motives for writing?

Humanistic Motives

Beyond its pragmatic uses, writing also has personal and humanistic virtues. To write cogently, you must think cogently. To write effectively, you must understand people—both your readers and yourself. Learning to write well is part and parcel of developing your most human potentials, both rational and intuitive.

Writing is a discovery process as well as a communicative process. The act of writing usually forces you to explore, clarify, integrate, and sharpen your ideas. As you write you often must verify information and resolve contradictions. You must also organize ideas and perceive interrelationships. By the time you have your thoughts down on paper and revised, you usually have emerged with a deeper understanding—which is why term papers and essay tests are such important parts of a university education. This is why keeping a diary or journal can help you understand your own life. Academically, personally, and in many other ways, writing promotes insight.

To write effectively, moreover, you need a sense of audience. The ability to write is the ability to communicate with readers. Since not all readers are alike, the same message may have to be written somewhat differently for distinct groups of readers. To write effectively for readers who are not like yourself, you need to develop the sensitivity and empathy that will allow you to understand them. To write for readers who are part of some special community—be they engineers or mountaineers, auto mechanics or university graduates—you need to understand that community and its ways of using words.

To write honestly, you must also understand yourself. The tone of your writing, like the tone of your speaking voice, inevitably projects an image of who you are. To make this tone accurately and honestly reflect your motives and personality, you must have some sense of yourself.

Thus learning to write well means developing insights into your subject matter, your readers, and yourself. This is what Isocrates meant when he said, "True, just and well-ordered discourse is the outward image of a good and faithful soul." This is why writing is such a crucial part of a humanistic education.

You may achieve minimal competency at some particular, specialized type of writing—such as business writing, technical report writing, or news reporting—by just memorizing rules, practicing techniques, and following formulas. But the ability to write perceptively, thoughtfully, critically, and sensitively is more than a technical skill. To develop your ability to write excellently in any area, or to write even competently as a generalist, you must also develop your mind and heart.

At its highest development, writing is the creation and communication of insight. When Percy Bysshe Shelley wrote, "poets are the unacknowledged legislators of the world," he was asserting the creative power of language to shape the perceptions—and hence to influence the actions—of readers (as well as writers). That is the ultimate power of writing. Here the practical and humanistic reasons for learning to write well merge.

Writing 1a   Write a short letter or memo to your writing instructor outlining your motives for writing and for taking a writing course now. Be sure to mention what types of writing you have done in the past and expect to do in the future.

How People Write

When we speak of improving the mind we are usually referring to the acquisition of information or knowledge, or to the type of thoughts one should have, and not to the actual functioning of the mind. We spend little time monitoring our own thinking and comparing it with a more sophisticated ideal.

JAMES ADAMS

Good writers . . . guide their own creative processes.

LINDA FLOWER

The best way to improve the quality of your writing is to improve the process by which you create it. To be sure, the writing process is a means to an end: once the process of creation is complete, it is the written text that must communicate. Whether your goal is to evoke a feeling or to provoke a bureaucracy into taking action, it is the written text that must get the job done. But the quality of the written product depends on the quality of the creative process. A person who is having trouble writing or who wants to learn to write better should focus on the writing process.

Much of the guilt people feel about writing, moreover, is centered not on the written product itself, but on the writing process.

> I always procrastinate until the night before the deadline. Then I don't have any time to revise, and what I hand in is not my best work.
>
> I don't usually know what my thesis statement is until after I've written my draft. I can never produce an outline. There must be something wrong with me.

If your writing process is failing you—either because you are not producing the quality you want or because you spend too much time and suffer too much in the process—you should modify parts of your process. But remember that writing is very personal. What works best for one individual may or may not work well for another individual. Many would-be writers want formulas, and many textbooks offer such formulas. But there is no one right way to write. What works best for you is best for you.

Consider, for example, the outline, which makes many inexperienced writers feel guilty. Although some writers find outlining so useful they rarely start drafting without producing a detailed outline first, many writers use the first draft to discover what they are going to say—so they cannot produce an outline in advance. That is why many students, when required to hand in an outline, write the paper first and the outline second. Most writers actually make no more than a rough list of probable subtopics before starting their drafts. And Prof. Janet Emig's now classic study of student writers indicated that students who use outlines do not get better grades than those who do not use outlines.

The point is not about outlines, which have a number of uses (see pages 120–29). The point that *different people write differently*. What's more, the same writer may use different procedures for different types of writing. John Ciardi, for instance, uses outlines when he writes essays but not when he writes short stories.

Despite all the variation from one individual to another, we can make certain useful generalizations. We can define some basic guidelines to help each individual develop an effective writing process. Writing, of any type, is a creative process; and human creativity has been well studied in both ancient and recent times, by both scientists and practitioners. The writing process itself has also been much studied, recently with considerable rigor. Slavishly following a textbook formula may actually interfere with successful writing. But you can get good ideas about how to improve your writing process by learning how other people write.

Case Histories

Writing 1b Think of something you wrote recently (perhaps Writing 1a). Write down everything you did from the time you first got started on the topic (or received the assignment) to the time the written product was complete and ready for its readers. *After* you have drafted this narrative, revise it by inserting passages that explain how this particular writing was typical or atypical of the way you usually write.

Be careful: many people have a tendency to idealize the way they usually write and to think their processes are closer to the ''standard'' textbook procedure than they actually are. And be sure to consider various types of writing you may have done in the past few years (letters, a diary, school essays, reports, proposals, or whatever). *Note*: What you are doing here is a process analysis using the narrative as an example (see pages 282–91 on narration, pages 294–99 on examples, and pages 342–49 on process analysis).

In this analysis, details matter. Be sure to include enough detail so that readers get a good sense not only of what happens on paper but also of what you really do—and feel—when you write.

Generally, I stop while I am writing and revising the first draft to "putter about" the house. I straighten the cushions on the couch, vacuum the front room, or wash the dishes. I sometimes even begin a completely new activity, such as reading the newspaper, a magazine, or material for another course. While I am busy with these activities I may mull over ideas about the essay in my mind. If I do not have a lot of time before I have to start typing the final copy, I feel guilty about doing these various activities, which seem to delay what I really should be doing.

Because we had visitors while I wrote Assignment 1a and I wanted to complete the essay as quickly as possible, I wrote the first draft straight through, stopping only to make some minor revisions (correcting spelling errors and changing one or two words). I typed

the rough draft and left it until the night before the assignment
was due. I then made more major revisions, deleting or completely
changing some sentences, but not moving or deleting whole
paragraphs as I usually do when I have time to make such revisions.
As I typed the final copy (at about 1 a.m. on the due date), I made
some final revisions at the same time. I have found last semester's
pattern of having the final draft ready a few days before the essay
is due much easier on my nerves and expect to resume it.

Jim Boorman

In this passage, Jim gives us quite a clear idea of what he does while he writes. "Puttering" and "mulling," incidentally, are quite common as writers prepare to write. And washing the dishes or taking a bath encourages mulling much better than, say, watching television.

Just as he mentions particular chores he does when he "putters about," Jim should have included a more detailed account of what actually happens on paper, especially during revision. He could, perhaps, have given examples of sentence revisions and what motivated them. Specifics make this analysis useful. Do not report merely, "and I made some minor revisions while typing the final copy." What kinds of revisions did you make, and why? Was it merely a matter of correcting spelling and punctuation? Did you replace some simple words with more sophisticated synonyms? Did you rephrase—or delete—sentences to get rid of awkward structures? Did you add transitions? Did you rewrite the introduction?

After you have done this writing—or if you do not do it, after you have thought about how you write—it will be useful to compare writing processes with other writers who are more or less your peers. Looking at their writing processes can help you evaluate yours more realistically, help you realize that you are already doing many things well, and give you ideas about how you might change.

Here are two advanced composition students' analyses of their own writing processes. Although both started the course as relatively good writers, they lacked confidence in their writing abilities and felt guilty about the difficulties they had getting started.

Picking My Own Brain:
The Masochism of Writing

The writing process for me nearly always includes pressures that
I create. I seldom begin assignments well ahead of time and have
broken this pattern only in rare instances. I am also a formula
writer, using as a guide what I can recall of my somewhat patchy
high school composition courses. My procedure in writing the first
assignment this term was typical of my approach.

The day before the assignment was due, I had nothing but free time;

however, true to form, I filled up the available hours with finding things to do around the house. That afternoon I decided to try using my daily meditation as a source of inspiration. This worked well, I thought, and having observed the scenarios that my subconscious unfolded before my inner eye, I settled upon a topic—— "The English Class." Thereafter I discussed my choice with my husband and finally at 5:30 in the afternoon I sat down to write.

Once I have a vague idea of what I want to express in an essay, I jot down a rough outline. Usually I do not have an ending in mind. My outlines are little more than lists of words, each word or couple of words representing the main point in a paragraph. The word order corresponds to the order I intend to follow in arranging my paragraphs. Beginning with the first line on the list, I start work on the introductory paragraph. I may get as far as writing one or two sentences and then the revision begins. The rest of the exercise continues in similar fashion——I write, revising as I go, until I'm satisfied with the result. As the crossed-out and scratched-over streaks thicken and begin to obscure my vision, I write out a corrected copy on a clean page. For as long as the fresh page and neat writing remain free of marks and arrows, they help to clarify the form of the composition. In writing "The English Class," I revised the opening paragraphs about half a dozen times and in doing so ended up with a very different viewpoint from the original. This in turn altered the direction of the rest of the essay.

Closing paragraphs are not one of my strong points. I tend to deal with them when I get there. Then, in accordance with my formula, I attempt to sum up. My closing paragraphs are usually too brief and consequently do not adequately cover the overall theme of the writing. My formula requires organizing paragraphs in a logical sequence and concluding with an appropriate summary. In the case of "The English Class," this meant going from a general description of a room and a group of people to a description of a specific individual and ending with my subjective opinion of the whole lot put together.

Vicki Workman

What follows is excerpted from a piece entitled, ''Why I Cannot Write This Paper.'' (No less a writer than the journalist Tom Wolfe, incidentally, testifies that such explanations can be a good way to get a difficult assignment started.)

The process by which I construct my essays may be divided into four main stages: a gathering stage, a kernel stage, a general overhaul stage and a fine tuning stage (pardon the mixed metaphor).

The gathering stage is prior to any actual writing, aside from note-taking, and is mainly the period during which I gather thoughts and information pertinent to the general topic which my paper will be dealing with. I then organize the information within my mind and draw a conclusion which in turn becomes the central idea or theme of my essay.

Converting this central idea into a kernel sentence initiates the second stage of my writing process. I build my first draft about this kernel sentence, selectively incorporating the information gathered in stage one, i.e., quotes and paraphrased material. I then conclude the first draft with a summation of the general points of the essay.

During stage two I pay little or no attention to sentence structure, paragraph formation or transitions, and the organization is very loose; the overhaul of structural and stylistic defects is attempted in stages three and four. At stage three I try to structure my ideas according to a coherent pattern, which I have been formulating in my mind since stage one; this usually entails a degree of reorganization at every level from sentence structure through to whole sections. Also, it is at this stage that I reappraise the amount of information and expand or edit as deemed necessary.

Fine tuning is the fourth or final stage. In essence this stage is a continuation of stage three but on a more superficial level, my main concern being with the mechanical aspects of the paper, i.e., grammar and spelling.

Tom Longridge

The first problem for writers is getting started. This may be, in part, reluctance—though sometimes exhilarating, writing is usually strenuous—but some difficulty getting started is typical of creative processes.

The writing process begins with *purpose*, with reasons for writing. That may mean something you want to express, be it an experience, a feeling, or an opinion. It may mean that something you want to get or to do can best be obtained or accomplished by writing. It may mean that you have been assigned to write something, perhaps by a teacher, a supervisor, or some group to which you belong. Purpose is usually what brings you together with your pencil, pen, typewriter, or word processor in the first place. For Vicki and Tom, purpose included both the desire to improve as writers and a course assignment.

Within the parameters of purpose, writing logically begins with having or discovering something to say. That is what Vicki was doing as she found things to do around the house, meditated, and spoke with her husband. That is what Tom's gathering stage is about, whether he does it in the library or in his mind. Sometimes a purpose is so specific, it leads you immediately to your material. But writers often need to muck about a bit.

Many writing students, quite correctly, conceive of their writing problems as starting here: "But I don't have anything to say about that topic," or even more basically, "What should I write about?" These students are right. Except when a piece of writing is just an exercise, no one is likely to care how well it is written unless what it says is interesting, useful, or otherwise valuable. Even when your purposes define your topic and establish your thesis— as they often do in the workaday world—you still need something to say on the topic in support of the thesis. And that something may take some finding.

The main distinction between students and more experienced writers is that experienced writers have come to accept some difficulty getting started as an inevitable part of the writing process and no longer feel guilty about it. Instead, they allow time for it by starting well before the deadline. And they have techniques to help them discover their material more quickly and reliably (see Chapter 2).

Of course, having something significant to say is not enough. The word *composition* comes from the Latin verb *componere*, meaning "to put together." In a sense the central aspect of writing is the literal composing, the "putting together," of a pattern of meaning. Much of the meaningfulness of a piece of writing (as of any conception or communication) comes from the way information is organized. Information is not really information until it has been focused and put *in formation*.

This is what Tom is doing during stages two and three. This is what Vicki is doing as she jots down a rough outline and works and reworks her opening paragraphs. Many writers find the beginning hardest to write because they use the beginning to structure the rest of the piece. Tom's "kernel sentence" (i.e., the first sentence of the excerpt) structures the whole writing. It is not just another sentence, so it is not surprising that it takes him a long time to come up with it.

Other writers find it easier not to worry about structure (or make an outline) until after a draft has been completed. Sometimes they do not write an opening paragraph until the rest of the draft is done. Not surprisingly, such writers usually have an easier time getting started. This is because they have postponed problems of organization. They generate their material first and worry about organizing it later. Often they make outlines after the draft is written.

The difference is largely a matter of timing. Either way, the shaping— the giving form to substance—is basic to any creative or communicative process, and especially to writing. The process of ordering exposes the gaps and imbalances in the material being presented (and thus contributes to the discovery of more substance). The need to supply transitions for readers forces the discovery of interrelationships.

Similarly, some writers worry about language and style right from the beginning. Like Vicki, they revise as they go. Other writers, like Tom, try to postpone such matters until questions of substance and structure have been settled. For him, all but the most basic, substantive revision comes after drafting.

There would seem to be—and, up to a point, is—a certain efficiency in dealing with substance first, organization second, and style third. But real writers' composing processes rarely divide so neatly into stages. The common notion that we first collect information, second think about it, and third write it down is reductive and erroneous. To be sure, in the early phases "gathering" often predominates, but not to the exclusion of thinking or "wording." In intermediate phases, "thinking" and organizing tend to become primary. And "actual writing" may come later. But it is a mistake to separate thinking from writing, to imagine that one should wait until one's thinking is totally in order, and then "just writes it out."

Real writers rarely work that way. Tom, who is in this sense typical, is forming his thesis sentence between stages one and two; he is still developing and organizing information through his stage three. Rare indeed is the writer for whom composing sentences and paragraphs is not part of the process of forming and interrelating concepts. Most writers are playing with potential sentences, perhaps even revising sentence structure, during the earliest phases of composition. Trying to "think and *then* write" gets many would-be writers in trouble. In fact, it seems to contribute to writer's block (see pages 43–44). More typically, writers assert that they do not know what they think until they read what they have written.

All writers have to deal with matters of substance, structure, and style; but the appropriate process for doing so varies considerably from individual to individual. For other case histories, see pages 289 and 346–47.

Classical Rhetoric

The first great teachers of what we now call composition were Greeks and Romans of Classical times—Corax, Gorgias, Isocrates, Aristotle, Cicero, Quintilian, Augustine—and many of their insights remain useful today. They called their subject rhetoric, by which they meant using words persuasively. In keeping with the times, they taught their students to compose speeches, not written documents; but the kind of public speaking they taught began with speeches written out in advance and memorized. Though delivered orally, the speeches were very much written compositions. These rhetoricians, especially Isocrates, were also the great Classical educators, and they made rhetoric the core subject of advanced education because they believed that articulating and defending one's ideas develops both mind and heart. "A rhetorician," wrote Cicero, "is a good man speaking well."

Interestingly enough, the writing processes of real writers match the teachings of the classical rhetoricians more closely than they match traditional textbook procedure. In part this is because the classical rhetoricians emphasized that different individuals and circumstances require different strategies.

In the rhetorical tradition, which goes back to classical Greece, composition is conceived as beginning with the discovery or invention of arguments (Latin, *inventio*; Greek, *heuresis*), roughly equivalent to Tom's "gathering stage." The rhetoricians taught their students techniques for discovering what to say (see Chapter 2, especially pages 89–98).

The second major emphasis of classical rhetoric is the literal composing, the "putting together," of the invented "arguments" into an effective pattern (Latin *dispositio*; Greek, *taxis*). This is roughly equivalent to what Tom does in stages two and three. Although they emphasized the importance of remaining flexible and adapting to particular audiences and occasions, the classical rhetoricians taught specific structures to help their students arrange their compositions (see pages 385–91).

The choosing and combining of words and phrases, correctly and with style—what most people think of as "actual writing"—is the third emphasis of classical rhetoric (Latin, *elocutio*; Greek, *lexis*, *hermeneia*, or *phrasis*). Tom leaves most of this to his fourth stage. It is here that the emphasis of many modern English composition classes and textbooks has fallen, especially on correctness.

Although it is sometimes overemphasized, this aspect of writing matters. A poorly chosen word may not convey the intended concept. Awkward sentence structure may confuse readers. "Bad grammar" or nonstandard usage, moreover, conveys a significant message about the social background of the writer (which is why the upwardly mobile, lower middle class is typically most concerned about correctness). Style and correctness not only facilitate communication; they are also part of the message (see Chapter 4, pages 193–206, and Chapter 5).

For the classical rhetoricians, who were primarily concerned with formal speech, not with writing or ordinary conversation, there were two more aspects to the composing process: memory (Latin *memoria*; Greek *mneme*) and delivery (Latin, *pronuntiatio*; Greek, *hypokrisis*). Except as it contributes to invention, memory does not have much importance in respect to writing because permanence is in the very nature of the medium—indeed, one of Plato's arguments against writing, which he discouraged, was that it weakened people's desire to memorize.

Delivery as related to writing might well refer to such matters as format, neatness, and so forth. It is important that you use the proper format, achieve good penmanship or neat typing (including clean keys and a good ribbon), proofread carefully, and so forth. Several studies have demonstrated that such matters have a significant effect on grades in school writing. In one study, typewritten papers averaged half a letter grade higher than handwritten papers, and such factors make a similarly important impression in other writing situations. The classical rhetoricians did not consider the process complete until the message was successfully *delivered* to its audience. A lot more will be said about this in Chapter 4.

The division of classical rhetoric into invention, arrangement, style, memory, and delivery did not imply that these are "stages" in some ideal writing process. The writing process encompasses a number of functions: generating material, focusing, organizing and articulating that material, formulating sentences and longer passages, adapting, and delivering to particular audiences. All successful writers take care of all these basic functions, but not all in the same order. The various subprocesses of writing coexist, intertwine, interact, occur and recur as writers write. The linear division is made so that students can concentrate on learning one thing at a time (see Chapter 8, pages 345–49).

Improving Your Process

Writing is both strenuous and satisfying. The process can be frustrating, even painful. It can also be tremendously fulfilling, even exhilarating. Many writers—especially relatively advanced writers—see an uncomfortable, inefficient writing process as one of their primary writing problems. In the end they produce relatively good writing—writing that succeeds, writing they feel pretty good about. To produce that writing, however, they spend more time and feel more pain than they should. The following was written by a university student who generally received A's on her papers.

> I am a third year university student and a competent writer—so why is my composition process so slow and why do I struggle so long over an introduction? The flow of my writing is inhibited by several factors: a stubborn anxiety about my ignorance of composition principles, a tendency to work under poor writing conditions, and a peculiar mental block which habitually occurs before I draft. . . .
>
> Too often I'm writing when I'm overtired and under extreme pressure. . . . I incessantly find myself attempting to compose in ridiculous places: in front of the TV set, in the student union common room—or worse, at home before my four-year-old daughter has gone to bed. . . . [Among] other resolutions I must make are restricting my drafting locations on campus to the library and confining my studies at home to thinking, reading, and drawing notes and outlines . . . .
>
> My pre-drafting period [tends] to overlap excessively into my drafting stage. Often I'm still engrossed in research when I'm composing my final draft, but this isn't due to my not having

accumulated enough data or ideas; rather it's because I have an insatiable curiosity that goes wild whenever I set it loose. What happens after this is predictable. I overwhelm myself with a vast amount of material and broaden my focus so much that it's hard for me to maintain control over my ideas. To complicate matters, I nurture compulsion of having to express all I know in my essays. . . .

Yet serious problems set in during my drafting stage, and they usually start with my introduction. I revise as I compose, so my writing process goes like this: I write a sentence—and read it and revise. I write another sentence—read it, and revise. I read from the beginning—revise. I commence all over again. Often I spend over ten hours on my introduction. What I develop out of this process is not only a coherent structure of sentences, but an organization of integral phrases which flow together. I demand nothing less. Unfortunately, this gets me into a lot of trouble because I lose valuable time through the practice. Sometimes I try to speed up my process by not allowing myself to reread my draft as I write it; this doesn't help. I only end up rewriting the entire thing when I reread it later. Sometimes I try writing the body of the essay first, but if it deals with complex issues, which it usually does, I depend on my introduction to coordinate my ideas; I rely on it even more than I do on my outline. The structure of my final piece, though, is usually identical with that of my introduction and outline; in fact my introduction is really just a more sophisticated version of my outline.

When I finally master my introduction, I find it's getting uncomfortably close to the deadline. Then other poor habits contribute to my project's tardy finish: I stay up too late and drink too much coffee. Consequently, I enter a vicious cycle: I develop insomnia; I get sick, short-tempered, and depressed. By the time I've reached my conclusion, I've fizzled out mentally, physically, and spiritually. What ultimately baffles me about all of this is that I still turn out relatively good work. I don't understand how I can produce decent writing under such hellish conditions. How can this be? But more importantly, how can I change my situation?

Irene Louie

Irene's goal is to produce writing of equal quality with more efficiency and less pain. Monitoring her writing process was a good first step. Now she has to change it. To begin with, as she herself notes, she must make clear-cut resolutions about where and when she will write (and about how much coffee to let herself drink).

Irene also needs to make a clearer division between generating and revising. In Irene's case, much of the pain seems to arise from excessive overlap between "pre-drafting," "drafting" and "revision." For a while at least, she should set an arbitrary deadline when research stops. And she should restrain her tendency to revise sentences while drafting. That may mean doing major revision (and writing a new introduction) after she finishes drafting. She probably will also end up going back to the library for some additional research after drafting has refocused her attention. But she will have saved enough time to do that late research and still come out ahead. The time saved will also allow her to set another deadline, well before the project is due, when she must stop drafting and turn to serious revision. Such a sharp division between generating and revising is somewhat arbitrary, but often useful, at least temporarily. It can help writers gain control of the process, increase their efficiency, and reduce their pain.

Which aspects of your writing process create problems? Where do you usually bog down? How could changing certain aspects of your writing process allow you to write more productively (or less painfully)? How could changing certain aspects of your writing process help you compose more efficiently and effectively?

Before changing your process, however, you should look also at the strengths and weaknesses of the writing produced by your process. Improving your writing also means improving the quality of that written product. And an improved writing process can yield better quality output.

Setting Goals ─────────────────────────

The rules in textbooks of rhetoric cannot by themselves make expert those who are eager to dispense with study and practice.
DIONYSIUS OF HALICARNASSUS

People learn better when they have specific goals instead of vague intentions. Some goals may follow from your motives for studying writing in the first place. You may, for instance, want to master a particular type of writing.

```
Because my professional goal is to be an urban planner, I want to
sharpen my report writing skills. Perhaps I'll do a little of that
in my journal, but I think what will really help me in this regard
is to read planning articles and write about the ideas expressed
in them. . . . This will (a) let me see how planners write, (b) let
```

me practice writing the way planners write, and (c) give me insight
into how I really feel about some planning issues.

Elisabeth Arnold

Another kind of goal may follow from an analysis of your writing process. If
you suffer from procrastination, lack of time for revision, or the sort of inefficient,
painful writing process described in the previous section of this chapter (pages
16–18), your goal may be to learn how to write more quickly and pleasurably.

A third type of goal is defined when you determine to overcome whatever
weaknesses presently recur in your writing. To do that effectively, you should
understand those weaknesses and devise a plan for getting rid of them without
undermining your strengths.

Defining Problems

Although most writing students have had their weaknesses marked for
years, they often cannot state precisely what their main writing problems are.
No wonder they have difficulty solving them. As you start working on improving
your writing, you should have more precise goals than ''I want to write better''
or ''I want to improve my style'' or even ''I need to learn more grammar.''

If you understand a problem only vaguely, all the hard work you can
muster may bring you no closer to solving it. You can work and work, but if
you are working the wrong way, your writing may just get worse as you get
more and more frustrated. Defining a problem is often the key to solving it.

Most students have had their ''errors'' pointed out to them innumerable
times. They have been told very specifically about a comma error in this or
that particular sentence, and they have a general sense that they do not punctuate
well. They know that some particular word does not mean quite what they
wanted to say, and they have been told that they often use ''wrong words.''
They feel that a particular draft is not well organized, and they know that
they have a problem with organization. But all this knowledge is either too
specific or too general. The problems are not defined on the level that is the
key to solving them.

Most people who are trying to learn to write cannot say things like, ''I
tend to oversimplify my main point—or to choose a simple thesis in the first
place.'' They cannot say, ''My writing is actually well organized, but readers
have difficulty because I don't use enough transitions.'' They may be confused
about punctuation, but they usually cannot say things like, ''I do not know
how to use commas with conjunctions.''

Yet that sort of precise analysis is the key to setting clear goals and
devising effective solutions to writing problems. The person who says, ''I
don't know how to punctuate,'' is referred to several dozen rules and often

learns nothing. The person who says, ''I don't know how to use commas with conjunctions,'' is referred to one particular rule, which can be mastered in half an hour or less by doing a few exercises and writing a few sentences. Though punctuation may seem a trivial example, many writers feel insecure because they are not sure about punctuation, grammar, and usage. As one student wrote,

> I've finally learned how to use commas with coordinating
> conjunctions. Ha–ha! I'm elated over this. (Would you believe that
> was my original reason for signing up for your class?) You were the
> first instructor to define the problem for me, and that's what did
> it. All my previous instructors simply inserted little red commas
> where I had omitted them or crossed out those which I had erroneously
> inserted.

Looking back at writing you have done in the past year or so can help you define your strengths and weaknesses. After reviewing the papers she had written during her first two years at university, a student wrote:

An Optimistic Analysis of My Own Writing

In re–reading my work I discovered some things about my writing that I had never really considered before. The first and most surprising thing I discovered was that I actually liked my own writing. With the exception of correspondence, I have always written to fulfill assignments and to get marks. It had never seemed important whether or not I really liked my own work; the important thing was whether or not the instructor liked it. In recognizing that I genuinely liked my own writing, I felt an encouraging incentive to work at problem areas until even I am satisfied that they are as good as I can make them.

Another thing I discovered was that my use of punctuation and grammar had greatly improved since I started writing university level essays two years ago. I have never thought of myself as being very good at either grammar or punctuation, and remember wondering in high school if I would ever learn their respective rules and restrictions. Recognizing my own mistakes and realizing that I had ideas about revising and rewording were good signs that I had improved in these areas and that even I was capable of learning grammar and punctuation with a minimum of pain.

By re–reading my old essays I was also able to recognize three problem areas that have always bothered me in a vague way, but which I had never actually pinpointed or articulated before. The main problem I saw was that I have a tendency to cling to material that I have written in the first or second draft even when it doesn't really fit in with my argument or thesis statement. Since I often don't decide exactly what I am going to say or how I am going to say it until after the essay has been drafted, I need to be able to discard or radically revise much of what I've written up to that point.

Another problem area I noticed was that the organization of my essays seemed to be getting less structured and less clear as the topics were getting more complicated and more abstract. I always thought that I had good control of organization in my writing; it wasn't until I compared recent essays to those I wrote one or two years ago that I realized the organizing skills I prided myself on had not kept up with the advances I had made in thinking. Now that I am aware of this problem I will spend more time revising structure, sequence, and overall organization in my essays.

In re-reading my essays I also became aware of my habit of oversimplifying the topic I am discussing in an attempt to make the subject matter and argument as clear and straightforward as possible. This habit has caused me to lose marks in the past, and instructors' comments about oversimplification and lack of detail are noted on quite a few of my old essays. I think this comes from my desire to keep everything neat, tidy, and in its proper place in my writing and in most other aspects of my life.

If recognizing a problem is the first step to its rectification then I am already on my way to better writing. The fact that I do like my own writing and have seen some improvement over the past two years is encouraging and makes me optimistic about working on the problems I have recognized. I am going to concentrate on being less sentimental about early draft writing, being more concerned about structure and organization, and being extra careful not to oversimplify for excessive clarity.

Jan Melton

Jan has made two wonderful discoveries: that she likes her own writing and that her writing has been improving. Jan has also clearly defined three problem areas (and her instructor noted that she should review the rule for using commas with introductory modifiers). In fact, most of the weaknesses Jan discusses do not show up in this clear, well-organized, and well-controlled piece of writing, perhaps because the material was not abstract, perhaps because Jan was paying special attention to them.

Recognizing a problem is often *only* the first step. Since the solutions to Jan's difficulties seem to turn on large-scale revision—at which time she should delete digressions, consider reordering, check transitions, add details and qualifiers—she might find useful the revision techniques discussed in Chapter 3, especially pages 112–29.

It would have helped readers understand more precisely—and helped her instructor suggest solutions—if Jan had included some examples. Here is an excerpt from a more detailed paper.

> My major writing handicap is an inability to express thoughts concisely in a direct, penetrating fashion. My tendency is to enlarge sentences to include often redundant information. Such excessive verbosity is for show rather than effect and results in bulky, awkwardly structured sentences. For example, one sentence in my definition essay reads
>
>> The problem with scientific explanations for supernatural activity is that all truths, and the knowledge that follows are not dependent on a state of consciousness because there are many things one knows that he is unaware of such as the knowledge that the ceiling will not cave in while sitting under it.
>
> This sentence rewritten reads,
>
>> Scientific explanations for supernatural activity create a problem. Knowledge does not depend on a state of consciousness. For example, someone sitting under a ceiling unconsciously realizes it will not cave in.
>
> Ann Morrison

Notice that Ann's "excessive verbosity" and awkwardly complex sentence structure led to grammatical problems as well as stylistic difficulties. More importantly, note that her style here denies her thesis: she does have the ability to express her thoughts "concisely in a direct, penetrating fashion."

Some writing problems can be solved simply by paying attention to them; others require information as well as awareness.

> Because I did not know how to use semicolons, when I tried to avoid short, choppy sentences, I would simply connect two independent clauses with a comma. Semicolons and colons have also helped me be more precise. When I used a comma where a semicolon should have been, I would also use a lot of unnecessary transition words; I was trying to make words do what should have been done by a punctuation mark.
>
> Eve Edmonds

Eve got rid of her comma splices by spending a little time reading about semicolons in her handbook.

Although writers often exaggerate their ignorance of usage, grammar, punctuation, spelling, and mechanics, such problems can be serious, especially when readers, rightly or wrongly, take them as signs of ignorance and "illiteracy." They can also undermine your confidence and your style. If the last time you studied punctuation was in high school, you may now be using more complex sentence structure, which requires types of punctuation you did not learn in high school.

> I have a smooth rhythm and syntax to my writing, but I am often hampered by grammar and spelling problems. I can hear complex sentence structures and words in my head, but I don't have the tools to write them down. What I have often done is to write them down as best I can or replace them with something simpler.
>
> Elisabeth Arnold

Problems of organization and development can be more difficult than sentence-level problems.

> A major fault that runs consistently through my essays is the problem of fully developing themes and ideas. The problem is usually due to laziness in elaborating rather than a lack of knowledge. A comment that I got on a second-year English essay said:
>
>> The conclusion is "cruel" in that it holds a promise it does not fulfill. . . . How tantalizing to raise these questions and then leave your reader without a clue to the answer.
>
> I make false assumptions that the reader clearly understands my ideas and can read between the lines.
>
> Janice Carroll

Note that, again, the problem being described does not exist in the particular passage where the writer's attention is focused on it. But knowing how much development readers need is not always simple. Nor is it always easy to generate the missing detail. And the remarks of editors, writing instructors, and others who comment on your writing may help you only to locate—not to solve—such problems.

> I am a developing writer experiencing growing pains. I've noticed the symptoms for years: unreasonable anxiety over essay assignments, ingenious ploys to postpone beginning work, suffering during writing, dissatisfaction with work handed in, confusion about instructors' remarks on returned papers, and a continual frustration with the quality of my product. My problem is that my

ideas have developed beyond my ability to express them effectively
in writing. This comment is typical of the well-meaning little notes
professors attach to my papers:

> Lynn—this essay comes in conception and content very close
> to the ideal. You have difficulty expressing your good critical
> ideas in convincing prose and so your good ideas remain partly
> hidden.

This observation (and those like it)—which rarely offered
strategies to solve the problems—did little to bolster my writer's
ego. I agreed with what my professors said; I just did not know what
to do about it.

Lynn Upton

Such comments usually do identify real problems, but not very precisely.
Someone who specializes in teaching writing can often suggest appropriate
strategies for defining and solving such problems.

> My papers on complex or controversial issues are not well thought
> out. Sometimes this is due to the fact that I hastily rushed through
> my paper, but at others times this is due to, as one of my markers
> put it, my "limited perception." When he mentioned this, I started
> wondering how I could deepen my perceptions; suddenly I began to
> see the light, thanks to your heuristic.
>
> Ruby Stroshin

At any event, once you have located and defined a writing weakness,
you should restate it as a goal. That focuses your attention and helps you
think positively.

Listing Strengths

Though it may seem immodest, listing your strengths is important. Remembering your strengths helps maintain your self-confidence while you deal with
your weaknesses. And you certainly do not want to solve your writing problems
in ways that might undermine what you already do well.

> The most obvious strength in my writing is clarity of style and
> structure. It is structured with clearly organized sentences,
> paragraphs, and headings. Yet it is this strength that also
> contributes to my weaknesses. My thoughts are inhibited and bound

Table 1.1   Goals

Once you have located and defined a writing weakness, you should restate it positively as a goal. Goals for the students whose analyses have been excerpted above might read something like this:

> Irene (page 16–17): I will gain control of my writing process and learn how to produce the same quality in less time and with less suffering.

> Elisabeth (page 18–19): I will find out what kinds of writing urban planners do, then analyze and practice each kind.

> Jan (page 20–21): (1) I will learn to tighten my writing by discarding material irrelevant to my main point.
> (2) I will explain complex subjects accurately and fully.
> (3) I will develop my ability to organize complex essays.

> Ann (page 22): I will learn to express myself with penetrating directness by
> (1) breaking up or restructuring excessively complex sentences and
> (2) resisting the temptation to use big words to impress.

> Eve (page 22): I will learn to use semicolons and commas with parenthetical elements.

> Elisabeth (page 23): I will master sentence structure and punctuation principles that will allow me better to communicate my complex thoughts.

> Ruby (page 24): I will produce fuller and more perceptive interpretations.

Restating problems as goals in this way focuses your attention and helps you think positively.

---

by the structure and organization I consciously make for myself. Ideas and thoughts do not flow easily because I am afraid to take a chance at how they may sound. Thinking too much about the audience makes me afraid to let go and take risks where creativity may lead me. Therefore, I choose to play it safe and stay within my boundaries. Unfortunately, my writing has been sacrificed.

   This approach makes my writing imprecise, overly simplistic, and not fully developed.

                                                            Debora Turtan

   My greatest strength is that I rarely lack ideas when I begin to write. When I understand the topic, I usually argue my point of view well. Generally, I keep my style under control and come up with good conclusions. . . .

I tend to be overambitious when writing an essay; I try to handle too many ideas at once. I should make a habit of setting the best and most relevant ideas aside and expanding these to their utmost. That means throwing away good but irrelevant pieces of writing. And after separating the relevant ideas from the rest, I should elaborate on each point, using concrete, specific detail and clear, concrete examples—thereby ridding the paper of vagueness and abstract ideas. Making a clear thesis statement before revising and keeping that (and the audience) in mind as I'm revising will help to clarify the difficult decision of which ideas to keep and which to throw away. If the relevance is not clearly evident, showing the connection between the idea and the main point will clarify it for the reader. The best way to find out whether the connection is visible is to give the paper to friends to read. . . .

Although I'm good at coming up with ideas, I'm terrible at eliminating good pieces of writing that have no place in the paper. I usually tend to <u>make</u> them fit when they really don't, and it shows. So the next time I revise, I'll force myself to be ruthless—and I'll keep the good but useless pieces of writing for a time when they can be useful.

Nicole Duelli

While Debora is certainly right to want to learn how to let loose her creativity and explore the full complexity of what she is writing about, she does not want to end up with chaotically disorganized, stylistically obscure writing. Similarly, Nicole wants to achieve more control, but not at the expense of inhibiting her creative ability to generate ideas and supporting arguments.

Writing 1c   Describe as specifically as you can the strong and weak points of your writing. Wherever you can, give concrete examples.

Be sure to list strengths as well as weaknesses. Be sure to consider not only sentence-level strengths and weaknesses, but also strengths and weaknesses in such areas as finding good material, insight, organization, and adapting to particular audiences.

A good way to approach this assignment is to review ten or twelve fairly recent writings. If you are a student, it would be particularly useful to use papers written for courses you took from several different instructors in the past year or two. If you write at work, try to choose writing that has been revised or commented upon by several different supervisors.

Then generalize any feedback you received and any insights you now have about the strong points and flaws of those writings.

Do this analysis to the best of your ability, and be prepared to discuss it in order to define your problems and goals more precisely. (*Note*: What you are doing here is analysis by classification and exemplification; see pages 310–15 and 294–99).

Making Plans

Once you have defined your goals, what you need is a plan for how you will achieve each. It also helps if you set yourself a time limit or schedule. And you should have some way of checking your improvement, a somewhat objective measure of the extent to which you actually achieve what you set out to achieve.

Restated positively and fully, a problem like

    I make too many unsupported generalizations.

becomes

    From now on I will underline each generalization in my draft. I will
    make sure I have explained how I know each is true. And I will give
    an example. By next month I will no longer receive complaints about
    unsupported generalizations, and by the end of the year I will no
    longer need to use this underlining procedure.

A goal like

    I will produce more developed and perceptive interpretations.

becomes

    I will produce more developed and perceptive interpretations. After
    I have done my research and formulated a tentative interpretation,
    I will check the accuracy and fullness of my observations by asking
    myself the questions suggested in Process, Form, and Substance,
    pages 264–65.

Writing 1d   Reduce your previous writing (1c) to two lists. List your major strengths as a writer. List the type(s) of writing you want to master and your main problems (in rough order of priority). Rephrase those problems positively as *goals*, including

(a) means for achieving each without undermining your strengths,

(b) a time limit or schedule, and

(c) criteria by which you will be able to judge whether you have reached each goal.

Remember that successful goal statement depends on precise problem definition (because that leads to specifying *achievable* goals).

To devise effective means by which your goals can be achieved, you may need help from a writing instructor or someone else who specializes in solving writing problems. Sometimes the solution is learning how to fix the problem while you are revising. But often the best way to solve a writing problem is to change your writing process so that the problem never arises in the first place.

Process and Product

The most perplexing and challenging writing problems are often best solved by making some change in *how* you write. So figuring out how best to achieve your writing goals means looking at your writing process. After all, the process produces the product (including the weak parts). Even if a particular problem, such as punctuation, can be resolved just by getting some information or doing some exercises, you will still have to decide when during your writing process you want to focus attention on that problem. One student put it this way:

> If a professional tennis player were having trouble with his serve, there would be a number of procedures he could follow that might aid him in correcting it. However, before any correction could begin, the tennis player would need to know specifically when and where the error took place, not just how the ball missed. This would require a detailed analysis of his actual serve. Perhaps the most effective procedure would be to break down his serve by having a sequential series of photographs taken of it. Because the actual serve is dependent upon a vast number of different stages, ranging from backswing to follow-through, it might then be possible to analyze each photograph and thus pinpoint the error directly responsible for the "bad" serve.
>
> While tennis service and the essay writing process may initially seem totally different, there is a quality to them that makes them similar: both involve a series of stages that lead to a final and

```
definite result, whether it be the serve itself or the final draft
of a paper.
```

Andrew Crosse

Writing is a far more complex process than serving a tennis ball, but Andrew's point is well taken. To improve your writing, you should try to pinpoint where in your writing process the problems arise, or where they can be readily corrected. Consider the following instance.

```
    The problem of organization is foremost in my writing of in-class
essays. I go about writing this type of paper by studying as many
facts as I possibly can, which usually ends up being a vast array
of facts which are spilled out during the exam in a confused order.
The facts are down on the paper but are not clear: instead of focusing
in on the central theme, I cover a number of areas surrounding the
main issue. The issues I do raise are not well enough developed. A
comment on a first year in-class history paper states, "Your paper
really needs to be more clearly organized. Also, you might have
been much clearer in your discussion of the Gregorian Reform
Movement. Furthermore, you needed to cite more specific examples
throughout your paper. You raised a number of interesting points,
but you have failed to develop them."
```

Janice Moulton

Janice's problem is her written product, which satisfies neither her nor her professors. The solution is to change the process by which she produces those essays, a process that really begins with her study habits, which in a sense constitute the first phase of writing an in-class essay. In general, studying should be structured to match what one will be asked to produce on the exam, and this case is no exception. Instead of studying as many facts as she possibly can, Janice should practice organizing those facts under more general statements *during her study process*. There are also several changes Janice could make in how she writes essay exams that would probably improve her grades. For one, she should take a minute or two to plan each essay before starting to write it. And she could ask herself after each generalization, "How do I know this is true?" and "What is a good example of this?" Those questions would generate the logical support and concrete instances her professors find lacking (see pages 81–82).

Modifying the writing process is also the key to the following case:

```
    Very often when I don't express myself well at the start, the rest
of my ideas suffer for it. I feel that sometimes I'm playing with a
```

conceptual puzzle which has too many pieces and has more which can't
be used until a later stage. This is my first writing dilemma.

Whether it is due to subject matter or to my rigid conceptual
boundaries, my writing tends to be blatant and choppy. Once my
initial thinking process is completed, my conceptual field is
narrowed so that I do not always see all the facts or subject matter.
Sometimes I cut pieces to fit the puzzle for the time being. Later
I pay for it because a struggle arises between my conceptual
boundaries and those of the reader. My ideas often become more
blatant when put on paper.

Colin Grady

In one sense Colin's problem is not a problem at all. If you do not sometimes
feel as if you are "playing with a puzzle which has too many pieces," you
are not doing the sort of writing from which people learn, the sort of writing
that is basic to a humanistic education—which *should* expand your conceptual
boundaries.

In another sense, Colin's problem is that he tries to think first and write
second. He wants the thinking to be finished by the time he writes his first
sentences. But for most writers, the process of verbalizing thoughts on paper
is part of the thinking process. For most writers, ideas do change and develop
as they are being written. Introductions often have to be written or rewritten
at the end, after the conceptual puzzle has finally come together. Colin probably
needs to let himself do more exploratory writing before locking onto a thesis
and structure. He needs to think of his conceptual boundaries as tentative
and to let his drafts run over those boundaries. He needs to revise his drafts,
especially the introductions and conclusions, to match conclusions he ends
with, to qualify his blatant ideas after he discovers their limits. Several ways
to do that sort of revision are discussed in Chapter 3, pages 101–6 and 112–
18.

Experienced writers understand writing as a generative process. They
expect to get new ideas and insights as they write. They may work from
outlines (usually very rough ones), but they do not feel bound by them. They
know that writing is often a chaotic process and do not expect it to occur in
neatly defined stages. They understand, for example, that the search for a
better word may lead to rethinking a concept and thus to redrafting or reorganizing. At best, rather than making sharp boundaries, they try to focus on certain
functions during certain phases of the writing process.

Of course, writing your way through to a sophisticated understanding
of your subject and then revising your draft to match that complex understanding
is strenuous as well as rewarding. Certainly, it is harder than sticking with
your original concept and cutting the pieces to fit the puzzle. But it also
produces better results.

My last paper was the best example of an emotional struggle. To begin with it was supposed to have a simple title: "My Childhood in the Port City of Gdansk." But because of the emotional process I went though, it ended up with the more appropriate title: "Growing Up in Poland." As with most of my papers, I began by writing down on a piece of paper words which in my mind I associated with my childhood. Because of my familiarity with the topic, it was a simple routine. Very quickly I jotted down a somewhat chaotic list of sugary adjectives which I regularly use when thinking or talking about my childhood.

But soon I realized that something was wrong. I wasn't in the right frame of mind for this pleasantly nostalgic type of reminiscence. My memory of a carefree childhood was heavily overshadowed by the vision of the troubled Poland of today. After several painfully unsuccessful attempts to recapture the magic of perceiving the past through a child's rose-tinted glasses, I finally resigned myself to a very detached description of the mechanics of living in Poland, hoping that in this way perhaps I would eventually warm up to my memories. After numerous attempts to rewrite, I still found my description completely lifeless. By then I was feeling hopelessly angry. Midnight was approaching and I hadn't accomplished anything. Ignoring the dangerously late hour, I decided to go for a walk in a nearby park. I ended up running all the way there and back, partly to get rid of my frustration, partly because I realized the foolishness of walking alone at that late hour.

Half an hour later, sitting behind my desk, I was able to approach the topic with relative calm. Realizing the impossibility of reaching completely behind the barrier of the dramatic changes which my country has endured since my childhood, I decided to compromise by focusing on those aspects of yesterday's Poland that are responsible for the Poland of today. I concentrated on the issues from which I was protected as a child but which I took in stride as a typical Polish teenager. Thus, as with most of my essays, I ended up with a piece of work which resembled the initial plan very little.

Maya Kaplinowski

Writing is more strenuous than most romantics would have you believe, and Maya, like Colin, is to a certain extent describing the way it is. Having to write your way through to a final focus is quite normal. In fact, one reason for writing is that it often forces writers to reconceive their subjects. Having to articulate ideas in words on paper encourages precision. Having to adapt to a particular purpose, audience, and situation, moreover, often forces a writer to reframe ideas and make new connections. A more experienced writer might have taken that run in the park a littler earlier—or used some of the techniques for finding focus, clarifying thesis and purpose that are discussed in Chapters 2, 3, and 4 below. And because she would understand that some fumbling for focus is normal, a more experienced writer most likely would have felt less frustration.

Writing 1e Combine your analysis of your own writing process (Writing 1b) with your analysis of your own writing strengths and weaknesses (Writing 1c). Try to create one coherent piece of writing—because making your two analyses cohere should help you understand the relationship between your writing process and the strengths and weaknesses of the writing you produce. It should also give you an assessment of your present writing abilities. Thus it will provide both a platform from which you can grow and a way to evaluate that growth later.

Work your lists of motives (Writing 1a) and goals (Writing 1d) into what you have written. This will further define the tasks before you and help you motivate yourself. You will, in effect, have written a project proposal—complete with an analysis of existing situation, a definition of goals and the means by which they will be achieved, and a procedure for evaluating the project after completion.

With your personal writing project thus defined, you should be able to maximize the benefit you get from the rest of this book and from the writing course in which you are using it.

In the follow excerpt, a student defines two interrelated problems, one in her process, one in her written product. Using techniques discussed in Chapter 2, she develops a detailed plan for overcoming both.

My greatest problem is time management. By leaving writing assignments until the eleventh hour, I have only time for a hastily written, mediocre paper. There is no time for revision, let alone a second draft. Consequently, everything suffers—organization, detail, development, sentence and paragraph transitions—producing physical and mental anguish for the writer.

I see difficulty getting started as a problem. It takes me a long time to come up with an opening sentence that I like. And I have difficulty moving on with the piece until I have that opening sentence or sentences.

Past papers indicate a major weakness of my writing to be a need for elaboration ("develop," "more detail"). While this is directly related to time management, I am listing it as a separate problem as well.

I am proposing a solution of time management, focusing on the positive. This will take the form of a schedule of mini-deadlines designed to break the task into smaller pieces where the goal is more likely to be within sight, therefore achievable. This will provide shortterm success—positive feedback which should encourage movement to the next deadline—rather than procrastination resulting from feelings of frustration and guilt in trying to cope with a final deadline. For a paper due in two weeks, the schedule will be:

Days 1 to 3: Incubation (legitimate procrastination)

Day 3: Preliminary Draft (ideas and thoughts)

Day 6: First Draft

Day 10: Major Revisions (reformulations)

Day 12: Minor Revisions (language changes)

Day 13: Typing

The elaboration problem would probably best be corrected by using a heuristic [see pages 78–82 for an explanation of heuristics]. By using questions designed to focus attention on developing paragraph ideas logically and with adequate support, comments like "more detail needed," "develop," and "elaborate" will hopefully be avoided. Looking at one last paper, I see that the journalist's 5Ws would have provided elaboration of a report on group dynamics. I used a modified version of a heuristic in our text to organize the contents of this letter.

Another problem, that of getting started, I handled in this letter by ignoring the opening and jumping straight into part two of the heuristic. I will continue using this strategy and am also aware of techniques like freewriting, talk-then-write, brainstorming, meditation, keeping a journal, and research.

I see these techniques and strategies as reasonable solutions to my writing problems. They are of a practical nature, things that I can actually DO, formulas that I can apply, forms to develop substance. They should help me achieve my goal for this course, that of approaching a writing task in a positive manner—maybe not in joyful anticipation, but at least not with dread—because I am armed with strategies to get the process moving and techniques to improve the product.

                                                                Pat Dales

Exercise

1. Write a short essay explaining why writing matters (or will matter) in your life. If you have chosen your profession, find out what kinds of writing that profession involves. Consider the various types of writing you might do as a consumer and citizen and in your personal life. Use this essay to help focus your goals as a student of writing.

2. Do Writing 1b (page 9). Compare your writing processes with those of other writers (e.g., other students in a writing class).

3. Start a writing journal and record, among other things, observations of your own writing process and of whatever you do to try to improve your writing. Use this journal to respond to the continuing discussion of the writing process in the following chapters of this book, to bring that discussion to bear on your writing process.

4. Keep a writing folder in which you collect everything you write for the next while (and perhaps also anything you have written recently). As you develop your understanding of what makes writing work well, look back through this folder from time to time. As your writing abilities develop, you will see ways your earlier writing could have been improved. Consider doing some late revision, for no textbook exercise is so well adapted to what you personally need to learn as is the exercise of strengthening your own writing. (*Note*: This can be a good way to check how well you have achieved the goals you set for your development as a writer.)

5. Interview some successful writers to find out how they think they write (see pages 53–54 on interviewing). Interview some average and below-average writers. Can you detect any pattern of differences? (*Note*: This is a good project to undertake collaboratively, perhaps with other students in your writing class.)

6. Compare your ideal writing process with your typical writing process. Consider the implications.

7. Consider the divisions of classical rhetoric. What, if anything, can you learn from them that might help you as a writer? Does your writing process fulfill all the functions identified by the classical rhetoricians? If not, would it help to add something to the process?

8. List your immediate goals as a writer. Determine which parts of this book and of your handbook will help you achieve those goals. Set yourself a schedule for reading those pages and applying what you learn.

C·H·A·P·T·E·R 2

The Creative Process

I must confess that, personally, I have learned many things I never knew before . . . just by writing.

AUGUSTINE

I have never started a poem yet whose end I knew. Writing a poem is discovering.

ROBERT FROST

Writing and rewriting are a constant search for what one is saying.

JOHN UPDIKE

Writing is not simply a game of chance you play with your muse. Writing is a thinking process. To be more specific, it is a problem-solving process. . . . Good problem solvers—such as master chess players, inventors, successful scientists, business managers, or artists—typically have a great deal of knowledge and a large repertory of powerful strategies to use in attacking their problems. Good writers are the same. They are people who have developed better ways of attacking the problem of writing.

LINDA FLOWER

THE creative process of writing requires both inspiration and perspiration, both creative insight and strenuous creative work, both invention and revision.

1. We must creatively generate and articulate ideas, words, and strategies for approaching our readers.
2. We must critically select, arrange, and revise so that our words represent what we mean accurately and communicate with our intended readers effectively.

The creative process is thus a contradictory process. A good piece of writing is the result of both inspiration and revision.

Imagine that you have within yourself both an inspired Creator, who generates all sorts of ideas, words, and strategies, and a careful Critic, who evaluates, selects, arranges, and revises what the Creator has generated. To write well, you should know how—and when—to encourage both the Creator and the Critic within you. Too strong a Critic can stifle creative generation; too weak a Critic, and the seed of inspiration may never come to fruition.

We know that most experienced, effective writers spend much more time generating material and communicative strategies than most student writers do. We also know that experienced, effective writers spend a lot more time revising. And they know how to manage these two contradictory aspects of the creative process. They know when to listen to the generative voice of the Creator and when to listen to the evaluative voice of the Critic.

This chapter is about the first aspect of the creative process, about getting started, encouraging inspiration, invention, and discovery of words and ideas. In order to concentrate on one function at a time, we will postpone until Chapter 3 discussion of focus, structure, and revision. Issues of purpose, audience, and communicative strategies will wait for Chapter 4. Style, diction, and syntax are postponed to Chapter 5. The creative process of writing cannot really be separated so neatly into stages, but it is easier to learn if you concentrate on one function at a time.

This chapter begins with a short discussion of human creativity and the importance of managing one's writing time effectively. It then presents a variety of techniques for getting started: talk-then-write, freewriting, brainstorming, meditation, keeping a journal, and research. The second section considers ways to overcome the perceptual, conceptual, and attitudinal blocks that can interfere with the creative process. The third section presents structured techniques that can be used to guide discovery processes in predictably fruitful directions.

This chapter discusses many more techniques for getting started and generating material than any one writer is likely to use. Different techniques work best for different people and for different types of writing. You should have in your writer's tool kit at least one effective technique for getting started, at least one structured technique for generating the sort of material you need for the sort of writing you usually do. As you read this chapter, you should treat it as a catalog: do not feel you should master every technique discussed; select several techniques that might work for you, think about how they might fit into your writing process, and try them out.

Getting Started _____

He that sings a lasting song
Thinks in a marrow bone.

WILLIAM BUTLER YEATS

Writing depends on both strategy and intuition.

WILLIAM IRMSCHER

How can you write the beginning of something till you know what it's the beginning
of? Till you know what it's leading up to? But how can you know that till you
get your beginnings?

PETER ELBOW

Guiding Your Creative Process

Managing your time effectively is one of the quickest ways to improve your writing—because it allows you to take full advantage of the writing abilities you already have. Discovering what to say and how to say it takes time. So does revision. Getting started early enough to allow time for that discovery process and finishing a draft soon enough to allow for proper revision are two keys to writing successfully.

Writing often depends on inspiration, which cannot be ordered up on schedule like a pizza. There is no formula for instant inspiration. Productive writers, nonetheless, generally write regularly and on a schedule. They depend on inspiration, but they have ways to encourage it. They may run into writing blocks, but they have techniques for dealing with them. They often indulge idiosyncratic habits, but only because those habits help them get started. Not only do they spend more time generating material than most student writers do, but they have organized techniques for doing so. They know writing is a chaotic process, and they know how to live with that chaos. Though they do not work in neat stages, they try to focus on particular functions at particular times during the process.

Inspiration cannot be controlled, but it can be encouraged. As a writer, you should know a bit about the human creative process, for that knowledge can help you to tolerate the chaos out of which inspiration so often arises. It can also help you figure out what to do when your creativity seems to be blocked. The basic pattern seems to be something like this:

1. A period of preliminary work, using various techniques such as those discussed in this chapter. This work sets your mind to the topic or problem and gathers necessary information.
2. A period of doing ''nothing,'' of incubation.

3. Inspiration (which often occurs at some unexpected moment when conscious attention is focused elsewhere).

4. Another period of hard work during which the inspiration is articulated in detail, criticized, verified, and so forth.

The periods of hard work can be scheduled and controlled. Incubation and inspiration can only be guided and encouraged. Gertrude Stein compares the process to having a baby.

> You cannot go into the womb to form the child; it is there and makes itself and comes forth whole—and there it is and you have made it and have felt it, but it has come itself— and that is creative recognition. Of course you have a little more control over your writing than that; you have to know what you want to get; but when you know that, let it take you and if it seems to take you off the track don't hold back, because that is perhaps where instinctively you want to be and if you hold back and try to be always where you have been before, you will go dry.

A student wrote about it like this:

> I usually write at intervals, deliberately allowing time for ideas to settle and, if I'm lucky, to synthesize. In fact, I consider the times when I'm not pushing a pen an integral part of the writing process. By the same token, I prefer to "coax" rather than to "force" the process. Even when the deadline is close, I try to generate a positive working environment in which it's possible to coordinate writing time and "creative mulling." Certainly that effort can't be separate from the "lift" I feel when plodding is rewarded with words that encapsulate a thought or, even better, reshape and "explode" a thought.
>
> Monika Hilder

That part of the creative process which is most quintessentially creative—the moment of inspiration—is not subject to willpower or rationality. It cannot be directly controlled or forced. But it does not arise out of nothingness, and one can learn how to create space for it, to encourage it. One can develop ways of working and habits of mind that are conducive to creativity.

Getting started is easier when you know where you are going. Often writers do not know where a piece of writing is going until after they have been writing it for a while. But the more clearly you can define your destination, the more efficiently you can get there. Explain the task to yourself. What is this piece of writing supposed to do? What could it say in order to do that?

You can begin to answer the first question by looking at your own motives for attempting this particular writing—or at the assignment if the motivation is coming from someone else (such as a teacher or supervisor). The answer to the second question is often less apparent, but it should lie within the parameters defined by the first.

Knowing exactly what you are trying to do and how you will do it makes for a kind of efficiency, but a more flexible, open-ended process— Monika's "creative mulling"—will more likely "coax" quality inspiration.

Sometimes inspiration comes in the nick of time, perhaps the night before a paper is due, and sometimes just *after* the nick of time, for example, five minutes after the examination is over. Even when inspiration comes at the eleventh hour—"just in the nick of time"—it is actually late. By the time that inspiration has been turned into a draft, no time remains for revision. The full potential of the inspiration is never actualized. Errors and weaknesses remain that a writer knows how to correct—and would have corrected given a bit more time.

Managing time is especially important for students. Too often students hand in writing that is not their best work, writing that is filled with typographical and mechanical errors, is awkwardly organized and sloppily articulated—papers the students themselves are perfectly capable of improving. Late the night before the paper was due, however, eyes were too bleary to see the errors; reorganization was clearly in order, but it meant creating new transitions as well as recopying the whole paper; and there certainly was no time to refine the concepts. Then the instructor, concentrating on what seems most basic or most elementary, marks a set of problems of which the students were well aware and *from which the students have little to learn*. The whole purpose of the writing class is undermined and everyone feels bad.

One key to writing efficiently is learning how to tell the difference between incubation and procrastination. Though a certain amount of "not writing" is part of the writing process, it can easily get out of hand. One student writer had this to say about how poor time management undermined his writing:

```
For me, essay writing is a painful chore which I am unwillingly
forced to carry out. If something is painful, you try to avoid it;
therefore, when faced with an essay assignment, my first response
is to put it out of my mind for as long as possible. As a result of
this procrastination, my essays are handed in either late or in a
semi-completed form. Even when I decide that I can no longer
procrastinate but must now sit down and get on with it, this desire
to escape persists; suddenly, in mid-sentence of course, I get the
urge to make coffee, read the newspaper, clean up the apartment or
take out the garbage. Escaping into this other activity disrupts
my writing process; for each time I get up and sit down again I have
to regain my train of thought, and in order to do so I must reread
```

what I have previously written. Not only does this stalling ritual take up even more of what little time I have left before the deadline, but it also contributes to a lack of coherence in my essays.

Another form of escapism which affects my writing process occurs once I have begun to write. Because of my desire to "get this painful process over with," I rush through the actual writing. It is this tendency to rush which accounts for the remarks made on my essays, such as "should have made this point clearer" or "expand," which reflect that I have not fully expressed my ideas. It is also for this reason that most of my papers are under length. Furthermore, a great many surface errors and awkward sentences are a direct result of too much haste, for example, unnecessary punctuation errors such as leaving out apostrophes which show possession or placing commas in the wrong place, and careless spelling mistakes caused by leaving out letters or running words together. Also, since this need to "get the chore over with" extends to the revision process as well, most of these errors are carried intact to the final draft.

Finally, my negative attitude toward essay writing affects the manner in which I approach each essay: rather than viewing each paper as being part of a continually evolving process, I view each as a separate task. When my essays are returned, although I look over the comments, I make no conscious effort to analyze the errors I make or what I could do to prevent the same type of error from recurring in my next assignment; therefore, any improvement in my writing is incidental.

Procrastination usually occurs at the beginning, but it can also pop up later.

When I am given a topic for assignment, I am usually eager to get my thoughts onto paper. I mull the assignment over in my mind, loosely organizing the essay there. Certain phrases and sentences are seen as effective, and these are jotted down. After a day or two of this process, I sit down and write until I feel that I have written a general overview to the topic. It is at this point that I hit a snag. No matter how much time I have in which to complete the assignment, the actual draft is not written until the night before the essay is due. Until the pressure of the deadline finally forces me to, I just don't want to write.

Margaret Atwood once spoke of finding her nerve to write. That is how I feel. Words which sound perfectly splendid rolling around in my mind sound like lead when they are written down. Perhaps it is fear of failure which has caused my recent aversion to writing, but the result of this aversion is always a hurriedly written paper which is written for a deadline rather than for my own enjoyment. These papers usually lack any revision, and so are rife with simple errors of grammar and speech. Any proofreading that is done is too superficial to correct major errors in sentence construction and organization.

Most of the faults in my writing could be corrected through careful re-reading and revision. However, revision is difficult at five o'clock on the morning that an essay is due. For most people, a solution to this problem would be to manage time more effectively so that the essay would not be rushed. However, my problem is not one of time-management. My essays are not ready in time because I really dread writing them. I put off the task of applying pen to paper for so long that I cannot possibly do the topic justice.

As these examples indicate, problems of attitude and motivation often underlie the misuse of available time. But that only makes effective time management even more important. The writing process should be started early enough to allow for proper incubation (not to be confused with stalling). Your draft should ordinarily be completed in plenty of time, so that it can be put aside for a while, thus permitting you to see it afresh during revision. A final copy should be completed early enough so that it can be proofread carefully and alertly.

Start the preparation phase as early as possible. Gather your information, jot down notes, and perhaps do some very rough writing. Such preparation starts the incubator. As ideas "pop" up, jot them down. Try to do at least a rough draft well before the deadline. Get the drafting completed and start revising soon enough so that you can make major changes, such as modifying ideas, reordering paragraphs, or writing a new introduction.

Most people are incapable of following the advice of the preceding paragraph without a schedule. So *make a schedule* as soon as you know you are going to write something. Do not worry about sticking to it too rigidly— inspiration may not come when you scheduled it (perhaps it will even come early)—but make a plan for how and when you will write (see page 133).

Starting early and managing your time effectively does not mean expending much more time on a given piece of writing; it just means dividing that time over a longer span. You will probably save some time during the early phases, perhaps by doing some thinking on the bus or getting an inspiration in the shower. If the writing involves library research, you may actually have time to obtain all the materials you really need. You will probably save some time while drafting, too, because you may be a little more organized or have a few key phrases ready. And you will probably find yourself putting more time into revision because you will have the time to do so. Most student writers expend well over half their time drafting; experienced writing teachers generally recommend spending 30% or 40% on preparation and preliminary writing, 20% on drafting, and 40% or 50% on revision.

Many student writers who have trouble with procrastination or with insufficient time for revision find it useful to divide their writing time arbitrarily in half. They then allot the first half to the Creator for preparation and drafting, the second half to the Critic for revision and editing.

> While writing the previous assignments for this course, I began to wonder why I procrastinate. Surprisingly, I discovered that my tendency to procrastinate is caused by more than a simple lack of self-discipline. I found that I use a highly ineffective writing process. My writing is compressed into a single stage, during which I organize my thoughts, commit them to paper, and revise as I go along. I procrastinate because I dread going through the agony that accompanies this single-stage process.
>
> I hope, in this course, to divide my writing process into stages. I want to use freewriting as my first stage. I believe I have a talent for freewriting, and therefore it should be an easy way to start my writing process. It will allow me to generate ideas and commit them to paper without having to worry about grammar and punctuation. . . . Once those ideas have been expressed on paper, it will be easier for me to pick out the main ideas and plan an order in which I wish to discuss them in my essays. Normally I write my essays with no definite plan in mind; freewriting should allow me to plan my essay before beginning to write the final draft. . . . In an effort to learn how to use freewriting effectively I have already read the relevant material [see pages 44–48]. I have also read some portions of Peter Elbow's book, <u>Writing With Power</u>.
>
> Hank Bouwman

The extra time you put into revision may be more than the time you save earlier. Instead of spending twelve hours on a paper by staying up all night just before it must be finished, you may put fourteen hours into it over the course of a week. But those hours will be less strained, and you will probably get a lot more satisfaction out of the final product. In a writing class, moreover, the criticisms you receive later will much more likely be criticisms from which you can learn (instead of criticisms that just make you feel bad).

Generating the First Words

The very first problem a would-be writer may encounter is *writer's block*, the inability to write anything at all. Actually a certain difficulty getting started is typical. Most writers experience it. Most writers must struggle against procrastination at the beginning. There are a number of well-established techniques for overcoming this difficulty and generating the first words. If you have difficulty at the beginning, you should try several of the half dozen described in the following pages to see which help you. You almost undoubtedly will not want to use all these techniques, but one or several may make good additions to your writer's toolbox.

One reason for writer's block follows from the very nature of writing. In ordinary oral communication, one gets feedback from listeners. Even if the listeners do not say a word, a speaker can tell pretty well from facial expression, head movement, body position, breathing patterns, and so forth how well communication is proceeding. As a speaker, you are probably not very aware of this nonverbal feedback because your conscious attention is focused on what you are saying (as it should be). Nonetheless, unconsciously you depend on nonverbal feedback.

Writers do not have the advantage of immediate feedback. Writing is, in this respect, very much like speaking into a radio microphone without the presence of a studio audience; and writer's block is much like *mike fright*. When feedback is delayed, it is hard to continue verbalizing. But delayed feedback is in the very nature of writing: you write a sentence; then, before receiving any indication of whether that sentence has been understood, you have to write the next. To write effectively, you must *imagine* how your readers will respond to each part of what you have written. (See Chapter 4, especially pages 146–57.)

A second reason for difficulty at the beginning follows from the nature of the writing process. Like any creative process, writing has two contrary aspects. In the first place, writers need to generate material (or even before that, to discover topics). But much of what is generated will not be usable: images and concepts that are not quite accurate or correct; malformed sentences and sentences that do not fit with what has gone before or what is to follow; nonstandard usage in standard contexts; idiosyncratic punctuation that would confuse readers to no purpose; misspelled words; and so on.

Thus, in the second place, writers must criticize and select, reorder and correct. Dissatisfied with a sentence, a writer rephrases it several distinct ways and then selects the version that will work best. Uncertain about an argument, a writer tries it out on a friend and, in the process of receiving criticism, modifies it. Uncomfortable with the way a word looks, a writer turns to the dictionary and finds the correct spelling.

Any creative process—from biological evolution to musical composition—must involve both generation and selection. The problem for writers is that sometimes the second aspect becomes so dominant that everything is censored, and the would-be writer is left with a blank page. If your critical side is so strong that it totally censors all starting points, you have writer's block. The solution is to give it your word of honor that it will have its turn, but insist that it must go off and take a nap first.

Technique 1: Talk-then-Write

One technique commonly used to overcome writer's block and to generate the raw material for a piece of writing follows from our understanding that difficulty getting started arises partly because writers miss the feedback that is a normal part of conversation. This technique involves nothing more difficult than finding a listener or two and talking about what you want to write about. In the process, you will discover more about what you want to say, partly as a result of having verbalized and partly because of the feedback from your listeners. Questions they may ask about the substance of what you say are likely to be particularly good indicators. Do not ask your listeners, "Was that okay?" If they are your friends, they will probably be supportive and say, "Sure it's okay." Instead check to see how well they have understood. Ask, for example, what they think your main points are. If they do not know—or do not get them quite right—you may not be communicating clearly.

A variation on this technique is called nutshelling. Here you begin, "In a nutshell, what I want to say is . . ." and state the essence in three or four sentences. Then you imagine yourself teaching those ideas as you continue talking.

If you leave a tape recorder on as you talk, you will be able to listen to yourself afterwards and take notes on whatever was useful. Or you can take notes from memory after you finish. But even if you keep no record at all, the process of talking it out is a good way to generate your material without having to "actually write."

Another variation on this technique is suggested by some writers' experience that they seem to be more productive when they "hear" in their minds the words they are writing. If your writing is coming too slowly (or not at all), imagine yourself talking instead of writing to your readers, listen to your inner voice and write what you "hear."

Technique 2: Freewriting

Another technique for generating material and getting some words on paper is suggested by our understanding that difficulty getting started can arise partly because a writer's critical faculties are too strong too early. This technique, with which you may already be familiar (for it is one of the most widely taught), is called freewriting. Freewriting is very effective because it forces you to write from the very start. It follows the advice of Gertrude Stein, who said to

> think of writing in terms of discovery, which is to say that creation must take place between the pen and the paper, not before in a thought or afterwards in a recasting. Yes, before in a thought, but not in careful thinking. It will come if it is there and if you will let it come, and if you have anything you will get a sudden creative recognition.

Freewriting works like this. You set a time limit, usually ten or fifteen minutes for beginners, but eventually as long as forty-five minutes or even longer. You sit down with pen and paper (or at a keyboard). You think of your writing task or topic if you have one (or of whatever comes to mind if you do not), and you start writing. The only rule is that you must keep writing constantly, without censoring. If you cannot think of anything to write, you write "Nothing comes to mind" or (better) you recopy the preceding sentence until something does come to mind. You do *not* worry about spelling, punctuation, grammar, or usage. You are allowed to misspell, mispunctuate, and violate the rules of grammar and usage. You do *not* worry about style. You do *not* worry about whether one idea or sentence has any connection with another. You do *not* even worry about making sense—yet.

If you compose on a word processor, there is a variation on freewriting called "invisible writing." To do this, you simply turn down the brightness of the screen until no letters are visible. Since you cannot see what you have written, you are not even tempted to think about what is wrong with it or how you might revise it. After you have written freely for the set time, you turn up the brightness or print what you have produced.

Most people soon find that they can fill a handwritten page in less than fifteen minutes. Occasionally, a writer gets lucky and has a page of good writing—or at least a draft that can be revised to suit her or his purposes. Not surprisingly, freewriting also produces a considerable quantity of garbage. That is no problem, however, if you have access to a wastebasket. Think of the garbage as compost (a word which has the same Latin root as *composition*). Among it you will usually find at least one well-phrased sentence, one good idea, one provoking image which the rest of the page helped to fertilize.

Here are two examples of freewriting which worked. Neither is a finished piece of writing, but both are very good starts. Each is good, honest self-expression. Although neither is written in Standard English or adapted to other demands many readers might make, each writer's voice is clear and the feelings come across. Each writer has generated good contrasts and good particulars. The first begins with little sense of purpose. The second seems to be written more to express and clarify strong emotions than to communicate with readers.

Whatever faults these writings might seem to have if judged as finished pieces of writing, both are successful freewritings with excellent potential.

> Fifteen minutes at the library. The steam is streaming out of the thermos of that girl. No, . . . out of the girl's thermos. She is pretty. Should I say something to her? She has no rings on her left hand. Why is she sitting at this table in front of me and not some other seat, there are plenty around. I should get on with my home work. What time is it? Plenty of time till 2:30 class. I should be thinking about science. Not girls. What makes her so beautiful? No, not that kind of science. Let light trigger a sort of chemicals like CO_2 and H_2O, to simulate photosynthesis. Why did she turn sideways? What is she thinking? How beautiful she is. Should I ask her to read this? Maybe she'll like it. She has a nice profile. Would the professor laugh at this? Great! Ten seconds to go.

> & today riding back from the grocery store on my bike, going past men working on the sidewalk—stares, one whistle & one man repeating hi there til I turned the corner. i can't describe the leering look on his face or the tone of his voice, but i know it so well, i've seen it heard it, countless times & it makes me ashamed——less ashamed now & more angry, but still ashamed.
>
> we've a mirror in the bedroom, attached to the dresser—i liked the way i looked in it this morning. i liked the sunshine around me——our room is on the south side——i liked my clothes which were clean, functional & recycled & i liked me——clean, no more makeup, glasses instead of contacts, hair that does what it wants——clean.
>
> & those men made me feel dirty
>
> converted me to an object for their pleasure. i could tell them i'm intelligent, i have consciousness, mostly i wanted to tell them they have their heads up their asses——but i didn't cuz i was scared——around the corner & i was home.
>
> Sharon Dowe

After you have done one or more freewritings, take a short break. Then look for that good idea, provoking image, or well-phrased sentence. Copy it at the top of a blank page, and use it to start another freewriting. Let it take your mind and your pen where they will.

Probably this second freewriting will be more fertile (and possibly even more organized) than the first. Again, after a short break, look for another starting point. Very likely, you will find several potential starting points. Use at least one to do yet another freewriting. Do not feel committed to your starting point, and do not yet aim for organization.

By now you have "wasted" almost an hour on these freewritings—but you probably have enough material to form the basis of a 500-word essay. If you are lucky (and people who do relatively longer freewritings are more likely to be lucky), a "center of gravity" has started to emerge. That is, you may have found something that you can use as the center or main point of a paper. If it has not emerged, look for it; make it emerge. Reread what you have written, and ask yourself what "it" is trying to say. Attempt to sum it up, or at least most of it. That center of gravity may be a rough version of the thesis statement of your final paper (or the main event of your short story, the central image of your poem). You may be able to use it to organize the rest of the material you have salvaged from your freewritings. You may now be ready to start drafting your paper in a more conventional manner.

Professor Peter Elbow, probably the foremost advocate of a freewriting approach to composition, suggests the following four-hour procedure (here rephrased) for producing a short paper:

1. Do a forty-five minute freewriting in which you try to write down every-thing which comes to mind about your subject. Spend fifteen minutes reading it over and looking for an emerging center of gravity.

2. Start from that center of gravity, and do another forty-five minutes of freewriting. Sum it up again.

3. Start from that summation, and do another forty-five minutes of writing. This time make it semi-free. Try to develop that emerging center of gravity. Aim for a bit of coherence, but still let new ideas or images flow.

4. Spend fifteen minutes making your meaning clear to yourself. Perhaps make an outline. Definitely focus on a single assertion that can serve as a thesis.

5. Now spend forty-five minutes writing the paper and fifteen minutes editing it.

(*Note*: These time lengths may be "stretched or squeezed"; the clock is being used because most of us need it to discipline ourselves.)

At first you may feel silly doing freewritings. After all, you are intentionally producing "bad" writing. Or perhaps you may have trouble identifying those kernels of usable material in the sea of compost, so you may well need a little help from your friends or from a teacher. Also at first, especially if you do not let yourself really loose, you may not be very fertile. (Even experienced freewriters occasionally produce several in a row with no apparent value).

Freewriting is hard for many people because it requires that the writer tolerate chaos. Chaos is a necessary phase of any creative process: order (what the Greeks called *cosmos*) can be formed only out of chaos; even the transition from one order to another requires at least a brief transitional period of chaos. Unfortunately, most of us are so strongly socialized to believe in order we have difficulty tolerating even that chaos which is a necessary phase of the creative process.

Freewriting liberates writers from several contradictions: How can I write the beginning until I have written the middle and know what I am introducing? How can I start writing when my mind is still in chaos? How can I think of everything—ideas, transition, logical support, examples, diction, spelling, punctuation—at once? Freewritings can start anywhere, they are supposed to be chaotic; and you are supposed to ignore transitions, diction, and mechanics—even supporting details can be found later if they do not come immediately to mind.

Experienced writers often use freewriting as a general problem-solving device, not just to generate material. If they are having unusual difficulty with a particular piece of writing, they may do a freewriting about why they are having difficulty. Such a freewriting often leads to insights that get the writing process moving again. They may also freewrite about the audience or whatever other aspect of the context seems to be creating difficulty. Clarifying one's understanding of audience, purpose or situation often unblocks the flow of writing (see Chapter 4).

The underlying principle and point to be remembered is that freewriting helps you generate both material and focus by allowing you to postpone the criticizing, selection, and editing until later. In the extreme case, you can start writing even before you know what you are writing about. You can use freewriting to develop and sharpen a vague conception, to discover your focus. You can use it to explore the implications of a key term or proposition. Freewriting allows you to start with whatever you have and to develop from there.

Technique 3: Brainstorming

Brainstorming is a well-established group technique, in some ways similar to talk-then-write, in some ways similar to freewriting. Like talk-then-write, it is oral and based on interaction among people. Like freewriting, it is a way of generating chaos in the hope that somewhere among the chaos will be a germ of inspiration.

Brainstorming is especially appropriate for collaborative writing. When people write collaboratively, especially when they are producing writing to represent a corporate or collective position, the group often tries to generate material and reach a preliminary consensus before individuals start drafting. Beginning with brainstorming and then seeking consensus (see pages 138–40) allows the group to give individual writers direction for drafting.

Brainstorming works like this. You need a small group of people—perhaps students starting on the same assignment or several people doing a collaborative writing, perhaps you and several friends who have agreed to help you start your paper. In the first stage of brainstorming, members of the group think of the topic, problem, or assignment and then free associate. Each person calls out any idea or image that comes to mind. Nobody does any evaluating, but one person's idea may suggest another idea to some other person. Meanwhile, one person has been assigned to take notes (or a tape recorder is running). The group collects as many ideas as possible in whatever order they come from the tops of everyone's heads. It is often useful to set a time limit on this stage before starting—or someone in the group can be assigned to decide when "enough" material has been generated.

In the second stage of brainstorming, the ideas are evaluated, and the wheat separated from the chaff. This stage is also a time for finding focus. If the group feels it does not yet have enough material or has found a focus that redefines the task, it can return to freely generating more ideas. If the group has generated enough material, it can go on to organizing by clustering related ideas and images, looking for patterns, perhaps even creating a rough outline. This latter stage of brainstorming resembles mindmapping or clustering.

Although originally devised as a group problem-solving technique, brainstorming can be applied to topics that are still too vaguely defined to be called problems in the proper scientific sense. This method can also be used by an individual, who simply jots down as many ideas as possible as quickly as possible. Individual brainstorming may be less fertile than group brainstorming, but it is still a valuable discovery technique. It is to ideas what freewriting is to words.

Technique 4: Meditation

Professor Edward Corbett suggests meditation as a discovery process. At first that may strike you as a bit odd. Given the nature of the human creative process, however, it actually makes a great deal of sense. Inspiration cannot be forced, but we can "make space" for it, and meditation is a good way to make that space.

In the Eastern traditions, meditation is often described as an *emptying* of the mind. Inspiration comes to those who wait, provided they wait properly; and the relaxed yet disciplined "wide focus" of the meditator is a proper state in which to wait for enlightenment or any form of inspiration. In the Christian tradition, to use Corbett's words, "the technique consists in taking a short passage from the Scripture or from the text of the day's Mass and, in an atmosphere of silence and freedom from distraction, thinking about it in a serious persistent way, trying to see the relevance of the passage to one's own life and spiritual growth."

Inspiration literally means *inhalation* and is derived from the image of breathing in the divine breath of the gods. The basic principle that underlies meditation is a good basis for opening yourself to the divine breath of inspiration. Even without taking up meditation in the full spiritual sense, you can apply the underlying principle to writing and to learning. You simply take the central idea or topic of the potential writing and use it instead of the scriptural passage. You start with your attention focused on the topic, but you do not try to think about it in any structured way. You let your thoughts go where your associations take them, only bringing your attention gently back to the topic from time to time. Thus you reach insights that a more controlled, structured kind of thinking might overlook.

Technique 5: Keeping a Journal

Many serious writers use another technique: keeping a journal. A writing journal is not the same as a diary, although it can be combined with one. A writing journal is a lot like a basket in which you can collect bits and pieces which may later be useful in one way or another.

Given the nature of the creative process, a writer may find a usable image or a potentially meaningful bit of information at any time. Often it is not clear just when, where, or how that image or information will be usable. Inspiration, moreover, can strike at any time. The writer's journal is a place to collect these images, bits of information, and inspirations. It can also be the place to do short freewritings when the impulse strikes. Its virtue is that it is bound, so what is collected is not likely to be lost (as it often is if left in the mind, told to a friend, or jotted on a scrap of paper). The notebook in which you keep the journal, incidentally, should be large enough to work in but small enough so that you will actually carry it around with you—after all, it has to be there when you discover an interesting item in the newspaper or are struck by that unscheduled inspiration. (*Note*: You can paste things in journals as well as write in them.)

A journal is especially useful for academic and other types of intellectual writers because it aids the most important kind learning. If you are learning new information which fits neatly into concepts you already have, it is easy to take organized notes and to incorporate the information quickly into your image of the world. But if you are learning new concepts, which may require you to reorganize information you already know or even to change beliefs you already have, then it is more difficult to make them your own. You have to play with them and discover their implications if you are to develop the ability to use them. This sort of learning is what a broad or humanistic education is all about. Using the new concept in a written paper is one of the best ways to get a hold on it (which is why writing—usually in the form of essay examinations and term papers—is basic to a humanistic education).

If a concept is genuinely new to you, at first you may not have enough control over it to use it precisely in a paper. But a journal entry, because it is essentially for your own edification and future use, is like a freewriting in the sense that it does not have to be "good" and certainly does not have to be correct. A journal is a place to play with ideas and images.

It is sometimes useful to structure journal entries, especially if you are starting your first journal. Make the first part of the entry a report: restate an idea, describe an image, narrate a potentially significant event (even if you do not yet understand how it may be significant); the first part of the entry might even be a quote or a statistic. Then make the second part of the entry a comment: explore the implications of the first part, give an example of it, argue with it, relate it to your own life or to some other concept.

Here are some sample journal entries.

> According to the structuralists, a sign can be divided (for analysis) into signifier/signified; and a single signifier can represent more than one signified. I want to cut down on my smoking (because cigarettes signify cancer), but I realize I have a problem. Last year a psychologist friend of mine showed me a picture an eight-year-old boy had drawn of his father: the man was smoking a cigarette; the boy felt that was an important aspect of his father. In my self-image I see a "cancer stick"; I think it is from a Marlboro commercial. I want to give up smoking, but I need a replacement for this signifier of masculinity.

> Definition: I listened to Carly Simon's first album for a long time before I realized what was bothering me: all the songs were about men. Does that say anything about how Carly defines herself (as a person? as an artist?)

> The Principle of Perfection
>
> Perfection does not always have to have a positive result. . . . Burke refers to Freud's use of the term "repetitive compulsion." For example, Joe has many relationships which always end by his girlfriend leaving him and calling him absolutely useless. Joe does not have a problem finding a new girlfriend, but he does have a problem going out for more than three months with the same person.
>
>> Observation: Joe gives his life FORM by shaping the outcome of events always to follow the same emotional pattern.
>
> This is what Burke calls a drive to make one's life "perfect." Thus for Burke the "repetitive compulsion" is not antithetical to the perfection principle. This view leads to Burke's stating "man is rotten with perfection." Rotten, possibly referring to morally

```
corrupt or worthless in some sense, lends an ironic twist to the
concept of perfection.
```

                                        Leslie Teresa Taylor

```
Robert Pirsig does not balance his philosophizing with his story-
telling. I'm taking a British drama course, and I think Pirsig should
have used George Bernard Shaw as an example. Shaw had ideas which
were far ahead of his time, but managed to put them across in
conjunction with highly entertaining literature. Pirsig's Zen and
the Art of Motorcycle Maintenance is a textbook masquerading as a
novel.
```

Journal entries can also be structured in other ways. For example, you can create dialogues, real or imagined, among people or among points of view; you can write letters, often the sort you know you will never mail; you can write down clever responses that you did not think of soon enough to say; you can record dreams and fantasies, perhaps together with interpretations; you can make lists, perhaps of goals or fears or things to do; you can write character sketches, real or imaginary. What you collect in your journal and how you structure it should depend on what you are trying to understand and what types of writing you plan to do. The virtue of the journal is that it allows you to write a little about something one day, then return to it another day, and perhaps another, as your understanding deepens. When you are finally ready to attempt a fuller and more formal writing, you have some material to start with. You also have a record of how your understanding developed, which can be useful when you are thinking about how to make that understanding clear to your readers.

It is often helpful for writers and writing students to make journal entries *about their writing*. You can use your journal to get started on a piece of writing and also to keep track of how you write it. Thus you use the journal to develop and understanding of your own writing processes. Later you can look back to see what sorts of approaches seem to lead to your most successful writings, which problems you have put behind you, what works and what does not work, and so on. A writer's journal can help you develop an understanding of whatever you are writing about, and it can also help you to understand and develop yourself as a writer.

A journal is a source book. When you are about to start writing, you turn to your journal for a topic, for material, or for concepts that can suggest how to organize your writing. (*Note*: If you are about to keep a journal for the first time, you will be wise to make a rule about the minimum number of times a week you must write in it—perhaps three. Once the habit is established, you can drop the rule.)

Technique 6: Research

Research (literally, *re-search*, to search again) is a most respectable technique for getting started. Most people interpret the word *research* much too narrowly, thinking of it only as a process that takes place in libraries and laboratories.

In a sense, any form of observation that is structured as a search should be considered research. For instance, going to see a hockey game (or three) prior to writing a paper on violence in hockey is research. Usually, however, we reserve the word *research* for somewhat more structured forms of observation.

The first and easiest place to search for material is your own *memory*. Especially if your subject is personal or one with which you are very familiar, you may find much or all the material you need right there in your own mind. And the heuristics discussed later in this chapter can help you re-search you own memory fully and efficiently (see pages 78–98).

Interviewing is another good research technique and a relatively painless way to gather material: when you interview, the interviewees present your material to you. You can interview experts or participants. Prior to writing about "functional illiteracy," for example, you might visit an adult basic literacy program to interview both teachers and students.

Conducting an effective interview is itself a craft. You must create an atmosphere and ask the right questions to get the person you are interviewing talking, and talking to your point. At the same time, you must give that person enough room to say things you would never have thought to ask about and even things with which that person may well expect you to disagree. A good interviewer is open and perspicacious, sensitive and perceptive. (Learning to be a good interviewer, like learning to be a good writer, is good for your character.)

One key to a successful interview is preparation. It helps to know something about the topic—not necessarily a great deal, but something—so you can know what questions to ask. It also helps to know something about the person you will be interviewing, so you can know *how* best to ask those questions.

It helps to have a strategy—not just a random list of questions, but a plan about the order in which you will ask them. You may start with a general question and use the answer to focus on particulars. Or you may start with particulars and build toward more general implications. Of course, if the actual interview takes off in unexpected and fruitful directions, you may decide not to follow the plan. What is most important is to establish rapport, so the person you are interviewing opens up and speaks freely.

Once the person is talking, be sure you are getting specifics. Do not be embarrassed to admit you do not understand something. Do push for specifics, dates, names, anecdotes, details, supportive evidence. Do not interrupt—you want the person to keep talking—but remember to come back to key points. Always remember the purpose of the interview, which is for you to get information; express your own point of view only enough to get responses. And, since you may not have asked all the right questions, a good closing question is, "Is there anything important I haven't asked?"

Experiments, although most common in the sciences, are good for gathering all sorts of material. One student at Central Michigan University, for example, turned a question into an experiment by giving three versions of it to students in his dormitory. The question was simple: "Should a girl [sic] ask a guy out?" The variants were " . . . if she has known him for over two years?" and " . . . if she just met him within the last two weeks?" The responses were not surprising (for 1973), but the student was not centrally concerned with the responses as such. His hypothesis was that the results of polls and other questionnaires are influenced by the ways the questions are worded. Indeed, the answers to the first question seemed to indicate that there was considerable disagreement on the campus. However, the two follow-up questions revealed that the apparent disagreement was the result of what the question did not stipulate: Central Michigan students in those days apparently thought that women should ask men out only if they had known them for a long time.

In the same writing class, an assignment on nonverbal communication led to a number of papers based on informal experiments. What these students each did was to pick an unspoken rule of behavior and violate it. For instance, one writer went to a party and made a practice of standing about six inches closer than usual to other people. These papers, perhaps because the students used concrete, structured experiences instead of writing "out of their heads," were among the best the class produced.

Such experiments are not conclusive. They are similar to the preliminary experiments that scientists (and educators) do prior to designing the serious experiments that are supposed to produce reliable results. But even an informal experiment, especially when combined with other forms of research, is an excellent technique for getting started on a piece of writing. It may not prove anything, but it is very likely to suggest a lot.

Reading is not usually listed in textbooks among the other discovery techniques. But reading about your topic is a way of consulting other people (in this sense like interviewing). Reading is a way of gathering information and a way of setting your mind to work, of preparing the incubation process, which will result in inspiration and insights. When done properly, reading is one of the best ways to start writing. The details of library research we will leave to Chapter 10 because most of those details have to do with the selection process, not with the generation of material: the library is filled with information, the writer's main problem is to find the relevant sources. The point here is that reading and responding to what you read—by discussing it, by freewriting responses, by commenting on it in your journal—is a good way to get started writing.

Databases are another place to look for material. Strictly speaking, any collection of information, including a book, is a database. But computerized databases have one major advantage: a computer can scan the database with incredible speed, locating key words that may indicate material on your topic. Most academic libraries have access to a variety of databases.

Computer Variations

Computers allow fruitful variations on these techniques for getting started.

Some writers simply find it easier to start writing on a word processor than on paper. As images on a screen, mere electronic blips, the first words seem less permanent than they would on paper. Thus they do not need to be so perfect. And if they turn out to be "no good," they can be erased with the flick of a switch.

Word processors also allow an extreme variation on freewriting, known as "invisible writing." Simply turn the monitor's brightness control all the way down until nothing is visible on the screen. Then write freely whatever comes to mind. Since you cannot see what you are writing, there is no possibility of stopping to revise. Later you turn the brightness back up, save what is potentially useful, and erase the rest.

Computer networking, forums and bulletin boards allow variations on brainstorming and the talk-then-write technique. Sometimes it is easier to try out ideas on people you do not have to face (on a forum or bulletin board), perhaps even people you will never know except via computer). And networking allows brainstorming even when a group cannot get together physically.

Keeping a journal, taking research notes or freewriting on a word processor is not essentially different from doing the same activities with pencil, pen, or typewriter. But it does save the work of recopying the parts you later decide to use. Similarly, you may be able to save work by transferring information directly from a database to your word processor.

As more and more "data" become available on computerized databases, it becomes increasingly possible to use the computer for time-consuming sorts of analyses as well. Statistical analysis of quantifiable data is the most obvious instance. But software that searches text for key words—or more interestingly, combinations of key words—can help lawyers, historians, rhetoricians, or literary critics trace a theme through a very large text or set of texts. And shunting such time-consuming searches onto the computer creates time for people to do the more sophisticated and interesting levels of analysis and interpretation.

EXERCISE

1. When next you write, keep track of how you manage your time. What effect, if any does this have on your writing process or on the quality of the final written product? Would it help you to make a schedule or to divide your writing time in half, reserving the second half for sharpening focus, deleting irrelevant material, organizing and reorganizing, making additions to fill gaps, checking transitions, fixing awkward structures, finding precisely "right words," correcting usage, grammar, punctuation, spelling, and mechanics?

2. Do a fifteen-minute freewriting that is totally free (no topic). Do two more, either totally free or following from a kernel you discovered in the first. Reread them. Share one with a small group. Let people in the group ask questions, pick out good points, and offer compliments (no negative responses allowed at this stage).

3. Keep a journal. Record what happens as you write papers. Record ideas from this book; play with those ideas and relate them to other experiences and ideas you have had. Record ideas and happenings from your writing class or workshop and speculate about their implications. Carry your journal with you always. Jot down notes for writings as they occur to you. Jot down intriguing quotations and statistics. Do freewritings. Write in this journal at least three times a week.

4. Try at least two of the following techniques: talk-then-write, freewriting, meditation, journal writing, and brainstorming. Compare your experiences with those of other writers. Consider ways in which you might adapt one or more of these techniques to your own writing needs.

5. Try using a research technique as a way of getting started on a piece of writing. Compare your experience with those of other writers. Consider various ways you might use research in the kinds of writing you are likely to be doing in the near future.

6. Use Peter Elbow's freewriting procedure (page 47) to write a short paper. How well does it work for you? Could you modify it to make it work better for you? If you know other people who are trying this procedure, compare your results with theirs. Are there particular types of writing for which it seems to be most appropriate?

7. Compile a list of common beliefs—eating spinach makes you strong; an apple a day keeps the doctor away—and consider how you might research their accuracy and origins.

8. Do some reading on human creativity. Consider the implications for yourself as a writer. Consider also how these implications might vary somewhat for the different types of writing you do.

Negative Invention _____

May God us keep
From Single vision & Newton's sleep.

WILLIAM BLAKE

There are many notable aspects of language, such as classification, specification, abstraction, which have their analogues in purely nonverbal behavior. But the negative is a peculiarly linguistic resource. And because it is so peculiarly linguistic, the study of man as the specifically word-using animal requires special attention to this distinctive marvel, the negative.

KENNETH BURKE

Conceptual Blockbusting

In order to create a new idea or image, one must destroy—or at least temporarily set aside—old perspectives and concepts. James Adams, a humanistic professor of engineering, calls this process *conceptual blockbusting*. It is a form of what we will call *negative invention* because it negates the old conception in order to create the new one.

Negative invention is formally negative but creatively positive. Conceptual blockbusting can explode a stereotypical conception that may be blocking a more useful view of the subject or problem. Consider, for example, the following story-riddle:

A father and son were in an automobile accident. The father was instantly killed. The son, seriously injured, was rushed to a nearby hospital for emergency surgery. The surgeon entered, apparently ready to operate, and then declared, "I can't operate. This boy is my son!" What is the relationship between the boy and the surgeon?

The answer, which *ought* to be obvious, is that the surgeon is the boy's mother. But when a writer, using experiment as a discovery technique to prepare an article for an early issue of *Ms.*, asked this riddle of 51 people at a cocktail party, only two could answer correctly. Forty-nine people's view of the obvious was blocked by a stereotype of surgeons as male. Nowadays that stereotype has been significantly undermined, so a much higher percentage of people can solve the riddle quickly.

Stereotyping—that is, perceiving what one expects to perceive instead of what is really there—is an example of *perceptual block*. A person who is "blocked" by a stereotype literally does not "see what you mean" if your meaning contradicts the stereotype.

Closely related to stereotyping is the failure to look at a topic or problem from various perspectives. The ability to switch viewpoints is often crucial to successful rhetorical invention (i.e., to generating the material and devising the strategy for successful communication). The ability to perceive from various relevant perspectives is often crucial to scientific discovery, to technical design, and to almost any sort of humanistic vision. That is why William Blake prayed to be saved from "Single vision." It is also why much of the rest of this chapter is devoted to a catalog of rhetorical techniques for generating a variety of perspectives.

The surgeon riddle exemplifies the sense in which *attitudes* may underlie perceptual stereotypes and thus block creative discovery. In that example a sexist stereotype is allowed to exist because a sexist attitude has not been eradicated. Consider the following paper, very much like a freewriting, which was written by a basic writing student at Boston University. Notice how it circles round and round an attitudinal block, getting ever closer to a conceptual breakthrough it does not quite reach.

I really don't know what to make of today, Liz trying to give me the money for her prom ticket. I really don't see why she even thought I would take it. I mean if I wanted her to pay for her ticket I would have said so when I asked her.

But this really put me to thinking, she's said things about when we go out, yet I never really paid much attention to them. I guess it's because I feel that the guy should be responsible for the date, after all he's the one who did the asking. Ah, but that brings up a good point I've never thought of before, what if the girl should do the asking. I guess I'll worry about that if the situation ever comes up. Meanwhile I should worry about the situation at hand, sooner or later Liz is going to say something since I don't take her out as often now that I don't have a job. But there isn't too much you can do with little or no money, even less on weekend nights. Another point is transportation, since I don't always have a car it gets to be a pain, because then we either have to walk or get a ride with someone else. That can be a hassle especially since you're then limited to where you can go and what you can do. I've often wondered about that, I always decide what and where we go to. But occasionally I've heard girls say they don't always want to go where their date is taking them. Yet they never say anything, or if you ask them where they'd like to go they say, you decide. That's sort of a pain because generally if the guy has asked his date where she'd like to go it's probably because he doesn't want to resort to the old standby movie or bowling and can't think of something different to do.

So I guess I'm saying that when asked out on a date the girl shouldn't have to pay for any of it, or worry about where to go unless

the guy asks her were she'd like to go. I also believe the guy should
be responsible for the transportation and definitely should be the
one to ask. Furthermore if the girl has a curfew the guy should see
that she's home on time.

This is all quite interesting because I've just decided I really
don't know if Liz agrees with these views. As a matter of fact I
know she doesn't agree that the guy should have to pay for the entire
date. She probably wouldn't hesitate to suggest something if I asked
her, although it would more likely than not be the movies. She's
also said she doesn't think the guy should always be responsible
for the ride. However I know she agrees that the guy should see to
it that the girl gets home on time, although her parents would do
nothing more than ask if she wasn't out kind of late last night.

That's weird because I never realized just how much people
disagree on certain issues of this nature. Why I'd probably bet
that no two people have the exact same image-model of anything. I
guess this all just goes to show that no man is like any other.

Edward Scanlon

In this case, the block is a cultural attitude men have about women and
so causes difficulty only for this topic. There are also more general cultural
blocks, which can interfere with problem-solving and creativity. Many North
Americans, for example, feel a need to be always rational, orderly, and "in
control." These personality traits can prevent a writer from tolerating the
period of unconscious incubation and conscious chaos that so often precedes
inspiration and insight. Writers may block because their internal critics are
too strong.

The Revolt Against Anxiety

My problem with writing is directly related to the disappointment
I have with myself as a thinker. During the past six semesters I've
inundated my mind with information to compensate for many years
of academic vacuity, but I have yet to develop skills to clear and
critical thinking. I can imitate a competent thinker by coughing
up appropriate bits when necessary, and I can also imitate a
competent writer. Consequently I have acquired very superficial
knowledge but little understanding.

. . .

The sense of confusion and disappointment, and the pressure of
an internalized critical and hostile audience, permeates my
attempts at writing, causing anxiety. My main task in writing has
generally been to win <u>A</u>'s and good cheer by impressing that audience

with uncommon topics; I would try to 'say it with flowers,' which
overshadowed and inhibited the adventure of learning. But upon
reanalysis of my writing process, I had to admit that gnawing
audience is, for the most part, me—and I'm not impressed.

What all this means is that I have a head full of unreconciled
ideas, delusions of grandeur, and a disorganized thinking/writing
process (I can't distinguish between the two); the anxiety incurred
is indicative of this mess. I tend to edit and revise continuously
as I write—before, during, and after an idea hits the paper—
working arduously from beginning to end without a genuine grasp
on what I'm trying to say. I go from paragraph to paragraph, reworking
sentences from general to specific and vice versa, searching for
the magic combination that will get me on a roll, as it were. The
peculiar thing is I concentrate on sound—I say to myself, "This
sounds horrible, it doesn't make sense," or "I feel good about the
way this sounds"—constructive thinking is somehow buried beneath
or triggered by sound and feeling. And when I'm almost finished, I
begin typing the paper for distraction, or to see how it looks, but
continue revising by supporting generalizations, reordering, and
deleting (usually metaphors), whatever it takes to make the paper
sound better. My endings are always contrived in haste over the
typewriter, and upon proofreading, things are altered once again
to comply with the sense of the ending.

Marjorie Doll

As this passage of self-analysis makes clear, Marjorie is both a skillful writer
and a subtle thinker. Though she can undoubtedly get better at both writing
and thinking—who can't?—her immediate need is to quiet the internal critic
that sabotages her writing process.

To what extent do you share common attitudes that may be interfering
with your development as a writer? Do you believe that playfulness and humor
should always be kept apart from ''serious'' work, that fantasy and reflection
are often signs of laziness (if not craziness)? Do you share the common Anglo-
American anti-intellectualism that rejects any theoretical knowledge unless it
has *immediate* practical applications? Putting some effort into overcoming such
blocks may be a very important part of improving your writing abilities.

A writer may also suffer from an *emotional block*. To what extent does
the fear of failure interfere with your development as a writer? In the extreme,
such an emotional block can prevent someone from writing at all.

In our conversation, I confessed that my ambition is to write. I
also told you that, except for one other occasion, I had not let
this out. When I made this statement, did you notice that the earth

did not move; that the sky did not open; that you did not prostrate
yourself before me babbling in tongues?

I did.

And I don't mean this to be humorous or trite: I do mean that because
of the paradoxical combination of my conviction that I can write
with my desperate lack of confidence, the level of reassurance I
seek is infinitely great. Without this insane level of adulation,
which I never receive, I cannot succeed. Therefore, publicly
risking my most precious belief—that I'm a writer—is a chance
I'm unwilling to take.

Fear can also interfere with particular types of writing.

However serious my other difficulties may be, it is beyond doubt
that my most serious writing problem is in-class essays. Whenever
I am forced to write under these circumstances, I go into a state
of paralyzing anxiety which not only affects my ability to see or
make sense of the essay questions but also affects the quality of
my writing. I end up freewriting my essay because that is all I am
capable of when anxiety gets in the way of my ability to think
clearly. If you asked me after the in-class essay what I wrote, I
would not be able to tell you.

Ruby Stroshin

Since leaving home almost six years ago, I have written very few
letters. I have kept saying that this was just because I hated
writing. However, I don't think this was completely true as I often
wrote friends and loved writing in my journal. So the question,
"Why don't I ever write home?" remained a mystery to both my family
and myself. We have all spent time searching for repressed
resentment that would make me want to reject them. Consciously, I
did want to write them, but something was blocking this
communication.

While reading Elbow's Writing with Power, particularly the
chapter on audience, it struck me that there was another element
at work: acute audience awareness. When writing my parents, I
thought it was necessary to give them a complete summary of my
physical and emotional bearings from the time I left them until
the present. This seemed like such a major undertaking that I shied
away from it; the longer I put off writing them, the more I felt I
owed them this kind of explanation.

Eve Edmonds

Fears can also prevent a writer from learning. Although we say, "Nothing ventured, nothing gained," some students and even some professional writers will stick with one formula they have mastered (e.g., for a five-paragraph essay, a term paper, a newspaper report) rather than experiment with other forms and develop their writing abilities more broadly. Even in a writing class, where the main point is to develop one's writing abilities, many people are tempted to play it safe.

We are all human; we are all more comfortable with our old conceptions, just as we are with our old slippers. But a writer who is too comfortable with old conceptions is not likely to have anything new to say, nor even a significantly fresh way to say something old. To be competent at negative invention one must be open, able to tolerate contradictions and new ideas— even new *ways* of thinking—at least long enough to genuinely comprehend and consider them.

Problems do not exist autonomously. A problem is a problem only *for someone*. Sometimes an apparently intractable problem or contradiction is best overcome by changing *the problem-solver*. This may mean you.

Interestingly, this assertion has its roots in antiquity. Quintilian and Cicero both asserted that the good orator (or writer) must be the good person! To be good at negative invention, beyond narrow and specialized bounds, writers must display certain personality traits which we ordinarily consider "mature" or "good." Such traits include openness, tolerance, and empathy, as well as a balanced development of emotional, intuitive, and rational faculties—traits that are also among the goals of a genuinely humanistic education. Negative invention is crucial to the development of writing abilities beyond certain narrow bounds, so in this sense the classical rhetoricians were correct when they said a good writer must be a good person.

The Power of Negative Thinking

One of the mottos of our culture is "Think positively!" Positive thinking certainly has its uses, as when we insist on believing something can be done and therefore persevere until we discover a way to do it, or when we insist on defining a concept in positive terms (see page 324). A less-than-positive thinker might have given up before the task was accomplished or accepted a definition that did not really expose the essence of the concept.

But negative or critical thinking is often the basis from which positive concepts are developed. Thus negative thinking can produce positive results. Each type of thinking has its uses.

The epitome of negative thinking is the *law of contraries*. It is as old as Taoism, Buddhism, and pre-Socratic Greek philosophy. It is as new as relativity and quantum physics or modern dialectics. It is basic to thinking about change and process—because any process involves change, and any change involves the replacement of the old with the new, the development of the new from its contrary, the "not-new."

Greek teachers of philosophy and rhetoric, beginning perhaps with the Eleatics, taught a critical technique called antithesis (in Greek, *antilogike*), which embodies the law of contraries. To apply the law of contraries as a discovery technique, they assumed that *if any statement is true, there must be some sense or some context in which its contraries are true.* (Likewise, if any statement is true there must be some sense or some context in which it is to some extent false.)

On the face of it, the law of contraries seems to fly in the face of common sense, which asserts that a statement is either true or false. That particular common sense, however, is common mostly in Western logics, so it would be wise to suspend judgment long enough to consider how the law works as a discovery technique.

Just at the point when you have reached your conclusion, when you have decided that a certain generalization is true, this discovery technique forces you to pause and rethink. It forces you to look from other perspectives, to see other sides. It forces you to search for contexts in which your generalization might not apply, for exceptions to your rule. It turns any statement into a potential "problem" or contradiction by juxtaposing it with its contraries. It demands, at least provisionally, that you *blockbust*.

After you have applied this law, you often decide that your original generalization was and still is basically correct. Having considered the exceptions, you decide that they "prove the rule." But your understanding is fuller and deeper for having turned full circle, even if you have in a sense returned to your starting point. And very often you end up qualifying your original generalization, thus making it more nearly correct (and defensible).

Take, for instance, a proposition that seems obvious:

The best place to begin is at the beginning.

Clearly, this is correct, at least in some senses. Consider nonetheless, some contrary propositions:

The best place to begin is in the middle.
The best place to begin is at the end.

Are there senses or contexts in which these statements are also true?

The best place to begin is at the end. When you start a piece of writing with a thesis statement, in a sense you are starting at the end. That is, you are starting with your *conclusion*, with a generalization that sums up your thinking on the subject, with the end result of your thought process. It might sometimes make more sense to lead up to your conclusion and to put it at the end, as Socrates usually does (to cite just one example). Often, however, the most effective place to state your thesis is at the beginning of a piece of writing (see Chapter 4, pages 107, 173–75). When you do that you are, in a sense, beginning at the end.

The best place to begin is in the middle. That is precisely where many good fictional narratives do begin. There is even a common Latin term, *en medias res*, for beginning in the middle. The *Iliad* begins in the middle. So does *Oedipus Rex*. So does much modern literature. So for that matter do many movies. The importance of earlier events is often clear only in the context of the crisis, which precedes the climax. So it often makes narrative sense to begin in the midst of that crisis and introduce earlier events (including the beginning of the story) as flashbacks. (Some modern literature seems to go one step further: Samuel Beckett's *Waiting for Godot*, for example, is in a sense all middle; essentially it has neither a beginning nor an ending, so it could not possibly begin at the beginning.)

Of course, there is a sense in which one always begins at the beginning. Literally, the fact that a text begins there makes it the beginning. And if we understand ''beginning'' to mean the rhetorically effective place to begin (as opposed to what-happened-first or what-logically-comes-first), then the beginning is where one should begin. The original proposition is in several senses correct, but our understanding is much more full for having considered the ways in which it is not so.

Thus biologist Marston Bates begins his essay on ''Biotic Communities'' by writing,

> I have been trying to think about an organism living alone, in isolation.
> It is not an easy condition to imagine, but perhaps the attempt will
> make a good start toward understanding the interdependence of organ-
> isms in communities.

The great American rhetorician, Kenneth Burke, seems to apply this discovery technique almost constantly. Reading his essays, one gets the feeling that he almost never makes an assertion without also considering the senses in which its contraries are correct. Much of the admirable fullness of his conceptions seems to come from his application of the law of contraries. In *Language as Symbolic Action* (California), for example, he explicitly bases an entire essay on the ideas generated by applying this discovery technique to the proposition, ''Words are signs for things'':

> There is so much that is substantially correct in this common sense
> view (summed up in the proposition that ''Words are the signs of
> things''), we tinker with it at our peril. But we would here ask, if
> only as a tour de force, if only as an experiment tentatively tried for

heuristic purposes, what might be said for the reverse proposition, "Resolved: That things are the signs of words." And even if we didn't dare assert that it should flatly replace the traditional view, we still might hope that it could supply a needed modification of that view, like adding an adjective to a noun.

And, indeed, Burke goes on to reach many important insights about language and communication from this starting point.

The law of contraries can be a powerful discovery technique. It can help you open yourself to perspectives that you had not considered. It can help you improve the substance of your writings, the strategies you devise for communicating that substance, and even your writing processes. There is much more to be said about this law as a rule of logic or dialectic, but that goes beyond the purposes of this book. What has been presented here is difficult enough. Play with it, work with it, learn how to use it. It may lead you to more sophisticated, more useful, and more effective writing.

On Contradiction

Contradictions take various forms that can be useful to you as a writer. Though most recently derived from modern problem-solving methods, it has venerable antecedents. In classical Greece, it was the method of Zeno, Socrates, Isocrates, and the early Sophists. Truth was to be discovered through discussion, with one speaker representing (literally, *re-presenting*) each perspective on the subject. Through discussion, the group of speakers and listeners might approach a fuller and more accurate truth than any of those represented by any of the original viewpoints.

According to Aristotle, certain truths can be known definitely. Other types of truth can be only approached and are best reached by the method of discussion or *dialectic*. Rhetoric—in Classical Greece, the craft of persuasive public speaking—could be a servant of truth because certain truths are best reached through the discussion of contradictions and best made known to the citizenry through convincing verbal presentations. Two or more minds are better than one, and two or more minds interacting are better than the same number of minds operating in isolation. The process is *interaction among people* and the contradiction is *between ideas*.

In other cases, the contradiction may be between an established abstract principle or generalization and a concrete instance. That is, an apparent "fact" may call into question a previously held belief, theory, or opinion. Karl von Frisch, for example, describes the beginning of forty years of research in this way:

About 1910 a famous ophthalmologist, Professor C. von Hess asserted that . . . fishes and invertebrates, and in particular bees, are totally

color-blind. If this were true, the colors of flowers would have no
biological significance. But I could not believe it, and my skepticism
was the first motive which led me to begin my studies of bees about
forty years ago. I tried to find out whether bees have a color sense.

Certain types of contradiction are generated by writing. For this reason—
because the writing process concertizes various types of contradiction—writing
is a learning process. For example, writers often run into a contradiction *between
words and ideas*, as when semiformed ideas seem not to "fit" into the available
words or sentence structures. This is a problem, and it often leads to better
or fuller development of the words, the ideas, or both. Once ideas are in
words, moreover, writers often feel "distanced" from them and, therefore,
better able to criticize and evaluate what is being said.

It may seem that contradiction is negative, not in any way positive.
Logically, a contradiction *is a negation* of one statement by another. We all
know that it is "not nice to contradict." Logical contradiction, however, is
not negative in any moral of judgmental sense. Logical contradiction can be
a positive process, which can lead to the discovery of positively new ideas.

The technique of contradiction can also be used to improve ideas. At
some point during the writing process, often early on, you know what you
are going to write about, you have decided roughly what you are going to
say about it, what your main point is going to be. But you may not have
considered your subject or thesis from enough angles. A "rush to judgment"
can cut off or diminish inspiration and insight. Often it can lead you to reach
conclusions based on a stereotyped image or idea. It can interfere with your
ability to approach a subject from several perspectives; it can interfere with
your ability to develop a genuinely new conception—to see the contradictions.
A "rush to judgment" can interfere with the creative process, can destroy
that "attitude of suspended conclusion" which typifies the mature writing
process and often leads to success. Applying the technique of antithesis to
your tentative thesis statement can help you sharpen it, can help you produce
a more qualified, subtle and sophisticated version of that thesis.

The Utopian U

The Utopian U was developed by a college instructor to help writers
write about an unsatisfactory situation and how it might be changed. It is
often applied in collaborative writing when a group of people agree that something is wrong and want to propose a change. The Utopian U helps writers
move from a negative ("what is wrong") to a positive ("what would be
better"), from *what is* to *what should be*. That is to say, writers using the U
start by describing a "negative" situation; then, through careful analysis and
diagnosis, the U helps writers figure out how to negate that negative situation,
thus

Utopian U

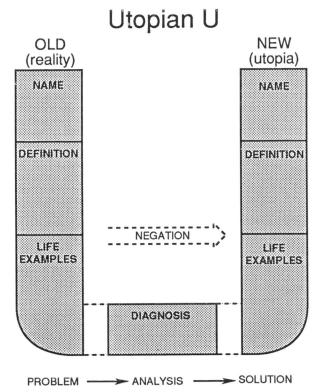

Figure 2.1. The Utopian U. To start using the U, you need only some real life examples of the unsatisfactory situation. Having listed these examples in the box at the bottom of the left arm of the U, you work up, defining and naming the problem. Then you investigate why the problem exists; you diagnose it. *On the basis of this analysis*, you imagine some specific workable alternatives, which you list in the box at the bottom of the right arm of the U. You then work up again, defining and naming.

inventing a positive alternative. If you are trying to convince people to change something, the Utopian U can help.

One application of the Utopian U would be to apply it to your own writing. The U would help you move from a description and analysis of how you write now to a set of pragmatic goals about how you will be able to write in the future (see pages 18–33).

What Is. You begin by describing, defining, and naming what exists. You can start with particular examples or with a word or phrase that names the problem situation. But it is crucially important that you describe concrete instances of the problem. Do not name a problem with which you are only vaguely familiar— say, world hunger, about which you have read a few newspaper articles—unless you will be able to observe or research the problem in detail. Only after observing (or getting detailed reports from those who have) and describing particular instances should you generalize and define the problem. The name, definition, and examples constitute one arm of the U. At this point, you know what the problem is.

Diagnosis. To get to the other arm, you must investigate and diagnose the problem. Without a careful diagnosis, your proposed alternatives are likely to be utopian in the derogatory sense of the word. Why is the existing situation a problem? Since it is such a problem, why does it still exist? On the basis of answers to these questions, you construct a resolution by starting with particular instances of the problem and imagining specific, *workable* alternatives.

What Should Be. Your proposed solution must take into account all the factors that presently contribute to the problem. If the problem exists in part because of a shortage of funds, you cannot suggest an expensive solution (unless you also explain where the money will come from). If the problem exists in part because of a shortage of time, you cannot suggest a time-consuming solution (unless you also explain where the time will come from). You look at the first arm of the U, which describes, defines, and names the problem. Then you imagine a workable alternative—that is, an alternative consistent with your diagnosis of why the problem exists. The specifics of that alternative constitutes the base of the second arm of the U. Like the particular instances of the problem, they also need to be defined and named.

The Utopian U can be applied to any problem from getting better food in the cafeteria to improving a personal relationship to imagining a utopian society to making yourself a better writer.

Some students at Staten Island Community College did apply this heuristic to the problem of unsatisfactory food served by the campus cafeteria. First they listed specific *examples* of cafeteria food they found unsatisfactory:

burgers, fries, canned fruits and vegetables,
packaged cereals, cookies, donuts, candy.

Then they abstracted to reach a *definition*:

mass produced food, usually low in nutrition, that can be cooked easily and quickly or bought already packaged.

Then they found a *name* for it:

Junk food.

The first arm of the U filled, they faced two tasks: to explain why the campus cafeteria stocked so much junk food and to imagine practical alternatives.

Focusing on the hamburger as the archetypal junk food meal, they diagnosed the reasons for the existing situation:

> Junk food is quick, convenient and makes a cheap meal. It fits in with the auto culture, the youth culture, and suburbia (drive-ins, shopping malls). It creates high profits because it uses cheap labor—little skill needed to cook and serve it—and allows standardized portions, frozen ingredients and a limited menu. It is easily disguised and varied with pickles, relish, cheese, etc.

With such a diagnosis in hand, the problem becomes how to fill in the second arm of the U—to think of food that is quick, convenient, and nutritious—and to figure out how it can be sold cheaply in the student cafeteria. It is not hard to start by naming the second arm "nutritious food," defining it as food that provides relatively high nutrition per calorie, and giving examples such as fresh fruit and vegetables, salads, fish, and so forth; but the Utopian U demands that the alternatives be practical, consistent with the diagnosis of why the problem existed it the first place. Thus the task becomes to imagine how more nutritious food could be made convenient, attractive, and cheap. The Staten Island Community College students suggested that the cafeteria should be a nonprofit student cooperative run by the College as an educational program to train students to work in the food industry. Student involvement and control, they thought, would change attitudes; student interns working in the cafeteria could receive not only wages but academic credit.

Once you have filled in both arms of the U, you can easily create a thesis statement from the two top boxes by writing

The existing [Name[1]] should be replaced with [Name[2]].

Using your definitions and examples, you can easily write a contrast demonstrating the superiority of your alternative. Using your diagnosis, you can explain why the problem exists and demonstrate that your alternative is workable. (See pages 210–19 on naming, pages 302–9, 317–31, 294–99 on comparison/contrast, definition and exemplification, and pages 350–70 on causal explanation.)

Images and Metaphors

Discovery through contraries can be applied to images as well as to propositions (although in a sense we do so by converting the image into a statement). Imagine, for example, the stereotyped image of "the writer" in its Romantic extreme: a gaunt young man, lonely and suffering, dressed in his only suit of threadbare black clothes, starving and unappreciated in some dark garret, torturing his soul over each line of lyric poetry. There are many

Figure 2.2. Images of "the writer."

potentially contrary images we can think of (the idea that each term, image, or statement has one-and-only-one opposite is a conceptual block that also needs to be "busted"). One will serve. Imagine "the writer" now as a *group* of people, male and female, of various ages, adequately fed and clothed, excitedly creating an extended argument. In what senses or contexts is this second image accurate or useful?

In fact, this second image is in several ways accurate: much writing these days *is* done by groups, is explanatory or persuasive, pays quite adequately, and involves somewhat less suffering than our Romantic image of "the writer" suggests. Collaborative writings are produced by groups of people in various ways, but the basic fact is that much of the writing you read is produced by more than one person. Most newspaper and newsmagazine articles are collaborative productions, either because they combine the work of several reporters or because one person discovered, organized, and drafted the report and then another person revised, edited, titled, and perhaps reorganized it. Certainly most corporate reports are produced corporately. The same is true of government reports and press releases. Academic reports usually come out of committees (and are typically drafted by subcommittees). Scientific papers are often co-authored. Political and union leaflets are often written collectively. Many popular novels are written by teams of writers, though only one name usually appears on the cover (because the publisher's marketing department defers to the public stereotype). There are even "factories" where large numbers of writers, editors, and typists produce many books simultaneously under the direction of one or two people who approve the ideas and control the publishing contracts.

It remains true that certain types of writing, such as poetry, are still written predominantly by individuals. And the actual drafting of a given passage of prose is almost always done by a single person. But if the substance of that passage was invented by a group interaction, if the draft was reorganized and revised by a group or by anyone other than the person who drafted it, if it was combined into a single written product with other passages drafted by other writers—then the final written product is in several significant senses a group production.

More important, especially for its potential as a discovery technique, is the sense in which every metaphor is a contradiction. Traditionally, metaphor has been defined as comparison—and distinguished from simile by the absence of *like* or *as*. A simile makes an explicit comparison:

Finding words to convey your thoughts is like finding clothes to dress your body.

Samuel Johnson made that a metaphor when he said,

Language is a dress that thought puts on.

Without making an explicit comparison, Johnson juxtaposed the abstract idea of using language to represent ideas with the more concrete idea of putting on clothes. Because language is not literally a dress, the metaphor is logically a contradiction. To make figurative sense of the metaphor, one must resolve the contradiction. One must say,

> I know Johnson doesn't really think words are made of cloth, so he must be asserting that words share some feature we associate with clothes. Let me think about how a dress might be like language. Clothing has various functions. It keeps us warm in cold weather. Does Johnson mean that words keep ideas warm? No, that doesn't go anywhere. Well, then let's see. We dress before appearing in public in order to make ourselves socially acceptable and as attractive as possible. Perhaps Johnson is suggesting that we have to dress our thoughts before we let them out of our minds and that finding the right words makes our ideas more attractive.

Thus the apparent contradiction created when Johnson juxtaposed two words that literally do not make sense together—*language* and *dress*—is resolved in the minds of those who read his metaphor.

Over a century later, I. A. Richards attacked Johnson's metaphor in *The Philosophy of Rhetoric* (Oxford). No, he said, we do not create finished thoughts in our minds and then find words to dress them in. The process of developing our thoughts and the process of verbalizing actually go together, intertwine. The words we use help shape our thoughts. Making meaning is not like dressing; it is an organic process, a growing.

The point here is not about who is right—though Richards' metaphor is a lot closer to the mark than Johnson's—but about how metaphors stimulate our minds. Do you think of the writing process as finding words to dress your thoughts? Does that mean you should finish thinking before you start writing? Can you plan your writing process as you can plan what you will wear tomorrow? Or do you think of writing as more like growing a plant, as a process in which words and ideas interact and meaning develops? Do you fertilize and encourage, then prune and graft? Or to go back to Gertrude Stein's metaphor (see page 38), do you think of writing as growing a child in your womb, a process you can initiate and influence but not fully control or direct—a process whose outcome is not entirely predictable?

Metaphors cause shifts in perspective, direct our attention to particular features of the subject. Playing with metaphors, trying out different metaphors by juxtaposing your subject variously is a wonderful way to generate various perspectives and discover various aspects of your subject. Even just calling a cliché metaphor into question can create insight:

> Is toast the warmest thing you know?

MAY SWENSON

> People talk about love as though it were something you could give,
> like an armful of flowers.
>
> ANNE MORROW LINDBERG

Succinctly, Lindberg reminds us that "to give love" is a metaphor and makes
us consider how giving love is different from giving flowers.

Thus it can be useful to start with metaphors other people have used,
even cliché metaphors, then try to generate some alternatives. The cliché metaphor for revising a piece of writing is polishing. What does that imply about
revision? Is it accurate? What other metaphors might you apply? What do
they suggest?

Another technique for using metaphors is serendipity: pick a noun at
random, perhaps by closing your eyes and sticking your finger in a dictionary.
Can you make that word work as a metaphor for your topic? Engineers use
this blockbusting technique to generate new ways of thinking about design
problems. Professor James Adams reports using it while doing early design
work for the United States space program. It works for writers too.

When you are using metaphors to encourage invention, you can even
mix them. Stylistically, mixed metaphors can be disastrous,

```
If this idea ever catches fire, it will snowball across the land.
I wouldn't be caught dead in that pornographic movie with a ten-
foot pole.
```

But mixed metaphors sometimes represent substantive contradictions. The classic example of such a contradiction comes from physics, where light was
usefully conceived both as a stream of particles and as a wave; the resolution
of this mixed metaphor took decades, but it led to a better understanding of
subatomic physics.

In short, metaphors are not just a way to decorate your writing or to
give it more emotional impact. Metaphors are figures of thought, not just
figures of speech. They can sometimes trap you in a trite perspective, but
you can also use them to create radically new insights. You can use serendipity
and invent random metaphors. You can start from existing metaphors and
generate alternatives. Here are some thoughts one student generated by paying
careful attention to some ordinary metaphors:

What Would You Say?

```
I was sitting in a movie theatre a few weeks ago, passing the minutes
before the show began glancing through a movie magazine, when I
came upon what was--for me at least--a relatively new term, which
apparently referred to a woman pictured nestling in Harrison Ford's
arms. The term, which I had seen twice before, was "squeeze," and
for some reason--which I still don't understand well--I found it
```

repulsive. My reaction was so intense that I could not ignore the dilemma it presented, and even after the show began, I found myself thinking about it. I mean, why would anybody call a woman——any woman——a "squeeze"? The more I thought about it, the more puzzled I became.

The next morning I was much more tuned in to the conversation of my friends, and as the day went on I tried to listen to all the people around me. What I began to notice was that a great many people have a great many names for other people. Because of my problem of the night before, I was especially interested in words men used to refer to women, and over the course of a few days of thoughtful listening, I compiled quite a list of names. I thought that by making a list I might be able to figure out why men used certain words to refer to women and what they <u>really</u> meant——if anything——when they used them.

. . .

When I had finished compiling this list and read it over a few times, there was one particular point I noticed right away: some men like to refer to women as animals. Now this might sound a little outrageous, but it was true. Men weren't just saying "that woman reminds me of a goose," they were <u>calling</u> that woman a goose. Men's conversations concerning women often contained references to "foxes," "fillies," and "doves"; to "chicks," "chickies," and "old Mother Hens"; and to "cats" or "bunnies." And there were other less complimentary names, words that named specific barnyard animals and members of the canine corps but referred, I supposed, to characteristics men saw in women. But why did men use these words? Clearly, the women referred to were humans, not animals! What did the use of these words mean——if anything——for women (or for men)?

After reviewing the list again and recalling past conversations, one thing seemed fairly clear: there were "good" animal names and "bad" animal names, certain names for women who were considered attractive and different names for women who were not (whether for physical or temperamental reasons). The "good" names, used to describe attractive women, were the names of passive animals (chicks, doves), or animals soft to the touch (bunnies, foxes, cats), or animals considered elegant and spirited (filly, gazelle, tigress). Conversely, the "bad" names, names probably meant to deride the women they were used for, were the names of animals considered to be foolish (goose, fool-hen, old foolish hen) or animals considered awkward or ungainly (cow, hippo). What did this suggest about the men who used those words to name women? Clearly, whether they realized it or not, they were using value-laden terms.

Now it may seem as though I am suggesting that nearly every time a man uses one of these terms to refer to women, he makes a conscious

decision on a term that is appropriate to that woman. That is not
entirely true; in fact, it would be misleading. I have used enough
of these words myself to know how this kind of language is generated.
What happens most of the time is that the "right" word just "pops"
into your mind, and you use it. So do your friends and many of the
people within your community. That is probably why the words "pop"
into your head--because they are considered acceptable and
appropriate by those around you. But are they really appropriate
or acceptable--or harmless?

. . .

In times past--at least when their use was novel--the words were
recognized by the user to be allusions; but now, after years and
years of increasingly common usage, these terms have been reduced
to mere labels. Today, when a man uses one of these terms he doesn't
necessarily think consciously about the woman; he just sticks on
a label. The danger is that, once he has labelled the woman, he may
be so satisfied with the label that that is all he can see her for.
In effect, if he has labelled her an animal, she becomes less than
human to him; he may even begin to notice the characteristics in her
that support the label. Now this may seem a little farfetched--
I can imagine that you might be saying, "This is ridiculous. It's
silly. I mean, so what? Who cares? What does it matter? Everybody
does it!"

Well that's not entirely true; not all men still use these labels,
and a lot more women are aware of their use and meaning than you
probably suspect. You see, many people have known for a long time
that labels are suspect and powerful, that they can hide the truth
and inhibit understanding by being misleading. That is why labels
have been commonly used by people during times of war and economic,
political, or social crisis to persuade or influence public
opinion. That's probably why I reacted so violently to the term
"squeeze" when I saw it in the magazine. Clearly, the woman it
referred to was much more than she was being credited for. The term
was misleading and demeaning; it could cause you to think about
that woman, and other women, in an unkind way; in fact, using labels
could cause you to think, period, in a particular way.

Now this last point may sound a little strange, maybe even scary.
Can using labels really control the way you think? You might not
think so, or you may be unsure, so I have thought of a way that you
can test yourself (for yourself) and see the extraordinary power
of labels. it's really very easy and informative, and it has worked
for me. Whenever you feel as if you're going to say, "she's a
_____," stop and say to yourself instead, "I want to call her
a _____ because she makes me feel _____ when she does

_____." Then ask yourself, "What is it I intend to gain by calling this woman a _____?" (Is it a feeling of superiority? Will your use of this label make your friends appreciate you as one of the gang?) If you do this, a surprising thing often happens: you may discover your motivation for wanting to label the other person, and you realize that labelling another person is just a way of copping out on yourself, of avoiding placing blame for your actions—and people's reactions—on yourself. You will probably still see the other person as another human being, maybe not your favorite human, but a human just the same. And that's important because it means you can still communicate with that person and learn to understand them.

So next time you feel the urge to label someone, what would you say? And how might that differ from what you might have said? And how does that make you feel about yourself?

Mitchell Sulkers

Writing is exciting and important in part because the words we choose are one major factor in shaping our perceptions, thoughts, feelings, attitudes, and insights. For more on how the metaphors and key terms we use to name and discuss a subject can tautologically shape our perceptions and conclusions—and about how writers can take advantage of this fact—see pages 154–56, pages 210–19, pages 261–62, and pages 331–39.

EXERCISE

1. Pick several propositions that matter to you. Apply the law of contraries. What type of insights, if any, do you get?

2. Examine some lists of new words, such as those published to update dictionaries. Note how many are created through metaphors. What implications can you draw?

3. From each of the following lists derive the underlying metaphor. (Note that we often have several basic metaphors for one concept.)

This gadget will save you hours every year.

He's wasting her time.

Is this book worth your while?

Can't you give me a few minutes of your time?

How do you spend your free time?

Your carelessness cost me an hour.

I've invested a lot of time in her.

To succeed you need to budget your time.

She's living on borrowed time.

Use your time profitably.

Thank you for your time.

Put aside some time for ping pong.

Time is . . . ?

It is important how you package your ideas.

She won't buy that.

That idea won't sell.

There is always a market for good ideas.

That idea is worthless.

She's a source of valuable ideas.

I wouldn't give a plugged nickel for that idea.

Such flimsy ideas don't have a chance in the intellectual marketplace.

Ideas are . . . ?

She has a keen mind.

She's sharp.

He has a razor wit.

She cut his argument to ribbons.

That's an incisive idea: it cuts right to the heart of the matter.

That was a cutting remark.

Ideas are . . . ?

4. As you prepare to write on some particular subject—say, computers or death—consider the standard metaphors people use when talking or writing about that subject. What are the implications of those metaphors? How do they direct your attention? What are some alternative metaphors that might direct your attention to a fuller view or to overlooked features of the subject?

5. Exploring the key terms people use when the talk or write about a subject can also lead to insights. Read pages 210–19. Then, as you prepare to write on some particular subject, examine those terms and consider alternatives, just as you did with metaphors in the previous exercise. Looking up key terms in an historical or etymological dictionary is also often seminal—and citing etymology can rhetorically effective in your writing as well.

Heuristics

Every writer confronts the task of making sense of events in the world around him or within him . . . and of making what he wants to say understandable and believable to particular readers. He uses a method of invention when these processes are guided deliberately by heuristic procedures, that is explicit plans for analyzing and searching which focus attention, guide reason, stimulate memory and encourage intuition.

RICHARD YOUNG

One of the chief differences between good and poor writers . . . is the repertory of strategies or heuristics on which they draw. Good writers . . . have a large repertory of powerful strategies [and] sufficient self-awareness of their own process to draw on these alternative techniques as they need them.

LINDA FLOWER

What Are Heuristics?

If you find yourself encountering the same type of problem regularly, it makes sense to devise a procedure for approaching it. Otherwise you have to start from scratch each time.

In the more mathematical and precise disciplines, certain problems, after they are well defined and reduced to some recognizable pattern, can be solved mechanically by applying a standard procedure. Such procedures are called *algorithms* (after the ninth-century mathematician, Muhammad ibn-Musa *al-Khwarizmi*). An algorithm leads mechanically to a solution. Writing "problems" are not often so easily handled.

In rhetoric, standard procedures for discovery are called *heuristics* (from the Greek, *heuresis*, to discover or invent). A heuristic is a guide that increases the probability of discovery and decreases the likelihood of overlooking relevant material. A heuristic replaces neither thought nor intuition. Instead, it makes both thought and intuition more effective and comprehensive, encouraging what Kenneth Burke has called "methodological inspiration."

Because heuristics focus your attention in particular ways, each heuristic is good for a particular type of invention. Whenever you meet a heuristic, you should ask how it will focus your attention and thus what sort of writing tasks it is good for. The **Utopian U** (see pages 66–69), for instance, is a heuristic that can help generate workable alternatives to an unsatisfactory situation.

This section will introduce you to a number of well-known heuristics, each of which is useful for a particular type of writing.

1. The **journalists' 5Ws** is excellent for generating news reports in particular and narratives in general. If you are writing a story, the 5Ws can help you.

2. **Burke's Pentad** is a powerful heuristic for investigating motives, both of real people and of fictional characters. If you are trying to explain why someone did something—or to interpret motives in literature—the Pentad can help you.

3. The **tagmemic grid** is useful for analytic description, especially when the ultimate purpose of the analysis is problem solving.

4. One version of the **classical topoi** functions much as the tagmemic grid; another (Aristotle's) is good for generating persuasive arguments.

Some heuristics—like the 5Ws and the general version of the topoi—are relatively easy to master. Others take some effort. Which heuristics you should use depends on what sorts of writing you expect to do regularly. If you often find yourself trying to generate a full analysis of some object or concept, the tagmemic grid or the general version of the *topoi* can help you. If you more often write arguments, perhaps you should try Aristotle's *topoi* instead. If, however, you need to understand people's motives—in literature or in life—Burke's Pentad will focus your attention most usefully.

Equally important is the more general point: if you do any particular type of writing regularly, a heuristic can help you do it more efficiently; the right heuristic can also help you avoid overlooking important aspects of a familiar subject. One or more of the heuristics described here may be right for you. If not, once you understand what heuristics are, you can easily make up your own heuristic for any type of writing you do regularly.

Question Heuristics

Heuristics often come in the form of questions. Even when a heuristic comes in some other form, it can usually be translated into a set of questions. Probably the most well-known question heuristic is **the journalists' 5Ws:**

who?	*when?*
what?	*why?*
where?	*how?*

By answering these questions, a reporter discovers the information needed to begin a news story.

The formula is not automatic. The questions can be answered in various ways, and reporters use a combination of experience and intuition to pick answers that will be considered appropriate at their particular newspapers. It is, moreover, not always appropriate to answer all the questions (*why?* and *how?* are those most often left out). The writer must also decide how to order the answers. Nonetheless, an experienced reporter usually can quickly generate the opening of a news report with these questions.

> Protesting U.S. military occupation of their land (*why*), fishers from the Puerto Rican island of Vieques (*who*) last week (*when*) stymied military maneuvers (*what*) in the area (*where*) for more than five hours.

Since a newspaper report usually tries to catch readers' attention by putting the most important or dynamic bit of information first, the reporter could have begun, "Military maneuvers were stymied for five hours last week . . . ." In this case, however, she decided to avoid the passive sentence and put the emphasis on the protest. She also decided that *how?* was not an important question to answer in the first sentence (and that using the unfamiliar "fishers" was better than implying that all the protesters were fisher*men*). Although she used the heuristic, she still had a lot of decisions to make.

The journalists' 5Ws is useful for generating narrative reports of various types. It is one of a large number of question heuristics that are available to writers for various purposes. Some of them are rather broadly applicable to a wide variety of writing tasks. Others are quite specific. (Grade school teachers, for example, often make up a specific question heuristic to guide pupils through a particular writing assignment.)

You can make up question heuristics to meet your own special needs. For any particular type of writing task you face regularly, you can devise a set of questions that will help you generate the substance of such a writing and help you avoid leaving out anything important. Such questions can also help you choose an effective rhetorical strategy. Here, for instance, is a heuristic devised by three students who were trying to teach themselves how to write journalistic movie reviews (see pages 419–21 for the analysis from which they derived the heuristic):

1. What kind of film is this:

   Genre – musical, western or science fiction?

   Period – contemporary, WW II, biblical?

   Plot – romance, mystery, adventure?

   Script – original, a play, a novel?

   Actors – female, male, famous, unknown?

   Origins – sequel, remake, true-story?

2. What angle does the press kit use; what is the focus of other promotion hype, gossip, or critical response?

3. How does the film rate in terms of:

   Believability?

   Accuracy?

   Place, climax, resolution?

   Production values, cinematography, location?

   Acting?

4. What consumer information does your audience want?

Nationality (of film, director, actors)?

Entertainment level?

Viewing time?

Violence?

Sex?

Social issues?

5. Are the expectations your audience brings to the film fulfilled? reversed? manipulated? What is suprising? predictable? disappointing? inventive?

Vicki Coupland, Tim Shireman, Rebecca Soles

You can also devise a personal heuristic to help yourself overcome particular shortcomings in your writing. One advanced writing student at the University of British Columbia, for example, had a problem with under-, over-, and mis-developed paragraphs. She always chose good topics, generated clear and complex theses, wrote detailed sentence outlines which contained topic sentences for her main paragraphs, and organized the writing effectively. But some of her paragraphs had inadequate support, some concepts were supported more than necessary, and much of the detail in her papers did not seem clearly attached to anything. In her university courses, her papers generally received B's and B-minuses, grades which did not satisfy her. But even when the flaws in a particular paper were marked, she did not seem able to correct them. Finally, after doing the self-analyses of her writing process assigned in the preceding chapter, she devised for herself the following heuristic, which she applied to each topic sentence in her outline:

1. What do you mean?
2. Explain that!
3. Give details!
4. Give an example!
5. This means that . . .
6. Why do you believe that?

This heuristic may sound like a bit of overkill, and it does sound as if she is yelling at herself; but it produced an immediate qualitative leap in her writing (and A's on term papers just weeks later).

This heuristic worked because it matched the particular individual's problem and personality: it suited her purpose. A simple heuristic for turning a topic sentence into a developed paragraph with logical and exemplary support is:

1. To what extent is this true?
2. How do I know it is true?
3. What is a good example of it?
4. So what?

You can devise heuristics to focus your attention on whatever aspects of your writing are weakest, from discovering a topic to revising punctuation. There is no guarantee of an immediate leap in the quality of your writing. But *if you insert the right heuristic at the right point in your writing process*, you should see significant improvement soon.

The Pentad

One of the better-known heuristics, superficially similar to the journalists' 5Ws, is Kenneth Burke's Pentad. Designed for investigating motives, it is particularly useful for writing about human behavior, either as it actually occurs or as it is represented in literature, cinema, and so forth. Thus the Pentad could help you write a sociological case history or a critical analysis of a novel. It is less likely to help you if you are writing about nonhuman matters (unless you are writing about them as they relate to human beings).

This heuristic was derived from the metaphor ''human drama'' and is sometimes called the Dramatistic Pentad. Here is Burke's own introduction to the Pentad from *A Grammar of Motives* (California).

> What is involved, when we say what people are doing and why they are doing it? . . .
> We shall use five terms as generating principle of our investigation. They are: Act, Scene, Agent, Agency, Purpose. In a rounded statement about motives, you must have some word that names the act (names what took place, in thought or deed), and another that names the scene (the background of the act, the situation in which it occurred); also you must indicate what person or kind of person (agent) performed the act, what means or instruments he used (agency), and the *purpose* .... [A]ny complete statement about motives will offer *some kind* of answer to these five questions: what was done (act), when or where it was done (scene), who did it (agent), how he did it (agency), and why (purpose).

The terms of the Pentad should be understood rather broadly. Anything a human being does, has done, or might do can be considered an *act*. Thus a thought, a decision, or a statement is an act. A piece of writing was an act when it was written and continues to be an act whenever anyone reads it. A poem, when it is read, is a communicative act, what Burke calls ''symbolic action.'' So is the body posture of an excessively proud person. Identifying an act involves not only discovering the facts (what happened, is happening, or might happen) and making inferences from them, but also *naming* the act. Attaching a name to an act (is it love?) means making a judgment, putting it in a category.

The *scene* or context of an act can be narrowly interpreted as equivalent to the journalists' *where?* and *when?* In Burke's usage, however, it also includes other sorts of contexts— historical, social and psychological. The scene of a novel might include the literary traditions in which it was written and is read. The scene in which a person chooses a vocation might include the economic situation, social trends, and family situation of that individual. The background of the act should be explored on various levels.

The term *agent* also can be considered on several levels. In the case of a drama, for example, a character in the story could be considered an agent. In another sense, the playwright or the actor is the agent. The term agent can be subdivided: a person's act might be modified by friends (co-agents) or by enemies (counter-agents). Aspects of a person's character could, by extensions, be represented as agents. One might say, for instance, "Her stubbornness made her hold out for a better contract" or "His good looks cause him to act so uppity."

Agency raises the question *how*. What means were used to perform the Act? How was it done? If a judge made a decision, agency might refer to the lawyers' briefs, legal procedures, and logical "tools" used in thinking it through. On another level, it might refer to the means by which the decision was made known to others. When the act is communicative, agency can refer to the medium: thus the agencies by which world news is made known include newspapers, radio, and television.

Purpose raises questions about intention and function. What purposes were served by the act? What did the agent intend to accomplish? The agent's intentions and the actual function need not, of course, be the same. All of the terms in the Pentad are ultimately aimed at discovering motivation, at answering the question *why?* Purpose refers to a narrower version of the same question. The distinction is best made clear by explaining how Burke uses all five terms together to explore motivation.

As stated thus far, the Pentad adds little to the journalists' formula. Burke, however, is primarily concerned with the predictable relationships among the five terms, not with the terms themselves. He calls these relationships *ratios*. The ratios are the ten pairs that can be made from the terms. Burke begins by discussing the "scene-act ratio." By that he means the predictable ways in which the *scene* or context can motivate the *act* (and *vice versa*, the ways in which the act can modify the scene). The influence of the social context on the development of an individual is an example of the scene-act ratio in action. That ratio is particularly clear in the novels of Thomas Hardy and other regionalist authors, where much of what happens must be explained in terms of the geographical and cultural environment.

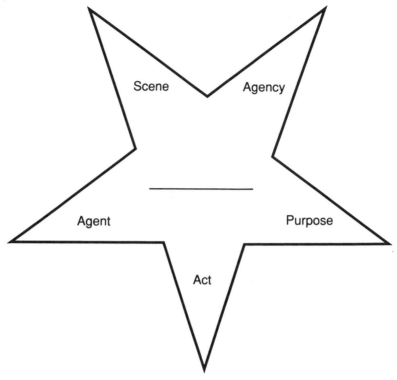

Figure 2.3. Burke's Pentad

Any pair of terms from the Pentad can form a ratio and thereby suggest an explanation or argument. Ordinarily, using the Pentad means investigating five ratios. The five-pointed star in Figure 2.3 can, therefore, help you use the Pentad. On the line in the center, write a word or phrase that represents whatever you are trying to explain. Decide whether what you are trying to explain is an act, agent, agency, purpose, or scene, and write that underneath the line.

Suppose you are trying to explain, "Why can relatively few university students write well enough to satisfy their professors?" The act to be explained is unsatisfactory writing. So you write "unsatisfactory writing" above the line and "act" below the line. By looking in turn at the relationship between each point of the star and the center, you explore the five act ratios. Table 2.1 lists those five ratios together with some tentative answers generated from them.

The Pentad is, of course, only a guide. It will help you generate a large number of explanations. Then you must judge the validity of each and decide which to use. The Pentad, moreover, is primarily a heuristic for explaining

Table 2.1   The Pentadic Act Ratios

Ratio	Definition	Example: "Unsatisfactory Writing"
Scene-Act:	The act follows from the nature of the circumstances.	Since employers are demanding more and more years of schooling for all sorts of jobs, an ever-larger percentage of the population has to attend college including many "underprepared" students.
Agent-Act:	The act follows from the nature of the person.	Many students are unintelligent, untalented, "underprepared," "culturally deprived," or whatever.
Agency-Act:	The act follows from the nature of the available means (or tools).	Schools are underfunded and understaffed. Professors judge writing by unrealistically high standards. Many English teachers and most English professors, having been trained primarily as literary critics, do not know much about teaching writing.
Purpose-Act:	In order to achieve the desired act, such-and-such needs to be done.	In order to develop all students' writing abilities to the desired level of competency, we would need to make a financial and intellectual commitment which would not be cost-effective (according to current standards of social accounting).
Act-Act:	The act in question follows from another act.	Students can't write well because they have not been taught "the basics."

motives, not a system for classifying motives. The main idea is to generate as many explanations as possible, not to worry about whether a particular motive is best classified as agent-act or purpose-act. Ordinarily, you will not use these terms when you write up what you have discovered.

Like many heuristics, the Pentad may seem awkward at first. Once mastered, however, it can be used to generate quickly a large set of explanations from which a writer may pick and choose. As will be seen in Chapter 4, it can also be used to analyze an audience. That is, a writer can use the Pentad to discover which sorts of arguments are likely to be effective with a particular group of potential readers. It can also be used to analyze arguments that a writer might want to refute and thereby to suggest effective refutations.

The Pentad is *not* designed to produce simple explanations. People act as they do for reasons that are typically complex, ambiguous, and multiple;

and the Pentad is designed to explain human motivations. Rarely, if ever, is a single, simple reason adequate to explain any human action. Burke takes it for granted that

> there must remain something essentially enigmatic about the problem of motives, and that this underlying enigma will manifest itself in inevitable ambiguities and inconsistencies among the terms for motives. Accordingly what we want is *not terms that avoid ambiguity*, but *terms that clearly reveal the strategic spots at which ambiguities necessarily arise*.

Such a perspective, although quintessentially humanistic, is not likely to be popular among those who demand simple explanations. But writers who want to write for and about human beings must be prepared to deal with ambiguities and complexities if they are not to oversimplify their subject matter.

A particular entity, for example, may be classified in various ways, depending on the points of view. Thus a person's body might be seen by a coach as a means to a winning season (i.e., as an agency), by a doctor as an object (i.e., as scene), by a painter as an expression of personality (i.e., as a property of the agent), by a nutritionist as the result of an unbalanced diet (i.e., as the result of an act), and by a deodorant manufacturer as a potential customer and hence as a potential profit (i.e., as defined by the manufacturer's purpose). A single individual, moreover, might view that same body from more than one perspective, even in a single moment. Such is the complexity of human affairs.

To master the Pentad requires a certain amount of study and practice. It is, however, a particularly seminal heuristic, and people's motives are easily misunderstood or oversimplified. So mastering the Pentad is well worth the effort.

The Tagmemic Grid

One key to successful invention is the ability to look at the same subject from varied perspectives. Originally developed by a linguist, Kenneth Pike, to describe and analyze languages, the tagmemic grid can help you describe and analyze an object or concept by looking at it nine ways. Tagmemic invention includes a number of heuristic devices, and the grid allows writers access to all of them.

Using a metaphor from physics, Pike asserts that anything can be viewed as a particle, as a wave, or as a field. That is to say, whatever you are analyzing can be looked at

1. as a thing in itself, static, in a moment of time;
2. as something dynamic, changing through time;
3. in context, as part of a larger system or network.

If you are describing and analyzing a building or a political system—perhaps for the purpose of designing a similar but better one—you can

1. describe the building as it exists;
2. analyze how it has changed since it was first constructed and how it will likely continue to change into the future;
3. look at how it functions in relation to its physical and social environments.

Pike also asserts that within each perspective the object or concept should be analyzed three ways:

a) by looking for the contrastive features that distinguish it from similar objects or concepts,
b) by considering how the object or concept is subdivided into various divisions or types, and
c) by considering the contexts or classifications in which the object or concept normally occurs.

That is, Pike says one should (a) define (by contrast), (b) divide, and (c) classify or contextualize whatever object or concept you are investigating.

When Pike went to a foreign country and saw people bowing, he wanted to know:

a) What defines bowing for these people, how is it differentiated from such acts as inclining one's head in greeting someone?
b) What are the different types of bows and what is the significance of each?
c) In what contexts do people bow: when? where? to whom? What responses do they normally expect?

Having answered these questions, Pike had solved the problem facing him as a polite visitor to that place. He knew when and how to bow, what it meant when someone else bowed, and how he should respond when someone bowed to him.

The tagmemic grid leads writers through the process of looking three ways—as particle, as wave, and as field—and analyzing each by contrasting (defining), dividing, and classifying or contextualizing. Thus it generates nine perspectives (see Table 2.2). A writer may use whichever combination proves useful for a particular writing task.

Table 2.2 The Tagmemic Grid

	Contrast	Variation	Distribution
Particle	1a. View ____ as an isolated, static entity. What features distinguish it from similar things and serve to identify it?	1b. View ____ as a group or set. What is the range of variation? How much can ____ change before it becomes something else?	1c. View ____ in context. How is it normally classified? Where does it occur in sequences?
Wave	2a. View ____ as dynamic. What distinguishes it from similar events? What is its most typical or representative form?	2b. View ____ as a dynamic process. How is it changing?	2c. View ____ in dynamic context. How does it interact with its environment? Are its borders clearcut or hard to define?
Field	3a. View ____ as a system. How are its components interrelated?	3b. View ____ as a type or set of systems. How do particular instances vary?	3c. View ____ as a system within a larger system. What features make it part of the larger system? How is it interrelated with the larger system?

Aristotle's Topoi

Aristotle lists in his *Rhetoric* twenty eight common *topoi*, or general lines of argument. One way to use this heuristic is simply to try to invent arguments of each type in support of your thesis. Some of the arguments you produce will be arguments you intended to use before you tried Aristotle's heuristic. Others will likely be weak—not all types of arguments work for any particular thesis. But you will probably invent a few new and strong arguments that you can use. Thus Aristotle's heuristic helps you discover additional arguments in support of your position.

Aristotle's first *topus* is a line of argument based on opposites, and he gives the following example:

> If war is the cause of our present sufferings, peace is what we need to relieve them.
>
> ALCIDAMAS

If you were arguing in favor of reducing the federal deficit, one parallel line of argument might be,

> If a tax cut and a radical increase in military spending caused the excessive national debt, perhaps a tax increase and a radical cut in military spending will cure it.

Aristotle's third line of argument is that if one side of an action is just, so is the other, and he gives the following example.

> If it is not wrong to sell something, it is not wrong to buy it.
>
> DIOMEDON

If you were writing about tax loopholes, a parallel line of argument might be,

> If it is not wrong for the government to offer tax loopholes, it is not wrong for individuals to take advantage of them.

Another line of argument Aristotle suggests is what logicians call *a fortoriori*: if something is true in the stronger case, it is likely true in the weaker. If you were arguing in favor of helping the victims of the Vietnam War, a parallel argument might be,

> If you believe that American veterans of the Vietnam War deserve help, surely you must agree that all the victims of that war, especially noncombatants, deserve help.

Not all of Aristotle's types of arguments adapt readily to persuasion in modern English. What follows, therefore, is a modern version of Aristotle's common *topoi*.

Remember the point is not to invent twenty eight arguments, one from each of Aristotle's topoi, but to generate as many arguments as possible. Nor is it necessary to classify your arguments or to worry about whether they parallel Aristotle's exactly, just to invent as many as possible. Once you have generated a variety of arguments, you can decide—on the basis of both ethics and effectiveness—which to use.

The lefthand column presents Aristotle's topoi, including selected examples (where Aristotle provided examples). In the righthand column are arguments invented by applying Aristotle's *topoi* to the Classical argument about whether rhetoric serves or undermines truth.

Socrates and Plato argued that rhetoric was bad because people should be convinced by logic, not by eloquence. Cicero, among others, responded that rhetoric is necessary because people do not necessarily recognize the plain truth when they hear it. Suppose we take Cicero's position as our proposition to be proven and use Aristotle's heuristic to seek supporting arguments.

If truth were self-evident, eloquence would not be necessary.

CICERO

Thesis: Rhetoric (eloquence) is necessary because truth is not self-evident.

Opposed: Socrates, Plato, et al.

1. *Opposites.* If *A* is the opposite of *B* and something is true of *A*, the opposite is likely true of *B*.

If war is the cause of our present sufferings, peace is what we need to relieve them.

ALCIDAMAS

If truth were self-evident and eloquence unnecessary, no one would worry about hiring a good lawyer, politicians would not waste money on speech writers, nor would advertisers spend huge sums on the best advertising agencies. The existence of such institutions demonstrates that truth is not self-evident and eloquence necessary.

2. *Inflection.* One may equate different grammatical forms of the same root word.

Justice does not mean that which is beneficial. For one cannot be said to have been treated beneficially if one is executed justly.

Most speakers would like to speak eloquently. How then can eloquence be undesirable?

3. *Correlative terms*. If one side of an action is just, so is the other.

If it is not wrong to sell something, it is not wrong to buy it.

DIOMEDON

4. *More and less* (*a fortoriori*). If something is true in the stronger case, it is likely true in the weaker.

If we know a man lost his temper and struck his father, surely we should believe him capable of striking other people as well.

5. *Time*. If something was true (or you would have agreed to it before) you should accept it now.

If before doing the deed I had demanded a statue in payment, you would have given it to me. Now that the deed is done, how then can you deny me the statue?

IPHICRATES

6. *Turning an Opponent's Argument*.

When Iphicrates was accused of betraying the Athenian fleet for money, he took advantage of general opinion that his accuser, Aristophon, was less patriotic and more greedy than he and argued that if Aristophon would not betray the fleet for money neither would he.

When Odysseus [in Sophocles' *Teucer*] uses the argument that, because Teucer's mother was sister to the King of Troy, he is friendly to the Trojans, Teucer replies that his father was an enemy of the King of Troy.

It is generally accepted by the opponents of rhetoric that an eloquent speaker can make the worse appear the better case. Why then do they not accept the corollary that people may fail to recognize the truth until it is communicated skillfully?

Even when the truth is genuinely self-evident, many people do not perceive it until someone explains it well. How much more must eloquence be necessary when the truth is not self-evident.

If, as Socrates argued, Gorgias and other rhetoricians led their audiences to false conclusions, the truth must not be self-evident. Therefore, eloquence is necessary to win people to the truth.

That favorite assertion of Socrates—that every man was eloquent enough upon a subject he knew—has some plausibility but no truth: it is nearer the truth to say that neither can anyone be eloquent upon a subject that is unknown to him, nor, if he knows it perfectly and yet does not know how to shape and polish his style, can he speak fluently even upon that which he does know.

CICERO, *De Oratore*

If eloquence, as Socrates suggests, is what wins ordinary people to truth, how can anyone who believes in the value of truth argue that rhetoric is unnecessary?

7. *Definition.* If something follows from an accepted definition, it is true.

True nobility is goodness. There was nothing noble about Harmodius and Aristogeiton until they had done noble deeds. Insofar as my deeds are akin to those of Harmodius and Aristogeiton, I am noble despite my lowly birth.

Iphicrates

If rhetoric is using words to persuade, then all naming is rhetoric; for if we give something a derogatory name, people value it less, and if we give it a eulogistic name, people value it more. Since rhetoric is inevitable when people use language, we may as well use it well.

8. *Ambiguity.*

If a statement is true, we say it is right. If an action is just, we say it is right. Truth, therefore, is justice, and justice is truth.

Though *rhetoric* is sometimes used as a derogatory term to mean "verbal tricks," Aristotle says rhetoric means knowing how to discover how to persuade in any given situation. Thus rhetoric can serve truth.

9. *Division.* If there are a limited number of possibilities and all but one can be eliminated, that one must be true. If all can be eliminated, the contrary must be true.

All men do wrong from one of three motives. In my case, the first two are out of the question; and even the prosecution does not allege the third. So I must be innocent.

Either eloquence has no effect, in which case it need not be opposed. Or eloquence is effective, in which case it should be used in the service of truth.

10. *Induction.* If something is true in a whole series of cases, it is probably true in general.

If we do not entrust our horses to men who have mishandled other people's horses, nor our ships to those who have capsized the ships of others, and if this is our way with everything else, then beware of employing for the safety of our State mercenaries who have ill protected the safety of others.

Theodectes

There have been many court cases in which a poorly defended innocent person was unjustly convicted—only to be found innocent later when a better lawyer took over the case. The first time I, myself, went to court, I made a rhetorical error and was fined. The second time, I hired the best lawyer available and suffered no consequences other than his fee. Without eloquence, we may suffer injustice.

11. *Precedent.* If something was just in a previous case, it is probably just in the present case.

The dread goddesses were content to submit to the judgment of Areopagus and you are not?

AUTOCLES

Death is an evil; the gods have so judged it, or they would die.

SAPPHO

If it was correct for Socrates, in the *Phaedrus*, to use eloquence and rhetoric in his arguments against rhetoric, why is it incorrect to use rhetoric in other cases? If Socrates needs eloquence to convince the youthful Phaedrus that eloquence is bad, how much more necessary must eloquence be to demonstrate truth to more difficult audiences.

12. *From parts to whole.* What is true of the parts (or particular cases) is likely true of the whole (or in general).

Socrates has honored all the gods recognized by the State. He has profaned no temple. Therefore, Socrates respects the gods.

THEODECTES

Rhetoric is the effective use of language. If words are not bad, then the effective use of words is surely also not bad.

If Socrates thinks it all right to use rhetoric in particular cases, it is likely that rhetoric itself is not intrinsically bad.

13. *Consequences.* If something has bad consequences, it is bad.

If it is good to be popular and if educated people are unpopular, it is bad to be an educated person.

Those who decline to use rhetoric on behalf of truth abandon eloquence to the proponents of falsity, thus leaving the audience in danger of being swayed against the truth. To abandon rhetoric is not to serve truth.

14. *Cris-cross consequences.* You should not speak in public, for if you speak honestly, men will hate you; if you speak dishonestly, the gods will hate you.

Socrates says people recognize truth when they hear it because our souls glimpsed the truth before we were born. That is, he says people do not discover truth; they only recover it (from their prenatal memories). If so, there is no danger that rhetoric will lead people to recover what is not there.

15. *Inner thoughts / outer show.* Where there is a distinction between what people say and their real motives, one may address one's arguments to either.

If you want to win, you should use rhetoric, speak eloquently.

People often say they favor truth and justice, when they are actually motivated by self-interest.

16. *Proportion.*

If you are going to assign public duties to my young son because you count tall boys as men, then you will have to treat short men as boys.

IPHICRATES

If you give citizenship to mercenaries like Strabax and Charidemus for meritorious service, should you not exile mercenaries who have cause irreparable harm?

THEODECTES

Literature influences how readers perceive and feel about the realities it represents. Aristotle, for instance, says that the cathartic experience of tragedy makes it less likely that people will take action in response to the social and political contradictions portrayed in the plays. If we allow literature, surely we should also allow other forms of eloquence.

17. *Results and antecedents.* Similar results indicate similar antecedents.

To affirm the birth of the gods is as impious as to say they die; either way, you suggest a time when no gods exist.

XENOPHANES

Rhetoric—public debate of political issues—is the means by which democracy functions. To oppose rhetoric, therefore, is to oppose democracy.

18. *Altered choices.* What we decide now should be consistent with what we decided before.

When we were exiles, we fought to return. Now that we have returned, it would be monstrous to choose exile rather than fight to defend our home.

LYSIAS

When his life was at stake, Socrates used eloquence to defend it (in the *Apology*). How can he and his followers object to the use of rhetoric in other cases?

19. *Attributed motives.* Discredit your opponent's position or action by attributing a selfish motive.

Diomedes chose Odysseus as his companion not for honorable reasons but because he wanted a companion to whom he could feel superior.

When Socrates, Plato, and others attack rhetoric, they are attacking the means by which democratic decisions are made. This is because they really favor aristocracy over democracy.

20. *Incentives and deterrents.* We should act to our advantage.

To say rhetoric should not be used is to leave all that can be gained through eloquence to our opponents.

21. *Incredible occurrences.* Though what I am suggesting is improbable, more improbable things have happened.

Though fish are bred in brine, they need salt to preserve them; and though olive cakes are made from the source of olive oil, they need olive oil. Likewise our laws need a law to correct them.

ANDROCLES

People once believed it self-evident that the earth was flat. People once believed it self-evident that the sun rotated around the earth. People once believed that Caucasians were intellectually and morally superior to other human beings. We now know that what seemed to them self-evidently true is actually false. Since truth is not self-evident, we need rhetoric to debate and discover it.

22. *Conflicting facts.* My opponents contradict themselves.

He says he loves the people, but he conspired with the oligarchy against democracy.

In the *Gorgias*, Socrates says rhetoric is evil, a form of flattery, and to be avoided. But in the *Phaedrus*, he says that ordinary people cannot be won to the truth without rhetoric (and uses it himself to convince Phaedrus).

23. *Explaining a slander.* Provide a reasonable explanation for evidence used against you or your position.

Plato says rhetoricians do not value truth because they are willing to argue all sides of a question. In fact, they are willing to do so because they understand that the whole truth is a synthesis of various perspectives, that debate leads to a fuller understanding of the truth.

24. *Cause to effect.* If the cause or motive exists (or does not), so must the effect.

Why would I have erased your name from the list of criminals when leaving it there would make the oligarchs trust me?

LEODAMAS

Were truth self-evident, all people would agree. Since people actually disagree, truth must be difficult to discern and rhetoric necessary to achieve consensus.

25. *Better course.* Propose a course of action superior to what your opponent suggests.

If pure logic and evidence alone could win people over, would not those who wish to persuade take this simple course. Logic and evidence alone must be insufficient or only those arguing falsehoods would ever use eloquence.

26. *Consistency*. If you chose one thing, your other choices should be consistent with it.

If you think Io became a goddess, you should not sing a dirge; if you think her a human who died, you should not worship her.

XENOPHANES

If truth were self-evident and rhetoric unnecessary, no one would use eloquence to argue that eloquence is unnecessary.

27. *Previous mistake*. Discredit an opponent by mentioning previous errors.

In the *Phaedrus*, Socrates retreats from the view of rhetoric he had asserted earlier in the *Gorgias*. If Socrates was wrong in the *Gorgias*, perhaps he is also wrong in the *Phaedrus*.

28. *Meanings of names*. Argue from the etymology of a name or key term.

And rightly does the name of the goddess of Love [Aphrodite] begin as does folly [aphrosyne].

HECUBA
in Euripides' *Troades*

Rhetoric comes from the Greek *eirein*, "to say, speak"; *eloquence* comes from the Greek *eloqui*, "to speak out." Rhetorical eloquence is nothing more than speaking well. And only thus can we make clear both truth and the reasoning by which it was established.

The Classical Topoi and the Forms of Discourse

The English word *topic* comes from the Greek *topos* (plural, *topoi*), meaning *place*. In classical rhetoric, the *topoi* were "places" one could "go" in search of substance or strategies for a speech. There were special *topoi* for particular subjects and types of speeches. There were also common *topoi* for more general use.

The common *topoi* are frequently summarized by five basic questions:

1. What is it?
2. What is it like and unlike?
3. What caused it?

4. What can come of it?

5. What has been said about it?

Even by themselves, these five general questions make a useful heuristic. Asked about almost any subject, they generate a broad range of information. Whatever you may be writing about, the first question can lead you to describe it, define it, classify it, and divide it into its parts or aspects. The second question can lead you to compare and contrast, make analogies and give examples. The third and fourth can lead you to consider it as part of a process, analyze its functions, explain why it exists, perhaps tell a story in which it plays a part. The fifth can lead you to quote authorities, cite statistics and precedents, and refer to proverbs, parables, and other common wisdom.

The classical rhetoricians enumerated the common *topoi* in great detail. A Greek or Roman teacher of rhetoric provided his students with a list of *topoi* and examples of each. Much of the suggestiveness of the common *topoi* follows from their having been developed in such detail. But the version of the *topoi* encapsulated in these five basic questions, based on essential tendencies in human thinking, is sufficiently generalized to be very generally useful.

The modern equivalents of the common *topoi*—known as forms of discourse or patterns of development—are presented in Chapters 6, 7, and 8 of this textbook. Although they are discussed there primarily as ways to structure and develop writings (i.e., as patterns of arrangement), they are also *topoi*. They can help you discover both substance and structure. These chapters discuss description, narration, exemplification, comparison/contrast, definition, analogy and process analysis, causal analysis, and logical progression. If you use them and describe something, say what it is like and unlike, define it, classify if, divide it into its part or aspects, make some analogies, give some examples, tell a story in which it figures, analyze it as a process, explain why it exists and what its functions are, discuss its implications, and so forth, you will have generated a great deal of material, probably more than you could use in a short paper.

You may detect a similarity between the modern patterns of development and the classical *topoi*. The Greek rhetoricians apparently understood the connection between persuasive tactics and rhetorical forms, for the word they used for selection and arrangement of arguments is *taxis*, from which the word *tactics* is also derived. Both the modern patterns of development and the classical *topoi* are based on how human minds work. The basic structures that give *form* to our speech and writing reflect the processes of the human mind (as it has evolved on this planet). Although there is great variation from culture to culture in how human minds work, there are also basic commonalities—captured by both the modern patterns of development and the most general version of the classical *topoi*.

The form of a piece of writing can function as a heuristic for the discovery of its substance. The patterns of development discussed below in Part II are both structures that can give shape to your writings and also ways to develop the substance of those same writings. Chapters 6, 7, and 8 deal with very general patterns, the equivalents of the common *topoi*. Chapters 9 and 10 deal with more specific patterns, modern equivalents of the special *topoi*. If you are writing a scientific report, for instance, the standard formal structure leads you to invent (1) an introduction that reviews previous work on the subject, defines a problem and states hypotheses, (2) a detailed description of your methodology, (3) a report of your findings, and (4) a discussion of the implications. Use these forms and you will discover that your attempt to follow a particular pattern helps (and even forces) you to discover appropriate substance. Form can play a crucial role in writing not only by constraining, but also by generating substance. Hence the title of this textbook: *Process, Form, and Substance*.

EXERCISE

1. Practice using one or more of the heuristics discussed above, perhaps in your journal.

2. Devise a question heuristic which meets one or more of your own needs, perhaps one to generate a particular type of writing you need to produce regularly (be that something for your field of special interest or a letter to your parents). Then use this heuristic to generate a piece of writing.

3. Devise a heuristic that will focus your attention on a particular writing problem you have. Use it next time your write or revise.

4. Research and study a formal heuristic. This could be one from the discipline of rhetoric, such as Aristotle's *topoi*, the Pentad, or the tagmemic grid. Or it could be one from your field of specialization. (*Remember*: Any set of questions designed to generate information needed in your field is a heuristic, a set of special *topoi*, even if it is not so titled.) Whichever formal heuristic you choose, use it to generate a piece of writing. Submit the heuristic and the piece of writing together.

C·H·A·P·T·E·R 3

Drafting and Revising

The only justification for our concepts and system of concepts is that they serve to represent the complex of our experience.

ALBERT EINSTEIN

A search for a better word is a search for a better vision.

GARY TATE

Rewriting is the difference between the dilettante and the artist, the amateur and the professional, the unpublished and the published. William Gass testifies, "I work not by writing but rewriting." Dylan Thomas states, "Almost any poem is fifty to a hundred revisions—and that's after it's well along." Archibald McLeish talks of "the endless discipline of writing and rewriting and rerewriting." Novelist Theodore Weesner tells his students at the University of New Hampshire his course title is not "Fiction Writing" but "Fiction Rewriting."

DONALD MURRAY

BECAUSE writing, like any creative process, begins by discovering potentials, Chapter 2 emphasized getting started, generating words and ideas. For a variety of reasons, however, some of the material writers generate does not serve their purposes. After careful thought, it may even appear to a writer that some of the generated material is not entirely true. Or perhaps the words do not accurately represent what they were intended to. Or perhaps the words and ideas are good, but not as they stand; perhaps the generated material needs to be focused, rearranged, put in a more meaningful pattern. Like any creative process, writing is brought to fruition by critical selection and arrangement.

Like a gardener whose seeds have sprouted and whose young fruit trees are starting to branch, a writer must cut, thin, transplant, graft, prune, and even refertilize. Aside from surface changes in sentence structure and word choice, inexperienced writers' final drafts are usually not much different from their initial drafts. Successful, experienced writers generally do much more revision and make much more radical changes in their drafts. Because they know how to revise, they spend much more time revising. Hence a common rule of thumb among experienced writing instructors is that, on major writing tasks, 40% to 50% of the writing time should be allotted to revision. This makes sense, however, only for writers who are skillful revisers. This chapter (as well as much of Chapters 4 and 5) is designed to help you develop the ability to revise fruitfully.

In reality, of course, the two processes—generation and selection, creation and revision—interpenetrate: writers do not first uncritically generate a complete set of potential words and meanings, and second select and arrange the ones that serve their purposes. Many of the discovery techniques discussed in Chapter 2 actually embody principles of selection. To constrain a set of freewritings toward an emerging "center of gravity" is to select. Any research process requires the researcher to select information. Certainly any heuristic embodies a principle of selection that constrains the writer toward discovering relevant information.

The two contraries coexist within the composing process. Very often it is precisely the rejection of a phrase that leads to the generation of an alternative. Even if we cannot treat them as two distinct stages, however, the distinction between generation and selection is useful for thinking about writing. The generation or discovery of material does usually predominate in the early phases of writing, and the critical selection and arrangement does usually predominate in the later phases. Inexperienced writers, or writers who are blocked, often find it useful to separate the two because they can impede each other. Certainly, it is useful for writing students to think of the writing process as having two complementary, but contradictory aspects—the Creator and the Critic, if you will—and to study them separately.

To revise effectively, one must have a sense of purpose. To decide one version is more effective than another, one must know what effects the particular piece of writing is supposed to achieve. A sense of purpose and function is crucial to the decisions one must make while revising. Consider this analogy:

> As wolves cull the caribou herds, they have a clear principle of selection: They select the aged, the deformed, the weak, the slow, and the poorly protected young. Their principle of selection constrains them to take those caribou that are unfit for survival. They remove certain genes from the genetic pool of the herd and create space for caribou that are more fit. Thus, by selecting out caribou who are unfit, they serve *the natural purpose* of strengthening the caribou spe-

cies. The Inuit who hunt the caribou therefore say, "The wolf and the caribou are one."

In the same sense, Creator and Critic are one in the writing process. To have a healthy caribou herd, you need some wolves; to have good writing you need not only creative inspiration, but also a skillful Critic function as editor. Indeed, what frees a writer to be fruitfully creative during the generative phases of the process is confidence that the Critic will revise and edit well.

What in the writing process is the equivalent of "the natural purpose"? On what principle or principles should writers select and reject, arrange and rearrange? The key is a clear sense of what the writing is supposed to accomplish. If you have a sharp sense of purpose, then you have a basis for making decisions about focus, organization, style, and even mechanics.

This chapter will begin with drafting and the problem of finding focus. Then the most basic kind of revision: revision as genuine re-seeing, revising to make your drafts more true and accurate, subtle and sophisticated. The following section discusses logic and organization, for one of the most powerful types of revision turns on a clear sense of structure, on filling gaps and reorganizing what you have generated. Revising for readers, to make your writing work with particular audiences, will follow in Chapter 4. Revising words and sentences will be discussed in Chapter 5.

Drafting

The artist must contain his critic, must recognize the validity of contraries.
KENNETH BURKE

I think at the typewriter.
ARTHUR MILLER

Drafting—what most people think of as the "actual writing"—makes a transition from the purity of creative generation to critical evaluation and revision. In early drafts, the creative voice usually predominates. A first draft may not be very different from a focused freewriting—indeed, for those who use freewriting, it is often not clear where freewriting leaves off and drafting begins. But drafting is also where writing starts to find focus and take form, where writers start to select (and reject), to order (and reorder). The potential conflict between Creator and Critic is strongest during drafting.

Perhaps for this reason, it is often not easy for writers to get themselves started drafting, or even to decide when they are ready to start drafting. You can waste time by starting to draft too soon, when you should still be getting ready, perhaps doing the sorts of initiating and heuristic activities described in Chapter 2. It is also easy to confuse preparation with procrastination and put off drafting too long, thus wasting time and leaving too little time for proper revision.

You may be ready to start drafting when you can sense the crux of a piece of writing and know the main elements that will go into it, when you can feel its "center of gravity" and the general direction it will take. Or you may want to put off drafting until you can write out your main point at least tentatively as a thesis statement and list the major subtopics.

At any event, it is usually best to think of early drafts as part of the discovery process. Drafting for perfection—trying to get it right the first time— may seem efficient. In fact, by forcing you to think about too many things at once, it usually costs both time and quality. Trying to get it right the first time slows down the writing process to the point where it loses its flow. Trying to get it right the first time usually weds you to your first ideas—for admitting a new idea in the middle would mean going back and changing the beginning you sweated so much to perfect.

It is better not to rob yourself of the joy of discovery, better to listen mostly to your creative voice, to let your draft take tangents and fill itself overfull. If you think of two or three alternative words and cannot decide which is right, write them in a stack (or if you are using a typewriter or word processor, with slashes between them), and decide later, during revision, which one to use. If you think of two or more directions the draft could take, follow whichever seems best at the moment—but jot a note to yourself so you will be able to come back to the other(s) later.

Often it helps literally to listen for your own voice, to imagine your audience and talk to them in your mind, taking dictation from yourself, so to speak. You may even find yourself muttering aloud, not unusual behavior for writers.

As you draft, it is important to pause from time to time and reread what you have written. This is what makes a draft more coherent than a freewriting. You reread to sense the pattern you are creating, to decide where to go next. If as you reread you see an error or problem, circle it or jot down a quick note to remind yourself to fix it later. But now is not the time to get sidetracked into revision and lose the flow of the draft. Only on later drafts, when you already have the gist and the main elements written, does it make sense to indulge in extensive, detailed revision.

Experienced writers feel free to write very rough drafts because they have confidence in their ability to revise. They can trust their creative voices because they know they will be able to turn rough drafts into good written products by revising extensively.

On a major writing task, drafting may take only 15% to 20% of a writer's time. One rule of thumb says to allow a third of your time for invention and half your time for revision—which leaves only a sixth of the writing time for drafting, the so-called "actual writing." For a short, familiar writing task, the proportions can be very different. To an executive writing an ordinary business letter, invention may mean just a few minutes rereading previous correspondence, thinking and jotting down the main points to be included in the letter. And revision may mean just rereading the draft once, pencilling in a few minor corrections. So even ten minutes spent drafting that letter may be two-thirds of the writing time. But as writing tasks get longer and more substantive, the proportions shift. For a book, thesis, or major report, to allot only a third of the time to invention may be a gross underestimate.

Drafting may be the crux of the writing process. Certainly, it is where creative generation merges into critical evaluation, where the two contradictory aspects of writing come together. But fruitful drafting is made possible by proper preparation, and you can draft freely only if you have the time and ability to revise skillfully.

Finding Focus

Good writing is always, in one sense or another, focused writing. It achieves its purposes, fulfills its function, because it is focused. Of all that can be written about a particular topic, a writer with a clear sense of purpose knows what to include and what to leave out, what to emphasize and what to deemphasize, what to say first, what to say last, and how to arrange the material in between. Within this crucial principle—that focus follows from purpose—there are two common techniques for achieving focus.

In the traditional textbook procedure for writing a paper, the second step—after finding (or being assigned) a topic—is to *narrow and focus*.

Narrowing reduces a large topic to one that can be covered in a relatively short paper. Suppose, for example that your topic is "The Literacy 'Crisis' in North America." Clearly, you cannot say all there is to say on that topic in 500 words or eight to ten pages (or even 80 to 100 pages) without being very general. So you narrow to one separable *part* of the topic—for example, "The Literacy 'Crisis' in New York City Schools."

Simultaneously, you focus on a particular *aspect* of the topic, like "What are the dimensions of the 'crisis?' " or "What should be done about the 'crisis?' " The combination of this narrowing and focusing results in a topic like "What should be done about the literacy 'crisis' in New York City schools?"

Good start, says the textbook, now keep narrowing. The final topic for a short paper eventually becomes "One remedy for increasingly poor punctuation among Stuyvesant High School seniors." This topic—which was reached by carefully following the instructions of one widely used handbook—has several virtues. It is likely to make the writer deal with the concrete realities of the problem instead of writing a paper filled with vague generalizations. It is specific and easily manageable. It is the sort of limited topic that scientists and other academic researchers often choose.

On the other hand, it is in grave danger of becoming trivial. Thus,

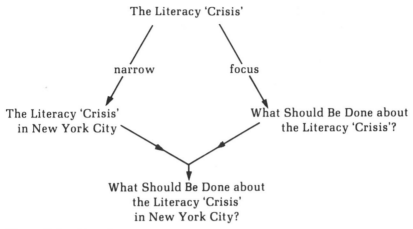

Figure 3.1. Focusing.

even as an exercise, it is not likely to interest many readers. Worse, the narrowed topic will likely be considered out of context. When you use the narrow-and-focus method, *make certain that you narrow and focus on a topic that is not only specific, but has broad implications.* Make certain that your solution to the punctuation problems of first-year students at Stuyvesant High School is not one that will interfere with other, more important, aspects of their writing. Make certain that you discuss this very narrow topic in such a way as to clearly imply (or explicitly state) its broader implications for responding to problems of literacy in general. Scientists and other academic researchers who choose such limited subjects often do so because they know that other members of their research community are doing related research and that the combined weight of a number of limited studies will likely have significant implications.

Of course, a writer who has just started on a topic might not be ready to narrow or to focus. Sometimes it may be better to delay trying to focus until you are a little further along in the writing process. Perhaps you may let the writing "find its own focus," for example, after a few freewritings. Perhaps you may use the technique of narrow and focus but only after you have done a considerable amount of preliminary writing and even drafting.

Focusing to Solve a Problem

A casual survey of almost any anthology of "great essays" will demonstrate that it is often acceptable to write a short piece on a very general topic. The master essayists, of course, were capable of various feats which should not be lightly attempted by ordinary writers. Still, their example raises the question: How else may one focus a piece of writing?

One other way to focus, although it does have ancient antecedents, has recently been derived from research on problem-solving methods. Here is how it works.

As you gather material on your chosen (or assigned) general topic, you look for a "problem." That is, among the various statements you collect or generate, look for two or more that seem to contradict each other (or for one that seems to have contradictory implications).

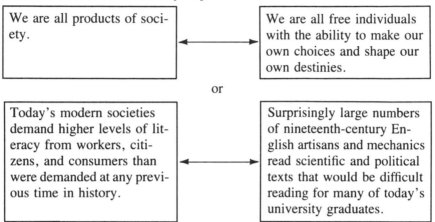

An apparent contradiction between two statements may be dissolved by disproving one of the statements: perhaps we are not free individuals; perhaps late twentieth-century industrial societies do not demand such high levels of literacy as is ordinarily believed. A genuine contradiction is resolved by generating a statement that combines the two originals and demonstrates the extent or sense in which each contains some truth. It is this sort of contradiction that constitutes the sort of "problem" which can focus a piece of writing (see pages 62–66).

Often the awareness of such a problem is what motivates the writing in the first place. On other occasions, however, writers discover the "problem" as they write. The resolution of the "problem," which often occurs during some middle phase of the writing process, generates the thesis of the piece of writing. You might, for example, discover that nineteenth and late twentieth-century industrial societies demand distinct *types* of literacy. You might decide to argue that human beings are *in a certain sense* products of society but *in another sense* free individuals—or that people have freedom to choose *within certain constraints*.

Finding a problematic contradiction focuses your attention on certain aspects of the original topic—the ones that are relevant to resolving the contradiction, hence to solving the problem. It gives you a basis for deciding which aspects of the topic need to be discussed and how much emphasis to give each. When Karl von Frisch discovered the contradiction between his belief that consistent patterns in nature (e.g., flowers being colorful) are biologically functional and the assertion of a famous ophthalmologist that all invertebrates are colorblind, his research found its focus. When he observed and wrote about bees in the context of this problem, he could focus on how they found pollen and ignore everything else. For this purpose, he did not have to "cover" the topic of bees.

Resolving the contradiction also complicates your viewpoint. To argue that we are in one sense products of society but in another sense free individuals is more complicated than to argue *either* that we are just products of society or that we are simply free individuals. Thus one reaches a more complex understanding and discovers a more sophisticated thesis.

The complex thesis is harder to think about and may also be harder to write about. Initially, it forces you to look at your topic from at least two perspectives and to articulate it in a way that more closely approximates the complexity of the real world. Thus it is consistent with the values of a broad or humanistic education, and the technique that generates such theses is especially appropriate for writing which forms part of such an education. It is from wrestling with complex theses that one learns how to think without oversimplifying.

This discussion of problem solving as a way to focus a topic has just exemplified itself. The opposition between *narrow and focus* and *problem solving for focus* has just been resolved: each has its assigned role, and the relationship between them has been defined. Narrow and focus is a narrower technique, often appropriate for specialists and academic researchers. It should be subordinate to problem solving in the same sense that "facts" are subordinate to the "opinions" they support—indeed, the limited research report often provides the facts upon which later analysis and recommendations will be based. Both techniques are useful, and sometimes both can be used together on one writing task.

From Focus to Thesis

If you search and research a topic until you find a contradiction which interests you, that contradiction will focus your attention and your writing. It will lead you to theses that are both specific and complex. It will encourage what John Dewey called "an attitude of suspended conclusion" and help you avoid simplistic conclusions that can become overly simple thesis statements. Such an attitude of suspended conclusions typifies the mature writing process and helps produce first-class writing. In university classes, incidentally, the sort of thesis and tone likely to follow from such an attitude generally secures excellent, as opposed to merely good, grades (see pages 449–52).

A topic can be named, stated as a noun phrase:

The Literacy "Crisis" in New York's Schools.

A thesis says something about the topic, is stated as a complete sentence:

> We have a ''literacy crisis'' in our schools not because our educational system has deteriorated, but because an ever increasing percentage of our students go on to college or university and then to ''white collar'' jobs where someone notices how well they can read and write.

When a topic has been focused, you can go beyond naming it to asserting something about it—to a thesis statement. And the crux of your writing task is then defined: to explain and validate the thesis.

In many types of writing, the thesis should be stated explicitly, often in the first or second paragraph. In other types of writing, the thesis may be left implicit. In either case, it is useful for the writer to know explicitly what the thesis is.

Similarly, the thesis statement is sometimes developed into an explicit thesis paragraph. This means stating not just the thesis, but also the gist of the arguments, evidence, or explanations that will support the thesis. Ask yourself, how do I know this thesis is true? how will I make this thesis clear? Stating the main points you will make to validate and clarify your thesis completes the thesis paragraph.

Some writers spend hours drafting and revising and re-revising the thesis paragraph before writing anything else. They are not, however, really spending hours on just one paragraph. What they are doing, in effect, is planning the structure of the whole piece. Other writers leave drafting the thesis paragraph until the rest of the draft is finished, until they have discovered what their main points will be (and in what order they will come). The second option is, in principle, more efficient and, if you find yourself spending too much time drafting that first paragraph, you might try it.

A thesis paragraph is, in effect, a summary. In some types of writing, readers expect such a summary near the beginning. On other writing occasions, it may be optional or even undesirable. In any case, a one-paragraph summary can provide an overview and thus help a writer revise.

EXERCISE

1. Working in a small group, pick several broad topics of general interest. Focus each by narrowing and focusing. Then focus each by finding a contradiction or ''problem.'' Compare and contrast the results. Imagine communicative contexts for which each focused topic might be appropriate.

2. Explain the statement (on page 106), ''This discussion of problem solving as a way to focus a topic has just exemplified itself.'' Consider whether having a piece of writing exemplify its content is ordinarily useful.

Revision Means Re-envision _____

Re-vision—the act of looking back, of seeing with fresh eyes, of entering an old text from a new critical direction.

ADRIENNE RICH

In baseball you only get three swings and you're out. In rewriting, you get almost as many swings as you want and you know, sooner or later, you'll hit the ball.

NEIL SIMON

For most inexperienced writers, revision is largely a matter of (1) attempting to eliminate errors of usage, grammar, spelling, and punctuation, and (2) trying to find more accurate words to substitute for the "wrong words" in their drafts. Inexperienced writers often have a negative attitude toward revision: they imagine their least favorite English teachers looking over their shoulders and try to correct accordingly. But revision should really be much more than that. Experienced writers see revision as a time of opportunity, a chance to transform a draft into a more satisfying and effective piece of writing. Experienced writers spend much more time on revision—because they can see so much more to revise. Learning to see opportunities for revision is one of the most important abilities for a writer to develop. The rest of this chapter and the two that follow should help you develop this ability.

Revision is a combination of the root *vision* with the prefix *re-*, meaning "again." So *re-vision* is literally "to see again," "to obtain a new vision" of your subject—or of how best to present it.

The writing we most admire often flows so naturally when we read it that we assume it must have flowed just as naturally when the writer wrote it. But the writers who produce such writing generally spend much more time on revision than less experienced writers who produce less fluent writing.

Whoever said writing is not work was either lying or befuddled by some Romantic myth. Inspiration is real and wonderful and occasionally even easy, but it is not the whole story. Although there have been a few well-publicized exceptions, the revision of that inspiration generally takes a lot of time and effort. The more you know about writing, the more potentials you see, the more changes you consider. That is very exciting, both in the process itself and because of the quality of the resulting product. But it is also work.

Skillful writers can, of course, usually turn out a given quality of writing with less effort than less experienced writers need to produce the same quality. But as your writing abilities improve, you are not likely to be satisfied with that same quality. For any given writer, producing good writing is usually more work than producing bad writing—whether we measure that work in intensity of labor or simply in number of hours per page.

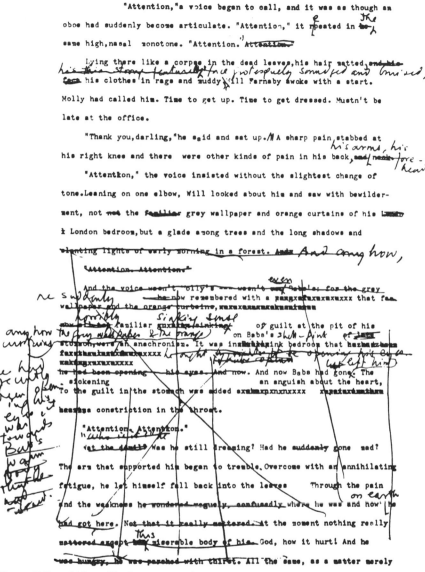

Figure 3.2. Aldous Huxley manuscript page.

Here is what some people who have produced publishable writing say about revision:

There are days when the result is so bad that no fewer than five revisions are required. In contrast, when I'm greatly inspired, only four revisions are needed.

JOHN KENNETH GALBRAITH

Each book is completely written three times and then given a polish and overhaul. . . . I start by combing the first draft through and listing every alteration. Then I rewrite, chapter by chapter. It takes about six months. Then I leave it aside for at least three weeks without looking at it. . . . This is where the book is cut, shaped, tightened up, discrepancies ironed.

MARY STEWART

After writing about twenty pages, I go over them and over them and over them, cutting and changing words to bring out the meaning more clearly. Sometimes I destroy the pages entirely. Or, at best, I rewrite them several times.

TAYLOR CALDWELL

To rewrite ten times is not unusual.

SAUL BELLOW

I do a great deal of rewriting. Almost never is a paragraph right the first time or the sixth or seventh time either.

PEG BRACKEN

After I've written two to three thousand words I go through the penciled copy and correct it and mark it up. Sometimes it looks pretty terrible. Then, when I can't read it any more myself because it is so marked up, I have it typed. I then go over the typed copy once; I may take out some material or put more in.

NORMAN VINCENT PEALE

I write my first versions in longhand (pencil). Then I do a complete revision, also in longhand. . . . Then I type a third draft on yellow paper. . . . Well, when the yellow draft is finished I put the manuscript away for a while, a week, a month, sometimes longer. When I take it out again, I read it as coldly as possible, then read it aloud to a friend or two, and decide what changes I want to make and whether or not I want to publish it. I've thrown away a few short stories, an entire novel, and half of another. But if all goes well, I type the final version on white paper and that's that.

TRUMAN CAPOTE

After the first draft is finished, I put it aside temporarily and work on other things. Then when I feel the time has come for me to really

(Later he goes into catalytic state in coffee pot where proprietor
thinks he's drunk and props him up outside where he can see and hear
muggers rob white-man looking for prostitutes; then he is rolled by these
two em lies helpless; then by cripple, then by child. Around corner

I walked back to Harlem at top speed, never slackening my pace until

black faces began to dominate the streets. God, what had come over me?

What had happened to people? couldn't they see me? Didn't they know that

I was nothing like what they ____er? First the eviction and now this.

One group as confused as the other. Had I become invisible? And then

had a terrifying thought; Perhaps I was everything and nothing, depending

upon who was looking name at the moment! Hadn't I acted the role of

priest as quickly as I had played ____? This was

most frightening, because I hadn't wanted to do either--or at least

part of me had ____. I had gone along and who knew what I would do

next? Perhaps ____ someone ____ whisper ____ a bank

robber--a Dillenger or Robin Hood-- ____ to find myself masked

and ____ gun ____ demanding all the banknoted ____ a teller. And what

if someone took the notion that I was a moron? I might find myself arrested

for indecent exposure. This would have to stop now, today, I thought as I

passed a shooting gallery. I knew who I was, perhaps, but not *what* I was.

And what I appeared to be to others was liable to get me into serious

trouble. ____ no doubt ____ the police were looking for me ____ this

very minute ____. But I wasn't sure; perhaps by now

had come to look like anybody and everyone and not even ____ could

look at a man and determine the quality of his voice. And yet I remembered,

stepping around a car that had stopped too far into the intersection,

that certain types of Negro did ____

many of our alto and contralto singers had tended to be short dark girls....

Anyway, they couldn't look at me at tell *what* I'd say in a speech, anymore

than the cover of Leroy's diary and ____ what he had to say inside. Be-

sides, I ____ know what I would say myself. Lord, how simple life had

seemed on the campus where everyone had had his name and his role

Well, I was tired, perhaps that was the explanation. Perhaps I was

Figure 3.3. Ralph Ellison manuscript page.

formalize it, I begin a second and final draft—and this part of the
process is strangely the most enjoyable of all. I cut each chapter drasti-
cally, seeing as objectively as possible what can be eliminated or
shortened (my manuscripts would be very long, sometimes twice as
long, if I didn't cut so severely), trying to read the work as if from
another part of myself, or from the point of view of another person.

Though the original, spontaneous part of writing can be very exciting, the real reward for me at least is this third and most conscious, most "intellectual" organization of material.

JOYCE CAROL OATES

The First Principle of Revision

The writing process has its own rhythms and its own internal logic. Very often it generates statements with which the writer, upon careful consideration, cannot fully agree. It is quite amazing what can happen to a draft if one stops at each assertion to ask, "Is this *really* true?"

The answer is usually "yes." Often, however, it takes the form of "yes, but. . . ." Thus the real question is "To what extent is this true? How true is it?" Very often the statement is true in the context the writer originally had in mind, but not always true. Then the correct response is to modify or qualify the original statement. And sometimes—especially in opening passages, for some reason—writers have to admit to themselves that they have drafted statements which are hardly true at all.

As rhetorical theorists from Plato to Richard Weaver have insisted, *the first principle of revision is truth.* Rarely is a generalization totally true— indeed, part of what we mean by *generalization* is *"generally* true." Though most generalizations contain at least some degree of truth, generalized and abstract statements usually need to be qualified. Next time you are about to start an introduction with a statement like,

```
Throughout history, human societies have always been characterized
by competition.
```

ask yourself to what extent it is true—or even if you know enough to know how true it may be. Probably you will end up qualifying the generalization— or perhaps even deciding that it is not necessary to the point you are trying to make in that piece of writing. Especially in explanatory writing, and most especially when the rhetorical context is academic, scientific, or professional, *one of the most important and common types of revision is qualification.*

Excessive qualification can reflect an excessive, even paranoid need to avoid responsibility for one's statements. But considerable qualification is often necessary if the meanings understood by readers are to match those intended by writers. Consider the qualifiers in the first two paragraphs of this discussion of the first principle of revision. The cues of the level of language include these: "Very often . . . upon careful consideration . . . fully . . . quite . . . usually . . . Often. . . . Very often . . . sometimes. . . ." Delete those qualifiers and you reduce the truth of the passage.

One can approach truth—or correctness or effectiveness—by adding, deleting, or substituting. This may mean no more than adding a qualifier to an excessive generalization or substituting a more accurate word for one that does not really represent the intended meaning. Sometimes, however, the reconceiving becomes so substantial that the statement should be radically redrafted. Sometimes an untrue statement which is tangential to the point of the writing should be totally deleted.

The following sentences, written by advanced composition students, are easily fixed:

> During the time that it was spoken, however, Latin gave root to new
> languages, such as Italian and English.

> I often have to interrupt the flow of the narrative when I find myself
> at a loss for the exact word to express a certain emotion or convey
> a feeling, etc.

There are two problems with the first sentence. First, although many modern European languages did evolve from Latin, English is not one of them; English is basically a Germanic language which was strongly influenced by Latin (through French) after the Norman conquest of England in the year 1066. One solution would be to substitute "Rumanian" or "French" for "English." Second, although the modern languages contain many words with Latin roots, "gave root" does not accurately describe the relationship. One solution would be to substitute "gave rise."

There are two problems also with the second sentence. First, "narrative" is not the right word because the writer is clearly referring to the flow of the writing process, not of the written product (and in context it was clear that the writer was referring to any sort of writing, not just to narratives.) A solution would be to substitute "writing process" for "narrative." Secondly, "convey a feeling" is redundant after "express a certain emotion," and "etc." is vague. Though one would have to ask the writer to be sure, it seems probable that he really meant "express a certain idea or convey a feeling."

Often one can detect an inaccurate expression only in context. In such cases, the problem is that the phrase or sentence or passage seems to contradict the gist of the whole piece of writing. For example, in a persuasive essay, reproduced in full on pages 409–10, a writer asserts,

> Even at the seventh grade level, many children are not mature enough
> to be told about sex. It is something they may not be concerned with
> personally for a good many years.

Since the writer goes on to urge parents to support sex education classes for seventh graders, it would seem that these sentences do not accurately represent her intended meaning. In context it seems clear that what she really wishes

Pincomb ? 5 B

day, the eighth, I had information that (Jones) would hold a mass meeting
at the centre.   And a phone call from the police at Lilmouth to look

out for trouble. The Lilmouth gang was on the way to East Tarbiton works
centre. Jones was going to talk. This was a gang that had made trouble
in Lilmouth - the only trouble they had.

The unemployment centre was a scheme by the Emergency Committee.
i.e. Nimmo. He had started it some months before, a plan for workshops,
recreation *rooms for unemployed, clothes mending*

~~rooms for unemployed, old-clothes distribution~~, canteens and nurseries,
scattered about in a lot of odd spots around East Tarbiton and Lilmouth.
An old chapel in Tarbiton and a sixteen-room villa just outside,
a half-ruined cloth factory at Batwell and the ~~Manor House~~ *old Hall* at Ferryport.
Countess of Lil mouth, & other laismend's
Lady Gould, chairman General Welfare Committee; ~~Countess of Lilmouth~~, *Mrs. James (odds*
chairman Canteen Committee; Mrs. William (Jones,) chairman Children's
Care. Nimmo's usual game, hang a nosebag on everyone, keep 'em quiet.

*Feeding their own fancies and ~~others their~~ falling in this
own own importance. But trouble, a lot of fun
th start. Mrs. Pincomb wanted to put Relihis
wit all the nurseries, lady Gould Red liberal
candidates full of high ideals, et to low
Suspicions and the centers Red a string of
Colonels widows quite ready to fight the mill
for the chap of the Cook to st' their Cat. Pen Pincomb*

?O

~~a string of colonels' widows,~~ Then Jones came in on the Workshop
Committee and appointed a Bolshy manager. One of Potter's old men,
carpentry instructor, ordered to get out first day. Next morning
Potters manager in th working shop, very well,
~~young Well~~ came down with a crowd of young fellows bringing the old
boy with them, and said if they wanted to put him out they'd have to

Figure 3.4.   Joyce Cary manuscript page.

to concede is that most of these children will not be engaging in sexual activity
for some years, that they may not have reached puberty, and that they may
not be thinking very much about sex yet. But she ends up inadvertently undercutting (in effect, contradicting) some of the arguments she will make later.

Similarly, to return to the example used above—"Throughout history, human societies have always been characterized by competition."—the solution is to narrow and qualify. Any of the following could be substituted, depending on the writer's knowledge and the point to be made.

> Our society is characterized by competition.
>
> Although not all societies are dominated by competition, some degree of competitiveness is part of all human societies.
>
> At least since the industrial revolution, those nations which have dominated the world have been characterized by competition.
>
> Every human society is based on both cooperation and competition.

Sometimes the qualifications and modifications become so substantial that the statement should be reexamined and redrafted.

Writing consists of pre-writing, writing, and re-writing.

This proposition, which from the late-1960s into the 1980s was a commonplace among professional writing teachers, contains a considerable degree of correctness. Certainly it is more correct than the propositions it tended to replace: "writing consists of finding the right words to represent one's thoughts"; "writing is what happens while a pen (or other writing implement) is moving on paper (or other writing surface)." But the proposition can still stand considerable revision.

The statement is in conventionally acceptable form, so it need not be revised on that level. "Pre-writing" is a bit of jargon, which is clear to most professional writing teachers. It refers to whatever precedes drafting, usually generating material and planning how to present that material. Chapter 2 of this book could be considered instructions on "pre-writing." If we assume the intended readers will know this term, the bit of jargon is acceptable.

On the level of language, however, the repetition of "writing" stands out. It suggests an ambiguity: how can "writing" be a stage of writing unless the word is being used in two distinct senses? And even if the ambiguity were acceptable, the repetition inevitably suggests that "writing" is the most important stage of writing. Let us try, therefore, to substitute "drafting" for the second "writing":

Writing consists of pre-writing, drafting, and re-writing.

A problem still remains. The prefix *pre-* (meaning "before") implies that "pre-writing" is a preliminary. Juxtaposed with the suffix *re-* in "re-writing," it connotes three distinct stages. But we know that, in one sense or another, discovery actually continues throughout the entire writing process; and we know that revision ("rewriting") begins very early on, usually before the start of "drafting." We know that drafting is itself a discovery process and that good writers typically do some revising while they are still drafting. So the proposition needs to be revised substantially for accuracy.

Note what has happened in the two preceding paragraphs because it represents one typical revision process of effective writers: problems on the level of language (the repetition of "writing" and the implications of *pre-* and *re-*) have suggested problems on the level of meaning and lead toward revision of the underlying concepts. As Professor Gary Tate says, "A search for a better word is a search for a better vision." Rewriting here leads to rethinking (and redrafting):

> Writing consists of two contradictory processes: we must generate or discover material; and we must focus, select and order that material. The first process usually predominates in the early phases, the second in the later phases of writing. Both are usually active when writers draft.

This is quite far from the original statement. The revision process which took us from the one statement to the other is certainly not trivial—and nothing one would want to attempt at 5 A.M. on the night before a deadline (see pages 37–42).

In a Nutshell

"Writing and rewriting are a constant search for what one is saying," asserts John Updike. "I don't know what I think until I see what I've said," declares E. M. Forster.

What one has written is often not what one meant to write. It is important to look back over each draft to see what *it* says. But that is very difficult because we tend to read into our own drafts what we meant to say. One way to find out what you have said is to write a brief summary statement or *nutshell*, which states your main point or points.

Such a statement should be short, perhaps only two or three sentences. For a ten- to twenty-page paper, aim at 100 to 200 words. A summary of this length is harder to produce than one of twenty or a thousand words. It requires more than a simple thesis statement, but it still forces you to pick out only what is most important. And the more difficult it is to produce such a summary statement, the more important it is to do so—because the difficulty indicates the extent to which you cannot articulate precisely what your own main points are.

If you are writing collaboratively, or if you have a really devoted friend or colleague, you might try having someone else produce a summary statement of your draft. Such a summary is more likely to be faithful to what the draft actually says.

Having created the short summary statement, having encapsulated the essence of what you are trying to say in a nutshell, you should then ask

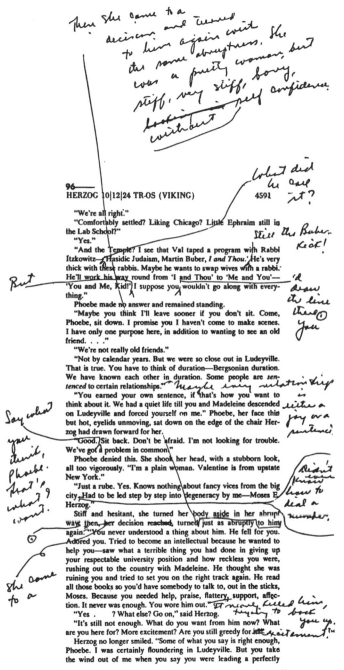

Then she came to a
decision and turned
to him again with
the same abruptness. She
was a pretty woman, but
stiff, very stiff, bony,
looking without
confidence.

96 ——
HERZOG 10|12|24 TR-OS (VIKING)   4591

*what did
he call
it?*

"We're all right."

"Comfortably settled? Liking Chicago? Little Ephraim still in
the Lab School?"

*Still the Buber-
Keick!*

"Yes."

"And the Temple? I see that Val taped a program with Rabbi
Itzkowitz—Hasidic Judaism, Martin Buber, *I and Thou*. He's very
thick with these rabbis. Maybe he wants to swap wives with a rabbi.
He'll work his way round from 'I and Thou' to 'Me and You'—
'You and Me, Kid!' I suppose you wouldn't go along with every-
thing."

But

*'d
draw
the line
there*

you

"Phoebe made no answer and remained standing.

"Maybe you think I'll leave sooner if you don't sit. Come,
Phoebe, sit down. I promise you I haven't come to make scenes.
I have only one purpose here, in addition to wanting to see an old
friend. . . ."

"We're not really old friends."

"Not by calendar years. But we were so close out in Ludeyville.
That is true. You have to think of duration—Bergsonian duration.
We have known each other in duration. Some people are *sen-
tenced* to certain relationships."

*Maybe every relationship
is
joy or a
sentence.*

"You earned your own sentence, if that's how you want to
think about it. We had a quiet life till you and Madeleine descended
on Ludeyville and forced yourself on me." Phoebe, her face thin
but hot, eyelids unmoving, sat down on the edge of the chair Herzog had drawn forward for her.

*Say what
you
think,
Phoebe.
That's
what I
want.*

"Good. Sit back. Don't be afraid. I'm not looking for trouble.
We've got a problem in common."

"Phoebe denied this. She shook her head, with a stubborn look,
all too vigorously. "I'm a plain woman. Valentine is from upstate
New York."

*Didn't
know
how to
deal a
number.*

"Just a rube. Yes. Knows nothing about fancy vices from the big
city. Had to be led step by step into degeneracy by me—Moses E.
Herzog."

"Stiff and hesitant, she turned her body aside in her abrupt
way then, her decision reached, turned just as abruptly to him
again. You never understood a thing about him. He fell for you.
Adored you. Tried to become an intellectual because he wanted to
help you—saw what a terrible thing you had done in giving up
your respectable university position and how reckless you were,
rushing out to the country with Madeleine. He thought she was
ruining you and tried to set you on the right track again. He read
all those books so you'd have somebody to talk to, out in the sticks,
Moses. Because you needed help, praise, flattery, support, affection. It never was enough. You wore him out."

*she came
to a*

*It nearly killed him,
trying to back
you up.*

"Yes . ? What else? Go on," said Herzog.

"It's still not enough. What do you want from him now? What
are you here for? More excitement? Are you still greedy for it
excitement?"

*you up.
excitement?"*

"Herzog no longer smiled. "Some of what you say is right enough,
Phoebe. I was certainly floundering in Ludeyville. But you take
the wind out of me when you say you were leading a perfectly

Figure 3.5. Saul Bellow's revisions on printer's galleys.

yourself certain questions about it. You might ask other people, too, for someone else is more likely to see flaws and exceptions than you are. If you are writing a term paper for a university course, you might show the summary statement to the professor. If you are writing an article for a magazine or journal, you might show it to the editor. Key questions to ask include the following:

> To what extent is this true? Does it need to be qualified or modified? Have I considered important exceptions?
>
> What has been left out? Have I considered all important and relevant aspects of the subject?
>
> How do I know this is true? What are some good examples of it?

The last two questions begin to take us beyond the simple consideration of truth and raise the consideration of *proof*. These two questions begin to imply a logical *order* by generating support, which is logically subordinate to the main points. They lead toward the second type of revision—reordering—which is the subject of the next section.

EXERCISE

1. Consider what *you* do when you revise. Write a narrative of how you revised a piece of writing recently. Expand that narrative into a process analysis by adding information about how you typically and ideally revise. Share this information with other writers (e.g., other people in your writing class or group) to see what you can learn.

2. Tape record yourself in conversation. Listen to the tape to discover how you revise while talking. Listen for overt corrections and also for sentences that seem to change midstream. Listen also for ideas that get restated—some of them will be restated for emphasis, but others will actually be revisions. How does revising in conversation differ from revising while writing?

3. Find out how other writers revise. Listen to your peers. Interview a writer about revision. If possible, watch a writer revise (preferably that same writer you interviewed). Find some manuscript pages from successful writers; what can you infer about their revision processes? Contrast a draft with final version of a piece of writing (e.g., James Joyce's *Stephen Hero* with his *Portrait of the Artist as a Young Man*).

4. Working in a group of three or four people, have each person bring in a short draft. Pass them around, and have *every* person do a quick revision of *every* draft. What can you learn from the ways other people revised your drafts?

5. As you continue working with this textbook, record your revision processes in your writing journal (see page 52). See if they change. Try to figure out what effects any changes have on the quality of your final products. Record also any suggestions made by other readers, especially your writing instructor or other students in your writing class. See if the types of suggestions change.

6. Keep a writing folder in which you collect all your recent writing. As you develop new revision abilities, look back at this writing and consider how you might now revise it.

Get Organized

The mature writer is recognized not so much by the quality of his individual sentences as by his ability to relate sentences in such a way as to create a flow of sentences, a pattern of thought that is produced, one suspects, according to the principles of yet another kind of grammar—a grammar, let us say, of passages. . . . The quality of an idea is not to be found in a nucleus or thesis statement but in the sentences that follow or lead up to that statement. An idea, in this sense, is not a "point" so much as a branching tree of elaboration and demonstration.

MINA SHAUGHNESSY

The recognition of structure gives the mind its ability to find meaning.

SUSANNE LANGER

Contrary to popular opinion, what makes us call a piece "well written" often has more to do with structure than with style.

For an idea to be true and accurately stated is not enough. It must also be properly related with other ideas. Though certain kinds of problems in a draft can be fixed by changing words or concepts, other problems have less to do with selection than with arrangement. In many contexts, including academia, you are allowed to express any opinion you like—so long as you support it properly. It is not so much *what* you say as *how* you say it. And as Professor Mina Shaughnessy emphasizes in *Errors and Expectations* (Oxford), the quality of individual sentences matters less than the pattern of thought communicated by a flow of sentences. The logic of the way you have developed and arranged your ideas reflects the quality of your thinking. Arrangement is so important that May Sarton, in *Plant Dreaming Days*, explains her revising process by analogy to arranging flowers.

After breakfast I spend an hour or more arranging and rearranging seven or eight bunches of flowers for the house. . . . Arranging flowers is like writing in that it is an art of choice. Not everything can be used of the rich material that rushes forward demanding utterance. And just as one tries one word after another, puts a phrase together only to tear it apart, so one arranges flowers. It is engrossing work, and needs a fresh eye and a steady hand. When you think the thing is finished, it may suddenly topple over, or look too crowded after all, or a little meager. It needs one more note of bright pink, or it needs white. . . . After the first hour I have used up my "seeing energy" for a while, just as, after three hours at my desk, the edge begins to go, the critical edge.

If a piece of writing is criticized as illogical, badly organized, or improperly developed, the problem is structure. If the problem is structure, the solution is not to change what you are saying, nor to change how you have phrased it, but to change the arrangement. In other words, you have to get organized—or reorganized. This is the second type of revision: *reordering*.

One of the clearest distinctions between experienced and inexperienced writers is that *inexperienced writers rarely reorder*. Inexperienced writers add, delete, and substitute, but they usually do not reorganize. Thus there is a whole type of revision most inexperienced writers do not even consider. Revising structure—to improve logic, organization, development—is often the key to successful writing, especially in academic and professional contexts.

Reordering is often the quickest and easiest way to improve a draft. Whole sections or paragraphs can be moved, and suddenly a seemingly incoherent writing reveals its true unity. The parts of a sentence can be reordered, and suddenly a whole passage flows. The reordered parts usually need to be recemented with new transitions (see pages 184–87), but the logic that mandated the reordering often suggests the transitions.

One of the great advantages of word processors is how easily they allow writers to move whole paragraphs and longer passages from one part of a draft to another. Good writers always did this type of revision (often with scissors and paste); word processing makes it quicker, easier and neater.

Outline Later

In order to revise structure, you must see it. This is often difficult, especially with longer pieces of writing, where the basic structure can get lost under a mass of details. The difficulty can be even worse on a word processor, for the screen rarely displays even half a page It is very hard to skim several pages of draft on a computer screen (which is why experienced writers print "hard copy" frequently).

To help yourself see structure, make an outline *of what is already written*.

Since the draft already exists, it is easy to make such an outline. And that outline represents the structure of the draft.

First, list the points you have made. One good way to do this is to go through the draft and try to find a sentence to represent each paragraph, either a sentence you make up or one which already exists in the draft. You will probably also need to make up or find more general summary sentences to represent larger sections of the draft.

Second, to transform that list of points into an outline, you need to classify statements according to importance (or level of generality). Mark the most general statements, the ones which seem to encompass the others. The traditional way to mark them, of course, is with roman numerals. The remaining statements may need to be subclassified. Try indenting and using capital letters, arabic numerals, and lower-case letters—tradition is often useful. What matters is not the particular format but that the outline allows you to see the *relationships* among the statements.

Try to keep the outline on a single sheet of paper. This may mean using a very large sheet. For very long writings, it may even mean making one general outline and then detailed outlines of each chapter or section. What matters is that you are able to see the pattern of the whole writing (or of whatever section you are considering).

By allowing you to see if your various points fit together into a *meaningful* pattern, the "outline later" technique reveals the structure of your draft and thus allows you to revise it. The key question is, "Does the pattern of meaning make sense as it stands? Or would it make more sense if reordered?" If any point is not where it belongs in relation to all the others, you can resolve the problem relatively painlessly by reordering.

While you are at it, you can easily produce or improve a thesis paragraph. In fact, one good way to create a thesis paragraph is to write out the gist of your outline in a few sentences and add it to your nutshell summary statement. Writing such a thesis paragraph is a good technique for establishing control of organization. It can help you turn the good idea in your mind into a "branching tree of elaboration and development" and to check for coherent development. It also helps readers anticipate and follow the pattern of meaning you have created.

You may also find it useful make an outline before the draft is complete, perhaps just before the conclusion is drafted, or at any point during the drafting when you are blocked and do not know what to say next. Looking at the outline, you can see the pattern of what you have drafted up to that point. If you are blocked in middraft, the emerging pattern often suggests what needs to be said next. If your conclusion is to be a summary, the main points of the outline often represent the substance of the conclusion.

The "outline later" technique allows you to evaluate the development of the piece of writing. Are some points left unsupported or supported less than they need to be? Are some points supported beyond their actual importance? Is the development balanced? Sometimes the answers to these questions are obvious as soon as you look over the outline. To make sure that each individual point is both true and well developed, you can ask of each point on your outline the same questions you asked about your nutshell summary statement:

> To what extent is this true?
>
> How do I know it is true?
>
> What is a good example of it?
>
> So what?

If the writing is well developed, the answers will be in the draft and in the immediate vicinity of the point. If they are not in the draft, you probably should add them. If they are in the draft but not near the point they support, perhaps you should move them.

You may also discover that some points are supported more than they need be or that some of what you have written is actually irrelevant to the point of the whole writing. You may then need to substitute (e.g., an appropriate example for an inappropriate one) or to delete. Deleting can be painful, especially if a lot of work has gone into what should be deleted, but it can be a crucially important revision process (see page 26). The blue pencil, used for deleting, was certainly a key to Ernest Hemingway's success as a writer (see pages 275–76).

Used together with nutshelling and reconsideration of individual points, the "outline later" technique can help revise your draft to represent the intended pattern of meaning accurately. It is not, however, the techniques that are crucial. What matters is the revision processes. Writers who already do these kinds of revision "naturally" need not adopt the techniques. But most inexperienced writers have a lot to gain from adopting these techniques.

Inexperienced writers typically look at a draft and—aside from changing a word here or there and looking for mechanical errors—cannot see what else to do. The "outline later" technique is particularly useful for breaking this block. It also directs attention to the crucial but often neglected questions of structure.

Consider, for instance, the following passage, written by a basic writing student.

To the poor man (lower class) living in the slums of the city, money signifies the comforts and luxuries he will never know but can only dream of because he can't even afford the necessities of food, medical care and clothing his family needs. The American population consists of immigrants from many countries. (The American Indian is becoming more and more non-existent). I asked my grandmother why she came to America, and her response was a common one which I learned in school, "America is the land of opportunity." My French grand-uncle wants his son and daughter to move to America so that they and their children can flourish in the land of plenty. The Irish, Italian, Armenian, Bulgarian, Chinese, Russian, German, Moslem, Hungarian, Japanese and the most recent example, the Vietnamese (and etc. . .) flowed and still flow into the dream land of prosperity. Although for the majority America turns out to be a better place to live compared to what they've left behind, the factory worker and unemployed worker can see but only dream of having the boy next door wash his Cadillac.

On first reading, this passage seems incoherent. If we try to pull out the main points, however, we discover three:

1. Almost all Americans are immigrants.
2. Immigrants come to the United States to seek prosperity.
3. But many remain poor in the United States.

If we reorder the sentences under these three points (and qualify the overgeneralizations), the passage becomes coherent.

With the exception of American Indians, the population of the United States consists of immigrants (and descendants of immigrants) from many countries. The Irish, Italian, German, Chinese, Japanese, Russian, Armenian, Bulgarian, Hungarian, Arab, and the most recent example, the Vietnamese, flowed and still flow into the dream land of prosperity. When I asked my grandmother why she came to America, her response was a common one I learned in school, "America is the land of opportunity." My French grand-uncle wants his son and daughter to move to the United States so they and their children can flourish in the land of plenty. Although for the majority America turns out to be better than what they've left behind, the factory worker or unemployed worker can see but only dream of having the boy next door wash his Cadillac. To poor slumdwellers, money signifies comforts and luxuries they will never know but can only dream of because they can't even afford food, medical care and clothing for their families.

The General and the Particular

One of the most important characteristics of a unified piece of writing is the proper relationship between generalities and particulars—or, to put it a bit more precisely, the proper relationships among various levels of generality. The proper relationship seems to vary somewhat according to genre and type of discourse. It may be very different for an expressive poem, a piece of explanatory exposition or a political persuasion, but it is always very important. Indeed, the propriety of the relationships is often crucial to the acceptance of a piece of writing—be that writing a fictional narrative or a scientific report. What has traditionally been called unity and coherence in writing is created not only by making certain that all particulars are relevant to the general propositions with which they appear, but also by observing proper relationships among various levels of generality.

There are certain exceptions. Within a personal relationship a speaker or writer may make a series of rather general, unsupported statements which will be accepted (or rejected) because the other person trusts (or distrusts) the first person's judgment on the matter. Likewise, people who have lived or worked together may understand the implications of a simple statement of fact so similarly that they do not need to state the implications. In face-to-face communication, moreover, people often can ask questions if they feel a gap in the message. Exceptions aside, however, the proper relationship among levels of generality is crucial to the success of your writing.

Two related rules of thumb encapsulate the point:

Generalizations should be inferred from particulars.

Opinions should be supported by facts.

These rules originate in scientific thinking, but they are generally enforced in most modern discourse, be it literary criticism, popular magazine writing, or sometimes even dinner-table conversation. Because they reflect the values of empirical science, these rules are particularly dominant in modern Western cultures. Lest we mistakenly think them universal, it is worth remembering that medieval Western culture was dominated by discourse rules quite antithetical to these (i.e., "Particulars should be deduced from generalizations," and "Opinions should be supported by authorities.") Almost anyone trying to learn from this textbook, however, is presumably writing in a modern, scientific culture and should be aware of the rules.

The first rule seems simple enough (the second we will leave for Chapter 6), but its application often is not. For one is rarely dealing with just "the general" and "the particular." More typically, writers are faced with various levels of generality (which may never get down to absolute particulars). The following paragraph, for instance, has four levels of generality.

One American Indian tribe, the Iroquois, consider themselves a nation apart from the United States, even though they are citizens. When the United States declared war on Germany, the Iroquois sent a message to Washington that they too had declared war. They intended to use bows and arrows, though. Since Germany made no separate peace treaty with the Iroquois at the end of World War I, the Iroquois didn't think it necessary to declare war again in 1941. Some other Indian tribes also think of themselves as separate nations.

The main point—that the Iroquois consider themselves a nation—is supported by two facts: the Iroquois declaration of war in 1917 and their decision that another declaration was unnecessary in 1941. Their intention to use bows and arrows, although not strictly relevant, is a supporting detail about the 1917 decision. And the final sentence goes beyond the apparent topic of the paragraph to make a more general point. If we reformat this paragraph to indicate level of generality by indenting, it looks like this:

> One American Indian tribe, the Iroquois, consider themselves a nation apart from the United States, even though they are citizens.
>> When the United States declared war on Germany, the Iroquois sent a message to Washington that they too had declared war.
>>> They intended to use bows and arrows, though.
>> Since Germany made no separate peace treaty with the Iroquois at the end of World War I, the Iroquois didn't think it necessary to declare war again in 1941.
> Some other Indian tribes also think of themselves as separate nations.

It is sometimes easier to understand how this principle works in a piece of writing by starting with the thinking process that generates the material for the writing. Suppose, for instance, you were writing an analysis of the following passage from Richard Wright's *Black Boy* (Harper & Row).

> Up or down the wet or dusty streets, indoors or out, the days and nights began to spell out magic possibilities.
>
> If I pulled a hair from a horse's tail and sealed it in a jar of my own urine, the hair would turn overnight into a snake.
>
> If I passed a Catholic sister or mother dressed in black and smiled and allowed her to see my teeth, I would surely die.
>
> If I walked under a leaning ladder, I would certainly have bad luck.
>
> If I kissed my elbow, I would turn into a girl.
>
> If my right ear itched, then something good was being said about me by somebody.

If I touched a hunchback's hump, then I would never be sick.

If I placed a safety pin on a steel railroad track and let a train run over it, the safety pin would turn into a pair of bright brand new scissors.

If I heard a voice and no human being was near, then either God or the Devil was trying to talk to me.

Whenever I made urine, I should spit for good luck.

If my nose itched, somebody was going to visit me.

If I mocked a crippled man, then God would make me crippled.

If I used the name of God in vain, then God would strike me dead.

If it rained while the sun was shining, then the Devil was beating his wife.

If the stars twinkled more than usual on any given night, it meant that the angels in heaven were happy and were flitting across the floors of heaven; and since stars were merely holes ventilating heaven, the twinkling came from the angels flitting past the holes that admitted air into the holy home of God.

If I broke a mirror, I would have seven years of bad luck.

If I was good to my mother, I would grow old and rich.

If I had a cold and tied a worn, dirty sock about my throat before I went to bed, the cold would be gone the next morning.

If I wore a bit of asafetida in a little bag tied about my neck, I would never catch a disease.

If I looked at the sun through a piece of smoked glass on Easter Sunday morning, I would see the sun shouting in praise of a Risen Lord.

If a man confessed anything on his deathbed, it was the truth; for no man could stare death in the face and lie.

If you spat on each grain of corn that was planted, the corn would grow tall and bear well.

If I spilt salt, I should toss a pinch over my left shoulder to ward off misfortune.

If I covered a mirror when a storm was raging, the lightning would not strike me.

If I stepped over a broom that was lying on the floor, I would have bad luck.

If I walked in my sleep, then God was trying to lead me somewhere to do a good deed for Him.

You would probably begin with a detailed examination of this somewhat strange list. What are the parts? What is the pattern? What is absent?

The list has 25 items. Almost all begin with an *if* and end with a consequence. The *if* clauses contain somewhat surprising things—

```
spit, urine, itching, elbow kissing, touching a hunchback, covering
a mirror--that do not seem to have any empirical causal relationship
with the imputed consequences. But however odd, the if clauses do
name things that are commonplace, events and actions that are
possible. The consequences generally have to do with health, luck
and death, but not success, money or power. None of the standard
formulas for success--e.g., if you work hard you will succeed or
"early to bed and early to rise makes a man healthy, wealthy and
wise"--are on the list.
```

In short, the list contains a series of *if-then*, cause-effect statements of the sort we call magic or superstitious because we have no empirical reason to believe these events or actions would actually have the stated consequences. The focus is on survival, not success; and good luck seems to be the best one can hope for.

Next consider the passage in context. The narrator is describing beliefs he had as a boy growing up in Mississippi during the 1930s. Immediately before this passage, he attempted to acquire some money by selling his dog; he not only failed to sell the dog, but he ended up being harassed by the police for being in a white neighborhood after sunset. Immediately after this passage, he tells the story of a black man who was lynched because he was perceived to have stared at a white woman in a store. In short, the narrator lives in a dangerous and irrational world where survival is a more immediate concern than success and where luck is the best one can hope for. In this context, his attraction to ''magic possibilities'' makes sense. Because his real environment is so bleak, we understand why he would loose his imagination to redeem it.

Having thus analyzed and explained the passage, suppose you reach a conclusion something like this:

```
The narrator of Black Boy lives in a dangerous and irrational world
where survival is a more immediate concern than success and where
luck is the best one can hope for. Because his real environment is
so bleak, he uses imagination to redeem it by envisioning "magic
possibilities."
```

From the point of view of someone who did not go through the thinking process with you, someone who perhaps has not even read the book (or at least, not recently), this conclusion by itself is an unsupported generalization. If you were to use it as a thesis statement in a piece of writing, you would be making the claim that it is true, and readers would expect you support it.

Main idea
for
analysis

```
In Wright's world, there is no logical connection
between what you do and what happens to you. It is not a
reasonable world and cannot be controlled by being reason-
```

able. The only kind of control that might work in this crazy
world where nothing but trouble seems certain is luck or
magic (control through non-rational means). Everything
is <u>not</u> up to you; it is up to something outside of you which
you can't control.

General
statement

The list of superstitions in Chapter 2 of <u>Black Boy</u> gives
the reader an idea of the kind of world that makes sense
to Richard—a world controlled by magic.

Explanation
of
statement

In magic there is no clear logical connection between what
you do and what happens to you, between an act and its consequences. In the so-called rational world, there *is* a connection. If a person works hard, he will probably be rewarded; if he shows imagination and ambition, he can go
far. His future is up to him, not to some mysterious outside
power.

Use of
observations
to
illustrate
statement

But in magic you never know. If you spit on something, it
may mean luck. If you urinate on it you may be dead. If
you kiss an elbow, pull a hair from a horse, tie a sock
around your neck or do any number of ridiculous things,
you may be dead or alive, sick or well, depending on the
superstition. Life cannot be figured out or controlled.
It is full of danger and terror, a crazy mixture of nuns
and devils, spit and stars.

Showing
connection
with
the rest
of the
book

This list of superstitions reflects the way the world looks
to Richard. It reflects a crazy world of lynchings and hunger and "Jesus Saves." The "logical" formulas for success in America hold no promise for him. If he has ambition,
he will be punished. If he reads books, he will be dangerous. If he develops fully his talents and powers as a human
being, he will most likely be dead. In a world surrounded
by the irrationalities of racism, it is no wonder that young
Richard feels safer and happier with magic. In a world of
"reason" he always loses. But in a world of magic, he
is bound to win some of the time. Magic, for him, opens up
the world of "possibilities."

We can understand the same principle also by seeing the implications
for revision in a piece that only partially follows the rule.

I started reading before I started school. My mother was the main
reason why I did so. When I was young she would take the time to
read to me and also try and teach me to read. I can remember the
first volume of <u>The Nancy Drew Mystery Stories</u> that my mother bought

for me, and my faithfully reading and buying the other volumes until
I had completed the set. In the fourth grade, my mother made a big
fuss with the principal of my school because my teacher would not
let me read if I finished my work early. In the fifth and sixth grades
I won first place in the school library contest.

The point that I'm trying to make is that I've been brought up
with the idea that reading is full of pleasure, not tedious as some
people think and say it is. Reading also expands vocabulary by
implementing new words that you can either understand from context
or by looking them up in a dictionary. Books expand your knowledge
by going into detail and initiating new subject matter.

DeAnne Paulis

DeAnne makes three general points (all stated in her second paragraph). The first—that she was brought up to believe writing is important and pleasurable—is well supported by the six sentences of the first paragraph. The second and third points—that reading expands both vocabulary and knowledge—are developed minimally. Once perceived, this imbalance suggests revision. Depending upon her purposes, DeAnne needs either to develop her second and third points or, if the first point is really the main point, to subordinate them.

Being Logical

The conventions of academic and professional discourse generally demand that writers assume—or at least pretend to assume—an ideal audience of rational readers who will be convinced by empirical evidence and logical proof. The basic structure of such discourse is *thesis statement + proof*. We call the thesis statement a *claim* because the writer's purpose is to claim this statement is true.

Most commonly, at least in modern Western cultures, we validate the claim with *evidence*. That is to say, we try to support a relatively general claim with specific facts. This is not the only way to validate a claim—one could logically deduce it from an established principle or authority—but our empirical culture tends to prefer evidence. In fact, the word *empirical* means a preference for trusting the evidence of our senses rather than authority or abstract logic.

Logically, however, there is still something missing. For a claim to be validated by evidence, we need an assertion that says something like "We know this evidence supports this claim because. . . ." Such a statement is called a *warrant*. Although the warrant is often obvious, hence left unstated, a complete logical proof includes claim, evidence and warrant. Claim, evidence, and warrant constitute the crux of any logical proof or argument. (For a fuller discussion of logical progression, see pages 370–79.)

Induction and Deduction

Logically, one can start from a general principle and deduce some specific implication. Or one can start with specifics and generalize. The sort of logic that goes down the ladder of generality, from general principles to specific implications, we call *deductive reasoning*. The sort of logic that goes up the ladder of generality, we call *inductive reasoning*.

The epitome of deductive reasoning is found in the formal logic. The philosopher says, "Here are my premises; here is my thesis. Grant me that my premises are true, and I will demonstrate that my thesis can be logically deduced from them." Writers, similarly, may start from generalizations their readers already believe—"All human beings are mortal"—and move by deductive reasoning to a conclusion they want those readers to accept—"Socrates was mortal."

The epitome of inductive reasoning is found in the empirical arguments of science. The scientist says, "Here is my hypothesis; here are the results of my empirical investigations. Grant me the validity of my experimental design, and my statistical calculations demonstrate there is a 95% probability (i.e., 19 chances in 20) that my hypothesis is correct." In practice, scientists do experiments to test hypotheses, which means they must have the hypotheses before starting to experiment and collect data; logically, however, their reasoning starts from the experimental findings and works inductively to confirm or reject the hypotheses.

The authors of the following example, eager to persuade readers to accept the first axiom of their theory of communication, use both deductive and inductive reasoning. The passage begins by deducing its thesis statement from an even more basic assumption. Represented as a logical syllogism, the first three sentences look like this:

> All behavior communicates.
>
> One cannot *not* behave (i.e., even doing "nothing" is behavior).
>
> Therefore one cannot *not* communicate.

Having reached its thesis statement in the final clause of the third sentence, the passage goes on to support it inductively and with examples.

> First of all, there is a property of behavior that could hardly be more basic and is, therefore, often overlooked: behavior has no opposite. In other words, there is no such thing as nonbehavior or, to put it even more simply: one cannot *not* behave. Now, if it is accepted that all behavior in an interactional situation has message value, i.e., is communication, it follows that no matter how one may try, one

cannot *not* communicate. Activity or inactivity, words or silence all have message value: they influence others and these others, in turn, cannot *not* respond to these communications and are thus themselves communicating. It should be clearly understood that the mere absence of talking or of taking notice of each other is no exception to what has just been asserted. The man at a crowded lunch counter who looks straight ahead, or the airplane passenger who sits with his eyes closed, are both communicating that they do not want to speak with anybody or be spoken to, and their neighbors usually "get the message" and respond appropriately by leaving them alone. This, obviously, is just as much an interchange as an animated discussion.

PAUL WATZLAWICK, JANET BEAVIN, AND DON JACKSON

Even in this one paragraph, the writers try to "prove" their point twice. The deductive proof is somewhat unusual in that it is fully stated. *Both* premises and the conclusion are made explicit (although not in the standard order of formal logic), and the more general premise is actually framed by, "if it is accepted that . . . , then it follows that. . . ."

More typically in persuasive writing, it is not necessary or even desirable to state all one's premises.

Democracy (from the Greek *demos*, the people + *cracy*, rule or govern) means government by the people; therefore Swiss women should have the right to vote.

Here three premises—that women are people (legally as well as biologically), that Switzerland should be a democracy, and that the right to vote translates in real political power—are at best probable. The premise that women are legally people, for example, was not obvious to the ancient Greeks who invented the word *democracy*; nor was it obvious in the United States, Canada, or Europe until the present century; and it was apparently not obvious to the men of Switzerland until 1971 (before that they periodically rejected referenda that would have given Swiss women the right to vote). The mere probability of the premises is reflected by the *should* in the conclusion.

If a premise is left unstated (or is only probable), we do not have a formally complete syllogism. What we have instead is an *enthymeme*, an incomplete syllogism. Aristotle says that an enthymeme is the equivalent in verbal persuasion of a syllogism in formal logic.

Aristotle's discussion of enthymemes has two implications for writers. First, it is often good tactics to leave premises unstated, either because the premises are so obvious that readers would feel "talked down to" or because the premises might be rejected if stated overtly. Second, and more important, the unstated premise is, according to Aristotle, often an attitude shared by the audience.

In the first sort of case, we write,

> If Socrates is human, he is mortal.

The warrant or major premise (''All human beings are mortal'') will be obvious to readers. Similarly, we write,

> This kind of corn takes five months to grow, so the corn planted in April should mature in September.

The premise that ''September is five months after April'' is so obvious it is not stated.

In these two cases, one leaves a premise unstated because readers will fill it in. Thus the readers participate in the reasoning process, and that participation has the psychological effect of making the writing more persuasive, even though the underlying logic has not changed. To have stated the obvious premises, on the other hand, would have seemed condescending and made the writing less persuasive. Watzlawick, Beavin and Jackson state both premises explicitly because they are not sure that the readers will fill in the missing premise, which is ''often overlooked.''

In making the argument that Swiss women should have the right to vote, the premise that Switzerland should have a republican form of democracy might be left unstated because it is ''obvious''—or because it might raise an issue which would otherwise not occur to the audience. More to Aristotle's second point, the three unstated premises—that women are legally people, that democracy is desirable, and that voting translates into real political power—are attitudes and assumptions we can expect modern, Western audiences to share. As Kenneth Burke has phrased this Aristotelian point in *A Rhetoric of Motives* (California), ''to change an audience's opinion in one respect,'' a writer must ''yield to that audience's opinion in other respects.'' That is to say, one must ''talk their language''; the argument must be based on premises with which they agree.

Writers often must deal with subjects where the premises can be known only probably. If a syllogism, whether completely stated or not, is based on a merely probable premise, then it is in another sense incomplete, hence the equivalent of an enthymeme. (''If we plant in April, we *should* have fresh corn in September; then again, corn worms might kill the plants in August.'')

The crux of Aristotle's point is that logical proof and rhetorical proof, although related, are not the same. Rhetoric, he says, is concerned with subjects where definite knowledge is impossible or unavailable. Rhetoric, moreover, is concerned with persuasion, with what will convince an audience. Writers should be concerned with logic, but not logic alone, not logic in the abstract. When Aristotle says that the enthymeme is the rhetorical equivalent of the syllogism, he is saying that speakers and writers must be concerned with logic in relation to the attitudes of real audiences (see Chapter 4).

As enthymemes are the rhetorical equivalent of deductive logic, examples are the rhetorical equivalent of empirical proof. This point, also from Aristotle, is especially important in modern times because empirical science and inductive reasoning now predominate. Rhetorically, we often support a thesis by giving not reasons but examples. Well-chosen examples can, however, establish the probability of a statement in readers' minds—at least if the readers do not think of counterexamples. Note that Watzlawick, Beavin, and Jackson supported their thesis statement with examples, not with statistically valid empirical evidence. (In any event, it is extremely difficult to provide empirical proof for a negative statement—for instance, that Zeus, Jehovah, or Allah does not exist or that "one cannot *not* communicate.")

Essentially, then, a logical argument consists of a statement plus proof. The proof that supports the statement may be either deductive (syllogism or enthymeme) or inductive and empirical (statistics or examples). In either case, a complete proof must include claim, evidence and warrant see pages 371–73). Writers must be concerned with both logic and the appearance of logic—that is, with making sure that their logic is apparent to their readers. Often effective organization is what makes the logic of a piece of writing apparent to readers.

Develop Your Own Revision Heuristic

One good way to improve the quality of your writings is to improve your revision processes. Especially if you are not a very experienced writer, you probably do not take advantage of all the revision opportunities available to you.

One way to help yourself see those potentials is to develop your own *revision heuristic* to guide your revision process. That means developing both a set of questions to focus your attention and a procedure for using them. The questions should pinpoint your weaknesses and focus your attention on flaws likely to appear in your drafts. Since your attention is limited, your questions should be grouped, thereby allowing you to concentrate on one type of question at a time.

The purpose of a revision heuristic is to direct attention during revision. Your revision heuristic should direct your attention to the kinds of problems that frequently occur in your drafts. Here are two examples of individualized revision heuristics. Note that each includes not only a set of questions but also a procedure for integrating them in the individual's writing process.

Revision Heuristic and Checklist

After writing the first draft--put it away for anywhere from 5 hours to a day. Now read it over keeping in mind the following questions.

Does this essay fulfill the assignment?
How does it fulfill the assignment?
Is its purpose shown clearly?
Does it communicate effectively to its chosen audience?

Now, outline the ideas and arguments in the essay.

Could your organization be improved?
Are your arguments reasonable and proven by facts?
Is your conclusion weak or indecisive?

Outline the levels of generality and complexity in your paper.

Is your essay too simple?
Is there another side to your viewpoint?
What idea or ideas could be added to improve the quality of your paper?
Did you use Burke's Pentad if your paper deals with human motivation? If not, why not?

Wait for another short period--then read the essay closely and ask these questions:

Are there meaningful transitions between paragraphs?
Does each sentence flow smoothly into the other?
Are the rhythms and structures of the sentences varied and interesting?

Finally--check for misspelling and punctuation errors.

Margaret Coe*

*No relation to author of this textbook.

Story Revision Heuristic

1. What is the purpose of this exercise?

2. To what extent have you fulfilled this purpose?

3. Can you title the piece of writing?

4. Who are you writing this piece for? Would the piece work for this intended audience?

5. Have you said everything that you wanted to say? Have you said more than you wanted to say?

6. Is the style obvious, repetitive, predictable?

7. Is the piece too sentimental, too dry, too vague, etc.?

8. Is there a consistency in tone? (Does it jump from a formal use of words to overly simple phrases? Does it try to be funny where humor is inappropriate?)

9. Can this piece be published while the characters are still living?

10. Do you feel good about this piece of writing? Do you feel good about showing it to another person?

The above heuristic is used after the first draft of the story has been completely written. A process of revision is going on while the first draft is being generated. This process involves removing words, sentences and whole paragraphs. It also involves changing words, rearranging the order of sentences and paragraphs, and adding to the body of what has already been written. This process takes anywhere from several hours to several days. No heuristic is used for the process, nor will it be.

After the first draft is completed I use the revision heuristic. In the case of ''Jude'' it resulted in a complete re-write. This is not always the case.

Sometimes I cannot answer the questions in the heuristic to my satisfaction, but choose to leave something in or take something out anyway because I like the sound of it. However, I feel that the questions are very beneficial and generally serve as an effective set of guidelines.

Virginia Louise Clesse

Remember, a revision heuristic with too many questions will be overwhelming, hence useless. Formulate questions only to match the weak points of your own drafts, particularly those weaknesses you want to concentrate on now.

Thus far, this chapter has discussed revising for focus, accuracy, and organization—that is, substantive revision. The final section discusses collaborative writing and editing, processes that influence revision. Then the following two chapters consider readers and language, two other factors that influence revision. As you read these chapters, you can develop your own, individual revision heuristic by considering which of the points discussed are relevant to problems that occur in your drafts.

Working with other writers—writing together, editing each other's drafts, or just reading and responding—can also focus your attention and help you understand how to improve your writing. The final section of this chapter will help you do that gently and effectively.

EXERCISE

1. Choose something you wrote recently. Use the "nutshell" and "outline later" techniques to consider how it might be revised.

2. Try the following activity, devised by Professor Peter Elbow, in a group of four or five writers. Read a piece one of the writers has written and then do the following:

    a. First tell very quickly what you found to be the main points, main feelings, or centers of gravity. Just sort of say what comes to mind for fifteen seconds, for example, "Let's see, very sad; the death seemed to be the main event; um . . . but the joke she told was very prominent; lots of clothes."

    b. Then summarize it into a single sentence.

    c. Then choose one word from the writing which best summarizes it.

    d. Then choose a word that isn't in the writing which best summarizes it.

3. Analyze some piece of writing you admire from your own area of special interest by looking at the levels of generality. Then analyze one of your own more recent writings in the same way. Is there a difference? If so, is there something you need to learn if you are to write effectively in this special area?

4. Take any extensive list or table and use it to generate a hierarchy of generalizations (as done on pages 125–28).

Collaborative Writing and Editing ⸻

Writers often invent by involving other people: as editors and evaluators whose comments aid invention; as "resonators" who nourish and sustain the inventor as well as the invention; as collaborators who interact to create new ideas; and as opponents or devil's advocates who provide challenges and alternate perspectives to work against. To create certain kinds of discourses such as contracts or treaties, two or more rhetors (often in adversarial positions) must collaborate. . . . Reputable [literary] authors regularly solicit opinions about their manuscripts from friends, colleagues, agents, and editors, and they often take those opinions into account during revision.

KAREN BURKE LEFEVRE

So much writing is co-authored or at least invented and revised collaboratively that writers often need to work collaboratively. Articles in newsmagazines or scientific journals, project proposals, political platforms, treaties and contracts, textbooks, environmental reports, and many other types of corporate, public, and published writing are typically written by more than one writer. Even when they are not co-authored, moreover, most corporate or public documents are guided and/or edited by someone other than the person who drafts them. The ability to work with others—to give and take criticism constructively, to write collaboratively—is very important for writers.

Some of the most sensitive writing tasks—say, a formal critique of a colleague's project proposal or an evaluation of a subordinate's performance—also require skillful constructive criticism. Even if you always write alone, the processes of writing and learning require taking and making good use of constructive criticisms from editors, supervisors, teachers, and so forth. If revision is really part of the writing process—and it is—then at least the final phase of most public writing is collaborative.

Writing Collaboratively

Though common, collaborative writing has not been much studied until very recently. So we know a lot less about the collaborative writing process than we do about the individual writing process. But collaborative writing is in many ways like doing any task in group, and has similar advantages and disadvantages.

Writing collaboratively can be very exciting. Getting started is often easier, and interaction stimulates invention. We say "two heads are better than one," but the point is really that two (or more) minds interacting will likely come up with better ideas than the same number of minds in isolation. Collaborative invention—generating both material and strategies for presenting it—can be one of the best parts of collaborative writing.

Another advantage is division of labor. Once the group has defined the task and settled on a strategy, research can be divided. Drafting can be divided, too, with individuals taking on different parts. Or one person can start drafting and pass the draft along when she or he gets stuck, thus evading even temporary writing blocks. Or individuals can take on the parts of the task that match their particular strengths.

Once a draft is completed, it is usually important that revision begin very collaboratively—otherwise one person may take the writing off in a direction the rest of the group does not like. But once consensus has been reached about how to revise, division of labor is again possible.

The drawbacks of collaborative writing are essentially those of doing any task in a group. If the group does not work well together, conflict may exceed cooperation. Or the work may be divided unevenly. Or one individual may prove unpleasantly domineering.

If at all possible, be selective about who you write with. Do they have the same level of motivation and commitment to the task that you do? Do they share your goals? Do you respect them and their opinions? Are their ways of working similar or complementary with yours? Do their strengths as writers complement yours? If you get the wrong answers to these questions, writing collaboratively is likely to be a frustrating experience.

Achieving Consensus

When a piece of writing is being written or edited by more than one person, those people need to agree about what the writing should accomplish and how. That can be done by appointing a boss, but several minds interacting are more fruitful than one mind dictating. So the writing is likely to be better if the group can reach a consensus.

The camel, it has been suggested, is a horse designed by a committee. A collaborative writing can be equally ungainly (and not nearly so well adapted to its environment) if it is not founded on consensus. Consensus means everybody (or almost everybody) is in essential agreement. It is achieved by extended discussion. Consensus is not majority rule and is not achieved by voting. Indeed, the need for voting and other such procedures indicates the absence of a consensus. When the goal is a clear and effective piece of writing, extend the discussion until all issues are resolved. The early majority may not be right, and an unconvinced minority may not cooperate wholeheartedly.

Achieving consensus is in certain ways similar to constructive criticism. The goal is not to win, but to improve the writing. Here are some guidelines for achieving consensus:

1. Keep the group's purpose always in view. Remember, the goal is not for any individual member's suggestion to ''win,'' but to make decisions

that will best achieve the group's purpose. Try to avoid egotism. Try not to argue for your own position just because you identify with it.

2. Insofar as time allows, avoid conflict-reducing techniques such as majority rule, averaging, compromises, and trade-offs. Avoid "changing your mind" only in order to reach agreement and avoid conflict. When the discussion locks, seek alternative solutions that synthesize the best of all the individual suggestions or offer a whole new approach.

3. View differences of opinion as helpful, not as hindrances. Try to involve everyone in the decision-making process because more information and more perspectives usually produce better decisions, and more involvement usually produces more commitment to follow through on those decisions.

Clearly making decisions by consensus is more difficult and time-consuming than making decisions by majority-rule (or dictatorship). Making decisions by consensus, moreover, is possible only when the group shares a common purpose. When conditions are right, however, consensus can produce better decisions. Collaborative writing produced by consensus can be more substantively more insightful and rhetorically more effective than writing produced in a hierarchical writing group dominated by one individual. (For examples of successful collaborative writing produced in a composition course, see Chapter 10, pages 419–21, 423–25, 429–33, 448–53.)

Here is an explanation of an editorial comment collaboratively written at one newsweekly:

It's often difficult to answer questions about who wrote an editorial, because the *Guardian*'s editorials are, more than anything else in the paper, collective productions.

In principle, the Viewpoints are an expression of the whole *Guardian* cooperative. When the subject of a Viewpoint is particularly controversial or concerns an extremely sensitive question, the whole staff is involved in producing the Viewpoint. First, we hold a discussion of the subject at a staff meeting, where we agree on a point of view and produce an outline of the Viewpoint, a draft of which is prepared by one staff member. The draft is reviewed by the 5-member elected Coordinating Committee, and a final version is discussed and revised by the whole staff.

Most Viewpoints are produced without participation of the whole staff because they are less controversial or politically sensitive. Such Viewpoints are initiated by the Coordinating Committee, often at the suggestion of the staff. The Coordinating Committee has a brief discussion of the points to be made in such a Viewpoint and then assigns it to a staff member.

The resulting draft is then revised by the Coordinating Committee, which can make minor editorial changes or major changes, as necessary.

In practice, the majority of Viewpoints are written by Coordinating Committee members. Other staffers are recruited to write Viewpoints concerning subjects they cover, such as labor unions, or economics or reproductive rights.

However they are produced, Viewpoints are subject to much greater scrutiny and contemplation than material in the rest of the paper. More people are concerned with their planning, and more people have a hand in making certain they say what they are supposed to. We put that extra effort into them because the Viewpoints represent the best expression of our political outlook, which we hope will carry far and wide, not only outside our cooperative, but beyond our regular readership as well.

Editing and Being Edited

Writers need feedback to improve. Positive feedback (''That's a terrific paper you wrote!'') makes writers feel good and encourages them to keep writing. In the long run, positive feedback can lead to growth: a writer who tries something different and is praised for it will probably try it again—thus positive feedback can reinforce positive changes writers may make. But it is negative feedback (''I don't understand that sentence'' or ''That report would communicate better with stronger transitions'') which induces change and directs improvement.

It is important for writers to learn to take criticism positively, to view it as an opportunity to improve. As a writer or writing student, your draft manuscripts will be read and criticized. To improve, you need to be able to take advantage of that critical response. It helps, of course, if the critical response is gentle and constructive.

If friends are giving you feedback on your draft, do not just ask if they like it. Friends usually say they do. Instead check to see how well they have understood it. Ask what the main point is. Ask for a summary. If that summary does not match what you were trying to communicate, revision is probably in order. And remember, writers who react defensively to criticism are likely to receive less of it, hence to have fewer opportunities to improve their drafts.

As a writer or writing student, you are very likely to be asked to read and respond to other writers' draft manuscripts. On the job, you may find yourself supervising writers—which means both defining their tasks and responding to their drafts. Your responses should be helpful, should help the writers make their writing better. That means telling them what works well and what does not work well—and doing so constructively, without undermining their self-confidence.

It also means thinking about the writers and their writing processes as well as about the strengths and weaknesses of draft manuscripts. Writers who need to undertake major revision—perhaps to find a sharper focus or reorganize—will often do better if not overwhelmed by negative comments about sentence structure, usage, or typographical errors. Often it is better to focus on just two or three of the most immediate revision tasks and to save other critical comments for later.

To give writers useful feedback, you must read in a special way. Editors are not ordinary readers—nor do they read as writers, judges, or critics. When you edit, you do not read as yourself; you make believe you are the sort of reader the manuscript is addressed to and you try to imagine how those readers will respond. In short, you read with an eye to gauging how well the manuscript will achieve its purposes with its intended readers on the occasion when they are likely to read it (see pages 146–56). If you are reading the draft of someone's university term paper, you must read as a professor does while grading (see pages 445–46). If you are reading the draft of a junior high school textbook, you must imagine yourself back in junior high school (as both teacher and pupil).

Before saying anything, be sure you understand what kind of response will be useful. If you are not sure, ask. Early in the writing process, for instance, many writers are concentrating on substance, general tone, and direction; they may not want to be distracted by comments about minor stylistic and mechanical flaws. At any event, begin by responding positively. And respond to the substance, to what the draft says, before you say anything critical about structure, style, mechanics, or even audience.

Be careful not to overwhelm. Concentrate on your most important responses. Present your response as one reading, one opinion. Questions are often more useful to writers than assertions. Ask questions especially where you have difficulty understanding the draft or think its intended readers might. Generally, do not correct the text; explain your response and suggest strategies for revision.

In most contexts, moreover, when you suggest revisions, you must take care that you are not transforming the manuscript into what you would have written: the highest compliment an editor can get from a writer is, "After your editing, this piece says and does what *I* wanted it to—but better." When you are an editor, you read critically, but unlike a critic, you are on the writer's side; you are helping, not judging the writer. Your criticism should be constructive.

Constructive Criticism

Constructive criticism aims not merely to be correct (thereby allowing the criticizer to feel righteous), but to persuade the criticized person or people to construct changes. Constructive criticism is a type of persuasion, closely related to Rogerian persuasion (see pages 395–411). Constructive criticism is especially important in a writing workshop, class, or group.

However useful it may be, criticism is threatening. Constructive criticism attempts to minimize threat. One way to achieve a reassuring context is to praise before criticizing. The praise should be genuine and specific: hardly anyone is taken in by the formula, "This is basically good, but. . . ." There is almost always something good about any piece of writing; by demonstrating your ability to find it and describe it, you earn your right to criticize. Another way to achieve a reassuring context is by self-criticism: "I can see what's wrong here because I often do (or used to do) the same thing myself."

The threatening nature of criticism can also be reduced if you make it clear that you are criticizing a particular action (or set of actions), not the person or people who did it. Criticism is most threatening (and least constructive) when it is not clear what can be done about it. If someone tells me, "Your paper is terrible," I do not know what to do (aside from feeling bad), so I respond defensively. If someone tells me, "This paper doesn't work as it stands, but if you do this, that and the other, it could be really effective," I respond constructively.

There is a formula for constructive criticism that helps keep the criticism specific, makes it clear that a particular action (not a person) is being criticized, and forces the criticizer to indicate what can be done about the criticism. It goes like this:

When you _____ , I feel/think _____ , so I wish you would _____ .

> *When you* use words like *chick*, *spic*, *welsh* and *gyp*, *I feel* angry and stop listening to what you're saying *so I wish you would avoid sexist and racist language*. [*Note: Gyp* is a derogatory term derived from *gypsy* and meaning "cheat"; *welsh* is derived from what used to be a widespread racist opinion in England that people from Wales do not pay their debts.]

> *When you* tell me my writing is "incoherent, ungrammatical, and confused," *I feel* stupid, discouraged, and angry, *so I wish you would* make more specific and constructive criticisms instead.

> *When you* hand me a sloppy manuscript, *I feel* insulted because I don't think you care enough about your work or my time, so *I wish you would* take the trouble to make the manuscript easier to read.

It is important that the first slot in the formula be filled with a specific criticism. Try *not* to say,

When you punctuate so ignorantly . . .

Do say,

When you use comma-splices . . .

The second slot should contain a response, not a judgment. Do *not* say,

> . . . I think you must be a bigot. . . .

Do say,

> . . . I feel angry and stop listening to what you're saying. . . .

The third slot should contain a specific and constructive suggestion. Do *not* say,

> . . . I wish you would start making some sense.

Do say,

> . . . I wish you would organize more carefully and supply clear transitions.

There are two other things you can do to help constructive criticism work effectively. The first is to make certain that the person you wish to criticize is prepared to receive criticism. If you have any doubt, ask. Say,

> I have a criticism of your writing. Should we discuss it now?

The second is to consider the other person's vested interest in receiving your criticism. What does the other person have to gain from your criticism? The third slot in the criticism contains your desire: your purpose is to encourage the other person to do what you are suggesting there. A constructive criticism ends, therefore, by emphasizing what the other person could gain by adopting your suggestion.

Antagonistic criticism plays to an audience. It is righteous. It passes judgment. Its goal is to demonstrate the superiority of the criticizer and the inferiority of those criticized. Constructive criticism is addressed to those criticized. Its goal is to minimize threat and induce change.

Though constructive criticism is appropriate for editing and collaborative writing, both types of criticism have their uses. For example, newspaper columnists usually write antagonistic criticisms of politicians; their purpose is to persuade the newspaper's readers to pass judgment on those politicians. Sometimes, however, newspaper columnists write constructive criticisms; they seem to assume the politicians in question will be among the newspaper's readers and they try to persuade the politicians to change. The material may be the same, but the tone and the form of the presentation shift distinctly. (The distinction between antagonistic and constructive criticism is parallel to the distinction between traditional and Rogerian persuasion; see pages 395–98.)

When you criticize, be clear about your purposes and use the appropriate kind of criticism. And when you are criticized, try not to react defensively: concentrate first on grasping whatever is constructive in the criticism.

EXERCISE

1. Apply the formula for constructive criticism to your analysis of *your own* writing weaknesses (see pages 19–24). Does it help you focus your own goals?

2. Select some newspaper editorials that make antagonistic criticisms. Practice transforming them into constructive criticisms.

3. In your writing group, workshop, or class, devote the last five minutes to criticizing the way criticisms were made during the preceding meeting. Try to put the emphasis on self-criticism (i.e., rather than criticizing others, try to say first, "I did such-and-such, but it would have been better if I had done this-and-that instead.")

4. Do a collaborative writing, and try to make decisions by consensus. How does the experience of collaborative writing contrast with the experience of writing by yourself? What gets easier? What gets harder? (See Exercise 4, page 118.)

C·H·A·P·T·E·R 4

The Communicative Process

Form . . . is an arousing and fulfillment of desires. A work has form in so far as one part of it leads a reader to anticipate another part, to be gratified by the sequence.

KENNETH BURKE

The author's whole art is bent on obliging me to create what he discloses, . . . so both of us bear the responsibility for the universe . . . . In order for the works to have any effect it is necessary for the public to adopt them.

JEAN-PAUL SARTRE

Writer and audience are Siamese twins. Kill one and you run the risk of killing the other. Try to separate them, and you may simply have two half-dead people.

MARGARET ATWOOD

The common ingredient that I find in all of the writing I admire—excluding for now novels, plays and poems—is something that I shall reluctantly call the rhetorical stance, a stance which depends on discovering and maintaining in any writing situation a proper balance among the three elements that are at work in any communicative effort: the available arguments about the subject itself, the interests and peculiarities of the audience, and the voice, the implied character, of the speaker.

WAYNE BOOTH

WRITING is a communicative process. We write not just for the pleasure of self-expression, nor just to clarify our own understandings, but also to communicate with readers. On this level, a piece of writing can be judged objectively by asking to what extent it achieves the writer's purposes with the intended readers. The first section of this chapter should help you evaluate your readers and also understand how readers read, hence how to write in ways that facilitate their reading.

Many of the qualities of "good writing" can be explained in terms of the needs and expectations of readers. The epigraphs that open this chapter all turn about one central point: writing is best understood as a communicative process; not as the production of text, but as interaction with readers. Many seemingly arbitrary writing conventions make sense when we think about writing as *addressed* to readers, when we understand writing not as a matter of getting words down on paper, but as a psychological, social, and rhetorical process.

You will find in this chapter material that you might have expected in the preceding chapter. The second and third sections discuss the structures that make a piece of writing coherent and help readers comprehend its structure and emphasis accurately: paragraphing and transitions, titles, openings, partitions, and endings. The last section emphasizes conventions, exemplified by certain usage and punctuation rules that are particularly problematic or important to advanced writers. Traditionally, these matters are discussed under the headings of "Organization" and "Editing." But in fact they make more sense when understood in terms of readers.

As you read this chapter, focus on the interrelationship between writing and reading. Try to master the devices that serve as signals to readers about the unity, coherence, and emphasis of your writing—and of the ideas it represents.

Writing to Be Read

Although ambiguous sentences seldom seem ambiguous to the writer (who knows what he means), . . . the effective writer learns to predict his reader's reactions to his words and to act accordingly.

RICHARD YOUNG ET AL.

The reader's perspective is bound up in the writing process itself, because . . . intended meanings are only fully realized through a reader's comprehension. . . . Written thought . . . emerges through writing into situational contexts.

LOUISE WETHERBEE PHELPS

Writers who wish to be read must often adapt their discourse to meet the needs and expectations of an addressed audience.

LISA EDE AND ANDREA LUNSFORD

Rhetorical Context

Certain writing tasks, including most school exercises and journal entries written to clarify ideas and feelings, allow writers to focus almost entirely on substance, on what they are trying to say. In addition to being a creative process by which writers discover and organize ideas, however, writing is also *a communicative process*. Most writing is written to be read, and the writing process is not really complete until the writing is understood by readers. In some cases, the writing process is not really complete until readers have believed and perhaps even acted.

As soon as the writing task includes among its goals that *readers* should *understand* its meanings, writing becomes an interpersonal transaction. When writers want their readers to go beyond simple understanding and to *empathize*, *believe*, or *do* something, writing becomes a rhetorical act. Successes and failures can be judged objectively according to how readers respond.

In all honesty, the first principle of selection should be truth, as the writer understands it. A writer's first concern should be whether the writing accurately represents the intended meanings and whether those meanings are true. But most ideas may be communicated in various ways. So the second principle should be effective communication.

When we juxtapose writers' purposes with the reality of readers, we discover *the rhetorical context*. Writers should ask themselves these questions:

What am I trying to accomplish?

With whom?

Under what circumstances and using what genre?

In terms of classical rhetoric, this means that decisions writers make about *how* to express their meanings should depend on *purpose, audience,* and *occasion*. Especially during revision, your decisions should not be based solely on how accurately the draft represents what you intended. Your decisions should be based also on how well the writing will accomplish its intended purpose(s) with its intended reader(s) in the real situation.

One of the major mistakes made by inexperienced writers is to evade rhetorical context by saying vaguely, "My purpose is to express my opinion to the general reader." Etymologically, the verb *express* means to breathe out. Unless one is writing entirely for oneself, the purpose is not just to express, but also to communicate. And any group of readers—even those, say, who read the editorial pages of a particular city newspaper—has specific characteristics writers should consider (though perhaps not to the extent that most advertisers and politicians do).

Because these readers have something in common that can be defined by their shared discourse, we call them a *discourse community*. A discourse community may be all the people who regularly read a type of writing—be that engineering proposals, the sports pages of a city's newspapers, postmodernist poetry, medical research reports, or detective novels. If you want to communicate with such a community of readers, it helps to be aware of their shared knowledge, values, and expectations.

A discourse community is, in essence, a kind of ongoing discussion. During the course of that discussion, the community has developed certain assumptions about the sort of substance, structure, and style that best fulfills the purposes of their "discussion." If you want to be taken seriously by those readers, you should write in a way that fits into the ongoing discussion. You do not necessarily have to follow the standard conventions of the community—indeed, if you want to write, say, a feminist detective novel or a post-modernist dissertation, you may have to violate *some* of those conventions—but you are not likely to succeed if you simply ignore readers' expectations.

How to Evaluate Rhetorical Contexts

Experienced writers are usually highly aware of rhetorical contexts, especially of audiences. They are usually able to explain quite specifically what they want a particular piece of writing to accomplish. They are usually quite articulate when asked about the audience or discourse community they are addressing. This awareness is one reason they generally revise so much: a writer who does not consider rhetorical contexts does not have much of a basis for certain types of revision. It is also one reason they succeed in getting published.

Student writers often have special difficulty identifying rhetorical contexts. To some extent that may be because they have not been taught to do so. To some extent it is because of the special nature of most school writing. The explicit purpose of most school writing is just to make meanings clear. Moreover, most school writing is done as exercise: the implicit purpose is not so much to communicate information (which the teacher-reader usually knows better than the student-writer) as to demonstrate the student-writer's knowledge and abilities and to convince the teacher-reader to award the desired grade or credit.

Yet the conventions of most school writing demand that students make believe they are writing not for the teacher, but for the "rest of the class" or for a mythical "general educated reader." Thus a double rhetorical context is created: a conventional one (often vaguely defined) and a real one (in which the student tries to obtain a grade or credit). In fact, the conventional audience for term papers is not a "general reader," but a modified version of a professional community, and instructors grade such papers largely according to how well they approximate the real discourse of that community (see pages 437–48).

Double rhetorical contexts are not unusual. A magazine or journal article must be adapted to the readers of that magazine or journal; but it must also convince the editors to publish it, or it will not reach those readers. A textbook must be adapted to the students who will use it; but it must also convince instructors to adopt it, or it will not reach those students.

Trying achieve the same writing purposes with distinctive audiences produces somewhat different pieces of writing. Whether you are writing to "the rest of the class," to the readers of the editorial pages of your newspaper, or to your instructor as representative of a professional discourse community will influence the selection, arrangement, and style of what you write. (And writing to each of these audiences is useful practice, for each exercises particular writing abilities.)

Just as you can make yourself more aware of what you are trying to say by writing out a short summary statement, so you can make yourself more aware of rhetorical contexts by writing down the purpose, audience, and occasion for each piece of writing. Then you will have an explicit and objective basis for deciding what should be emphasized, what should be deemphasized, and what can be left out altogether. You will also have an explicit and objective basis for deciding how to structure and phrase what you decide to say.

Your statement of rhetorical context should be brief. Here is an example:

My main point is that dolphins are a wonderful and endangered species. My purpose is to convince readers to support action to protect dolphins. Most of my readers (primary audience) will be residents of British Columbia. They will read what I have written on the occasion of a visit to the Vancouver Aquarium, where it will be handed to them as a leaflet [genre].

For a certain type of writing, usually called explanatory or expository, the primary purpose may be no more than that certain readers understand. A team of geophysicists publishing their results in a specialized geophysical journal will have succeeded as writers if other geophysicists read and understand those results.

To be sure, even such writers must take audience and occasion into account. The same geophysicists writing for a more general scientific journal (e.g., *Science*) could better fulfill their purpose if they gave fuller explanations and used less specialized jargon. Writing for an even more general audience (e.g., the readers of *Scientific American*), the same writers would be wise to choose yet a third representation of the same meanings, perhaps providing more analogies and examples, because some readers would be coming to the article with even less scientific knowledge and expertise.

In persuasive writing, where the purpose is to convince readers to believe or do something, it is even more necessary to consider audience and occasion. In expressive writing, where the purpose is usually to give readers a sense of the writer's experience and to have them empathize, the relationship is sometimes more subtle and complicated; but for the writing to succeed, writers must provide images, analogies, or other structures to which the readers can relate.

Purpose.   Outside of literary writing, writers do not usually have much trouble discovering and stating their intentions. Problems concerning purpose usually have to do with there being several distinct purposes for a single piece of writing—and two of those purposes may turn out to be contradictory. A writer who wants to communicate clearly about dolphins may also want to impress readers with technical terms and "big words." A writer may want an A on a term paper but also to demonstrate a sense of humor. An explicit statement of purpose thus can help writers choose between primary and secondary purposes.

Certain sorts of purposes, moreover, are built into a particular type of writing. Whatever the writer's conscious intentions, these purposes must be achieved for a piece of writing to succeed in that genre. One purpose of the methodology section of a research report, for example, is to provide all the information another researcher would need to repeat the experiment. One function of romance novels is to allow readers to fantasize that self-centered, domineering, emotionally inarticulate men (such as the ones they may be dating or married to) are really "good at heart," can become considerate and loving, can even learn to say, "I love you." One purpose of a five-paragraph essay is to make sure generalizations are supported by specifics. A writer who is not aware that a genre has some such built-in purpose may not fulfill it. Thus when we think about purpose in relation to a piece of writing, it encompasses more than just an individual writer's conscious intentions.

Audience.   The nature of one's audience may require a bit of thought or even investigation. What about those people who will be visiting the Vancouver Aquarium? What does one have to know about those people in order to communicate effectively with them about dolphins and to convince them to support political action to protect dolphins? Writers ask many questions about their readers—such as, "How old are they?" "What are their religious beliefs? How well educated are they?"—but the purpose of all such questions is to gain information that will allow you to answer the seven basic audience analysis questions listed in Table 4.1.

Table 4.1   Audience Analysis

---

1. Who are my readers (primary and secondary)?
2. What do they know about the subject?
3. What beliefs and attitudes do they have about the subject?
4. What vested interests do they have (or think they have) in the subject?
5. Are they part of an established discourse community?
6. How fluently do they read?
7. What are *their* purposes? Why will they be reading this?

It is often worthwhile to investigate your primary audience and occasion. Perhaps your stereotype of Aquarium visitors is inaccurate. Or perhaps it is just not specific enough. Perhaps you have not thought enough about how many of them speak Chinese, Japanese, or French as a native language. Perhaps people do not read leaflets as you imagine. Perhaps you should see if the Aquarium can give you some statistics or other information about typical visitors. Perhaps you should go to the Aquarium and talk with some visitors.

Few modern politicians prepare speeches without consulting polls, talking to important constituents, and so forth. One should not sell one's soul and allow readers totally to determine the nature of what one writes. But neither should anyone who wishes to communicate effectively ignore the nature of the audience. There is something to be learned from successful politicians and advertisers—so long as you remember the first responsibility of honest writers is to write the truth.

Your readers are not all alike. If you had time to talk with each of them individually, you would probably take a slightly different tack with each one, sizing up each individual as the discussion continued and choosing arguments likely to reach that individual.

As a writer producing a single piece of writing for a mass of individuals, you are less flexible. Like a politician, you have to think about the majority—about the *typical* reader. Even that can be problematic if the people you are addressing fall into several distinct groups. In such a case, a piece of writing aimed at the *average* reader might fall between the groups and end up convincing nobody at all.

You should, therefore, identify *primary and secondary audiences*. For the piece on dolphins, the primary audience will be residents of British Columbia who visit the Vancouver Aquarium. Most of them will be Canadian-born and speak English as their first language. Most will be adults, but a goodly number will be teenagers. Many will have friends or relatives involved in the fishing industry, and most will know how important that industry is to the economy of British Columbia. Many will be rather knowledgeable and sophisticated about ecological issues.

Some readers, however, will be immigrants to Canada, including a fair number of Asians. There will also be tourists from elsewhere in Canada, including some whose first language is French. And there will be tourists from other countries, largely from the United States, Japan, and Western Europe. These readers will probably have different beliefs, attitudes, and vested interests, will need more background information, and in many cases may not read English very fluently.

Generally, one should write to the primary audience and then make adjustments, additions, or deletions to appeal to various secondary audiences—insofar as one can without undermining the appeal to the primary audience.

What can one say, in general, about British Columbians who visit the Aquarium?

What do they *know* about dolphins and related subjects? (Do they think dolphins are fish?)

What *beliefs* and *attitudes* do they have toward dolphins, toward animals in general, toward ecological issues? (Do they believe animals have rights or do they believe animals should serve human beings?)

What *vested interests* do they have in how dolphins are treated? Will the protection of dolphins interfere with the fishing industry? Does the survival and well-being of dolphins in any way affect the quality of life in British Columbia?

How fluently do these readers read?

An estimate of your primary readers' knowledge about the subject, their relevant attitudes and beliefs, their vested interests, and their reading ability will enable you to make rhetorical choices more appropriately. Certainly there is a sense in which each reader is a unique individual, but it is possible to make generalizations about what they have in common.

Occasion.   You should also ask which appeals are likely to work *on this occasion*. The occasion in this case consists of the genre (a leaflet) and the situation in which it will be read. Since people tend not to read long leaflets or leaflets with a lot of small print, this occasion makes it particularly necessary to choose only the most salient appeals and to make them as succinctly as possible.

Here is one writer's estimation of a particularly difficult audience and occasion:

> I will be addressing my argument to an audience of fathers. These fathers have just signed the final documents pertaining to child custody, visiting rights, and support settlements.
>
> The long term causes that brought these men to these circumstances are various, but the common bond among them is that they have lost, to their ex-wives, custody of their children. The fathers have visiting rights and are required to make monthly payments toward the support of the children.
>
> The emotions of these fathers are chaotic. There is some relief and acceptance that the battle is over; there is also fear, loneliness, and pain at the prospect of a loveless future. Primarily, there is anger, frustration, and hate directed towards their ex-wives and towards the court system that has taken their children from them.
>
> Stephanie Legault

This analysis of audience and occasion helped Stephanie focus on the extraordinary difficulties of her writing task, an attempt to persuade these men to pay child support regularly and promptly. Is there anything else she should know about these readers?

Discover Mutual Purposes

Readers have purposes, too. Readers read for reasons. They have motives. Skilled readers especially read with focus, with a sense of purpose. As a writer you will do well to think about where your purposes overlap with your readers' purposes and to emphasize those areas. That is, you should try to locate *mutual purposes* that you share with your readers.

Sometimes a mutual purpose may be nothing more than your desire to convey information they wish to acquire. Other times you may find that readers have an objective vested interest in your subject, perhaps one of which they are not even aware. Perhaps the survival and well-being of dolphins is more important to them than they realize. In such a case, it would be good rhetorical strategy to make them aware of their objective self-interests, probably near the beginning of the piece of writing.

Burke's Pentad was discussed in Chapter 2 as a heuristic for generating subject matter (see pages 82–86). Because it is a heuristic for investigating human motives, the Pentad can also be used *to discover how to motivate readers.* That is, it can be used to discover how best to motivate your readers to fulfill your purpose.

With what sorts of appeals do the readers most easily identify?

What motives (i.e., purposes) do they already have? Why do they hold their present opinions on the subject?

How can you establish mutual purposes?

Burke says certain types of people respond best to certain types of appeals. And in general, people are most easily motivated by the same sorts of appeals they themselves use. If you want to convince people to believe or do something, it helps to use the sort of reasoning that already makes sense to them.

In *A Grammar of Motives* (California) Burke suggests that liberals tend to argue from social context or *scene* (e.g., crime is caused by poverty), conservatives from *agent* (e.g., crime is caused by immoral and degenerate people), pragmatists from *agency* (e.g., crime is caused by the availability of weapons), mystics and idealists from *purpose* (e.g., crime is part of the divine plan), and philosophical realists from *act* (e.g., crime is caused by permissive upbringing or by the experience of injustice).

Professor Charles Kneupper has applied this supposition to the problem of choosing appeals that will match the purposes particular groups of readers bring to a piece of writing. He presents the following example of how he uses the Pentad to choose appropriate appeals when addressing various groups within the university. His purpose is to get a new course approved. His problem is to discover how that purpose matches up with purposes his readers already have. Here is his solution.

> I tend to find my faculty colleagues liberal and idealistic on educational issues. They seem most receptive to scene and purpose ratios. In contrast, administrators seem dominantly realist and pragmatist and are correspondingly more attuned to act and agency ratios. Finally students seem conservative and idealistic and are moved by agent and purpose ratios. Put in more concrete terms, in proposing a new course the faculty is most moved by justifications concerning educational purpose and responsiveness to the social scene. Administrators are more moved by demonstrations of feasibility of the act within the constraints of agency. In other words, I need to show the course is staffable with minimal cost and will probably generate substantial Full-time Teacher Equivalents [the accounting unit by which many universities allocate instructors]. Finally, students are attracted to courses partially by their nature [purpose], but also by whom they are taught [agent] . . . .
>
> Faculty tend to be uninterested in the details of administration. Administration has some interest in purpose, but wants to get to the nitty-gritty questions of agency. . . . In a well thought-out proposal, a rounded statement of motive will include appeals to each respective decision-making group.

In other words, Kneupper appeals to the purposes and concerns of each of the three groups of readers. His decisions about which arguments to use are based on his analysis of his readers. His analysis is based on the Pentad.

Key Words and Root Metaphors

There is another Burkean concept writers can use to evaluate audiences. The basic idea is that peoples' assumptions, beliefs, and attitudes are often reflected in certain key words, metaphors or analogies. By analyzing the words your readers commonly use for important concepts, you can discover a lot about their attitudes.

One thing that makes a group of people a community is shared ways of naming what is important to them. These shared ways with words reflect shared attitudes. If one person talks about "the mother and unborn child" while another talks about "the woman and the fetus," it is not hard to predict how they will likely disagree about abortion. We know in advance that someone who talks about "women's libbers," "secular humanism," or "bourgeois democracy" is probably against it. If your readers refer to adult women as "babes," "girls," or "ladies" and use terms like "stewardess," "lady doctor" and "male nurse," you can make an educated guess about their attitude toward women in general, feminists in particular.

Certain metaphors are so common that people tend to accept them without thinking about them, perhaps even without realizing they are metaphorical. When such a metaphor refers to a key concept, we can expose underlying attitudes by analyzing the metaphor. Metaphors that reflect important attitudes are called *root metaphors* (see pages 69–73 and 333–39).

Root metaphors often live in clichés. When we speak of "falling in love," we make an analogy between a physical event and an emotional event. The juxtaposition of "love" with "falling" has implications: that "falling in love" is something which happens to you rather than something you do, that there is an element of danger involved, that it can be your "downfall" in one sense or another. Thus the cliché reflects standard attitudes.

What matters is not the analogy but its implications. In *The Philosophy of Rhetoric* (Oxford), I. A. Richards criticizes the assertion that language is "a dress which thought puts on" because he is worried about inferences being made by people who use or accept that metaphor. What he is really criticizing is the assumption that one thinks first and verbalizes second. When he argues that we should instead conceive of meaning "as though it were a plant that has grown," he is arguing for the assumption that we discover our thoughts in the process of articulating them.

Richards' audience brought to his lecture assumptions about thought and language that were built into their root metaphor. So he responded both by criticizing that metaphor and by substituting a new metaphor. Similarly, psychiatrist Erich Fromm begins *The Art of Loving* (Harper & Row) by discussing the implications of the notion that we "fall into" love and suggesting alternative phrases (see page 334). You can discover what assumptions your readers bring to a topic by thinking about the key terms and root metaphors they bring to it. Their clichés and standard analogies may be important clues to their attitudes and beliefs. Investigating your readers' key terms and root metaphors thus helps you to communicate with them.

If you think the assumptions built into those terms and metaphors are valid, you can use the metaphors. They will help establish a frame of reference you share with your readers.

If you think the assumptions built into your readers' key terms and root metaphors are not entirely valid, you have located specific beliefs and attitudes of your readers that you must try to change. Depending on the circumstances, you can try to finesse the situation by unobtrusively substituting your own terms and metaphors (and thus your own assumptions), or you can argue explicitly against the assumptions you consider invalid. Generally, the latter strategy is more honest, but it involves a sort of intellectualizing for which not all readers will sit still. (Consider the assumptions implicit in the root metaphor "revision is polishing," and look back at how "revision is re-seeing" was substituted on page 108ff.)

Here is an example from *Hamlet*, in which a student analyzes Shakespeare's metaphors for madness in order to uncover Elizabethan assumptions about the causes of mental illness.

Metaphors for Madness in Hamlet

In the tragic play, Hamlet, Shakespeare uses primarily two sets of metaphors to describe Hamlet's madness: the metaphor of disease and the metaphor of confusion. The metaphor of insanity as disease implies, according to Elizabethan belief, that madness is a condition or ailment which one acquires as a result of an invasion of the body by vapors or spirits. Hamlet exemplifies this belief system when he tells Rosencrantz, "My wit's diseased" (III, ii, 313). The set of metaphors comparing madness with confusion implies insanity is a state of distraction caused by extreme emotions of grief, love, or loss. For example, Polonius, a councillor to the king, explains that Hamlet's madness progressed from sadness to lightness, confusion and madness.

> And he . . .
> Fell into a sadness, then into a fast, . . .
> Thence to a lightness, and by this declension,
> Into the madness wherein now he raves.
>
> (II, ii, 146–50)

In Hamlet, the two sets of metaphors for insanity are similar in that they interpret madness to be a condition accidentally acquired, but the metaphors differ in the implied perceptions of the origins of Hamlet's madness.

Shannon Willow DiBassio

Write Reader-Based Prose

Reader-based prose is a key term used to focus writers' attention on the idea that good writing is well adapted to its readers.

Some writers believe the goal of the writing process is a perfect piece of writing. They think of what they are doing as "writing an essay," not in terms of "writing to readers." Much of their effort during revision is devoted to "polishing." Some other writers believe the goal of the writing process is "self-expression." Most of their effort is devoted to getting the ideas and feelings right. They usually present their ideas in the order in which they thought of them—which is not necessarily the order in which readers can best understand them.

With the possible exception of literary composition, aiming for "a perfect piece of writing" or for "self-expression" will usually focus your attention in the wrong place. What you really want to create is not a perfect piece of writing, but a piece of writing that communicates perfectly. Perfection is a relationship between a piece of writing and its readers. The only "perfect" piece of writing is one that accomplishes your purposes with your intended readers.

Such "perfection" can be accomplished only with the cooperation of your readers. It is impossible to create a text that no reader can manage to misinterpret. What you want to produce is a piece of writing that induces the cooperation of your readers, facilitates communication, and achieves your purposes as well as can be done with those readers.

Writing that does this is *reader-based* prose. To produce it, you should be aware of the significant differences between you and your readers. Although you decide *what* to say largely in terms of your purposes, you should decide *how* to say it largely in terms of their purposes. Reader-based writings present the information the readers need or want—which may not be entirely the same information that interests the writers. It is focused and organized according to the needs or desires of the readers. It is structured to facilitate the readers' discovery processes, not as a narrative of the writers' discovery processes.

How People Read

The principles of effective writing can all be derived from an understanding of how people read.

Fluent readers are always anticipating. They have a book in context, often before they pick it up. By the time they get to the first word on page one, they have gleaned a lot of information by skimming the blurb, introduction, table of contents, title page, even the index—or hy talking to othei people, reading rcviews, and so on. Because they have narrowed their expectations and are anticipating types of meanings that are likely, they can read more quickly (and usually more accurately) than can readers who start with the first word on page one and read sentence by sentence. And as fluent readers move through a text, they continue to focus their attention ever more sharply.

You may think that you read word by word, that you grasp the meaning of the whole text by adding up the meanings of individual words and sentences. Most people think that. But if you really did read word by word, your reading speed would be lower than forty words per minute, and you would not be reading a book as complex as this one.

The principle of anticipatory reading can be illustrated even on the level of the sentence. Suppose a sentence begins, "Is . . . ." As a fluent reader

of English, you have already anticipated that the sentence will be a question—
and not only that, but a particular type of question which can be answered
by "yes" or "no." You have also anticipated that the next word or phrase
will name the grammatical subject of the question. (You have done so even
if you do not know what a grammatical subject is.)

Suppose the sentence continues, "Is the book . . . ." You now anticipate
a word or phrase that will ask something about the book. You can accept a
variety of completions: "Is the book here?" "Is the book worth reading?"
"Is the book available in paperback?" "Is the book green?" But there is a
much larger set of potential completions which, for a variety of reasons, you
will not readily accept: "Is the book elephant?" "Is the book ill?" "Is the
book para mí?" "Is the book schmab?" "Is the book nicely?" All these
potential completions fall outside the range of your anticipations.

If while reading you run into something that falls outside the range of
your anticipations, it immediately throws you back—how far back depending
on the nature of whatever does not fit. Your assumption is that either the
writer erred or you anticipated falsely, and you look back to check the basis
of your anticipation. Perhaps you are reading a science fiction story in which
books are animate and can become ill. Perhaps you are reading a bilingual
Chicano poem in which sentences can contain both English and Spanish
words.

Except in special cases, such as writing intended to violate readers' stereotypes, writers should avoid throwing readers back like that. On the contrary,
writers should help readers read by helping them to anticipate accurately. In
many genres, including most academic and technical writing, writers use thesis
paragraphs and topic sentences to help readers anticipate.

Writers should also remember that readers read by creating clusters of
meaning. As ten individual letters, "t-h-o-u-g-h-t-f-u-l" overloads your short-
term memory. So you perceive it as two syllables, "thought-ful," or as one
word, "thoughtful." Similarly, to read a sentence you group words into phrases.
To comprehend a paragraph, you group sentences. Successful readers grasp
not individual meanings but patterns of meaning. When you have read and
understood, you remember the gist. In the case of expository prose, this means
you can summarize the main ideas.

Effective writing contains cues that help readers to cluster meanings into
the patterns intended by the writer. Without such cues, readers could correctly
read each sentence but still get the wrong *pattern of meaning*. The way you
use generalizations, headings, transitions, paragraph indentations, repetitions
and redundancies, introductions, conclusions, and so forth, are cues of this
sort. They function as signals to readers about how to pattern meanings.

The point to remember is that readers are not sponges: they do not absorb
meanings. Reading is an active process, a transaction. Readers not only extract
meanings, they also create them—by making generalizations, perceiving rela-

tionships, drawing inferences, and so on. The written text represents a message readers try to reconstruct.

Although a piece of writing may well say more than the writer consciously intended, effective writers create texts that guide readers toward intended meanings and constrain them away from misreadings.

What Is Readability?

What makes a piece of writing hard to read?

It is hard to read something that uses a lot of words you do not know, or even words you just sort of know. Most people, for instance, find it easier to read about heart attacks than about myocardial infarctions. It is harder to read complexly structured sentences than sentences that begin with the subject and verb and use few subordinate clauses (see pages 235–49). Similarly, it is harder to read long paragraphs with several subtopics than shorter paragraphs, each discussing a single topic. It is harder to read about unfamiliar and complex concepts than about familiar and simple concepts. It is harder to read large chunks of writing than writing that is broken up visually by paragraphing, headings and subheadings, illustrations, and charts. It is harder to read handwriting than typed or printed texts. It is harder to read small lettering or print. It is even harder to read when margins are skimpy.

Difficult vocabulary and complex sentence structure are the two most obvious characteristics that make a text hard to read. This does not mean that you should oversimplify your ideas by using only simple words and sentences. It does mean you should be aware that your word choice and sentence structure can cause difficulty for particular readers. With some readers you should take special care to choose words and structure sentences for easy reading.

Unfamiliar, abstract, and complex concepts also make a piece of writing hard to read. Familiar concepts are relatively easy to grasp no matter how abstract or complex—which is why writers often fail to realize how difficult a concept may be for readers (to whom the concept is new). New concepts, however, are easier to grasp if they are less abstract or complex, or when they are presented in relation with familiar ideas. This does not mean you should confine yourself to familiar or simple ideas. It does mean you should be aware of unfamiliar, abstract, or complex ideas that may cause difficulty for particular readers. It does mean you should think about *how many* unfamiliar ideas you are presenting per page. That is why publishers sometimes say even an innovative book should be 90% old hat.

Format, layout, and typeface also influence reading difficulty, and without changing your meaning. Thus it is often possible to make a piece of writing easier to read without simplifying the vocabulary, sentence structure or ideas.

In a sense, type size, margin width, illustrations, headings and subheadings, dropped lists, boldface and italic typefaces, and so forth have more to do with printing than with writing. But as the classical rhetoricians knew, *delivery* is an important aspect of the communications process.

The implications for writers seem apparent, but there are potential contradictions. What if what you want to communicate cannot be presented with familiar words or concepts? What if the pattern of meaning is distorted when the complex sentence or concept is broken down into a number of simpler sentences or ideas? What if you are trying to communicate that a certain subject is usually misunderstood because people do not grasp its full complexity? Sometimes you wish to communicate ideas that are both complex and unfamiliar to your readers. You may need to use unfamiliar and difficult words to represent some of those ideas because commonplace synonyms have the wrong connotations and implications. You may also need to use complex sentences to represent complex relationships.

To be sure, you should try to make your writing *as readable as you can without oversimplifying your meaning*. But when you write about certain subjects with some degree of sophistication, as-readable-as-possible-without-oversimplifying may be very complex indeed. Writers are sometimes tempted, therefore, to make their writing readable by oversimplifying. This is especially common in journalism and popular science, but the temptation exists in many writing situations. Virtually all the writing practiced at colleges and universities is written specialist-to-specialist and assumes highly informed, highly literate readers. Consequently, few writers know how to address a general, popular audience.

When should writers worry about readability? When it is likely to interfere with communication. If you are writing for an academic or otherwise highly educated audience, you probably need not worry about difficult vocabulary, complex sentence structure or paragraphs that exceed 200 words. You can also assume that your readers are used to dealing with complex ideas, perhaps even used to acquiring unfamiliar ideas. If you are writing for an audience of specialists, you can assume familiarity with technical terms and concepts. In fact, academic, scientific, technical and professional readers usually prefer precise technical vocabulary and detailed representation of complex ideas to easy reading.

If, however, you are trying to communicate with a popular audience, with generalists, or with people who are not so well educated, failing to worry about readability may mean failing to communicate what you want to communicate. Even for professional audiences, one rule of thumb is to keep sentence length down to an *average* of 20–25 words, to make sure you do not have too many sentences much over 30 words long, and to keep most paragraphs between 150–250 words.

How should writers estimate readability? First by looking at vocabulary and sentence structure. Vocabulary difficulty and sentence complexity correlate roughly with word length and sentence length, which can be easily calculated. Most measures of readability are, therefore, based on these two quantifiable characteristics (or on their correlates). Though we know that a short, awkwardly constructed sentence can be harder to read than a well-constructed long sentence, we usually estimate reading difficulty by assuming such cases will even out over a large enough sample.

Writers should remember, moreover, that readability varies with special audiences. Because the vocabulary, concepts, and format are familiar, for instance, an audience of auto mechanics may be able to read a car repair manual that most university professors would find unreadable. Similarly, someone who has never cooked may have trouble reading a cookbook no matter how simple the vocabulary and sentence structure.

Reading experts have established norms that define reading difficulty in terms of school grade levels. Though based on experience, these norms also represent a social judgment about what level of difficulty a person ought to be able to handle after a certain number of years of schooling. And the assumption that readability can be defined in levels rather than in terms of particular readers and circumstances is something of an overgeneralization. Despite these inaccuracies, however, writers can use standard reading scales as a rough guide to readability. Figure 4.1 explains the Fry readability scale, a relatively easy, moderately accurate way to estimate the readability level of something you have written.

Judged by such readability estimates, a typical North American newspaper is on about a sixth to eighth grade level of reading difficulty. *The New York Times* is about eleventh grade reading. Many government documents, allegedly written for the general public, are far beyond grade twelve readability.

When concepts are familiar and when layout, format, and typographical devices are used to make reading easier, people can actually read above their normal reading level. When concepts are new, abstract, and complex, however, people may need easier texts. When reading for enjoyment, moreover, readers may not want to read at their maximum level (which is why many university graduates find the *New York Times* "too difficult"). Thus writers sometimes need to make finer and more qualitative distinctions. As a rough measure, however, the Fry readability scale is usually good enough.

What can writers do to make their writing easier to read?

1. Try to use words your readers are likely to know. If they know several terms for the same concept, use the most familiar. Define terms they likely do not know, preferably in a short, unobtrusive phrase.

2. When possible, confine yourself to sentence structures your readers can handle easily. Consider splitting long, complex sentences into several shorter, simpler sentences. Similarly, consider splitting long paragraphs with several subtopics into shorter paragraphs, each discussing a single

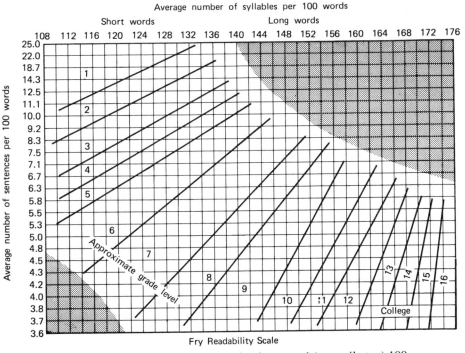

Figure 4.1 To estimate readability level, take several (normally ten) 100-word samples of the piece of writing. If the one hundredth word falls within a sentence, the sample ends at the end of the sentence. Calculate the number of sentences per hundred words (*not* per sample if your samples are not exactly a hundred words long). Count out the number of syllables per hundred words. Plot the results on Fry's readability graph.

Although Fry's readability graph is not the easiest way to measure readability, it is more accurate than the easier methods, and its results correlate well with the results obtained from more complex methods (e.g., Dale-Chall and Flesch). It is reasonably accurate from first grade through university senior (16th).

topic. (For most readers, many sentences longer than 30 words or many paragraphs longer than 300 words are likely to mean excessive difficulty.)

3. When possible, use concepts that are familiar to your readers. Minimize the number of unfamiliar concepts per page. When you do introduce unfamiliar or complex concepts, be sure to explain. If the new idea is complex, see if you can break it down into a number of simpler ideas without oversimplifying it. Try to relate it to familiar concepts, perhaps through the use of analogies. Try also to give concrete examples because readers can often grasp an idea through several concrete examples even if they cannot understand it when it is presented abstractly.

4. Consider using headings and subheadings. Consider whether a dropped list (such as the one you are now reading) may work better than the same information presented in a standard paragraph. In genres where it is acceptable, consider using italics (underlining) and boldface to emphasize key terms and concepts.

5. Consider using illustrations, graphs, charts, or tables, both to break up the text and to provide visual analogies for verbal information or concepts.

6. Generally type instead of writing by hand. If you are using a word processor, try to use a high quality printer. In any case use a dark pen or dark ribbon. Use relatively large type. Use relatively wide margins (at least one inch).

If you are using a moderately sophisticated word processing or "desktop publishing" program, you have lots of options for making reading easier through layout and typographical choices. With a typewriter, your typographical options are pretty much limited to underlining (and making sure the ribbon is dark), but you can still accomplish a lot by considering headings, subheadings, dropped lists, margins, and various sorts of illustrations.

The following was written as a brochure for visitors to a local museum; it would be distributed in a rack beside an exhibit of a shell midden. How effective do you think it would be? Would tourists who happened to stop in a local museum find it readable? If they started reading it, would they finish? Would they have a clear understanding afterwards? Can you suggest any revisions that might make it more attractive, effective, or easier to read?

What Is a Midden?

Archaeologists call a prehistoric garbage dump a midden. It is an area within an archaeological site, similar to the local dump in a town, where refuse of ancient cultures is buried. Although sites contain refuse scattered throughout them in addition to other features, middens contain only garbage in a confined space.

[Planview of a Site]

What Is in a Midden?

The contents of each midden depends on the culture it is related to, but it always consists of material that is no longer valuable or of use to the people throwing it away. Often middens are composed of items associated with cooking such as burned animal bones, plant remains, charcoal, broken pottery, and broken tools. Occasionally they contain human bodies. You would not expect to find gold, jade, or antler carvings in the midden of a culture valuing these items.

What Does a Midden Look Like?

On the ground, middens are shallow mounds ranging in diameter
from approximately one to four meters depending on the size and
the type of the site. A midden's most distinctive feature is its
unstratified and heterogeneous composition, unlike its
surroundings which are generally stratified and homogeneous.
[Cross Section of a Midden]

Are All Middens the Same?

No. Shell middens are a specific type. They differ from ordinary
middens because they are both a garbage dump and an archaeological
site in one. They are mainly composed of shells which are sorted
into layers (see cross-section on display). They are also larger
than ordinary middens, extending over an area of more than ten square
meters, and contain the same features as a site and not simply refuse.

Where Do You Find Middens?

Ordinarily middens are found throughout the world among different
cultures and in a variety of different locations, but shell middens
are found only near major bodies of water and ocean shorelines,
lakeshores, or riverbanks, where shellfish were easily obtainable.
In British Columbia they occur along the entire Pacific coast,
throughout the Gulf Islands, and along the banks of the Fraser River.
[Map Depicting Shell Midden Sites]

Why Are Middens Important?

Middens are important to archaeologists because they help them
to achieve their goal of discovering how people lived in the past.
For instance they can provide clues about what type of food people
ate or did not eat, what a group valued, what type of activities
they participated in, and even suggest the social structure of a
society. Archaeologists, then, are like detectives solving a
mystery, and middens are an informative tool that aids in this
purpose.

Dana Kwong

The questions in Table 4.2 summarize the practical implications of this
section. Consider whether you need to add any of them to your own revision
heuristic (see pages 133–35). Other important factors that affect readability

---

Table 4.2   Revision Heuristic: Writing to Be Read*

Is this written in a way that will accomplish its purpose(s) with the intended reader(s) on the particular occasion(s) when it will be read?

Is the presentation appropriate to the knowledge, beliefs, attitudes, and vested interests various readers will bring to it? Are the concepts presented in an order that the intended readers will find relatively easy to understand?

Does it appeal to a mutual purpose shared by writer(s) and reader(s)? Is it focused according to readers' needs? Is it organized to facilitate readers' discovery processes? Does it present all the information readers will expect and want?

Is the writing within the comfortable reading ability of its intended readers? Or does it demand the maximum reading ability? Are the concepts as familiar and concrete as they can be without oversimplifying the meaning?

Does the layout, format and typography facilitate readability?

* *Remember*: This is only a list of suggested questions. Choose from it questions that match your individual needs. Rephrase them more specifically, if possible, to focus your attention on your own particular weak points. Add any questions you need to. Use this list to continue developing your own revision heuristic (see pages 133–35). And do not rely on this list alone: read the sections of the text that explain the concepts behind these questions.

---

have to do with structure and style. These will be the focus of the rest of this chapter and Chapter 5 (and, in a somewhat broader sense, the rest of the book).

EXERCISE

1. Next time you write, generate a statement of rhetorical context (see pages 148–53 for a model), either before you begin or by the time you complete a first draft. State your main point(s) and your purpose(s). Describe your readers briefly, perhaps divided into primary and secondary audiences, and the occasion(s) on which you expect them to be reading. When you have both completed a draft and generated this statement of rhetorical context, apply the revision heuristic presented in Table 4.2.

After you have completed your revision, evaluate the usefulness of both the statement and heuristic. Is it really useful to *write out* the statement of rhetorical context? Can you modify the revision heuristic so that it better fits your needs? Compare your evaluations with those of other writers who have tried this exercise.

2. Take a short piece you have written recently. Imagine a rhetorical context radically distinct from the one for which you wrote it. Rewrite it for that new rhetorical context. Consider what types of changes you made.

3. Find a fairly long article with which you strongly disagree. Identify its key terms, analogies, and metaphors (including those hidden in clichés). How are the article's assumptions and attitudes built into its terms and tropes? How could you revise the key terms, analogies, and metaphors toward your own beliefs and attitudes? (See Exercises 3 and 4, pages 76–77.)

4. Look at a theoretical book or article about reading and also at a practical manual (of the sort used in college "reading skills" courses). What can you learn from them about how to *write*?

5. Estimate the readability level of your own writing. Take ten 100-word samples of your writing. If the one hundredth word falls within a sentence, the sample ends at the end of the sentence. Calculate the number of sentences per hundred words (not per sample if your samples are not exactly a hundred words long). Count out the number of syllables per hundred words. Plot the results on Fry's readability graph (see Figure 4.1).

Of what potential use is this estimate of the readability of your writing? Does the estimate vary from one piece of your writing to another?

6. Readability estimates are based on sentence length and vocabulary difficulty (often measured by word length). On the average, these two factors produce fairly reliable estimates. Write some short sentences using short words which would actually be difficult to read (e.g., "The id gyres, the ego mires, and I transpire.") Write some long sentences with long words which would actually be easy to read. (*Hint*: Try long independent clauses coordinated with conjunctions, colons, or semicolons, and long words that are combinations, of shorter words, e.g., "bookkeeper.")

7. Define a specialized abstract concept from an area of special knowledge (e.g., a craft, a sport, a profession, an academic discipline). Imagine a popular audience that lacks your special knowledge but has some reason for wanting or needing to understand the term you have defined. Expand your definition into an explanation, adding a motivating introduction, a contrast, an extended analogy, an example, and an appropriate ending. Minimize the use of terms and concepts with which your readers may be unfamiliar. Aim for a grade 10 readability level. (For advice about writing definitions, contrasts, and analogies, see Chapter 7.)

8. The following was written in response to the previous exercise. A brochure to be left in waiting and dressing rooms at health centers and clinics, it is addressed to friends and family of anorexics. The reading difficulty estimate is grade ten. How well do you think it would work? What are its strong points? How might you revise it to make it more effective?

What Is Anorexia?

Some people actually fear eating. These people are suffering from a disease called anorexia.

An anorexic is a person so afraid of being fat s/he refuses to eat enough to maintain body weight, resulting in life-threatening weight loss. Although the patient is interested in preparing food, s/he eats very little. The lack of nutrients causes different body illnesses, such as slow heart beat and low blood pressure. If an anorexic is forced to eat until s/he approaches normal weight, the disease is still not cured. Instead s/he has to admit having a problem and accept treatment.

What Do Statistics Tell Us? Anorexia is far more common in girls than boys—about 20 to 1. Nearly 1 of every 200 teenage girls has the disease. The chance of girls over 16 and young women in university is as high as 1 in 100. Among these patients, around 5% will die.

What Are the Symptoms of the Disease? Anorexics lose at least 25% of their original body weight. Even so, they continue to see themselves as too fat. Doctors call this false body image. Some of them may feel that they have finally arrived at an attractive weight. The onset of the illness commonly begins during early teenage. Being a little plump, they limit their eating to lose weight. Although the diet continues way too long, they deny having a problem that needs treatment.

Is Anorexia the Same as Dieting? No.

The purpose of dieting is most commonly for beauty or for better health. Dieting differs from anorexia in the following ways.

First, people who go on a beauty diet, for example, usually love food. They eat less for beauty reasons, not because they fear food. Anorexics, however, genuinely fear being fat. It is their false image of being fat that causes them to want to lose weight.

Second, most anorexics weigh within their normal range to begin with. But instead of aiming at improvement, a healthy body strong enough to fight against diseases, they go on the destructive side. As a result of serious weight loss, their weak bodies cause them to have different illnesses more easily.

What Are the Causes of the Disease? There are different explanations for anorexia. However, no one knows for sure which is the most accurate. The following four explanations are the most common:

1. Since anorexics are afraid of being fat, some people consider the disease nothing but a weight phobia. In other words, getting rid of the unreasonable fear of weight alone will cure the illness.

2. Others consider the disease a conflict between wanting to have independence and fearing to grow up. The anorexics face a choice: (a) to relax their control, thus admitting defeat; (b) to let themselves starve to death, thus gaining their so-called victory.

3. Others think refusing to eat shows a fear of increasing sexual desires. They consider eating a substitute for sexual expression.

4. Still others believe the part of the brain controlling eating, sexual activity, etc. is not working properly. (However scientists still have not found what exactly might be wrong.)

What Are the Treatments? The immediate goal is to help the patient gain weight to avoid further health problems and the danger of death. Sometimes doctors have to use intravenous feeding to save anorexics from dying.

The second goal of treatment is to keep the gains in body weight for a long term. However not all the therapies are successful in achieving this goal. Although self-help groups of anorexics seem helpful, the most effective treatment is family therapy. In family therapy, the therapist sees the families of the patients during mealtime (since the conflicts related to the illness are most evident then). One method is to tell each parent to try individually to force the patient to eat. The individual efforts are expected to fail. But after each parent fails, the mother and the father now work together to persuade the child to eat. Thus, rather than a focus of conflict, the child's eating will produce cooperation and parents become more effective in dealing with the problem.

An Example of Anorexia. Eighteen-year-old Ms. X weighed 120 pounds, within the normal range for her five-foot, six-inch frame. The year she was married she immediately began to lose weight (Photo A). Having had anorexia for a year, Ms. X weighed only 47 pounds when she was admitted to the hospital (Photo B). During the first treatment, she added 17 pounds in about three months, and then another 10 pounds in another eleven months. She reached a high point of 90 pounds in the second treatment (Photo C). However, anorexia is often a long-term illness. Sixteen years later, this woman weighed 56 pounds.

Anorexia—So What? Eating to anorexics is much the same as walking to little children—it is scary. But does this mean parents should stop teaching their little ones to walk? Does it mean that families and friends should do nothing to stop anorexics from damaging their bodies, or even let them starve to death?

Certainly not. You can help your anorexic friend(s) or family

member(s) by, first of all, persuading them to see the doctor. Ask
for referral to a mental health specialist when necessary. It is
important to encourage them to change themselves. That is why you
cannot cure the disease simply by forcing patients to eat. Once
they are willing to receive treatment, they have taken the first
step toward better health.

Genevieve L. Y. Ma

Note Genevieve's use of headings and graphics. How much do they contribute to making this piece readable? Among the possibly unfamiliar words or concepts Genevieve uses are *anorexia/anorexic*, *life-threatening weight loss*, *body image*, *intravenous feeding*, *therapy/therapist*, *mental health specialist*. Are they all clear in context? Without losing precision that matters, can you simplify the vocabulary any further? Genevieve also keeps her sentences fairly short, their structure straightforward. Are there any sentences you could make even more readable?

Does Genevieve supply all the information that friends or family of anorexics should get from an introductory brochure? Does she present any information that might better be left out of such brochure? How effective are the example, analogy and ending?

9. Think of an unsatisfactory situation with which you are personally familiar and invent a proposal for improving it, perhaps using the Utopian U (see pages 66–69). Imagine a popular audience to which you might address a proposal for improving the unsatisfactory situation. Write something that will convince them (a) there is a problem and (b) that your proposed solution is worth serious consideration. Aim for an estimated reading difficulty of grade ten or lower.

Beginnings, Middles, and Endings _____

An introduction is a passage which brings the mind of the auditor into a proper condition to receive the rest of the speech. . . . A partition correctly made renders the whole speech clear and perspicuous.

. . .

If you wish the first part of the speech to have a close agreement and connection with the main statement of the case, you must derive it from the matters which are to be discussed afterward.

CICERO

Following a paragraph is more like following a dance than a dash. The topic sentence draws a circle, and the rest of the paragraph is a pirouette within that circle.

FRANCIS CHRISTENSEN

Meaning and coherence are not inscribed in the text . . . but arise from readers' efforts to construct meaning and to integrate the details in the text into a coherent whole.

BETTY BAMBERG

Kenneth Burke defines form as "an arousing and fulfillment of desires." He says, in *Counter-Statement* (California), "a work has form in so far as one part of it leads a reader to anticipate another part, to be gratified by the sequence." Titles, openings and partitions, headings and subheadings, paragraphing, transitions, and endings are all devices for framing a piece of writing and marking its structure. They allow readers to anticipate, follow, and reaffirm structure, substance, and even tone.

Longer writings may also use other framing devices, such as tables of contents, prefaces, introductions, perhaps even afterwords. Skillful readers skim these parts of a text—as well as the indices, glossaries, blurbs, and so on—before reading the main body of the writing. This prereading allows them to frame their expectations, to anticipate the general shape of what they will be reading, and thus to prepare their minds for it.

Fluent readers do anticipate. The title and opening are your first chance to shape their anticipations and to help them to anticipate accurately. You can set the tone, indicate the substance and structure. As fluent readers read, they focus ever more sharply. They construe patterns of meaning and draw inferences. Headings and subheads, paragraphing and transitions and other cohesion devices allow you to guide this process, to reaffirm the structure, to clarify the relationships among the parts of the writing, to shape patterns and guide inferences. Endings allow you to reaffirm, emphasize, and correct, to constrain readers from misreading. Clear framing makes a piece of writing readable. It helps readers perceive the structure of the writing and thus the *pattern* of meaning.

Titles

Titles have two basic functions:

1. They make *contact* with readers, open a channel of communication, and encourage readers to read at least the opening passage.
2. They help readers to *anticipate the tone and substance* of the writing to follow.

Headings and subheadings are like titles—for sections and subsections. They serve the same functions as titles, especially helping readers anticipate the tone and substance of the section or subsections they head. In some types of writing, the heads and subheads also constitute an outline; in such cases, skimming the heads and subheads also allows readers to anticipate the structure. In other types of writing, such as newspaper and magazine journalism, subheads (called "slugs") serve primarily or even only to break up the text.

A title is a label, but it is also more than just a label. Like the label on a can of beans, it functions to inform readers what will be found inside. Thus students who write "Rhetoric Assignment, No. 1" or "English Theme" atop their papers do understand one of the functions of titles. But titles have another function also. Again like the label on a can of beans, a title functions also to *persuade* people to sample the contents.

The two functions of a title are not necessarily separate because anticipation of the substance is often what attracts readers' attention and convinces them to read on. Thus an apparently unattractive title may be a good title—if it announces tone and substance clearly. For instance, "The Application of Trans-formational-Generative Grammar to the Analysis of Similes and Metaphors in Modern English" will probably attract exactly the right readers (those interested in an academic treatment of the specialized topic) while dissuading readers not interested in a technical linguistic discussion of the subject. "Fun With Metaphors" might get more readers into the first sentences, but it would not attract the right readers for a technical linguistic article. The object is not to attract the maximum number of readers, but to attract those readers for whom the piece is intended.

The ideal title persuades the intended readers to read. Thus the nature of a good title varies according to two factors: the tone and substance of the writing and the nature of the intended readers. Without knowing the rhetorical context and the tone of the writing, one cannot say whether "Derrida's Platonic Assumptions" or "Derrida-da-da" would make a better title for an article deconstructing the assumptions of philosopher Jacques Derrida. Nor can one say whether ''A Proposal for Utilizing Recent Technological Innovations'' or ''Higher Profits: Capital Intensive Mega-Growth Opportunities'' would be the more effective title for a business proposal.

The two functions of a title do sometimes contradict each other. A writer may have to choose between an *attractive* title that somewhat misrepresents the tone or substance of the writing and an *accurate* but unattractive title. In such cases, remember that the relative importance of the two functions depends on the nature of the writing. An article in a scientific journal, to take one extreme, should have an accurate title; most of those who read it will do so because they are interested in the substance. A short story title, to take another extreme, need not indicate the substance of the story very specifically. With a satire, to take yet a third extreme, it may be most important to indicate the tone and genre.

Here are some titles from four magazines. What can you infer *about the readers* of each?

1. Bette Middler: Gutsy, Unique and *Divinely* Talented
   All About Shampoos
   Ways to Tell Somebody You're Mad
   What Every Girl Should Know About Wine
   The Eastern Way of Love
   How to Cope When Your Parents Are Suddenly *Old*

2. Paperback Romance
   Pets and People: Cat Grooming
   Big Tomato Cookbook
   Make Perfect Rice—Every Time
   How to Tell if Your Child Is Gifted
   Short Cuts to Summer Beauty
   How to Save Money on Jeans

3. 12-Meter Duel
   Dehydrated Foods
   Nor/West Passage
   Pacific Shell Collecting
   Pearson-323
   Racing Forum

4. Literacy as a Liberating Experience
   Discourse Analysis of Written Texts in an Overseas Teacher Training Program
   Answers and More Questions: A Survey of Computer Use in Composition Instruction
   Making and Remaking Meaning: Developing Literary Responses Through Purposeful, Informal Writing

Writing Across the Official Languages: Bilingualism and Rhetoric in the Canadian College

What can you infer about title writing if you assume that these titles are effective for their respective audiences and occasions? Why are the titles from the fourth magazine so much longer than the others?

Openings

Openings perform the same two basic functions as titles—and also a third. Like titles, openings appeal to readers and help them to anticipate tone and substance. In addition, the opening passage can help readers anticipate the structure of what will follow. The Classical rhetoricians called this last function *partition*: explicitly or implicitly, a partition indicates how the piece of writing will be divided in parts.

For some types of writing, the appeal aspect of the opening passage is crucially important. Newspaper and magazine readers typically move on to another article if the opening passage does not "grab" them, one way or another.

By contrast, other types of writing are virtually "assigned reading." Scientists, for instance, are expected to keep up with the latest research in their fields. In such cases, the opening passage should emphasize its other potential functions: to give readers a sense of what is to come and provide them with a framework so that they can efficiently reconstruct the meanings.

When it is desirable for an opening both to appeal to readers and to make very clear the structure of what will follow, these functions may be divided: a piece of writing may begin with an introductory paragraph designed to attract readers to the subject and then present a thesis paragraph, which helps readers anticipate the structure. As Cicero wrote, the introduction "brings the mind of the auditor into a proper condition to receive the rest. . . . A partition correctly made renders the whole . . . clear and perspicuous."

Consider the following opening passages from student essays. To what extent can you predict the substance and structure of each writing? To what extent does each make you want to read on? Why?

> Although political modernization is currently a popular fundamental concept in the social sciences, it is a malleable term whose definition and application often vary with the needs of its users.

> On March 17, 1978, Garibaldi Lifts Limited, the controlling voice of Whistler Mountain, officially announced that a new chairlift was to be built in the Alpine region of the mountain in the summer

of that year. Their announcement was subsequently met with disapproval from a host of organizations.

There are many approaches to coherence, but some are more effective than others.

Is our prison system a viable means of dealing with "crime"? I say, it is not!

Faith is defined in the Random House College Dictionary as "confidence or trust in a person or thing, belief that is not based on proof, belief in God or in the doctrines or teachings of religion, belief in anything."

Now consider the following opening passages of some articles from a popular magazine. To what extent can you predict the substance and structure of each article? What can you infer about the readers of the magazine?

If you've just now come into the market for an audio rig that will turn your wheels into a concert hall, you're in luck; there's a cornucopia of really spectacular sound equipment waiting for you at your neighborhood highway-sound store in a range of prices from the modest budget to the price-is-no-object level.

Victor Morrison is that success story uniquely of our times— intellectual, corporate strategist and gambler.

Now, with the same questions in mind, consider the following opening passages of articles from journals published by the U.S. National Council of Teachers of English.

We ask students never to judge ideas or events out of context, but fail to see our composition classes in any larger world. That is why they are such astonishing failures. For decades we have been smearing the bloody marks (sp, awk, gr) in the margins of what we call "themes." These papers are not meant to be *read*, but *corrected*.

In an age of overpopulation and underachievement, of instant credit and a growing knowledge industry, some processes still take time.

Style is the art of choosing, and one of our tasks, as writers and teachers of writing, is to identify as many compositional choices as possible.

If the new grammar is to be brought to bear on composition, it must be brought to bear on the rhetoric of the sentence.

What can you infer about the relationships between "a good opening" and intended audience? Assuming that many English teachers also read the popular magazine, what can you infer about the relationship between "a good opening" and the *occasion* on which the writing will be read?

Titles and openings are "good" insofar as they serve their functions. The first function can be deduced from a obvious fact: to communicate with people you must get their attention; you must make (and maintain) contact. The second and third functions can be deduced from the nature of the fluent reading process. Since readers anticipate meanings, the opening should usually help them do so. Since readers retain meanings in relation to what they understand to be the main points, openings should usually establish that emphasis.

There are, of course, exceptions to the general rule. If your readers violently disagree with your main points, you might do best to lead up to those points rather gently—even if that means you cannot state those points, or provide much of an accurate framework, until the middle or even the end of the piece of writing. The general principle is that good writing does what is necessary to achieve its purposes with its intended readers.

The extent to which the title, opening and headings of a particular piece of writing should perform each of these functions varies, consequently, from one rhetorical context to another. From an understanding of these three basic functions, however, you can deduce the right sort of title and opening for any particular writing.

Reminder. As was indicated in Chapter 3, it is often easiest to settle on a title and opening *after* the rest of the piece has been drafted, i.e., after you have discovered the substance, structure, and tone you are helping readers to anticipate.

Paragraphs and Partitions

If a piece of writing is divided into parts, it makes sense for writers to signal readers about where those divisions lie. Paragraphing is the most common device for doing so.

Not everybody—not even all good writers—will indent a given text in the same places. The following essay was handed in by a basic writing student who evaded the problem by presenting it as one long paragraph. Some of the slight discomfort you will probably feel while reading it comes from the lack of indentation. As a practiced reader of English, you subconsciously expect semantic and rhetorical units to be signaled by paragraphing. Because this writer did not provide those indentations, you as reader must figure out for yourself where the essay divides into sections. In other words, you as reader must do some of the work you ordinarily expect writers to do. And you may not have divided the essay as the writer intended. As or after you read "Danger! Shark!" decide where you would break it into paragraphs.

1 **Danger! Shark!**

2   I have an image-model of sharks that they are

3 very ferocious and vicious. As far as I can remember

4 I always read that sharks were the wolves of the sea.

5 In stories the shark always played the part of evil.

6 Last summer I saw the movie, "Jaws," and was even

7 more convinced of the terribleness of sharks. When I

8 think of sharks I conjure up in my mind a picture of

9 a large black tube with a point for a head and a

10 swooping tail. This shark seems to be made of steel,

11 and the beady gaze of its eyes strikes terror into

12 anything that passes its way. I see a large pearly

13 white smile with rows and rows of dagger-like

14 teeth. I see him cruising through the depths, master

15 of the sea, tearing apart any fish brave enough to

16 cross his path. As he glides through the water

17 there is a mysterious sound about him, like the

18 drone of a great industrial engine. A few times the

19 mystery of the shark has haunted me so much that I

20 was beckoned to the library in search of more

21 information about this curious devilfish. When I

22 saw pictures of sharks I was confirmed in my image of

23 them. I saw pictures of them with their great mouths

24 agape. I saw pictures of sharks hanging from a beam,

25 with fishermen standing beside them. It was easy to

26 see that the shark could have eaten the fishermen.

27 There were also pictures of victims of shark attacks,

28 dead and alive. Some were torn beyond recognition

29 and one man, who is alive, had teeth marks on his

30 belly. The movie, "Jaws," really made an image of

31 sharks in my mind. The movie was about a shark's

32 shark. There were lots of people being mangled by

33 the shark and everyone was terrified. There were lots

34 of scenes of the shark thrashing about in the water

35 and showing off his superiority. Even though "Jaws"

36 was a fictional shark, it had a big impression on me
37 because I had never seen a real shark. In books I have
38 read that sharks are generally very peaceful, except
39 when they are provoked or excited, but after all the
40 other image-models I had of sharks it was kind of hard
41 to believe. When I first got to Boston I heard about
42 the shark exhibit at the New England Aquarium. I was so
43 excited to see them. Now I could really see this
44 monster first hand. I even had a dream about what it
45 would be like. I dreamt of a brave Aquarium employee
46 carefully leaning over the shark tank and throwing
47 large chunks of fish to the snapping mouths of the
48 sharks below. I dreamt I saw a little girl,
49 overzealous in her desire to see a shark, lose her
50 grip and fall into the steaming water. Within seconds
51 the poor child was devoured and the weeping parents
52 just stared into the water where she had fallen.
53 Finally one day I made it to the Aquarium. After
54 paying what I thought was an overwhelming amount to
55 see a shark ($3.50) my girlfriend and I slowly walked
56 in the entrance with anticipation of a most terrifying
57 event. Much to our surprise that first pool we came
58 to was filled with brightly colored sharks. They
59 were very beautiful and handsome. I had expected
60 them to be dark black. As I watched them they seemed
61 to be lethargic. I had expected to see them darting
62 around, causing the water to churn. One shark which
63 was lying in a corner, very casually let two big sea
64 turtles walk right over him. My first reaction was
65 that this wasn't the same kind of shark I had heard
66 or read about. So we proceeded on to the next shark
67 tank, which is a huge cylinder that stands in the
68 center of the Aquarium. Besides sharks, there were
69 many other species and I couldn't understand how they
70 could leave those fish in the same tank with the

71   sharks. There are three levels to the tank and at the
72   bottom level we saw a few sharks, not as big as I
73   imagined, lying lazily on the floor. Not one of those
74   sharks paid the least bit of attention to all the
75   little fish swimming right in front of them. On the
76   second level we saw even smaller sharks. They looked
77   almost lifeless and perpetually swam in circles around
78   the tank. When we finally reached the top floor we
79   were looking at the surface of the water. On the wall
80   was a sign that announced that feeding times would be
81   in just a few minutes. I was really excited because
82   I thought that now I would get to see what I had been
83   waiting for. When time came for feeding I was really
84   surprised to see a man in a wet suit come walking out.
85   I couldn't believe he was actually going to dive into
86   the tank. When he did jump in we rushed down to the
87   second floor to see the fool eaten alive. Much to our
88   disbelief, though, the diver began to take food out
89   of a bag he had and push the fish into the shark's
90   mouth. I was totally confused. Where was the
91   awesome death machine I had imagined for so long?
92   What was this imposter before me? I came to the
93   conclusion that the poor shark had been drugged in
94   order to make it safe for captivity. My image-model
95   of a shark may be partly correct. I'm sure the wild
96   ones are more fierce than those in the aquarium, but
97   my image-model is a far cry from the real thing.

Tom Rindfleisch

In the opening three sentences, Tom presents readers with a partition, a frame-work for the first part of the essay (see page 173). The first sentence is on a higher level of generality than the second and third; logically the three form an introductory paragraph. After reading these sentences, one expects Tom to go on to describe his "image model" of sharks, his reading about sharks (factual and literary), and "Jaws," presumably in that order, probably with one paragraph for each subtopic. Probable points for paragraphing the first half of "Danger! Shark!" are in lines 7, 18 or 21, 30, and 37 or 41.

"When I think of sharks I conjure up in my mind" begins a group of sentences about Tom's image of sharks. From the word "mind," the level of generality remains very specific through the next four sentences. Then he makes a transition to the library and we move to what he has learned about sharks from books, a subtopic controlled by "When I saw pictures of sharks I was confirmed in my image of them." That relatively general sentence logically encompasses the next five sentences, which present particulars of the "pictures of sharks." Then follow, as one might expect, five sentences about "Jaws": a relatively general topic sentence, three specific sentences, and a concluding sentence that restates and amplifies the first—a classic textbook paragraph, if only Tom had indented.

If the essay were about to end, as the introductory partition might have led one to expect, the next sentence could stand alone as a concluding paragraph (albeit not an especially good one). Because the essay continues, however, and because "sharks are generally very peaceful" and "it was kind of hard to believe" foreshadow the second part of the essay, it is better attached to the paragraph immediately following. The second part then turns out to be a narrative, concluding with just a bit of analysis, which refers back to the opening sentence of the essay. Probable points for paragraphing the narrative are in lines 53, 64 or 66, 78 or 79, 90, and 94.

Tom's essay is structured. In each of the two major parts, he has provided verbal cues that allow readers to anticipate much of that structure, and his final sentence ties the end back to the beginning. What he has omitted is paragraphing that would help readers follow that structure (and perhaps an earlier, clearer hint to help readers anticipate and grasp the contrast that is the central point of the essay).

What Is a Paragraph?

Paragraphing (from Greek *para*, "beside," + *graphos*, "mark") was invented by the ancient Greeks. They indicated a noteworthy break in the flow of sentences by putting a punctuation mark in the margin or under a line of text. Paragraphing marks boundaries, thus signaling that a group of sentences can be read as a unit.

Though writers have been paragraphing for millennia, the doctrine of "the Paragraph" was created in 1866 by Alexander Bain. By analogy to the sentence conceived as "a complete thought," Bain believed that each paragraph should be "a developed idea." The belief that each paragraph should contain one main proposition and its development is Bain's rule.

Not all paragraphing matches the textbook descriptions of "the Paragraph." Some paragraphs serve as introductions, transitions, or conclusions— such paragraphs may not be much "developed," and there is no reason why they must be. Paragraphs also commonly contain two or more subtopics, and if each is developed only briefly there is no reason why they should not. Moreover, writers sometimes indent for emphasis or because a paragraph is getting too long.

A new paragraph can be started to signal:

1. A new subtopic.
2. The beginning or end of a passage with a distinct rhetorical function (e.g., an introduction, transition, or conclusion).
3. A point you want to emphasize (so much that you call attention to it by violating the ordinary norms of paragraphing).

You do not need to start a new paragraph for every new subtopic, functional passage, or point you wish to emphasize. But you have the option of doing so if you think it will help your readers. Frequent paragraphing enhances readability, but the development of complex, interrelated ideas often requires long paragraphs.

How do you decide whether to exercise this option? How do you decide whether to start a new paragraph at the end of an introduction or the beginning of a new subtopic? To some extent, that varies with the occasion. One should start new paragraphs more frequently in journalistic or popular writing than in academic or professional writing. To some extent, it varies with your personal "stylistic" preferences.

But the basic rule of thumb is this: modern readers of English perceive a paragraph as "dense" and "difficult" once its form on the page becomes longer than it is wide. A piece composed of shorter paragraphs thus appears more readable than the same piece organized into longer paragraphs. On the other hand, a piece composed of longer paragraphs appears more sophisticated (because longer paragraphs often contain and explain the interrelationship of subtopics). [Note that this paragraph is logically part of the previous one, governed by its opening sentence; but it is presented as a separate paragraph in order to emphasize the "rule of thumb," which might otherwise have been lost in the middle of a long paragraph.]

Whether a particular subtopic gets a paragraph to itself depends largely on how much development it gets. If the development is short, it will likely be combined with another subtopic into a single paragraph. But if you expand during revision, you will likely create a new paragraph. Furthermore, how many words it takes to make a paragraph "long" varies according to the type size and column or page width normally used when it is printed—which is why people who are not used to writing for newspapers usually draft paragraphs that look much too long when printed in narrow newspaper columns. In modern newspaper writing, a new "graf" starts every 35 to 70 words or so, almost irrespective of meaning, because newspaper columns are typically only two inches wide.

Paragraphing depends primarily on how writers perceive their messages dividing into subordinate units. Although various writers may paragraph the same text somewhat differently, however, there are places where no competent writer would start a new paragraph. Because it was written for educated readers, the following passage was presented as a single, long paragraph even though it makes several related points. One could break it into two or three paragraphs—but not after, say, the second or third sentence.

> There is an amazement proper to the experience of all great art, but the special amazement which *War and Peace* revives in me while I am reading it is like that of a child. The child does not expect the unexpected; that would already be a preparation against it. He does not for an instant doubt that a certain event had to happen; such a doubt obscures. He may even have been told beforehand that it was going to happen; such foreknowledge is as little a part of him as a label in his cap. He is able to look at the thing itself. The event reaches him radiant with magical causes but not yet trapped in sufficient cause. Tolstoy does not, as many do, achieve this freshness by transforming the reading into a never-never land. On the contrary his fictional mode is realistic; the people in his novel appear and behave like possible people in the world we daily live in. His achievement is the greater because he uses the mode of realism, for realism offers a threat to which other literary modes are not subject, the encroachment of mediocrity.

The paragraph makes three assertions: (1) *War and Peace* evokes a special, childlike amazement, (2) Tolstoy achieves this freshness within the mode of realism, and (3) his achievement is therefore greater. One could easily break this paragraph after the sixth sentence. With some revision, such as changing ''His achievement'' to ''Tolstoy's achievement,'' one could break it after the eighth sentence as well—though that would normally be done only if the ideas about realism were developed at greater length.

There is also general agreement on what should not go into a paragraph. One of the most important rules of English paragraph development excludes irrelevancies. As Professor Christensen puts it, the controlling idea of a substantive paragraph ''draws a circle, and the rest of the paragraph is a pirouette within that circle.'' Thus the fourth sentence of the following paragraph does not belong:

> We had fun at the lake last summer. We swam and waterskied. We sunbathed and picnicked. We got terribly sunburned. We fished and barbecued our catch. We flirted as only innocent youngsters can.

Getting sunburned lies outside the circle drawn by ''fun at the lake.'' One sentence of the following paragraph is similarly irrelevant.

> One American Indian tribe, the Iroquois, consider themselves a
> nation apart from the United States, even though they are citizens.
> When the United States declared war on Germany in 1917, the Iroquois
> sent a message to Washington that they too had declared war. They
> intended to use bows and arrows though. Since Germany made no
> separate peace treaty with the Iroquois at the end of World War I,
> the Iroquois didn't think it necessary to declare war again in 1941.
> Some other Indian tribes also think of themselves as separate
> nations.

However interesting, the Iroquois' choice of weapons is strictly irrelevant; it in no way supports the assertion that they consider themselves a distinct nation.

The controlling idea of a paragraph constitutes an implicit promise about what will—and will not—be discussed in that paragraph. "Responsibility" in writing is the fulfillment of such implicit promises.

A useful way to think about such responsibility is to think about questions implicit in a piece of writing. Occasionally, those questions are explicit. Then they are called *rhetorical questions*, because they serve the rhetorical function of setting up readers' expectations. But that function remains even when the question is not explicit. When revising, you should ask yourself, "Have I answered adequately all the questions I have implicitly raised?"

When a paragraph fulfills the anticipations it has aroused in its readers, it has achieved *closure*. If a paragraph or longer piece of writing achieves closure on all implicit and explicit questions, it can be said to be *complete*.

The following paragraph has two subtopics, both within the logical circle drawn by the opening sentence. Because it is under a hundred words, however, it would usually be presented as only one paragraph. If the same ideas were more developed, the paragraph might well be broken in two. (The opening sentence, however, would normally remain part of the first paragraph.)

> Although not necessary, a topic sentence at the beginning of a para-
> graph can help both readers and writers. Readers benefit most. Their
> attention is focused immediately, and they can anticipate what will
> follow. Writers benefit indirectly. When they write they can keep
> their reasoning clear and explicit. For example, a short controlling
> sentence at the beginning of a list narrows the choices a writer can
> make when completing the list and helps that writer avoid digressions.
> Thus a topic sentence to open a paragraph is a useful tool for writers.

This paragraph does not consist simply of a generalization (topic sentence) + specifics (support). The topic sentence is supported by two subgeneralizations ("Readers benefit most" and "Writers benefit indirectly"), each of which is specifically developed. And even the support for the second subgeneralization is itself supported with an example. Thus this paragraph contains four levels of generality.

Similarly, the following paragraph develops a single topic through three levels of generality:

> The native speaker may, of course, speak a form of English that marks him as coming from a rural or unread group. But if he doesn't mind being so marked, there's no reason why he should change. Samuel Johnson kept a Staffordshire burr in his speech all his life. In Burns' mouth the despised lowland Scots dialect served just as well as the correct English spoken by ten million of his southern contemporaries. Lincoln's vocabulary and his way of pronouncing certain words were sneered at by many better educated people at the time, but he seemed to be able to use the English language as effectively as his critics.
>
> BERGEN EVANS

Three examples are presented to support the point of the topic sentence, which is itself encompassed by the more general opening sentence.

There is also an alternative paragraph form, increasingly common in modern expository writing, called the *dropped list*. A dropped list may contain exactly the same sentences as the equivalent standard paragraph, but they are arranged differently on the page. A dropped list begins just as a standard paragraph would, but the subordinate points are arranged vertically. Thus the fact that a number of parallel points are being listed is made visually clear.

Dropped lists are especially common in technical writing and other contexts where the detailed information is more important that the generalization that announces it. The fourth paragraph of this section contained a such a dropped list:

A new paragraph can be started to signal:

1. a new subtopic,
2. the beginning or end of a passage with a distinct rhetorical function (e.g., an introduction, transition, or conclusion),
3. a point you want to emphasize (so much that you call attention to it by violating the ordinary norms of paragraphing).

You do not need to start a new paragraph for every new subtopic, functional passage or point you wish to emphasize. But you have the option of doing so if you think it will help your readers.

Although Bergen Evans' paragraph about dialect also contains three items of information (about Johnson, Burns, and Lincoln), it would not be presented as a dropped list because the emphasis is not on the examples, but on the generalization supported by the examples.

Paragraphing is neither so rigid, nor so purely logical as Bain's doctrine of ''the Paragraph'' would have it. However, it does make sense, if one thinks of it as a rhetorical device to signal readers about how best to break a long flow of sentences into readily readable units.

What Makes Writing Cohere?

Traditionally, writing that includes everything a writer has led readers to expect and contains no irrelevant material is said to have *unity*. *Coherence* refers to what writers do to make unity visible to readers. Paragraphing, for example, does not affect unity but can improve coherence because it *cues* readers to the structure of the writing.

Paragraphs and other such devices—e.g., chapters, headings and subheadings—cue readers about how to divide a piece of writing. Readers can then grasp each division as a whole, as a meaningful or functional unit. These divisions having been established, of course, readers then need to know how to relate each to what comes before and after. Division must be balanced by connection.

As the analysis of "Danger! Shark!" suggests, some of that connection is established by overview: if readers can anticipate the large structure of the whole, if they can see the overall pattern, they will often know how to relate each part to the whole. But sometimes such connections are not clear, and then writers should provide cues to help their readers make the connections.

Making Transitions Visible

Transitions are the most obvious way to cue readers about connections. A transition is a word, phrase, sentence, or group of sentences that makes the chronological or logical relationship between two or more parts of a writing explicit. They act as cues; they call readers' attention to the unity of the writing by indicating chronological or logical relationships. Ordinarily, we think of transitions as words or phrases, but even an entire chapter can be a transition if its primary function is to connect one part of a book with another.

Interestingly, we are so attuned to these verbal cues that, if enough coherence cues are supplied, we often imagine some unity of meaning where none exists.

```
Governor Romero advocates statehood for Puerto Rico. However,
there are no wild elephants in Colorado. That is why Einstein set
off a revolution in epistemology as well as in physics. Therefore
you must learn to communicate more clearly in writing.
```

The power of the coherence cues is such that one can start to imagine meaningful connections among these four sentences. Now, however, reread those sentences with transition words and paragraph format deleted.

Governor Romero advocates statehood for Puerto Rico.

There are no wild elephants in Colorado.

Einstein set off a revolution in epistemology as well as in physics.

You must learn to communicate more clearly in writing.

Most writers do not think very much about providing transitions. Usually, transitions come automatically, as in speech. If, however, your draft is criticized for a lack of coherence, one way to fix it is to add appropriate transitions. The trick is knowing when relationships will be obvious to your readers, when they will need a cue to guide them. The logical relationships are usually clear to the writer, but will they be confusing or ambiguous for readers? Writing rarely seems ambiguous to whoever wrote it, but as Richard Young et al. say in *Rhetoric: Discovery and Change* (Harcourt), "the effective writer learns to predict his reader's reactions." Knowing when you need an explicit transition turns on understanding your readers.

The simplest transitions create order by indicating *when* particular events happened: "One day last summer . . . Then . . . My first reaction . . . Finally . . . ." This particular type of cue (an adverbial) is typical of narrative writing (and also of most writing by less advanced writers). Such cues mark *chronological* development—either in an event being narrated or in the thinking process of writer or reader.

There are at least seven types of relationships that can be indicated with transition words and phrases. Table 4.3 lists common transition words according to the logical relationships they commonly indicate. This list is a useful guide— but only a guide. Depending upon context, a particular transition can often be used to signal more than one logical relationship. In one context, *since* may indicate sequence in time; in another context, *since* may signal a causal relationship. In one context, *in other words* may signal an explanation; in another context, a conclusion. In one context, *instead* may signal an alternative; in another context, a contrast.

One point that often does need to be made about transition words and phrases has to do with where to put them. Less mature writers tend to put almost all their transition words and phrases at the beginning of sentences— which does, in fact, tend to improve readability. The beginning of a sentence is relatively emphatic (as contrasted with some point in the middle). The beginning of a sentence is thus a strong position for the transition. It is also a logical position since it is exactly in between the proposition represented by that sentence and the one that preceded it. And it is a "natural" position because that is where transitions usually go in speech.

On the other hand, why fill an emphatic position with a transition when it could be used for the subject of the sentence? Why not put the emphasis on what the sentence is about? In speech, the listeners prefer the transition at the beginning because they immediately get the framework for the sentence

Table 4.3 Transition Words and Phrases

Logical Type	Epitomized by	Examples
Sequence	then	then, next, finally, afterwards, eventually, later, meanwhile, soon, presently, while, immediately, since, formerly, previously, last, at last, at length, subsequently, simultaneously, in the meantime, first, second
Coordination	furthermore, in addition, and	furthermore, in addition, and, also, besides, likewise, moreover, similarly, again, equally important, too, what is more
Contrast	but, however	but, however, on the other hand, at another extreme, yet, still, instead, despite this, nonetheless, for all that, on the contrary, conversely, although, notwithstanding
Causation	therefore, because	therefore, because, for, as a result, accordingly, because of this, hence, consequently, thus, so, if . . . , then
Inclusion	for example, that is	for example, for instance, in particular, specifically, to illustrate, to demonstrate, that is, namely, in other words, as a matter of fact, indeed
Alternation	or	or, either/or, another possibility, as an alternative, neither/nor
Conclusion	in conclusion	in conclusion, in short, on the whole, to sum up, in brief, to summarize

Note: Some of the words and phrases cited here actually fit more than one category, depending on how they are used. The words in each category, moreover, vary considerably in their connotations. Like a thesaurus, this list should be used with care, especially if you are not familiar with the normal use of the word or phrase you are considering.

or passage to follow. Readers, however, are more flexible because they have the freedom to go back if they miss something.

Consider what happens to the previous sentence if the transition word is moved:

```
However, readers are more flexible because they have the freedom
to go back if they miss something.
```

Either version is adequate, but the emphasis shifts slightly. It is of such choices that style is made. In the passage cited just below, for example, Prof. Corbett puts heavy emphasis on the contrast between the two paragraphs by beginning the second with "But." Consciously or subconsciously, he chose not to write,

```
Even this kind of rhetorical approach to writing disappeared from
our classrooms and our textbooks, however, sometime in the 1930s.
```

The most important point to remember about transitions is that they make explicit the structure and pattern of meaning. They are an important aspect of the framework that makes good writing readable.

Other Cohesion Cues

One very important way writers create coherence is to repeat key words and concepts. Appropriate *repetition of key words and concepts*, especially near the beginnings of sentences and paragraphs, cues readers to the unity of meaning. If your English teachers frequently wrote "repetitive" and "redundant" in the margins of your papers, this positive function of repetition may be hard to accept; but your English teachers were (one hopes) referring to excessive, unnecessary, or inappropriate repetitions and redundancies. (Note: Pronouns and synonyms can sometimes create conceptual redundancy without verbal repetition.)

Setting up and fulfilling readers' expectations creates both unity and coherence. Coherence can also be achieved with paragraphing and by repetitions of words and phrases, concepts, or sentence patterns. It can be cued by words and phrases that indicate logical or chronological relationships.

In these terms, consider the following excerpt from Professor Edward Corbett's "Survey of Rhetoric." The three paragraphs that precede this passage review "the first hundred years of the Boylston Professorship of Rhetoric at Harvard University," Corbett says, because that "reveals what happened to rhetorical training during the nineteenth century and early years of the twentieth century."

Part of the nineteenth-century development in the teaching of rhetoric, though not associated primarily with the Boylston Professorship, was the doctrine of the paragraph, stemming from Alexander Bain's *English Composition and Rhetoric* (1866) and fostered by such teachers as Fred Scott, Joseph Denney, John Genung, George Carpenter, Charles Sears Baldwin and Barrett Wendell. Barrett Wendell's successful rhetoric texts helped to establish the pattern of instruction that moved from the word to the sentence to the paragraph to the whole composition. Henry Seidel Canby reversed that sequence, moving from the paragraph to the sentence to the word. It is to these men that we owe the system of rhetoric that most students were exposed to in the first half of the twentieth century—the topic sentence, the various methods of developing the paragraph (which were really adaptations of the classical "topics"), and the holy trinity of unity, coherence, and emphasis.

But even this kind of rhetorical approach to writing disappeared from our classrooms and our textbooks sometime in the 1930s. With the clamor from parents, businessmen, journalists and administrators for correct grammar, correct usage, and correct spelling, rhetoric books began to be replaced with handbooks. By 1936 the study of rhetoric had sunk to such an estate in our schools that I. A. Richards, in his *The Philosophy of Rhetoric*, could say of it that it was "the dreariest and least profitable part of the waste that the unfortunate travel through in Freshman English," and W.M. Parrish, reviewing the situation in 1947 could say, in an article addressed to teachers of speech, "English teachers . . . have almost abandoned the very name of the rhetoric, and the classical tradition is now completely in our hands."

Classical Rhetoric for the Modern Student (Oxford)

Note that the two opening phrases of Corbett's first sentence repeat the words, "nineteenth-century," "rhetoric," and "Boylston Professorship," as well as the concepts of *training* ("teaching") and *what happened* ("development"), and thus help readers tie this passage to what preceded it. The phrase "the doctrine of the paragraph" announces the topic of Corbett's first paragraph, and the rest of the sentence adds particulars. The second sentence begins with a repetition of "Barrett Wendell," repeats the word "rhetoric," and also repeats the concepts of *English composition and rhetoric* ("rhetoric texts") and *teaching* ("instruction").

The third sentence parallels the second in beginning with the name of an influential teacher and repeats "the word," "the sentence," and "the paragraph," but in reversed order. Thus it has *iteration* of sentence structure but *alternation* of word order. It also repeats with variation the verb "to move" and the structure "establish the pattern"/"reversed that sequence."

The fourth sentence begins with a conceptual repetition ("these men"), repeats "rhetoric," refers to *teaching* ("students were exposed"), and moves from the "nineteenth century" to the "first half of the twentieth century."

Thus it introduces the new information which follows the dash (new information which does include repetition of "developing" and "paragraph"). The second paragraph then begins with the transition word, "But," which indicates *negation* and defines the relationship between the two paragraphs.

It is important to emphasize that *writers do not ordinarily think about these sorts of repetitions, transitions, and other coherence cues.* Corbett will probably be surprised when he reads this and discovers just how much cement he used to make the passage cohere. Knowing what makes writing cohere is useful, however, because that knowledge helps writers recognize, analyze, and revise incoherent passages in their drafts.

Endings

Like openings, endings provide framework. The purpose of framing at the end is not, of course, to help readers anticipate. Rather it is to reemphasize what you want to stick in readers' minds. Thus an ending is a final opportunity to indicate emphasis, to instruct readers about what you want them to remember, believe, or do.

A bit of popular wisdom about writing is "tell them what you are going to say, say it, and tell them what you said." In terms of efficient reading, this makes a lot of sense. "Tell them what you are going to say" means to give readers a framework which allows them to anticipate effectively. "Tell them what you said" means, at the end, to help readers pick out and remember the points you think are important. As long as you do not forget that the *telling* should not always be overt and explicit, this is good general advice.

The most common sort of ending, at least in expository writing, is the summary conclusion—in fact, many writers do not seem to know how else to end explanatory or persuasive writing. The summary conclusion, which restates the main points, makes sense if those points are what you wish to emphasize. If the purpose of your ending is to make sure readers remember the gist of your argument, a summary conclusion is appropriate.

But endings can serve other functions. Perhaps you want readers to remember just your main point. Then you might end with an image, example, metaphor, pithy saying or stylistically dramatic sentence which captures that essence. Perhaps you are more concerned with what your readers do than what they remember. Then you might end either by stating explicitly what you want, as is common in business letters. Or you might assume readers are already convinced by your analysis or argument and provide an ending that motivates them to do something about it. Such an ending often moves on to new material—implications—rather than reiterating what has already been said. A scientific report, for instance, often ends with suggestions for future research.

Which function takes precedence depends on the genre and purpose of the writing. If the purpose is to instruct, for example, an explicit summary is often a good conclusion. If the purpose is to arouse empathy, on the other hand, an image that concretizes and reevokes the central feeling may better fulfill the rhythm of the whole.

Endings also have a psychological function. They serve rhythmically to bring the writing to a close. Directly or indirectly, they announce, "This is the end." If a piece has an opening, this implies formally and rhythmically that it will have an ending. A sudden, unmarked stop after the last point usually disrupts readers and leaves them feeling unsatisfied. The absence of any ending is usually a failure to gratify a desire aroused by the writing.

Consider the endings of the student essays whose openings were cited above (pages 173–74).

> As a result, political scientists will continue to use the concept of political modernization in various ways, while hoping that a complete concise definition will crystalize from its transitional foundation.

> Through analyzing the constraints that limited Garibaldi Lifts' decision it is possible to see that their decision was the best alternative to an Olympic Run lift.

> For, whether we imprison one Joe Badguy or one million like him, we are not affect.ng any of the constraints which prevent individuals from obeying the law; therefore we are not solving the crime problem.

> Faith then is rested on God and trust put in Him alone. He is described as worthy to have faith placed in. And he is picturesquely expressed as my rock and my fortress and my deliverer; my God, my strength, in whom I will trust; my buckler, and the horn of my salvation and my higher power. Faith may be confidently rested on a God like that.

> Finally, coherence should be recognized not only as a quality of writing but also, along with unity and emphasis, as a basic principle of writing because the quality of coherence influences the clarity of meaning in composition.

It is difficult, of course, to evaluate an ending in the absence of the writing it ends, but these give some sense of the variety possible within the single genre of student essay. All of them serve both to create emphasis and to bring the writing to a close, although the balance between these two functions varies considerably.

In conclusion, then, we should note that titles, headings, openings, partitions, paragraphing, transitions, and endings all serve both logical and psychological functions. They provide a framework that allows readers to anticipate, follow, and remember the pattern of meaning. They open, maintain, and close the channel that allows communication. As philosopher Jean-Paul Sartre points

---

Table 4.4   Revision Heuristic: Beginnings, Middles, and Endings*

Is the title sufficiently attractive? Does it indicate the subject of the writing?

Will the opening appeal to the intended readers? Does it indicate the subject of the writing? Does it help readers anticipate the substance and structure of the piece? Does it give them a framework?

If you use headings and/or subheadings, does each accurately indicate what comes under it? As a set, do they indicate the structure of the whole? If you have not used headings or subheadings, should you?

Does each paragraph represent a unit of meaning or have some other function?

Is there sufficient—but not excessive—repetition (of words) and redundancy (of concepts) for the intended readers?

Does each paragraph answer whatever question(s) it implicitly raises? Does the whole piece of writing answer all implicit questions in the order readers will expect?

Does the paragraphing guide readers through the pattern of meaning? Are phrases and concepts repeated at important junctures in the writing, e.g., after paragraph breaks? Are chronological sequences and logical relationships adequately marked (e.g., with transition words, especially after paragraph breaks) to meet the needs of intended readers?

Are transitions clear? Do they indicate the intended logical or chronological relationships? Are transition words and phrases properly placed for intended emphasis? Have you left any potentially confusing or ambiguous relationships unmarked?

Is there an ending? Does it help readers catch the intended emphasis? Does it help them grasp implications? Does it motivate? Does it bring the piece of writing rhythmically to a close?

---

* *Remember*: This is only a list of suggested questions. Choose from it only those questions that match your individual needs. Rephrase them more specifically, if possible, to focus your attention on your own particular weak points. Add any questions you need. Use this list to continue developing your own revision heuristic (see pages 133–35). And do not rely on this list alone: read the sections of the text that explain the concepts behind the questions.

---

out in *What Is Literature?* (Citadel), "In order for the works to have any effect it is necessary for the public to adopt them," so "the author's whole art is bent on obliging me to *create* what he discloses." Titles, headings, openings, partitions, paragraphing, transitions, and endings are devices writers can use to guide readers toward recreating the meanings the writers intend to disclose.

The rest of this chapter considers the conventions of Standard English in terms of readers' expectations. The questions in Table 4.4 summarize the practical implications of this section. Before reading on, however, consider whether you need to add any of them to your own revision heuristic (see pages 133–35).

EXERCISE

1. Take some titles from published articles. Imagine the same articles with radically distinct purposes, audiences, and occasions. Rewrite the titles to suit the new rhetorical contexts. Then rewrite the openings and endings.

2. Look at some titles, openings, and endings that emphasize the logical function of a framework. Rewrite them to emphasize the psychological function.

3. Select an issue of a popular magazine that you normally read—or one that you strongly dislike. Look at the titles, openings, subheads (''slugs''), and endings of all the articles. Make as many probable inferences as you can about the typical readers of the magazine. Write a brief description of those readers. Expand that description into an analytical piece by using evidence from the magazine to justify your description. Try to obtain the magazine's own description of its readers (usually available to advertisers in one form or another); compare and contrast it with the one you inferred.

4. Retype a short article from a popular magazine *without making any paragraph indentations*. Ask a number of people to indicate where they would paragraph it. Then ask them to explain why. Analyze the results.

5. Select some passages, each two to three paragraphs long, from good writing by several different authors in your area of specialization. Analyze them. See if you can identify the types of repetitions and cues that make them cohere, the basis on which new paragraphs area started, and typical ways the paragraphs are organized. (Do they typically begin by stating the main point? Do they typically make only one point? Do they typically restate that point in closing?) Compare and contrast results with those obtained by others who investigated distinct kinds of writing.

6. Collect short articles from a newspaper, a popular magazine, three academic journals (one from the sciences, one from the social sciences, one from the humanities), a collection of readings anthologized for university students, a cookbook (or other manual), and several other sources. Compare and contrast the principles of paragraphing.

7. Take several paragraphs you have written in the past that you suspect are not very good. Analyze them for unity. Do they achieve closure on all implicit questions? Are they free of irrelevant material? Is there a pattern of levels of generality? Then analyze for coherence. Underline repetitions, redundancies, adverbials, transition words, pronouns, demonstratives, etc.

Do the same for several paragraphs you have written that you suspect are fairly good. Compare and contrast the results. Rewrite the paragraph you think is the worst of the lot.

8. Select several pieces of good writing from your own area of special

interest. Analyze them to discover what type of framework they provide for readers and what devices they use to do so.

9. Select several pieces you have written in the past that you suspect are not very good. Analyze them to discover how you used titles, openings, transitions, and endings. See if you can make them more coherent—if you think lack of coherence is what you do not like about them. Then analyze your use of titles, openings, transitions, and endings in some of your better writing. If you are keeping a journal, write these observations in your journal.

Conventions ⎯⎯⎯⎯⎯⎯⎯⎯⎯⎯⎯⎯⎯⎯⎯

> *For boys do not need the art of grammar, which teaches correct speech, if they have the opportunity to grow up and live among men who speak correctly. Without knowing any of the names of the errors, they criticize and avoid anything erroneous they hear spoken on the basis of their own habits of speech.*
>
> AUGUSTINE

> *The English language is a public code; as such it has rules.*
>
> RICHARD YOUNG ET AL.

The Importance of Conventions

Standard English has many conventions. Some make sense and seem useful. Some seem arbitrary but still useful. Some seem arbitrary and useless— at least to writers who have not learned them. But all of them matter. They are signals from writer to reader about how to read. They help readers read.

Some of the arbitrary conventions were imposed on the language, especially during the eighteenth century, by authorities who grossly misunderstood language processes. Several rules, for instance, were imposed by analogy from mathematics. For example, the rule against double negatives (e.g. "I'm *not* going to do *nothing* until he shows up.") is based on the mathematical principle that "two negatives equal a positive." In most languages, two negatives equal an emphatic negative, but the rule against double negatives is now well established in Standard English. The convention that tells you to say, "It is *I*," also based on a false mathematical analogy, is less well established but still preferred in certain social contexts.

Other rules were established by analogy with Latin. One such rule says infinitives should not be split: do not write, "to carefully compose" because that "carefully" splits the infinitive, "to compose." Latin infinitives are never split for an excellent reason. They cannot be: Latin infinitives are one word (e.g., *componere*).

Whether they make logical sense or not—and many of them do—conventions matter. In the first place, they create a certain stability in the written language. Language is more than just a tool, but it does function as a tool, a means of production; and like other tools in an industrial society, it must be standardized to some degree if communication is to be efficient and cooperation encouraged. In the second place, conventions make reading easier by allowing readers to anticipate accurately. In this sense, conventions are *reader expectations*. You violate them at the risk of confusing readers, and a confused reader may misunderstand—or simply stop reading.

All else being equal, therefore, you should *follow the conventions of format, usage, grammar, punctuation, and spelling that your readers expect.* Violate those conventions only when the violation positively serves your purposes or helps you be more accurate. Try to avoid unintentional violations. Try to use the conventions with which your readers will be comfortable. For instance, when writing to a British audience you might spell "labour" with a *u* and "tyre centre" with a *y* and *re*. For Canadian readers, you might stick with "labour," but change the *y* to an *i* in "tire centre." For an audience in the United States, "labor" and "tire center" will be less obtrusive. You usually want readers thinking about your message, not your spelling.

Since conventions are conventional and only sometimes make intrinsic sense, some people downgrade them: "Oh, you might as well get out your handbook and learn those silly comma rules; you'll have to do it sooner or later, and it will make life easier." But those comma rules are not just silly; they are signals from you to your reader about how to read your sentences. Like paragraph indentations and transitions, they are cues to your readers about how to divide and to interrelate your meanings. Once you have mastered the code, punctuation helps you to read and write effectively.

You already know many of the conventions of Standard English and probably use them accurately without even thinking about them. It is not particularly useful to review the handbook version of rules you already know. It is much more efficient to look at your writing—especially pieces that have been edited or corrected—to locate common errors. Then you can focus on just those conventions that cause problems for you.

Certain conventions are more important than others. Recent research indicates that only a few grammatical, punctuation and usage errors normally upset readers enough to reduce writers' chances of achieving their purposes:

Faulty agreement: subject-verb / pronoun-antecedent

Unclear or ambiguous pronoun reference

Ambiguous dangler

Faulty and ambiguous parallelism

Apostrophe errors

Sentence fragment or comma splice (of the sort that indicates a lack of "sentence sense")

Run-on (fused) sentence

Blatantly unidiomatic expression (especially of the sort that indicates second-language or "dialect" interference)

Why these particular errors are considered most grievous (and whether they logically ought to be) is not the immediate issue. If you regularly make any of these errors, you should deal with them posthaste because they might cause you to lose an opportunity. Less serious violations of convention matter too, at least if you commit a lot of them, but they are less urgent.

It helps to think of conventions not as arbitrary rules to be memorized, but as typical reader expectations, as a standard code that helps you communicate accurately and effectively with your readers. Unfortunately, few handbooks describe the rules in these terms, but you can easily translate.

Consider, for instance, dangling modifiers. Danglers are perhaps the most persistent of the "mortal sins": writers who have long since gotten past other serious grammatical errors often still dangle modifiers regularly. Here is an example:

When emotionally motivated, there is some evidence of a creative flair in my writing, and I believe fiction could be my forte.

The sentence opens with a modifier—"When emotionally motivated"—but it is not immediately clear what the modifier modifies. What is emotionally motivated? the creative flair? the writing? the writer? Read the sentence carefully, and you have no trouble getting the point. But halfway through the first reading— "When emotionally motivated, there is some evidence of a creative flair . . ."—things were not so clear. Such ambiguity, however brief, does not make reading easy. And some danglers remain ambiguous even on second or third reading.

A modifier must modify something. If it does not clearly modify something in particular, it is said to dangle (or to be misplaced). The difficulty is especially acute at the beginning of a sentence, when the subject has not yet been named. So readers expect—and have a right to expect—that such a modifier will be followed immediately by its subject: "When emotionally motivated, I . . . ." If the subject of the modifier is totally and immediately clear, most readers will not complain. But when ambiguity arises, a dangler becomes a more serious error.

Here is a dangler from a newspaper review of the movie *All of Me*:

> While handled in an amusing manner for adults, I don't think a lot of the sex jokes are for kiddies.
>
> PETER WILSON

Who was handled in an amusing manner for adults, Peter Wilson or the sex jokes? By the time you have finished the sentence, the answer is obvious, which is probably why the journalist got away with it. But ambiguity halfway through a sentence does not make for smooth reading.

The best way to fix a dangler is usually to rearrange the main part of the sentence so that the subject comes where readers expect it:

> While handled in an amusing manner for adults, a lot of the sex jokes are not, in my opinion, for kiddies.

The other alternative is to insert the subject in the modifier:

> When I am emotionally motivated, there is some evidence of a creative flair in my writing, so I believe fiction could be my forte.

Either way, the rule makes sense when understood as a statement about what educated readers expect and about the ambiguity that can arise, however temporarily, when those expectations are violated.

Colons, Dashes, and Semicolons

Colons, formal dashes, and semicolons—three punctuation marks especially important to advanced writers—are good examples of how conventions are best understood in terms of readers' expectations.

Colons. The colon is often said to be like an equals sign. In a sense it is. What follows a colon must be in some way equivalent to what precedes it. But there is more to it than that: readers also expect that what follows a colon will be more specific than what precedes it. (In the previous sentence, what follows the colon is equivalent to "more to it," but more specific.)

Colons are typically used in the following situations:

1. To introduce a series.
2. To introduce a quotation, especially a long one.
3. To add specific detail after a general statement.
4. When a second clause restates the meaning of the first but more specifically.

Note that the preceding sentence contained a colon, which introduced a series. Here are four examples to illustrate these four uses:

1. The Andes Mountains run through the following countries: Columbia, Ecuador, Peru, Bolivia, Chile, and Argentina.
2. In "Rhetoric and Literacy in American Colleges," James Berlin argues that rhetoric is always at the center of the educational enterprise:

    Rhetoric teachers are entrusted with the responsibility of passing on to young people a given society's sanctioned rules governing reading, writing, and speaking. The main business of rhetoric teachers is in fact to inculcate these rules and to determine who has learned them and who has not.

3. This applicant lacks one essential quality: literacy.
4. That is the nature of growth, at least among human beings: it is often accompanied by "growing pains."

In all four cases, what follows the colon is more specific than what precedes it. *The colon throws the readers' attention forward* toward the specifics.

Something else is true in all four examples, something that illustrates a rule about using colons: the colon is always preceded by an *independent clause*. To obey that rule, of course, you must know what an independent clause is. Most simply put, an independent clause is a series of words that *could* stand alone as a sentence. There are more technical definitions—for example, an independent clause verbally represents a complete logical proposition, or an independent clause contains both a subject and a predicate—but for writers with "sentence sense" the first definition will serve.

This rule about preceding a colon with an independent clause is beginning to develop exceptions. Traditionally, if what preceded the colon was not quite an independent clause, the clause was completed with a phrase like "the following":

Presidents of the United States who died in office after being elected in a year divisible by twenty include the following men: John Kennedy, Franklin Roosevelt, Woodrow Wilson, and William McKinley.

In many contexts, it is now becoming permissible to delete "the following." The rule still stands, but this ellipsis is becoming a partial exception.

Dashes.   The formal dash is the opposite of the colon. It too represents a kind of equation, but what follows the dash should be on a *higher* level of generality than what precedes it. It throws readers' attention *back*:

John Kennedy, Franklin Roosevelt, Woodrow Wilson, and William McKinley—all these Presidents of the United States died in office during the twentieth century after having been elected in a year divisible by twenty.

Literacy—that is the one essential quality this applicant lacks.

Dashes have other uses too. They may be used for emphasis, either in place of other punctuation or where no punctuation is needed at all.

What follows a semicolon and what precedes it are usually on the same level of generality—otherwise the writer probably should have used a colon or a dash.

They may also be used to set off parenthetical elements (i.e., as emphatic parentheses).

As individuals, we have to communicate—and to a large degree even perceive, think, and feel—with concepts that are provided by the languages of our societies.

And in colloquial writing or representations of speech, they may be used to indicate abrupt or ungrammatical breaks in the flow of the sentences—especially the sort of breaks that defy any other sort of punctuation. (That last dash set off a parenthetical element.)

On a typewriter, a dash is usually indicated by two hyphens, although it may also be indicated by space-hyphen-space; in handwriting, a dash is longer than a hyphen. In the nineteenth century, it was accepted practice to use a dash and a colon together (:—), but this is no longer standard.

Semicolons. The general rule about semicolons is that they join what could have been two separate sentences. Therefore, a semicolon usually requires an independent clause on each side of it. What follows the semicolon and what precedes it are usually on the same level of generality—otherwise the writer should, in most cases, have used a colon or a dash.

A secondary rule about semicolons states that they may be used to replace commas whenever a sentence gets too complicated. In this sense a semicolon is a ''strong'' comma. For instance, if you write a long sentence with a lot of commas, you can arbitrarily make the most important comma(s) into semicolon(s). If the items are long enough or contain commas, a list introduced by a colon is often punctuated with semicolons.

These punctuation marks are cues to the reader about the relationships among levels of generality: the colon is followed by a more specific meaning; the formal dash by a more general meaning; and the semicolon by a meaning of the same level of generality.

Generally a semicolon indicates the meanings it connects are so closely related that the writer preferred not to put them in two separate sentences. Often the writer wanted to emphasize an antithesis:

Some people use books; others collect them.

Those carrots cost the farmers only eight cents a pound to produce; nonetheless, they cost fifty cents a pound in the supermarket.

More often, however, the reason two ideas are "so closely related" can be understood only in context. For example, the following passage could have been punctuated as five sentences, but the semicolons make it easier for readers to note that there are only three points:

The order [of science] is what we find to work, conveniently and instructively. It is not something we stipulate; it is not something we can dogmatise about. It is what we find; it is what we find useful.

In the paragraph about *War and Peace* on page 181, the writer uses semicolons to confine each characteristic of childlike amazement to one sentence. Without that punctuation, the passage is more difficult to read.

There is an amazement proper to the experience of all great art, but the special amazement which *War and Peace* revives in me while I am reading it is like that of a child. The child does not expect the unexpected; that would already be a preparation against it. He does not for an instant doubt that a certain event had to happen; such a doubt obscures. He may even have been told beforehand that it was going to happen; such foreknowledge is as little a part of him as a label in his cap. He is able to look at the thing itself. The event reaches him radiant with magical causes but not yet trapped in sufficient cause.	There is an amazement proper to the experience of all great art, but the special amazement which *War and Peace* revives in me while I am reading it is like that of a child. The child does not expect the unexpected. That would already be a preparation against it. He does not for an instant doubt that a certain event had to happen. Such a doubt obscures. He may even have been told beforehand that it was going to happen. Such foreknowledge is as little a part of him as a label in his cap. He is able to look at the thing itself. The event reaches him radiant with magical causes but not yet trapped in sufficient cause.

(Probably for emphasis, the writer did break the pattern, using two sentences for the last characteristic on the list.)

The following sentences were drafted for an earlier section of this chapter:

This awareness of audience is one reason experienced writers generally revise so much. A writer who does not consider rhetorical contexts does not have much of a basis for making certain types of revisions.

Then another sentence was added, which followed logically from the first. Repunctuation made the relationships clearer.

> This awareness of audience is one reason experienced writers generally revise so much: a writer who does not consider rhetorical contexts does not have much of a basis for making certain types of revisions. It is also one reason they succeed in getting published.

The same principle applies also to certain compound sentences. The last sentence of the following paragraph could have been broken in two before the *but*. Having three examples in his list and having represented the first two in single sentences, however, Bergen Evans wisely chose to make the last example also a single sentence.

> The native speaker may, of course, speak a form of English that marks him as coming from a rural or unread group. But if he doesn't mind being so marked, there's no reason why he should change. Samuel Johnson kept a Staffordshire burr in his speech all his life. In Burns' mouth the despised lowland Scots dialect served just as well as the correct English spoken by ten million of his southern contemporaries. Lincoln's vocabulary and his way of pronouncing certain words were sneered at by many better educated people at the time, but he seemed to be able to use the English language as effectively as his critics.

With certain exceptions, such as the colon used to introduce a series, writers do not usually need colons, dashes, or semicolons until their sentences reach a certain level of complexity. Their sentences typically reach that level of complexity when their ideas do. In contemporary North American societies, this seems to happen at an intellectual level roughly equivalent to the second or third year of university.

Writers who fail to learn how to use these marks often run into problems. Sometimes they have trouble getting the full complexity and subtlety of their meanings into their sentences. Sometimes they fail to adequately qualify their meanings. Sometimes they write the sentences they need, but try to punctuate them with commas. The result then is a comma splice.

> The most common error seems to be that I do not use specific enough examples when writing papers, my references need to be better.
>
> Not much of Old English remains today in active language, in fact, over eighty-five percent of Old English words have been lost.

Both of those sentences become correct as soon as a comma is replaced with a semicolon.

Punctuation in General

The same principle here exemplified with colons, formal dashes, and semicolons holds for all punctuation and, indeed, for all conventions: they are best explained in terms of reader expectations and as signals from writer to reader about how to perceive the structure of the writing.

One of the most important comma rules, for example, says to put a comma in front of a coordinating conjunction that joins independent clauses. Suppose a sentence begins

She met his father and . . .

Whether or not that *and* is preceded by a comma tells readers whether to anticipate an addition to that proposition or a new proposition. Without the comma, the sentence is likely to end something like this:

She met his father and his mother.

With a comma, it is likely to end something like this:

She met his father, and then she understood Zhu De better than ever before.

That is why it is important to use a comma when a coordinating conjunction connects two independent clauses, especially in long sentences, and not to use a comma when one clause is dependent (unless another comma rule takes precedence).

The comma after an independent clause and before a coordinating conjunction is a signal to readers about what to anticipate. If you can follow this rule—which means being able to recognize independent clauses and coordinating conjunctions— then you can help readers read more fluently. There are seven coordinating conjunctions in English: *and*, *but*, *or*, *nor*, and (sometimes) *for*, *yet*, and *so*.

Another important rule says to use commas to enclose modifying clauses that do not restrict the meaning of whatever they modify. Loosely, this means put commas around modifying clauses that could be deleted without creating ambiguity. Thus the commas are a signal to readers about the nature of the modifying clause. Suppose a sentence begins,

The speaker who used sexist language . . .

Without commas, readers will infer that there were a number of speakers and that the modifying clause, *who used sexist language*, is there to identify the particular speaker who is the subject of the sentence. With commas, readers will assume that there was only one speaker and that the modifying clause simply supplies additional information about that speaker. The two versions might end like this:

> The speaker who used sexist language was criticized after the meeting.
>
> The speaker, who used sexist language, was nonetheless applauded by many feminists.

Punctuation is not the most important matter for writers to master. But standard punctuation does help readers read sentences, and sentences are the basic units of language. Remembering that conventions make sense if they are explained as reader expectations should help you understand punctuation rules as well as conventions of format, usage, grammar, and spelling. Doing some exercises, which you can find in most handbooks, will also help you understand the rules.

But this understanding is of no use unless you transfer it to your own writing. Educational research indicates that transfer should be expected only if you follow up your abstract understanding by writing *sentences of your own* that utilize the rules. If among your writing problems you have identified problems with particular conventions, you should look up those conventions in a handbook, do some exercises, and also *write sentences that use them.* Or go back to some of your own recent writing, find sentences that violate the convention, and fix them.

It may also be useful to rearrange your handbook. Most handbooks list punctuation rules according to mark, putting all the comma rules together, all the semicolon rules together, and so forth. But it is more logical and useful to group the rules according to function—because there are only four major functions. Punctuation serves to (1) link, (2) separate, (3) enclose, and (4) mark omissions. If you organize the rules in your mind according to these four basic functions, it is easy to remember that a parenthetical idea can be separated from the rest of a sentence by commas, parentheses, or dashes— and then to choose the punctuation that will work best in the particular sentence.

The Rhetoric of Punctuation

Under certain circumstances, writers can intentionally violate standard punctuation for rhetorical purposes. As signal from writer to reader, all punctuation is in a sense rhetorical, but some punctuation is specifically rhetorical because it is used to create special emphasis.

Rhetorical punctuation can be effective—or disastrous. Do not violate normal punctuation if the violation will create an awkward or confusing construction. Remember also that certain genres, academic and scientific writing among them, allow much less leeway for nonstandard punctuation than do others.

In each of the following instances, Lewis Thomas creates emphasis by adding an unconventional comma:

> Today's Delphi thus represents a refinement of an ancient social device, with a moral modification of committee procedure constraining groups of people to think more quietly, and to listen.

> The technical term for this arrangement is a "closed ecosystem," and there is the puzzle. We do not have closed ecosystems here, at all.

E. M. Forster similarly creates emphasis by using an unconventional comma and making an unusual choice between two standard punctuation options:

Conventional	Emphatic
How, then, can we put any trust in personal relationships or cling to them in the gathering political storm? In theory we cannot, but in practice we can and do.	How, then, can we put any trust in personal relationships, or cling to them in the gathering political storm? In theory we cannot. But in practice we can and do.

In the following instance, too, the lefthand version is punctuated normally, the righthand version for special emphasis:

Conventional	Emphatic
In 1977 Princess Mishaal and her lover were executed for adultery. She was shot and he was beheaded.	In 1977 Princess Mishaal and her lover were executed for adultery. She was shot; he, beheaded.

Comma splices and sentence fragments, normally violations of convention, can also be used occasionally for emphasis.

Conventional	Emphatic
Altruism, a jargon word for what used to be love, is worse than weakness; it is a sin, a violation of nature.	Altruism, a jargon word for what used to be love, is worse than weakness, it is a sin, a violation of nature. LEWIS THOMAS
The more highly public life is organized the lower does its morality sink. The nations of today behave to each other worse than they ever did in the past: they cheat, rob, bully and	The more highly public life is organized the lower does its morality sink; the nations of today behave to each other worse than they ever did in the past, they cheat, rob, bully and

Conventional	Emphatic
bluff, make war without notice, and kill as many women and children as possible.	bluff, make war without notice, and kill as many women and children as possible.

E. M. FORSTER

[The media advise us] to "seek professional help": get a checkup, go on a diet, meditate, jog, have some surgery, take two tablets with spring water. If pain persists, if anomie persists, or if boredom persists, see your doctor.	[The media advise us] to "seek professional help." Get a checkup. Go on a diet. Meditate. Jog. Have some surgery. Take two tablets, with water. *Spring* water. If pain persists, if anomie persists, if boredom persists, see your doctor.

LEWIS THOMAS

Rhetorical punctuation can be effective, but only as a variation from the norm. To use punctuation effectively for emphasis, you should first know the conventions. And remember not to violate convention in ways that create misemphasis, ambiguity, or confusion for your readers.

The questions in Table 4.5 generally summarize this section. Add to your own revision heuristic more specific questions that will call your attention to those particular conventions with which you have difficulty.

EXERCISE

1. Choose a rule of English usage, grammar, or punctuation that troubles you. Look it up in one or more handbooks. Rewrite it as a principle about reader expectations. Write three sentences of your own that correctly obey that rule. Write a question for your revision heuristic that will call your attention to that rule when you are revising.

2. Here are six danglers—three written by students, three by professionals. Explain and fix them.

    a. As a Communications major, the courses I have been exposed to have emphasized the message impact, with very little attention paid to the mechanics of the message.

    b. Six years after first seeing Tibet, it seems in many ways an incalculably better place for Tibetans.

    c. Since returning to school on a fulltime basis, writing has become a tedious chore—rewarding only when it is approved by the instructor, frustrating at all other times.

Table 4.5   Revision Heuristic: Conventions*

Have you upset readers with faulty subject-verb or pronoun-antecedent agreement, unclear or ambiguous pronoun reference, ambiguous danglers, faulty and ambiguous parallelism, apostrophe errors, sentence fragments or comma splices (of the sort that indicate a lack of "sentence sense"), run-on (fused) sentences, or blatantly unidiomatic expression (especially of the sort that indicates second-language or "dialectic" interference)?

Have you committed any of the errors you commonly commit? [Add to your revision heuristic specific questions to remind yourself of errors you typically make, e.g., "Have I used commas correctly with conjunctions?"]

Does your usage, grammar, punctuation, and spelling match the expectations of your readers? Are you following the format that matches the expectations of your readers?

Have you punctuated your sentences so as to give readers accurate cues about the interrelationships among meanings? If you have used nonstandard punctuation for emphasis, are you certain it will not cause misemphasis, ambiguity, or confusion?

* *Remember*: This is only a list of suggested questions. You will need to make up questions about format, usage, grammar, punctuation, and spelling that will call your attention to your own typical problems. Use these questions to continue developing your own revision heuristic (see pages 133–35). Refer to the preceding section of this text and to a handbook to help yourself understand rules and devise questions.

    d. There are obviously some jobs which individuals, because of their religious beliefs, are not able to perform. Without intending to be facetious, a Sikh obviously could not be employed as a male fashion model for a hat manufacturer.

    e. As an English minor, most of the class time was spent on analyzing the various techniques used by a particular author or the issues raised by that author.

    f. Nevertheless, the European photographers were quick to criticize the work of their counterparts. Feeling that the work looked odd, even "wrong," and noting the apparent "flatness and incorrect vantage points" the Indian photographers chose, they were excused as "learners."

If danglers are a problem for you, find several in your own writing and fix them too—no exercise is as perfectly suited to your individual needs as fixing weaknesses you yourself have created.

3. Read the following sentence beginnings, and explain what you can anticipate about how the sentence will continue:

    a. Julian's embarrassment amused Alice, and . . .

    b. The legislators will either reject the proposal or . . .

    c. The candidates were Jane Murray, Siddhu Neesham, and . . .

    d. Julian's embarrassment amused Alice so . . .

    e. Julian's embarrassment amused Alice, so . . .

    f. This shop caters only to tourists who . . .

    g. This shop caters only to tourists, who . . .

    h. Alice Munro's story is about a girl who . . .

    i. Alice Munro, who . . .

    j. Her approach is simple: . . .

    k. Her approach is simple; . . .

    l. Punctuation, grammar, usage and spelling— . . .

    m. In some instances—although no one will admit it— . . .

    n. When in the course of human events, . . .

    o. After looking in every imaginable place . . .

4. Write ten sentences that use colons correctly: two that use them to introduce a series, two to introduce a quotation, two to add specific details after a general description, and four in which the second clause restates the meaning of the first but more specifically.

5. Write four sentences that use the formal dash as the opposite of a colon, one for each of the four types of sentences you wrote using colons. Be certain that what follows the dash is on a higher level of generality than what precedes it.

6. Write two sentences using dashes for emphasis and two using dashes to set off parenthetical elements.

7. Write three sentences using semicolons to connect independent clauses (of the same level of generality) and three using semicolons to avoid confusion in complicated sentences with several commas.

C·H·A·P·T·E·R 5

Style and Voice

So much is done by good taste and style in speaking that the speech seems to depict the speaker's character.

CICERO

It is a ridiculous demand which England and America make, that you should speak so that they can understand you. . . . As if there were safety in stupidity alone. I fear chiefly lest my expression may not be extra-vagrant enough . . . so as to be adequate to the truth of which I have become convinced.

HENRY DAVID THOREAU

The writer is not physically present to his reader. He is all words. The writer has no resources at all for dramatizing himself and his message to his reader, except those scratches on paper—he has . . . no way of introducing himself beyond what he can make his reader "see" by means of abstract written words in various arrangements. To these words the reader responds much as he responds in a social situation—that is, he infers a personality—but he has only words to go on.

WALKER GIBSON

IN at least one significant sense, a writer's style is the equivalent of a speaker's voice. It creates tone. It gives readers a sense of the writer as person. Your readers' sense of who you are—and thus of whether they ought to trust you, believe what you say, respect your conclusions—depends very much on the stylistic choices you make. Thus style helps create the relationship between writer and reader.

What readers imagine behind a piece of writing is not the real writer, but an image. It is not a person's character, but a facet of that character. It may, moreover, be fictive. Be that as it may, it does help shape how readers will relate to the writing.

To distinguish this image, created by a writer's words, from the actual human being who wrote the words, we call it a *persona*, from the Greek word for *mask*. Thus when we speak of Shakespeare's sonnets, we distinguish between William Shakespeare, the person who lived from 1564 to 1616, and William Shakespeare, the persona we infer from the sonnets. There is a relationship between the two, of course, and the persona may be shaped in part by what we know about the historical person; but the distinction is important.

An honest person honestly trying to communicate may inadvertently create an evasive or bureaucratic persona, which readers will distrust. In writing, as in most things, good intentions are not enough. A reader who does not know you personally can judge you only by the persona created by your style.

We associate style with the personal. Each individual, we say, has her or his own unique style. Ask a number of people to do the same task, and each will do it slightly differently. These differences we take as signs of individual personality, and we call them style.

Of course, style is more than just personal. In fact, we sometimes talk about social styles: bureaucratic style, academic style, and so forth. The style of a piece of writing should be appropriate to its subject matter and its rhetorical context as well as to the individuality of its creator. Style can be substantive, especially the choice of terms and metaphors for key concepts: the decision to use one word rather than another may modify a concept in a significant way. Style is, to some extent, both substantive and social, an adaption to both the requirements of subject matter and the norms of a discourse community, the expectations of readers.

But within the constraints imposed by subject matter and rhetorical context, there remains some flexibility. Writers make choices among the various words that could represent their meanings to their readers. Writers make choices about how to combine those words in sentences. When we speak of style in writing we generally mean these word- and sentence-level choices.

An individual writer will not make these choices the same way every time. In the context of various relationships, an individual person may be a physicist, gardener, surfer, mother, wife, lover, do-it-yourself-er, political activist, homeowner, and so on. Each of these roles requires a somewhat different style. The physicist does not talk to her colleagues in the same way she talks to her youngest child. Just so, a writer will use different styles at different times.

Style should not be your first consideration. Worrying too much about style and self-image can impede the early phases of the creative composing process. Though it may not come first, however, style is very important. The substance you are trying to communicate can be subtly distorted by an inaccurate word choice or ambiguous sentence structure. An inappropriate style can also offend readers, sometimes even cause them to stop reading. If not earlier, by the later phases of revision, you should pay considerable attention to style.

Though traditional textbook style rules may be phrased positively, most of them are about how to avoid "bad style." A certain kind of "bad style"— students call it "BS-ing," but it also goes by many other names, such as bureaucratese, academese, gobbledygook—is so commonplace that it makes sense to figure out how to avoid it. This style is commonly used by people who are more concerned with impressing readers than with communicating substantively. It can also be used to evade responsibility, to intimidate, or to sell—a product, a candidate or even an idea. It can even become a habit: some writers do not seem to remember how to communicate in a clear, straightforward way even when they are not out to impress or deceive. It no longer occurs to them that they might write, "Look out for cars turning here," instead of "Everyone is advised to be cognizant of vehicles modifying orientation at this site."

Another common kind of "bad style" confuses readers with imprecise wording and sentences structured in ways that are unnecessarily ambiguous or difficult to read. English teachers and editors then respond by marking "wrong words" and "awkward sentences." But style really has more to do with recognizing potentials than with avoiding faults. Skillful stylists take advantage of opportunities others fail to notice—often because they go the extra mile during revision.

The first section of this chapter focuses on word choice, with some attention to avoiding "wrong words," but with a primary emphasis on the relationship of diction to substance and persona. The issue of sexism in language is treated here as an example. The second section discusses how to achieve an honest style, which communicates clearly and presents an accurate persona. The third section turns to sentence structure and also emphasizes the positive. There is considerable discussion of awkward sentence structure—what makes it "awkward" for readers and how best to fix it—but the focus is on developing your ability to use a variety of complex structures, when you need them, when they enhance communication.

A competent writer can use a variety of styles as various purposes and situations demand them. This chapter should make you aware of the options available to you. Stylistic revision depends on your ability to perceive and create alternative wordings. To take proper advantage of this chapter, practice the kinds of rewordings discussed in the first two sections and practice generating and transforming sentences as discussed in the third section. You will probably find it useful to have a writing folder in which you can save all the writing you are doing now (and as much of your recent writing as you have not discarded). Then when you want to practice a stylistic principle, you can use your own sentences as well as (or instead of) exercises from a handbook.

As you read this chapter, try to understand the effect of various styles in terms of the triangular relationship among your subject matter, your readers, and yourself. That understanding should help you make sense of the stylistic choices that you face as a writer.

Choosing Words _____

By words the mind is winged.

ARISTOPHANES

If thought corrupts language, language can also corrupt thought.

GEORGE ORWELL

Language is the mother, not the handmaiden of thought; words will tell you things you never thought or felt before.

W. H. AUDEN

Language is essentially a rich stew of implications saturated with other accents, tones, idioms, meanings, voices, influences, intentions. . . .

CHARLES SCHUSTER

Words and Ideas

As your ability to perceive, think, and feel grows, you are likely to find yourself needing a greater variety of words to communicate the full subtlety of those perceptions, thoughts, and feelings. Similarly, although to a lesser extent, as your vocabulary grows, you are likely to be able to perceive, think, and feel more precisely and subtly.

Insofar as words do not exist to represent meanings you wish to communicate, they can be invented. In 1948, for instance, as computers began to enter our social reality, Norbert Weiner coined the word *cybernetic* from the Greek root *kybernan*, meaning "self-steering." It now refers to computers and other devices that are in a sense self-steering (once they are programmed by human beings). English, like any living language, continually evolves to meet the needs of the people who use it.

Language, as I. A. Richards insists in *The Philosophy of Rhetoric* (Oxford), is not just "a dress which thought puts on." Language and thought interpenetrate; they animate each other. Our *terms* to some extent de*term*ine our ideas. That is what Auden means when he says language is the mother of thought. The process of "finding words" is also a process of developing and defining ideas. To articulate an idea is usually also to refine it. Your ability to think is to some degree dependent on the quality of your vocabulary. Your ability to think critically is to some degree dependent on your appreciation of the power of words.

'Wrong' Words

Students frequently list "wrong words" high among their writing problems. A writer has used a "wrong word" when readers can tell from context that the word the writer chose does not represent quite what the writer must have meant. To make matters more complex, word choice involves more than discovering words that represent meanings accurately; words should be appropriate to rhetorical context as well.

When we read,

High school kids often use jargon their teachers cannot understand,

we can tell from the context of the sentence that *jargon* is a "wrong word" for what the writer apparently intends (and that *slang* would be a "right word").

"Wrong words" are often not so much a problem as a growing pain. As you learn new words, you are likely to misuse them for a while; and if you never use them, you may never fully learn them. As your ideas grow, moreover, you may not have the words to represent them, so you may fumble around for a while with "wrong words."

Of course, "wrong words" can also result from laziness: often a writer knows that the word is not quite right, but does not want to bother finding a better one. The solution to this kind of "wrong word" is the proper use of the dictionary, thesaurus, or advice from a friend or editor. (The thesaurus is often a source of "wrong words"—if it is used without doublechecking connotations.)

But the main reason for worrying about "wrong words" is that they often camouflage sloppy thinking. Once found and placed in the sentence, the right word may expose an imprecision or contradiction in the idea. Thus the search for the right word often becomes a search for a more precise and accurate idea (see pages 112–16). Writers, for instance, should understand the distinction between *slang* and *jargon* because, although each refers to the special terms of an exclusive group, the conditions under which each may appropriately be used are quite different.

Connotation

In use, all words acquire implications and tones, sometimes subtle, from the company they habitually keep, the contexts in which they are usually found. To use a word accurately and effectively, you must know these connotations, which often extend beyond its dictionary definition.

Your choice of a certain word also connotes something about you. Thus it helps to shape your persona. It communicates something about your attitude toward your subject matter and thus suggests the attitude you want readers to take.

It was perhaps Jeremy Bentham, who first wrote systematically about what we now call *purr-words* and *snarl-words*, words which have distinctly positive or negative connotations. Thus when you want to express positive feelings toward the police, you call them "police officers"; when you want to express negative feelings, they become "cops" (or even "pigs"). You are still referring to the same people, but the connotations shift radically.

Bentham suggests that tyranny can be called "order"; fear of punishment, a "sense of duty"; lust, "love"; greed "industriousness"; and so forth—when we need "fig leaves" to cover unseemly motives. Likewise, courage on the part of your enemy may be called "rashness." Other countries may have war departments, but the U.S. has a Department of Defense. Other countries' armed forces may be offensive and conduct sneak attacks; the U.S. armed forces confine themselves to "rescue missions," 'peacekeeping," and "protective reaction strikes." My frugality I call "being careful with money" and "knowing the value of a dollar"; but another's is "penny-pinching" if not downright "cheap."

A U.S. Air Force press officer won the first Public Doublespeak Award in 1973 for rebuking reporters, "You always write it's bombing, bombing, bombing. It's not bombing! It's air support!" Of course, it was both bombing and air support—air support, after all, means dropping bombs in support of your troops. But Colonel Opfer did understand the importance of word choice and connotation.

Bentham believed that there were neutral words, halfway between the purr-words and the snarl-words, with which reasoned discourse could be conducted. In any particular rhetorical context, there may be. It used to be said, for instance, that "policeman" was a neutral term between the purr-word, "police officer," and the snarl-word, "cop." But then feminists pointed out that "policeman" has connotations too: it implies that the police are (or should be) male. Those connotations evolved, of course, because the police once were all male—and because seven centuries ago "-man," especially as in *wyfman* or *woman*, could refer to an adult of either sex. In the present, however, those connotations are hardly neutral.

All words have connotations. Word choices matter precisely because words both reflect and influence attitudes. The persona you project through your writing is shaped in large part by your word choices. Readers will perceive the words you choose as a reflection of your attitudes. The exactness with which you are understood will also depend on the precision with which you choose words. And if your writings are successful, your choice of words will influence your readers' attitudes.

Since there are no neutral words—no words *without* connotations—the best you can do as a writer is to choose words with connotations that suit your purposes. If you are honest, you will also choose words with connotations that accurately match what you believe to be true and that project a persona which honestly matches your attitudes. To whatever extent the words you use may influence the attitudes of your readers, you also have an ethical responsibility to choose thoughtfully.

As rhetoricians have been aware at least since Classical Greece, you should choose words that suit your audiences and the occasions on which you are addressing them. On one level, this is what my mother used to tell me: "You can use that language on the street if you like, but don't use it at home in front of me." The bottom line is that, if you use words offensive to your readers, they may stop reading. Above that bottom line, you should think about the image and attitudes your words will project.

Inclusive Language

The activities of feminists in the early 1970s created a renewed awareness of sexism and sexist bias in language, even among people who would never call themselves feminists. By the mid-1970s, many educational organizations, government agencies, and private publishing companies were creating guidelines to help authors avoid such biased language.

In positive terms, this became a call for *inclusive language*, for words with the connotation that all human beings are included. Except in situations where one is intentionally excluding certain groups, inclusive language means using words that include all people, regardless of sex, race, ethnic background, age, sexual orientation, or any other irrelevant category. Thus one says "mail carrier" instead of "mailman" because sex is not relevant to a person's ability to deliver mail.

Sexist bias in language is largely a matter of word choice and connotation. Social attitudes about women are changing and, instead of waiting decades (or even centuries) for the language to catch up, feminists are consciously inventing an antisexist vocabulary. What matters, of course, is not the words themselves, but the attitudes they reflect. Although attitudes are primary and words secondary, changing the words can help change the attitudes (or at least make people conscious of the attitudes).

For instance, it used to be—and in some circles still is— commonplace to refer to women as "girls." Intriguingly, *girl* originally meant a child or young person of either sex. The connotation of immaturity, frivolity, and so forth remains with the word *girls*. The choice to refer to an adult woman as a "girl," therefore, communicates a certain attitude toward either women in general or that woman in particular. The speaker or writer may or may not be consciously intending to communicate that attitude, but the attitude is implied by the choice of the word. The speaker or writer may not even agree with the attitude, but the word choice projects a persona who does.

Sometimes inclusive language means coining new terms: *Miss/Mrs.* becomes *Ms.* to parallel *Mr.* and avoid the connotation that marital status is more important when considering women than when considering men; *chairman* likewise becomes *chairperson* or *chair*, which some people find hard on their ears but only because it is unfamiliar. Logically, *department chair* is no more odd than *department head*. And *chairperson* does not violate English phonetics. As I. A. Richards has noted, certain authoritative people often object to such new words; in 1936 when Richards was making the point, the objectionable words included *psychology*, *tasteful*, and *colorful*. (*Colorful* apparently came into the language about 1890 as a controversial alternative to "full of color.")

More typically, the antisexist vocabulary involves using existing words that do not identify people by gender when it is not relevant. For example:

Old Usage	Alternatives
airline stewardess	flight attendant
bachelor	single person
businessman	business owner, executive, manager
cameraman	camera operator
career woman	doctor, lawyer, secretary, etc.
chairman	moderator, facilitator, chair, head
cleaning woman	housekeeper, office cleaner
coed	student
craftsman	worker, artisan
divorcée	single person, unmarried
fireman	firefighter
foreman	supervisor
housewife	homemaker
layman	layperson
maid	servant, housekeeper
mailman	mail carrier
male nurse	nurse
man and wife	husband and wife
man, mankind	humanity, human beings, human race, humankind, people
manhood	adulthood
man-made	manufactured, synthetic, artificial
middleman	intermediary
newsboy	newspaper carrier
policeman	police officer
primitive man*	hunters and gatherers, pastoral people, subsistence farmers, nomads, tribal peoples
salesmen	salespeople, sellers
spinster	single person
spokesman	spokesperson, representative
statesman	leader, public servant
waiter/waitress	server
weatherman	weather forecaster
workman	worker
women's libber	feminist

* Note that the problem here is not only "man," but the ethnocentric judgment implicit in "primitive."

The general point here is not about sexism, but about language. For Bentham, purr-words and snarl-words were "question-begging appellatives." He wrote in his *Book of Fallacies*

> Begging the question is one of the fallacies enumerated by Aristotle; but Aristotle has not pointed out . . . the mode of using the fallacy with the greatest effect, and least risk of detection—namely, by the employment of a single appellative.

Bentham's point was that purr-words and snarl-words are the equivalent of the logical fallacy called begging the question. To beg a question is to somehow assume or take for granted what should be proven (see page 375). Implicit in purr-words and snarl-words are judgments that Bentham thought should be made explicit and validated logically. If you think industrialized people are superior to pastoral people, say so and explain why; do not hide that moral judgement in the connotations of the snarl-word "primitive." If you object

Figure 5.1   Using inclusive language.

to feminism, say so and explain why; do not use the derogatory term "women's libber."

A greater difficulty for those who want to avoid sexist connotations in their writing is pronouns, specifically third-person singular neuter pronouns (he, him, his). Some languages have neuter pronouns for use when the gender is unspecified; since the eighteenth century, English has used the masculine pronouns, thus creating the connotation that all unidentified people are male. For example, "Each student must open *his* book," technically denotes nothing about the sex of the students, but the connotation remains (especially since few people say, "Each secretary must finish *his* typing by 5 p.m.")

There are a number of potential solutions.

1. Switch to the plural: "Everyone likes his bacon crisp" then becomes "All people like their bacon crisp."
2. Avoid the pronoun altogether: "Most people like crisp bacon."
3. Use both pronouns: "Anyone can fail if *he* relies on common sense alone" becomes "Anyone can fail if *she or he* relies on common sense alone." (Some writers then alternate *she or he* with *he or she*.)
4. Alternate throughout the text: "Students often complain about instructors, saying, 'She's a hard marker' or 'He requires too much work.' "
5. Use *he/she* or *s/he*.

Perhaps the most interesting solution is the one most common in people's speech: *they*, *them*, and *their* are starting to evolve into singular pronouns! In addition to retaining their traditional uses, these pronouns are becoming increasingly common in sentences like "Everyone likes their bacon crisp," or "Someone took my pen again, and they're going to get it." This usage is not yet generally acceptable in formal written English, although the U.S. National Council of Teachers of English and many major publishers are willing to accept it.

Another approach to the problem is simply to use *she* and *her* whenever a singular neuter pronoun is required—presumably on the grounds that turnabout is fair play—at least until there is no more sexism and no one cares. A small but significant number of published articles do this; reading them, most people are constantly reminded of their linguistic biases.

At present, there is no solution that will be totally acceptable to all contemporary readers. Some guidelines, therefore, suggest avoiding the problem whenever possible: "The editor uses his skills, tact, and common sense in making his changes on the manuscript" then becomes "The editor uses skill, tact, and common sense in making changes on a manuscript." An increasing number of apologetic prefaces indicate that many writers wish the problem could always be avoided so easily.

Jargon—Its Use and Abuse

In a very different sense, jargon is the contrary of inclusive language. *Jargon* itself is a snarl-word for the terminology that a group of specialists uses for discussing their special subject. Though it can serve as a kind of slang, excluding nonmembers from the group's discussion, the main function of jargon is to provide specialists with precise terms for concepts that other people may use more loosely—or not at all.

Thus *connotation* allows linguists and rhetoricians to distinguish a particular, subtle aspect of what most people call "meaning." *Person* and *persona* allow literary critics and rhetoricians to make another important distinction. And *grammar* means something quite different to a linguist than to a person who says, "I think I would write more confidently if I had learned more grammar in high school"—in fact, the linguist retorts, "As a native speaker, you already know English grammar" (a statement that leaves the ordinary person confused).

The difference between using and abusing jargon is quite straightforward. Jargon is abused when addressed to nonspecialists, who may not know the term, at least not in its technical sense. Jargon is abused when it is used to exclude people. Jargon is abused when it is used just to impress people: sometimes one has to decode a lot of jargon in order to discover that a writer was saying something quite simple. Jargon is abused when it is used in place of ordinary words that mean the same thing.

Often the abuse of jargon is quite unintentional. The people who work in a particular field—or even a particular office—develop special vocabulary and acronyms to facilitate their communication. Because they think in these terms, they may use them automatically, without even considering that their audience may have trouble understanding.

Thus a psychiatrist testified in court that the accused was not a pedophile— even though he admitted that the accused did have a sexual preference for children. According to the technical psychiatric definition, people with a sexual preference for children are pedophiles only if they are also at least partially impotent with adults and readily confess their crimes when confronted by authority. The psychiatrist's testimony was, therefore, technically accurate, even if it may not have given the jury the information needed for an accurate verdict.

Jargon is often abused when moved out of its specialized context. When an airline company stock report referred to a $3 million profit on the "involuntary conversion" of a Boeing 727, legal jargon was being abused. The jargon was accurate enough— if your house burns down or your plane crashes, lawyers do call it involuntary conversion (unless you did it on purpose). In a nonlegal document, however, "involuntary conversion" seemed more like a way to avoid saying, "Our plane crashed, killing everyone aboard, and we made a $3 million profit from the insurance."

Table 5.1 Revision Heuristic: Word Choice*

Do the words chosen have the desired connotations to represent your meanings accurately and without unintended implications? Do they have connotations that may be offensive to any of your readers? Is there any misuse of purr-words or snarl-words?

Is the style and tone (and hence the persona) of this piece consistent? Do the connotations of words chosen at one point in any way contradict the connotations of words used elsewhere?

If you have used any jargon, is it necessary? Will your readers readily understand it? Have you used it accurately? If you are writing on a specialized subject for an audience of specialists and have not used jargon, should you? Are the ordinary words you have used in place of jargon accurate?

* Remember: This is only a list of suggested questions. Choose from it only those questions that match your individual needs. Rephrase them more specifically, if possible, to focus your attention on your own particular weak points. Add any questions you need. Use this list to continue developing your own revision heuristic (see pages 133–35). And do not rely on this list alone: read the sections of the text that explain the concepts behind the questions.

Jargon, like abstraction, is useful. Not only does it facilitate communication within the group of specialists, it also represents key concepts those specialists use to gain insight into their subject. That is why learning specialized terms—and the concepts they represent—is one of the important parts of advanced education in virtually any field, from auto repair to neurology to rhetoric.

The general principle is that certain words belong in certain contexts. In those contexts they are appropriate and facilitate communication. In other contexts, the same words may be inappropriate or impede communication. Whether a word is "right" cannot be determined without considering both its connotations and the context.

The questions in Table 5.1 should help call your attention to the quality of word choice in your drafts. Add to your own revision heuristic any questions that can help pinpoint your own weaknesses.

EXERCISE

1. For the next day or two, listen for purr-words and snarl-words as you talk with people. Then find an official statement that purports to be objective (e.g., a government press release, a "fact-finding" report, a biography of a political figure). Search through it for purr-words and snarl-words. What questions do they beg? Revise a passage by substituting a snarl-word for every

purr-word and a purr-word for every snarl-word. What effect does your revision have on the statement?

2. Bertrand Russell made a point similar to Bentham's by offering the following "declensions":

I'm cautious. You're timid. He's chickenhearted.

I'm thrifty. You're a bit of a tightwad. She's a skinflint.

I'm human. You're prone to error. He's a blundering idiot.

Compose a similar "declension" of your own.

3. Underline the sexist usage in the following passage, and be prepared to explain why it is sexist. Then supply alternatives that could be substituted for the sexist words and phrases.

> Martha was a thirty-year-old salesgirl and dreadfully afraid of dying a spinster. Then she met George, a thirty-four-year-old mailman. Soon they were man and wife—and she was a housewife. One day, in her newfound boredom, she was convinced by her friends that there should be more to life than taking care of a husband. She told George that she wanted to study medicine and become a career woman. He said they couldn't afford to hire a cleaning woman. She suggested that he do half the housework, and soon she became a divorcée. Many people thought this was a tragedy. Mary, now a coed at the local university, disagreed. Mankind has long known unhappy marriages, but this disagreement about divorce was virtually unknown in feudal societies.

(If you want to try something more difficult, rewrite the passage to avoid heterosexual bias, i.e., to include the possibility that a gay couple might have this sort of experience.)

4. Inclusive language is prescriptive in somewhat the same sense that traditional grammar is prescriptive: both tell how language should be used; neither just describes how it is used. The difference is that traditional grammar is based in the past, whereas the antisexist vocabulary is oriented toward the future. Think of some common attitude other than sexism that you think is undesirable. How, if at all, does the English language embody that attitude? How could the English language be modified to help counteract that attitude?

5. Go through one of your recent writings that used jargon and underline each instance. Have you used it accurately? Will your intended readers understand it—and if not, can you insert a brief definition or example without creating awkwardness? Is there in no case an ordinary word that would be accurate? Is any of the jargon there primarily to impress?

An Honest Style

The ill and unfitting choice of words wonderfully obstructs the understanding.
FRANCIS BACON

The Official Style comes in several dialects, bureaucratic, social-scientific, com-puter-engineering-military, but all exhibit the same basic attributes. They all build on the same central imbalance, a dominance of nouns and an atrophy of verbs, the triumph of stasis over action. This basic imbalance is easy to cure—if you want to cure it.

But when do you want to cure it? Students today often feel—sometimes with justification—that they will be penalized for writing in plain English. In the academic bureaucracy, writing plain English seems like walking down the hall with nothing on.
RICHARD LANHAM

Abstract nouns refer to the world in a way quite different from concrete nouns. They do not point to a set of particulars. . . . They are relational. . . . Some important kinds of thinking can be done only with the help of abstractions.
RICHARD OHMANN

Although there is a sense in which dishonest writing can be effective— if it effectively achieves a writer's deceitful purposes—a good style is an honest style.

Dishonest writing is commonplace. Among students it is known as "BS-ing," but it goes by many names: bureaucratese, gobbledygook, legalese, medicalese, educationese, academese, public doublespeak. However unethical, this deceitful style can impress, can cover up a paucity of thought, logic, or integrity. Worse, it can become a habit: some writers actually forget how to use words in a clear, straightforward way.

Dishonest writing is often so abstracted from the realities it describes that readers may hardly notice what it is saying. Such writing avoids making an impact on readers by using generalities, abstractions, ambiguities, clichés, unintelligible jargon, passive constructions, and so on. Dishonest writing some-times has so little impact on readers that they barely notice whether it is true or false.

The "ho-hum" opening is often dishonest in this way. A student once began a paper,

```
    The automobile is a mechanism fascinating to everyone in all its
diverse manifestations and in every conceivable kind of situation
or circumstance.
```

That sentence has so little impact that most readers do not consider it carefully enough to notice that it is blatantly false. Concretize the statement by listing some of the less pleasant manifestations of automobiles (e.g., smog, middle-aged people so accustomed to driving that they grow tired if they must walk a quarter mile) or certain situations (e.g., a broken fuel pump on a lonely road late one cold and rainy night)—or simply ask, "Is *everyone* really *always* fascinated by cars?"—and the proposition becomes highly improbable. This writer in this instance did not take the trouble to think about what he was writing and whether he actually believed it. In Eudora Welty's words, this is "bad writing" because it "is not serious and does not tell the truth." Writing concretely and honestly, the same writer probably has something to say about cars.

In *Telling Writing* (Boynton/Cook), Professor Ken Macrorie contrasts this opening sentence with a short passage by a grade seven student:

> I'd like to be a car. You get to go all over and get to go through mud puddles without getting yelled at . . . that's what I'd like to be.

Whatever its stylistic flaws, this passage makes a meaningful comparison and speaks honestly (about getting yelled at, not about cars).

Honesty in writing, as in life, means more than not lying. Honesty means revealing what you actually think and feel, at least insofar as it may be significant and relevant. It may mean telling "the whole truth"; it may even mean getting in touch with thoughts and feelings that have been repressed. Honesty is often frightening (and in the context of certain power relationships, it can get one into real trouble). Powerful writing, however, is usually honest writing.

Honesty can be avoided by lying or simply by avoiding certain subjects. A deceitful style, however, is more devious. It allows writers to raise a subject, seem to discuss it (often at considerable length), tell no overt lies—but nonetheless avoid revealing their true attitude or opinion.

Some dishonest writing intentionally tries to miscommunicate or avoid communicating relevant information. Since the very act of writing can be taken as an assertion that one is trying to communicate, writing that strives to miscommunicate or avoid communicating is intrinsically paradoxical and dishonest.

Much dishonest writing is characterized by a lack of commitment. For some reason, the writer feels a need to write but does not really want to say anything. The situation is analogous to when your friend asks what you think of his terrible photographs, and you reply, "interesting, very interesting effect," in order to avoid giving your true opinion. The bureaucrat who does not want to make waves, the student forced to write on a subject perceived as irrelevant, the politician trying to avoid any assertion that might alienate a voter, the prude caught in some situation where it is necessary to refer to

222 / STYLE AND VOICE

sex, the schizophrenic who wants to avoid responsibility for any statement whatsoever—all of these are likely to produce dishonest writing.

Such writing is called bureaucratese, academese, doublespeak, euphemism, or schizophrenese—according to the context in which it is found. It varies somewhat: the schizophrenic is more likely to use concrete ambiguity, the student to use abstraction, the technocrat to use unnecessary jargon. But it is always an attempt to write or speak without saying anything for which one might be held responsible, to avoid both outright lies and clear, straightforward, accurate statements.

Dishonest writing, it must be added, may be an adaptation to a situation that demands it. On the basis of past experience, the schizophrenic probably believes (perhaps accurately) that definite statements will be punished. The bureaucrat's supervisor may demand bureaucratese, as the student's instructor sometimes demands academese. Euphemism can allow diplomats to communicate without forcing other governments to take offense.

Much as we might wish for a world in which it were never necessary, the point is not simply to condemn dishonest writing, but to understand it. Too many writers slip into a dishonest style even when they are honestly trying to communicate what they really believe. And too many readers are too easily fooled by gobbledygook (often because they are insecure about their reading abilities and assume that their failure to make sense of a passage is their fault, not the writer's).

Dishonest writing is often a matter of style. Thus an executive might write, "It is imperative to maximize potentials for synchronized management options," in order to avoid saying whatever that might specifically mean (perhaps, "We should not commit ourselves until we see what other departments are doing.") In either case, dishonest writing omits or obscures objectively relevant information. Typically, it also disguises or mystifies the writer's attitudes and biases.

Honest writing is literally effective writing: it has an effect on readers. It establishes a persona contemporary readers will consider reliable and trustworthy. On the level of style, honesty in writing often means being concrete and specific enough so that readers get the full impact and understand the full implications.

Honest writing, it should be added, calls only for the expression of those perceptions, feelings, opinions, and beliefs that are relevant to the writers' and readers' purposes. The readers of a literary biography of Robert Graves want to know about Robert Graves and probably not about the biographer's feelings. The readers of a scholarly journal of literary criticism do not ordinarily want to know the scholar-author's feelings about *King Lear*. The readers of a scientific article about butterflies are probably interested in butterflies, not in the scientists' feelings about butterflies. (This distinction is especially true in North America; the British literary essay, for example, allows much greater intrusion of the writer's feelings and unsupported opinions than would be tolerated in most North American publications.)

Sometimes you can achieve an honest style just by forgetting that you are writing and making believe you are talking to someone. Or you can use some of the techniques discussed in Chapter 2, such as freewriting. But if you or someone you are writing with or someone whose writing you are supervising or editing does draft some gobbledygook, you should know how to revise for clarity.

Concrete and Abstract

Show–don't tell is one of the basic slogans in most creative writing classes. That slogan, which is most directly relevant to expressive and literary writing, embodies an understanding that concrete words, phrases, and images affect readers in ways that more abstract terms and ideas do not. To *show* means to verbally recreate images that allow readers to re-perceive. That usually has more emotional impact and is more convincing than if you *tell* them *about* something.

Suppose, for example, you write,

His outrageous remark upset her.

You have told your readers what happened. In the telling you have included your interpretation of what you heard and saw: it is your *judgment* that the remark was outrageous; you have inferred from her response that the remark upset her. Even assuming that your inference is valid and your judgment correct, a description that quotes his remark and describes her response will generally be more effective because it will allow readers to interpret and judge for themselves. Not only will the more concrete description create more vivid images, but the readers' active involvement in the interpretative process will make the conclusions more convincing.

"Mrs. Hennessey has told me of a part-time job I could probably have," she said quietly, her eyes fixed on her knitting. "It would bring in a bit of extra money and give me something to do mornings while the children are in school."

"Woman's place is in the home" he said coldly, picking up his newspaper.

Her cheeks reddened, her fingers trembled and she dropped a stitch, though she still did not raise her eyes from the stocking she was knitting.

This bit of dialogue and description is slanted to bias readers toward the conclusion that "his outrageous remark upset her." But the bias is only in the writer's selection and juxtaposition of facts. The conclusion is unstated. Readers draw it themselves, almost as if they had heard and seen with their own ears and eyes. Such an unstated conclusion is more convincing. In Ernest Hemingway's words, "Anything you know, you can eliminate and it only strengthens your iceberg."

The sorts of words and phrases likely to create vivid images in readers' minds are called *concrete*. Concrete language usually refers quite specifically to objects or events that we could experience with our five senses. By contrast, *abstract* language usually refers to intangibles, such as concepts, relationships, and judgments. It usually has less impact on readers (and is sometimes used by writers who wish, for one reason or another, to downplay the impact of their reports).

To say that someone was "upset" is more abstract than to say that "her cheeks reddened, her fingers trembled and she missed a stitch." To say that someone is "lonely" is more abstract than to say that "sitting in his rented room, he longed to speak to somebody, anybody . . . even a door-to-door salesperson would have been welcome."

Each of the following series moves from the relatively abstract to the relatively concrete:

Fruit . . . apple . . . a mealy, red MacIntosh.

Environmental problem . . . polluted water . . . cancer-causing chemicals in the city's drinking water.

Moved . . . walked . . . strode.

Made . . . built . . . sawed and nailed.

Ten percent of writers . . . some modern novelists . . . Faulkner, Hemingway, and Fitzgerald.

Some textbooks flatly assert, "Use concrete language." Such advice can be useful, especially for inexperienced writers, who sometimes tend to confuse abstraction with profundity. An abstract term, moreover, is less likely than its concrete equivalents to have the same meaning for both writer and reader, so a concrete style tends to make communication more precise. A writer may write "bird" while thinking of a swan; a reader may imagine a magpie—or not imagine any concrete image at all.

But abstractions are useful. That is why Thoreau fears ordinary words may not "be adequate to the truth." As advertising agencies well know, a concrete image of one hungry child may have more emotional impact than statistics about hunger; but there are times when the abstract statistic that a quarter of the world's people go to sleep hungry each night is a more important fact.

A relatively abstract term, moreover, is sometimes more specific than a concrete description:

> He had the measles.
>
> His body was covered with a rough, red rash; he was feverish and itched terribly.

The second sentence is more concrete, but it could describe a number of diseases. Though it has less emotional impact, the first sentence is more specific and would be more useful to someone who had to prescribe a treatment.

The distinction between abstract and concrete should be used like that between general and particular—not to eliminate either type of language from your writings, but to choose in each case what will achieve your aims. You might, for example, use a relatively abstract style to present a rational argument and then follow it with a concrete illustration for emotional impact.

Abstractions can also be used to create meaningful insights. It is precisely by juxtaposing abstract concepts—like ecosystem or honesty—with concrete events that we make sense out of our experience. Indeed, this is one of the most important functions of technical terms (see pages 217–18). Often it is the interplay between abstract and concrete that makes a piece of writing work. Susan-Ann Green's description of North Bend (reproduced in full on pages 277–78) turns abstract when she writes,

> I was troubled by the idea that my world was linked to this other world by a cable. That constituted a connection and I found it hard to see the relationship, for my world seemed not as complicated.

Read out of context, these sentences do not have much effect. In context, the abstraction works because it is well grounded in the concrete description which preceded it and because the contrast between simplicity and complexity is a predominant theme of the essay.

The point to remember is that concrete terms have greater impact and communicate more vividly. They have *more* effect on readers and that effect is more precisely predictable—in this literal sense they are more *effective*. A concrete style can contribute to an honest persona. In general, all else being equal, writers should prefer concrete language, but all else is often not equal.

Clichés

A cliché is a linguistic preconception, the verbal equivalent of a stereotype (see pages 267–68). Indeed, the word cliché comes into English from the French, where one of its meanings is "stereotyped." In English, it refers to a phrase that has been used (and overused) to the point of extreme familiarity.

Such phrases are similar to abstractions in that, however concrete they may seem, they have little impact on readers and do not communicate vivid images.

Clichés are not always and automatically to be shunned. Much common-sense and conventional wisdom is stored in clichés. In certain contexts, the very familiarity of a cliché can make it persuasive, or at least reassuring. But clichés must be used self-consciously and with extreme caution.

To a writer the key point about clichés is the effect that they have (or do not have) on readers—and the nature of the persona they, therefore, create. The English lover who first compared his true love's lips to a red rose was using a metaphor that brought to her mind a vivid image; he was, we may presume, suitably rewarded, at the very least with a smile from those lips he so admired. A lover who attempted the same comparison today would more likely be rewarded with a grimace or a groan. The comparison is so familiar that it is called trite (from the Latin *tritus*, "worn out.") The persona it creates is almost embarrassingly inept and unoriginal.

Many clichés are "worn out" metaphors. "The spur of the moment" once brought to mind a vivid image of horse and rider. "Cash on the barrel-head" once referred to the barrel top in a country store where many a deal was consummated (probably because the store lacked a counter). Such clichés usually do not produce even a grimace or a groan; more often they are so familiar that readers barely respond at all.

Many nonmetaphorical phrases which were once powerful because they were fresh and vivid are now powerful only as soporifics. "Tried and true" once suggested that a person had passed tests of loyalty. "The humanities" and "humanistic education" once had specific connotations based on a contrast between the specialist and the whole human being—as the phrase "humanistic psychology" still does. The power "progressive" once had came from connotations related to "progress" (back when "progress" did not yet suggest "pollution").

Similarly, the first instructor who wrote, "This is basically a good paper, but . . . ," probably communicated the opinion that the paper was basically good. Instructors who use that introductory clause now might just as well save their ink: most students have come to take the remark as a perfunctory and essentially meaningless preliminary (which it often is).

A writer who wishes to communicate an image or idea with impact often must verbalize it distinctively. One way to do that is to coin a new and fresh phrase. Another is to revivify an old one. Clichés can be very powerful when brought back to life. A writer who can provide a verbal context that revivifies a dead metaphor sometimes creates a doubly effective phrase:

I feel the spur of the moment thrust into my side. The present is an inexorable rider.

HENRY DAVID THOREAU

A man's home may seem to be his castle on the outside; inside it is more often his nursery.

CLARE BOOTH LUCE

Likewise, Abigail Van Buren (of "Dear Abby") made a strong retort when she remarked that those who fight fire with fire may end up with nothing but ashes. One can also revive a cliché by inverting it, as in "tried and untrue" or "both gladder and wiser" (which takes its power from each and every time readers have heard or read "both sadder and wiser").

Effective writing generally avoids clichés or uses them in an extraordinary way. But writers do not always wish to communicate either specifically or vividly. If you are criticizing something in order to induce the person who created the situation to change it, you may wish to understate your criticism—to state it in a way that we would ordinarily call "ineffective." If you are writing a ceremonial speech for a politician who actually has nothing to say and wishes, more than anything else, to avoid antagonizing anyone, you may find clichés extremely useful. If you are a bureaucrat who needs to hand in a thick report but does not want to step on any toes, you may find "ineffective" clichés and other forms of excessive verbosity extremely effective.

Of course, many of the circumstances in which clichés and other forms of dishonest writing "work" are morally questionable. Perhaps we would all be better off—and the government deficit a lot smaller—if bureaucrats were occasionally more willing to step on a few toes. Perhaps speechwriters should quit their jobs before agreeing to produce misleading scripts for public figures. In general, moreover, clichés do not work well for writers, and unless a writer has specific justification, they are best shunned.

Writing with Nouns and Verbs

The traditional advice to prefer concrete terms generally emphasizes the choice of concrete nouns. Because one of the great banes of modern English style is excessive nominalization, the piling up of nouns upon nouns, the other important advice about nouns concerns when and how to minimize them.

Nouns are most precisely defined in terms of their grammatical function. Loosely, however, we may say that nouns (from the Latin *nomen*, name) are words that name things, people, places, acts, qualities, and concepts.

English, like other Indo-European languages, is noun-based. All the other words in an English sentence are attached to a noun or noun phrase, which names what the sentence is about and is called the subject of the sentence. (Certain other languages, e.g., Hopi, build their sentences around verbs and are therefore called verb-based; such languages tend to produce statements that at least sound more process- and relationship-oriented than English sentences.)

One can name a particular thing or concept by choosing a somewhat general noun and adding modifiers that limit its meaning. Or one can choose a noun that by itself precisely represents the intended meaning.

false statement	lie
baby dog	puppy
ritual purification	ablution
hired soldier	mercenary
excessive daring	rashness

Where a noun alone can represent either the same meaning or an even more specific meaning than a noun-plus-modifier, the noun alone will generally have more impact. This fact should not, however, be interpreted to mean, "Avoid modifiers." Indeed, one reason for preferring specific nouns over nouns-plus-modifiers is that more modification can then be added to the specific noun. Suppose the draft sentence reads,

Deciduous trees grew along the riverbanks.

Substituting "oaks, maples, and birches" allows one to add modifiers and produce a revision which reads,

Young oaks, sugar maples, and silver birches grew along the riverbanks.

Similarly, changing "baby dog" to "puppy" opens the potential of writing "hungry mongrel puppy." Changing "false statement" to "lie" opens the potential of writing "bald-faced lie." Thus using specific nouns allows writers to reach for more concrete images.

Sometimes, however, writers wish to minimize impact. It will be easier to get someone to admit to a "false statement" than to a "bald-faced lie." It is easier to defend "excessive daring" than "rashness." When impact is desired, however, seek the most concrete noun available—and only then consider modifiers. (But do remember, as with all maxims, that other factors may override this principle.)

The other important point about nouns is knowing when to avoid them. Piling up nouns is one of the most effective ways to create an unreadable or dishonest style. Though it may impress some readers, a sentence that begins with a noun phrase like "early childhood thought disorder misdiagnosis" is extremely difficult to read. And when a "ground hostess" announces "a flight overload situation," she avoids admitting, "Our airline sold a lot more tickets than the plane has seats." Similarly, one can probably sell a "hydro blastforce cup" for more than a plumber's plunger or rent a "natural amenity unit" for more than a portable privy. Whether such phrases are good style—or good ethics—is another question.

The nurse who said,

Insulin-dependent diabetics should perform self blood glucose tests,

was using a complex nominalization ("self blood glucose tests") when she could have said, simply and clearly,

Insulin-dependent diabetics should test their own blood sugar.

The solution to this common sort of nominalization is to make sure that the real action becomes not a noun, but the main verb of the sentence. Like nouns, verbs are most precisely defined in terms of their grammatical function; loosely, however, we may say that verbs are words that express action, occurrence, or existence. Since the action here is *testing*, the sentence becomes easier to read when *test* becomes the verb (instead of a noun modified by three other nouns).

Similarly, the journalist who wrote,

The government intends to release draft legislation dealing . . . with pension indexation,

could have written,

The government is drafting a law to protect pensions against inflation.

In general, use verbs—rather than nouns or noun phrases—to communicate action: *not* "It was my intention to . . . ," but "I intended to. . . ."

Often it is writers' choices of effective verbs that make narratives come alive, that make process analyses and causal explanations precise. (And it is difficulty with verbs that often makes narration a difficult mode for writers to whom English is a second language.)

As with nouns, so with verbs the most powerful are likely to be the most specific and concrete. Narratives that lack impact often rely too heavily on the verb "to be" (*am, is, are, was, were,* etc.). You should similarly be wary of verbs like "to have," "to make," "to go," "to come," "to move," and "to get." All of these are, of course, important English verbs, and no one could write very well without them. But inexperienced writers often rely on them where more particular verbs would carry more meaning and have more impact.

Consider, for instance, the following pairs of sentences.

She went up the mountain.
She climbed the mountain.

He was in bed.
He lay in bed.

He had the appearance of an assembly-line worker.
He looked like an assembly-line worker.

In barely a minute, she made her decision: she would handle the matter herself.
In barely a minute, she decided to handle the matter herself.

They went away together.
They eloped.

He came to the conclusion that there should be no taxation without representation.
He concluded that there should be no taxation without representation.

The baby walked across the stage in rhythm to the salsa.
The baby tottered across the stage in rhythm to the salsa.

In a morning's work, he got only two pages written.
In a morning's work, he wrote only two pages.

The prison was situated on a hilltop.
The prison stood on a hilltop.

In each case, the second sentence substitutes a more specific verb or transforms a verb-plus-object into a verb ("made her decision" becomes "decided"; "got written" becomes "wrote"; "was situated" becomes "stood"). In each case, the second sentence carries a more specific meaning or transforms the key word into the verb for greater impact. The underlying principle is well understood by advertisers, for example, whose products will rarely "make hair moist" when they could instead "moisturize hair" (and who make heavy use of verbs and verbals in variety of other ways).

Out of context, one cannot say definitively which version of each sentence is better. If a writer wanted to put emphasis on the making of a decision, "she made her decision" might be better than "she decided." In certain contexts, moreover, one might want a less empathic version. What can be said is that the second version of each sentence is more specific or emphatic and that it should be chosen when those qualities are desired.

Choosing nouns and verbs well is important. To use nouns and verbs effectively, however, is to use them in sentences with modifiers. For that, see the following section of this chapter.

In Short

You can go a long way toward an honest style by remembering the following rules of thumb:

1. Prefer concrete words—except, of course, when you are writing about something abstract or using an abstract concept to illuminate a concrete event. Avoid using a "big word" or technical term when an ordinary word will communicate the same idea. Watch out for clichés and other set phrases that have lost their impact. *Do not say* "vehicle," *when you could say* "car." *Do not say* "cognizant," *when you could say* "knows."

2. Get rid of "empty" words that can be dropped without changing the meaning of the sentence. Where possible, consider substituting a single word for a phrase. *Do not say* "written composition," *when you could say* "writing."

3. Try to use jargon only when writing for readers who will understand it. If you must use technical terms when addressing other readers, keep them to a minimum and work some sort of definition into your text.

4. Avoid piling up nouns into long noun phrases (except when they sum up what you just said). If such a compound noun phrase is standard jargon, at least be careful not to put another noun in front of it. *Do not say* "Early childhood thought disorder misdiagnosis often occurs because . . . ," *when you could say* "Doctors often misdiagnose a child's disordered thinking because. . . ."

5. Generally use a verb, not a noun, for the action—and make the verb as specific as you can. Generally try to make the real actor ("who" did it) the grammatical subject of the sentence—unless you are intentionally shifting the emphasis (see pages 237–38). *Do not say* "made" or "fabricated," *when you could say* "drew" or "baked." *Do not say* "a need exists," *when you could say* "we need" or "we must."

6. Watch the connotations of your words—especially key words—to be sure they accurately connote your attitudes (preferably in ways that will not offend your readers).

7. Try to keep most of your sentences under twentyfive words. Though the occasional longer sentence may be good, too many sentences with more than thirty words is reason to think twice about the burden you may be creating for your readers.

These are guidelines, rules of thumb, not absolute rules. And there is more to it. Nonetheless, if you understand them, these seven guidelines can take you a long way toward a clear, honest style.

The questions in Table 5.2 should help call your attention to tendencies toward a dishonest style in your drafts. Add to your own revision heuristic (see pages 133–35) any that could help you develop a more direct and effective style.

Table 5.2   Revision Heuristic: An Honest Style*

Have you left out any relevant information (thereby distorting the accuracy of your representation)?

Are any passages overly abstract or ambiguous?

Is there any jargon that is unnecessary? that readers may not understand?

Are there any clichés or trite passages?

Have you chosen words that will have the desired impact on your readers?

Can a specific noun be substituted for a noun-plus modifier?

Can a specific verb be substituted for a modified verb or verb-plus-object?

Is each sentence as "tight" as possible? Can you shorten any sentences without losing any meaning that matters?

Have you used examples and images to concretize abstractions or ambiguities you have chosen to use?

If there is any jargon your readers might not understand, has it been defined or explained?

Remember: This is only a list of suggested questions. Choose from it only those questions that match your individual needs. Rephrase them more specifically, if possible, to focus your attention on your own particular weak points. Add any questions you need. Use this list to continue developing your own revision heuristic (see pages 133–35). And do not rely on this list alone: read the sections of the text that explain the concepts behind the questions.

EXERCISE

1. The following was written to justify the creation of a new bureaucratic structure within a corporation. Rewrite it in a direct, readable style. What happens? Which version do you think would more likely lead to the creation of a Corporate Records Management Advisory Group?

> The 1987 Corporate Records Management Action Programme calls for the establishment of a functional Corporate Records Management Advisory Group. This group would assist individual departments in ensuring all retention requirements are satisfied before records are destroyed. While departments are able to review retention and disposal to meet their own operational needs, assistance is required to identify requirements beyond the scope of departmental operations. This means that each record series must be appraised for its legal, historical and informational value. The Records Management Advisory Group would fill that need.
>
> The group would regularly consist of representatives from Corporate Law, Internal Audit, Public Information and Records Management, with

representatives from specific operational and administrative areas as required. This concept has been discussed in past with the departments named, and each has agreed to participate in the review of records retention and disposal schedules.

Find another piece of gobblydegook or doublespeak produced by a bureaucracy. Rewrite it clearly and concretely. Contrast the two versions.

2. Here are some real examples of recent public doublespeak. Analyze and rewrite them.

Profits have been negatively impacted by lower sales—no question about it.

cadaveric donor

The six deaths were the result of systematic failure over a period of time involving various organizations and individuals directly and indirectly at all levels.

Bereavement Resource Centre

Further to your very kind offer of October 24, 1988, to Mr. G., he has asked me to follow up and put together an inventory of all the various prison education opportunities provided in the local area or in other parts of the jurisdiction which would be of interest to our inmates. Since I suspect you have this information at hand, we would be appreciative if you could provide us with this overview and any other information you think may be relevant. It would be our intention to promulgate this broadly to relevant correctional centres.

A 17% service charge will be added for your convenience.

The Bank is hereby authorized to credit the said account with all monies paid to the Bank (i) at the branch of account of (ii) at any branch other than the branch of account for the credit of any one or more of us, the proceeds of any orders to promises for the payment of money, of bonds, debentures, coupons or other securities, signed to drawn by or payable to or the property of, or received by the said Bank (i) at the branch of account of (ii) at any branch other than the branch of account for the credit of us or any one or more of us, and to endorse any of such instruments on behalf of us of any one or more of them.

The Youth Employment Strategy will provide assessment, counseling and employment for young people who are having difficulty achieving labor force attachment.

Hospitals should cut costs through labor productivity improvements and other efficiency improvements, staff hiring curtailments and, if necessary, service realignments.

3. Find a piece of "dishonest" writing you wrote sometime in the past. Rewrite it, adding details and concretizing to make it more honest. Contrast the two versions.

4. Study the doublespeak produced by a government around some historical event (e.g., U.S. government press releases about the Vietnam War, Chinese government statements about the takeover of Tibet, U.S.S.R. government statements about the invasion of Afghanistan). Try to show a relationship between the style of the doublespeak and the purposes it served in its historical context.

5. Create several series of three or more terms illustrating transitions from highly abstract to highly concrete (e.g., fruit . . . apple . . . mealy, red MacIntosh).

6. Look up the metaphorical origins of the following phrases:

a. cold shoulder	n. bang up job
b. going to pot	o. woolgathering
c. seamy side	p. land-office business
d. eavesdropper	q. steal one's thunder
e. dead as a doornail	r. weasel words
f. skinflint	s. keep your shirt on
g. brush up	t. fired up
h. kick the bucket	u. free lance
i. let the cat out of the bag	v. ham actor
j. clincher	w. bootlegger
k. to have one's work cut out	x. claptrap
l. to a T	y. freewheeling
m. read between the lines	z. seventh heaven

Write some sentences that revivify some of the original metaphors.

7. Collect some clichés by listening to the broadcast of an athletic event or examining the sports section of your newspaper. Why are there so many? What function do you think they serve?

8. Go through one of your recent writings and underline all nouns and verbs. In each case, ask yourself if you can substitute a more specific noun or verb and if you can then delete modifiers. If you can make some changes, what effect do they have on the tone of the piece?

9. Examine some of your own writing to see if the real action is in the verb, if the real actor is the subject of the sentence. When this is not true, would the sentence have been better if it were?

10. Pick an issue about which the facts are in dispute (e.g., nuclear power). Obtain reports written by proponents of distinct positions (e.g., a corporation that owns nuclear power plants, an organization opposed to nuclear power, a scientific commission evaluating nuclear waste disposal for the government). Examine the factual statements in each report to determine which "facts" are in dispute, where writers conveniently exclude facts harmful to their positions, and so forth.

Forming Sentences

A long sentence may be extremely simple in construction—indeed must *be simple if it is to convey its sense easily.*

HERBERT READ

Clarity and brevity, though a good beginning, are only a beginning. By themselves, they may remain bare and bleak. When Calvin Coolidge, asked by his wife what the preacher had preached on, replied "Sin," and, asked what the preacher had said, replied "he was against it," he was brief enough. But one hardly envies Mrs. Coolidge.

F. L. LUCAS

When you put one word after another, your statement should be more precise the more you add. . . . The noun, the verb, and the main clause serve . . . as a base on which the meaning will rise.

JOHN ERSKINE

A Few Words About Grammar

Many writers feel anxious about grammar. They believe that if they just knew more about grammar they could write better, or at least more confidently. In most cases this is a misapprehension. Though there may be a few rules of grammar—or more likely, usage—that you should learn, a comprehensive review of English grammar is not likely to do much to improve your writing.

A grammar describes how sounds and words may be combined within the system of a particular language or dialect. If you can speak and write English—certainly if you are a native speaker—you already know how to make almost all of these combinations. Noam Chomsky makes this point in *Syntactic Structures* (Gravenhage) with these two "sentences":

Colorless green ideas sleep furiously.

Furiously sleep ideas green colorless.

"Any speaker of English," Chomsky declares, will recognize that only the first is "grammatical."

Although both series of words are non-English on the level of meaning, a grammarian could call "Colorless green ideas sleep furiously" a sentence. Although, from a writer's perspective, it is not really a sentence because it is not meaningful, at least not literally, it does obey the rules of English grammar. That is why any native speaker, even one who does not know grammatical terminology, can recognize the first series of words as acceptable English word order and the second as unacceptable word order—can recognize the second as ungrammatical.

There are many types of formal grammars. Traditional English grammar is, in a sense, Latin grammar: historically, it began with the application to the English language of terminology taken from Latin grammar. Its study usually begins with the identification of eight "parts of speech": nouns, verbs, pronouns, adjectives, adverbs, conjunctions, articles, and interjections. Traditional English grammar is also a prescriptive grammar. Its rules prescribe how people are supposed to combine words into socially acceptable English sentences. The dominant goal is correctness.

In order to move beyond correctness to style, this chapter will use concepts from several types of modern English grammar, descriptive grammars that describe how people actually combine words in socially acceptable English sentences. As a writer, however, you do not need to learn these—or any other—grammars. With plentiful examples and minimal terminology, you can grasp their stylistic implications.

Sentence Basics

Sentences are both words and ideas. A sentence is clearest and easiest to read when the verbal structure of the sentence matches the actual structure of the idea.

An English sentence, like a logical proposition, has two parts. The first, called the subject, names something. The second, called the predicate, tells something about the subject. The essence of the predicate is a verb. The most basic sort of sentence states that somebody did or is doing something:

The dog shivered.

Siddhu loves Mary.

The lawyer is drafting a brief.

And the most basic principle about sentences is simply this: a sentence is easiest to read when the agent who is doing the "something" is its grammatical subject and when the action is expressed by its verb. Thus the following sentences are relatively difficult to read:

There is a brief being drafted by the lawyer.

Anxieties now play a large part in deterring prison inmates from entering basic literacy programs.

It is perfectly appropriate for literacy skills to be one of the factors considered in the granting of parole.

Such constructions are not intrinsically bad; in fact they allow writers to shift emphasis. The second sentence, for instance, puts the emphasis on anxieties, rather than on prisoners. But such constructions are harder to read than equivalent sentences beginning "The lawyer . . . ," "Prisoners . . . ," and "Parole boards. . . ."

Active and Passive Construction

The most common application of this principle of readability distinguishes between active and passive sentences. The most basic and common English sentence structure—subject + verb + object—produces sentences like this one:

Coleridge wrote the poem.
   s + v + o

This is known as an active construction because the grammatical subject of the sentence ("Coleridge") performed the real action represented by the verb ("wrote"). The sentence can be transformed, however, to read,

The poem was written by Coleridge.

And it can be further transformed (by deletion) to read simply,

The poem was written.

In these two versions, the grammatical subject of the sentence ("The poem") is no longer the real actor. Indeed, in the last version, the real actor has been deleted from the sentence altogether. These two versions exhibit what is known as passive construction (and the verb is said to be in the passive voice).

Traditional wisdom advises writers to prefer active constructions (just as it advises them to prefer concrete nouns). In this case, too, traditional wisdom is right—most of the time. For passive construction can muddle a perfectly clear idea: "There has been a displacement of goals" is one way to avoid saying, "We changed our minds." But there are also perfectly valid reasons for using passive structures.

The underlying principle is one of emphasis. To transform the sentence is to shift the emphasis from ''Coleridge'' (the real actor) to ''the poem.'' Since the intended emphasis of a sentence is usually on the real actor, active construction ordinarily puts the emphasis where it belongs. Reading is easier, moreover, when the grammatical structure (subject + verb) matches the real structure (actor + action).

Passive construction can be used to obtain a desired word order. Passive construction can be used to shift the emphasis away from whoever did it and toward what was done. The passive is commonly used, for example, in journalistic openings to get the key phrase right at the beginning of the first sentence:

A ''state of emergency'' was proclaimed Sunday by Gov. Romero, who is asking federal officials to declare a disaster zone.

Thus the key phrases, which tell what was done, are in the emphatic positions at the beginning and end of the sentence.

The passive is also commonly used in bureaucratese to avoid responsibility; for example,

The president made a mistake.

A mistake was made.

(In proper bureaucratese, a milder word, such as ''misstatement,'' would also be substituted for ''mistake.'')

This same passive construction can be put to good use when you have to criticize an action. Suppose your draft reads,

You made a mistake and you should do something about it.

If you are more concerned with preventing future mistakes than with assigning blame, you might transform that sentence into a passive construction:

A mistake was made and something should be done about it.

The second version is weaker. The emphasis is on the mistake, not on the person who made it. As a result, that person is less likely to respond defensively. Thus the purpose is more likely to be achieved. (If your actual purpose is to assign blame, however, the first version is preferable.)

A good rule of thumb is use active constructions—except when you have a good reason not to. Or, to put it the other way round, use the passive only when you have a reason to. More important, remember the underlying principle that, all else being equal, a sentence is clearest and easiest to read when the verbal structure of the sentence matches the actual structure of the idea, when the real agent is its grammatical subject and when the action is its verb. As will be demonstrated below, however, writers often should use other structures to create emphasis and to improve the flow from one sentence to the next, as well as for various other reasons.

Building with Modifiers

Reduced to its basics, an ordinary declarative English sentence can be just two, three, or four words:

They huddled.

He loves her.

She licked her lips.

Such a sentence is called a kernel sentence. If a kernel sentence becomes the basis for a more complex sentence, it is called the main or independent clause. However much more a sentence may convey, the basic information is usually represented by the nouns and verbs of the main clause. That is why nouns and verbs are so important.

But from another point of view, the words which modify the meanings of nouns and verbs are even more important. Consider, for example, what William Faulkner adds to "they huddled":

Calico-coated, small-bodied, with delicate legs and pink faces in which their mismatched eyes rolled wild and subdued, they huddled, gaudy, motionless and alert, wild as deer, deadly as rattlesnakes, quiet as doves.

The basic meaning of this sentence is "they huddled." All the words that precede this clause just describe "they." And all the words that follow just describe how they "huddled."

Looking at Faulkner's sentence, one can understand the sense in which the basic or kernel sentence—the main clause—serves as the base on which meaning rises. The modifiers which Faulkner has added qualify and particularize the basic information of "they huddled." The modifiers modify and add to the basic meaning of the sentence; what they communicate can often be more important than that basic information.

The following sentence comes from an article in *Fortune*:

Yet another source of instability in the Middle East is the resurgence of Islamic fundamentalism, itself partly a reaction against alien intrusions and the pressures of modernization.

DAVID B. TINNIN

The main clause, which begins the sentence, restates common knowledge. Typical readers of *Fortune* are well-informed corporate managers, and the idea that a resurgence of Islamic fundamentalism was a destabilizing factor in the Middle East had appeared frequently in the daily press at the time. What might have been news to *Fortune*'s readers is found in the long modifier that follows. The important information in the sentence is that the resurgence of Islamic fundamentalism is not just a religious phenomenon but also a reaction against sociopolitical and economic changes that have been imposed on the peoples of the Middle East. Grammatically, the sentence could well have ended with "fundamentalism." Had it done so, however, the nature of the resurgence might have been misunderstood by many readers.

This sort of sentence is called cumulative because modifiers are added on, or accumulate, after the main clause and refer back to it. You may be able to improve sentences in your drafts by adding cumulative modifiers. Adding such modifiers can affect more than your sentence structure; it often adds information, usually specifics, that were not in the original draft. Here are three cumulative sentences written by technology students:

> Connect the timing light to the battery posts, red lead to the
> positive, black lead to the negative.

> Lay the two grill pieces onto the heating element, placing the lip
> on the underside of the element.

> Energy is the ability to do work, to exert forces to move matter.

In the first two sentences, the cumulative modifiers add detailed information that will help readers follow the instructions. In the third sentence a cumulative modifier unobtrusively adds a brief definition for readers who may not know the technical meaning of the term *work* as used in physics. These sentences would not be "wrong" without the cumulative modifiers, but they are better with them.

Similarly, there is nothing wrong with the following paragraph:

> There was a stove in the shed and many shelves covered with cans,
> jars and bottles. Why would a man who coughed constantly spend all
> his days breathing fumes? At the time, such questions were not asked
> as often as they are now. Outside several old men sat gossiping,
> and some of these old men coughed all the time. The fact is they
> were dying of what was called "the foundry disease." They had
> worked all their lives at the foundry, and now they sat coughing.

But here is how Alice Munro actually wrote it:

> There was a stove in the shed and many rough shelves covered
> with cans of paint and varnish, shellac and turpentine, jars of soaking

brushes and also some dark sticky bottles of cough medicine. Why would a man who coughed constantly, whose lungs took a whiff of gas in the War (called in Rose's earliest childhood, not the first, but the last War) spend all his days breathing fumes of paint and turpentine? At the time, such questions were not asked as often as they are now. On the bench, outside Flo's store, several old men sat gossiping, drowsing in the warm weather, and some of these old men coughed all the time too. The fact is they were dying, slowly and discreetly, of what was called, without any particular sense of grievance, "the foundry disease." They had worked all their lives at the foundry in town, and now they sat still, with their wasted yellow faces, coughing, chuckling, drifting into aimless obscenity on the subject of women walking by, or any young girl on a bicycle.

The first version was created by removing modifiers. Removing the modifiers meant removing the details that give the description life and texture. Adding details, especially in the form of cumulative modifiers, can give texture to your writing.

The relationships among the parts of a cumulative sentence can be usefully analyzed according to level of generality, just as paragraphs were so analyzed in Chapter 3. The main clause is the most general. Each modifier is more particular than whatever it modifies. Thus if we label the main clause as level 1, whatever modifies it becomes level 2. Whatever modifies a modifier of the main clause becomes level 3. And so on, like this:

1 The jockeys sat bowed and relaxed,
    2 moving a little at the waist with the movement of their horses.

KATHERINE ANNE PORTER

1 They regarded me silently,
    2 Brother Jack with a smile that went no deeper than his lips,
        3 his head cocked to one side,
        3 studying me with his penetrating eyes;
    2 the other blank-faced,
        3 looking out of eyes that were meant to reveal nothing and to stir profound uncertainty.

RALPH ELLISON

1 He could sail for hours,
    2 searching the blanched grasses below him with his telescopic eyes,
    2 gaining height against the wind,

2 descending in mile-long, gently declining swoops when he
  curved and rode back,
2 never beating a wing.

WALTER VAN TILBURG CLARK

1 Joad's lips stretched tight over his long teeth a moment, and
1 he licked his lips,
   2 like a dog,
      3 two licks
         4 one in each direction from the middle.

JOHN STEINBECK

Each of these sentences could have ended after the main clause (level 1). Written by inexperienced writers, they probably would have. In Ralph Ellison's place, for example, an inexperienced writer probably would have produced something like this:

    Brother Jack and the other man regarded me silently.

That is not a bad sentence, but it offers the reader so much less than Ellison's.

The cumulative sentence, with modifiers added after the main clause, is important in all kinds of modern prose. It is especially important in description and narration, which is why so many of the cited examples come from works of fiction. The details that accumulate behind the main clause of a cumulative sentence provide readers with much additional information. Thus cumulative sentences allow writers to follow the dictum, "Show, don't tell." Faulkner's "they huddled" tells what they did, but the modifiers show them huddling.

The additions, as Faulkner's sentence indicates, can be added before as well as after the main clause. Thus, in the same *Fortune* article cited above, Tinnin writes, for example,

> Amid war, threats of war, and the drama of peace negotiations, relatively little attention has been paid to Israel's economic problems.

As in the other sentence, Tinnin is turning readers' attention toward the economic basis for events, but here he does so by adding the modifiers before the main clause. The preliminary modification throws readers attention forward toward the main clause and explains why "relatively little attention has been paid to Israel's economic problems."

Cumulative sentences are also usually easier to read than other sentences of equal length and complexity. Modifiers that follow the main clause (or whatever they modify) do not tax reader's shortterm memory very much. The following sentence is extremely hard to read:

Those who are appalled by the prospect of living in a universe which, for the first time in several centuries, has ceased to seem comprehensible may be somewhat reassured by the reminder that it is only the novelty of the modern instances which is disturbing and that they have all along been living with other irresolvable paradoxes which did not trouble them simply because they had been for so long accepted.

JOSEPH WOOD KRUTCH

Rephrased with cumulative modifiers, however, it is somewhat easier:

Certain people, who are appalled by the prospect of living in a universe which, for the first time in several centuries, has ceased to seem comprehensible, may be somewhat reassured if reminded of the fact that what is disturbing is only the novelty of the modern instances, that they have all along been living with other irresolvable paradoxes, which have not troubled them simply because they had been for so long accepted.

Cumulative sentences are easily practiced, and the practice of cumulative sentences has two virtues. One is that, with practice, cumulative sentences will come to seem "natural" (if they do not already); and once they seem "natural" to a writer, they start appearing in drafts, often quite without conscious effort.

The other virtue of cumulative sentences is that they often help writers discover the details, qualifications, and explanations that have been left out of their drafts. A writer who has drafted the main clause, "he could sail for hours," can articulate the details of "how he sailed" by adding modifiers to create a cumulative sentence. A writer who has drafted the main clause, "he licked his lips," might well discover "like a dog" if required to generate a cumulative sentence.

In other words, a writer can work on the level of meaning and ask, "To what extent is this true?" or "Have I shown this in sufficient detail?" The answers to those questions will generate the qualifications and details, which can then be added to the basic sentence. Or a writer can work on the level of grammar and ask, "What would happen if I tried to expand this sentence into a cumulative sentence?" Either way, writers have a good chance of discovering additions that can turn ordinary prose into more sophisticated and "meaning-full" writing. Professor Francis Christensen, who initiated and popularized instruction in the cumulative sentence, put it this way.

The additions stay with the same idea, probing its bearings and implications, exemplifying it or seeking an analogy or metaphor for it, or reducing it to details. Thus the mere form of the sentence generates ideas. It serves the needs of both the writer and the reader, the writer by compelling him to examine his thought, the reader by letting him into the writer's thought.

Note that Christensen's first and third sentences are cumulative. (For a student's assertion of the virtues of cumulative sentences, see pages 410–11.)

Next time you revise a draft, see if you can improve it with cumulative sentences. The best revisions will probably come when you do so by adding details that were not in the original draft. But you can also do it by combining two draft sentences, transforming one into a cumulative modifier and then adding it to the other.

Combining Sentences

```
Jane Thomas, the well-known editor, works hard at her chosen
profession.

For the seventeenth time, the dedicated writer edited the near-
perfect manuscript.
```

Logically, each of these complex sentences may be seen as a combination of a number of kernel sentences:

```
Jane Thomas is an editor.
The editor is well-known.
Jane Thomas works hard.
Jane Thomas works at her profession.
Her profession is chosen.

The writer is dedicated.
The writer edited for the seventeenth time.
The writer edited the manuscript.
The manuscript is near-perfect.
```

The type of grammar that describes how kernel sentences can be transformed into complex sentences is called transformational grammar. Although writers do not need to know the rules of transformation grammars, an understanding of the basic principle of such grammars can help you to improve your style and your ability to handle problems of emphasis within sentences. You can use this basic principle—that a complex sentence may be seen as a combination of kernel sentences—for at least three purposes:

1. To create complex sentences which indicate the relationships among ideas and, in particular, to subordinate secondary ideas.

2. To rephrase sentences for emphasis or to avoid awkward structures.

3. To transform passive constructions into active ones (and vice versa).

Although they are usually harder to read, complex sentences say more than do the equivalent kernel sentences. Each kernel sentence represents a single statement; but two kernel sentences combined represent two simple statements and the relationship between them. Sometimes the simple juxtaposition of the two meanings makes clear their relationship; other times the juxtaposition forces the writer to insert a connecting word to specify the relationship. In either case, the relationship between the two simple meanings can be the most important information in the complex sentence:

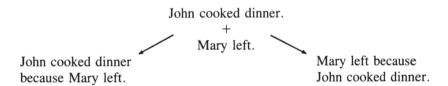

John cooked dinner.
+
Mary left.

John cooked dinner because Mary left.

Mary left because John cooked dinner.

Even where the relationship is fairly evident, the combination helps the readers to grasp it:

Many professors find my sentence structure to be somewhat elementary for a fourth-year student.

+

I use two short sentences when a longer, more complex amalgamation of the two would result in a more sophisticated version.

↓

Many professors find my sentence structure to be somewhat elementary for a fourth-year student because I use two short sentences when a longer, more complex amalgamation of the two would result in a more sophisticated version.

Does Jane Thomas work hard because she got to choose her profession or because she is a well-known editor (or despite the fact that she is a well-known editor)?

Because she works at her chosen profession, the well-known editor, Jane Thomas, works hard.

Because she is a well-known editor, Jane Thomas works hard at her chosen profession.

Although she is a well-known editor, Jane Thomas works hard at her chosen profession.

Consider the following excerpts from student writings in their original versions and as they might be revised by combining sentences. (In some cases the revision has also been tightened just a bit by deletion or substitution.)

Fort Nelson is a small town that is fairly isolated from other communities. It is surrounded by a beautiful green forest. There are two ways to get to Fort Nelson, one is by plane and the other is by the Alaska Highway. Most people prefer the plane rather than having to drive almost three hundred miles along a winding, dusty, unpaved road to get to Fort Nelson.

There are two ways to get to Fort Nelson, a small, fairly isolated community surrounded by a beautiful green forest: one is by plane and the other is by the Alaska Highway. Most people prefer the plane rather than having to drive almost three hundred miles along a winding, dusty, unpaved road.

The place where I grew up had no name and was not a community in any true sense of the word. It was just a few houses and a gas station that developed along a strip of the island highway between Ladysmith and Nanaimo. The people who lived there had little in common except location.

The place that I grew up in had no name. It was just a few houses and a gas station that developed along a strip of the island highway between Ladysmith and Nanaimo. It was not a community in any true sense of the word. The people who lived there had little in common except location.

Note how the recombination of the original meanings not only changes the sentence structure and style, but also subordinates certain information and thereby changes the emphasis. In the first example, the isolation of Fort Nelson is emphasized by subordinating ''surrounded by a beautiful green forest'' and focusing on how hard it is to get there. In the second example, the statement with the highest level of generality was incorporated into the first sentence to provide a framework for the paragraph. Although the remaining two sentences also could have been combined, this was not done because the separate sentences seem to create a more appropriate tone.

Revising Awkward Sentences

We call a sentence awkward when we know it does not read easily but have difficulty explaining why. Sometimes such sentences are ambiguous or violate idiomatic usage. More often the way the parts of the sentence are arranged overloads readers' short-term memories, usually because some important bit of information does not come until near the end.

```
This large current density suggests several lines of application,
miniaturization of components, very high power levels, or--perhaps
most interesting--a means of attaining the high "information
rates" required in electronic devices ranging from fast
oscilloscopes to compact X-ray machines for studying high speed
phenomena, to the electrical engineer.
```

This sentence is hard to read, but not just because it is long. Right after "application," comes an ambiguity: is "miniaturization" one of the "lines of application" or is it something else suggested by the current density? To make sense of the last phrase, moreover, readers must relate "to the engineer" all the way back to "suggests." Moving the last phrase and punctuating to remove the ambiguity makes this sentence easier to read:

> To the electrical engineer, this large current density suggests several lines of application: miniaturization of components, very high power levels, or—perhaps most interesting—a means of attaining the high "information rates" required in electronic devices ranging from fast oscilloscopes to compact X-ray machines for studying high speed phenomena.

There is still a lot of information in one sentence. But the colon, by signaling a list, removes the ambiguity. And everything readers need to frame the detailed information on the list now precedes it.

Here is another awkward sentence, carefully crafted to give readers all framing information as late as possible, thus overloading short-term memory and making it hard for readers to focus:

```
If what going to a clearly not very adequately staffed school really
means is little appreciated, we should be concerned.
```

If we bring the framing information forward, we end up with a longer, but much more readable sentence:

> We should be concerned if there is little appreciation for what it really means to go to a school that is clearly not very adequately staffed.

Generating Alternatives

This type of revision has two basic steps: first, you break the original passage or sentence down into kernel or near-kernel sentences; second, you recombine these elementary units in various ways until you discover a version that creates the desired effects. Consider the following sentence:

> It was a small community, mainly French; but it had a bit of international flavour because various ethnic groups had settled in the area.

To generate stylistic alternatives, first break the sentence down into kernel or near-kernel sentences, like this?

> It was a community.
>
> It was small.
>
> It was mainly French.
>
> It had a bit of international flavour.
>
> Various ethnic groups had settled in the area.

Then recombine the kernels in various ways, and choose the version with the desired emphasis.

In principle, there are three distinct ways to build a complex sentence after one has chosen a main clause: information can be embedded in the middle of that clause, added to the beginning, or added to the end. If the central point of the sentence is to be "it had a bit of international flavour," one could add the rest of the information at either end:

> A small, mainly French community, it had a bit of international flavour because various ethnic groups had settled in the area.

Likewise, if the central point is to be "the community was small":

> Although it had a bit of international flavour because various ethnic groups had settled in the area, the community was small and mainly French.

Other possibilities include these variants:

> It was a small, mainly French community, which had a bit of international flavour because various ethnic groups had settled in the area.
>
> Although it was mainly French, the small community had a bit of an international flavour because various ethnic groups had settled in the area.

Moving "mainly French" to a position before "community" or coordinate with "small" makes the sentence easier to read. Other recombinations primarily change the emphasis of the sentence. (Note that the grammatical subordination of a clause has an effect similar to reordering; that is because, logically, it changes the order of importance.)

Out of context, it is impossible to say which of the four revised versions would be preferable. Choosing the best version means choosing the one which

1. Is as readable as possible.
2. Indicates the correct relationship among the ideas.
3. Provides the desired emphasis.
4. Fits smoothly into the larger passage which contains it.

Consider the first revised version in the following passage:

> I grew up in a town in northern Quebec. Although it had a bit of international flavour because various ethnic groups had settled in the area, the community was small and mainly French. There were immigrants from almost every country in eastern Europe and a few from Asia, too.

The part of the second sentence which repeats meanings from the first is at the end (community = town; Quebec = mainly French). The first part of the second sentence, on the other hand, matches the meanings which are to follow in the third. Thus the passage is a bit awkward and harder to read than it need be. Another variant produces a better fit.

> I grew up in a town in northern Quebec. A small, mainly French community, it had a bit of international flavour because various ethnic groups had settled in the area. There were immigrants from almost every country in eastern Europe and a few from Asia, too.

The term "awkward" is an awkwardly vague concept. Generally, it means that the person who describes a passage as "awkward" knows there is something wrong but does not have the time to, or cannot, figure out just what is wrong with the passage. Simply put, an awkward sentence is hard to read, often because of its structure, i.e., because of the way words are combined in that sentence. In such a case, reordering the sentence can solve the problem. (In other cases, the problem may be word choice; then the solution is to change the words.)

Balance and Parallelism

Common in public oratory and aphorism, the balanced sentence is a special device to be used on special occasions. A balanced sentence has a "ring" that makes it memorable. It stands out. Parallel structures and verbal repetitions are juxtaposed—like weights on a balance scale. Readers feel the stylistic symmetry and anticipate a symmetry of meaning. When you deliver that symmetry—whether with parallel ideas or with antithetical ideas—the sentence has impact.

Politicians often make use of balanced sentences. U.S. President John F. Kennedy is perhaps best remembered for this one:

> And so my fellow Americans, ask not what your country can do for you; ask what you can do for your country.

Here the balance point is the semicolon, and the beginning of each of the parallel structures is marked by the repetition of "ask." The symmetry is antithetical: Kennedy was contrasting two attitudes. The antithesis is marked by the "not," and the contrasted elements—"you" and "your country"—exchange positions.

Here are some other balanced sentences from political speeches:

> The test of our progress is not whether we add more to the abundance of those who have much; it is whether we provide enough for those who have too little.
>
> FRANKLIN ROOSEVELT

> Let us never negotiate out of fear, but let us never fear to negotiate.
>
> JOHN KENNEDY

> Extremism in the defense of Liberty is no vice; and . . . moderation in the pursuit of Justice is no virtue.
>
> BARRY GOLDWATER

Balanced sentences have been used for millennia, in verse as well as prose, to serve a variety of purposes. Here are some more examples:

> Many are called but few are chosen.
>
> MATTHEW XXII:14

> Where there's marriage without love, there will be love without marriage.
>
> BENJAMIN FRANKLIN

> Parting is all we know of heaven, And all we need of hell.
>
> EMILY DICKINSON

The effect of a balanced sentence can most easily be understood by rewriting it to express the same ideas without the verbal repetitions or parallel structures. Suppose Franklin had written this:

Where marriage occurs without love, there will also be extramarital sex.

The idea remains the same, but the balance is gone—and so is the impact. Likewise, Kennedy's statement would not be so well remembered had it been composed thusly:

And so my fellow Americans, do not inquire how your government can serve you; instead ask what help your country needs.

A balanced sentence sometimes turns on a semicolon or comma.

The spoken word dies; the written letter remains.
When the going gets tough, the tough get going.

Other times, a coordinating conjunction is the fulcrum.

Hope for the best and prepare for the worst.

Occasionally, like other types of parallelism, balance may be marked by certain pairs of conjunctions: *both . . . and, either . . . or, neither . . . nor, as . . . as, not only . . . but, so . . . as.*

As a vessel is known by the sound, whether it be cracked or not, so men are provided by their speeches, whether they be wise or foolish.

Demosthenes

The general principle of parallelism, which underlies the balanced sentence, may also be used to structure phrases or clauses within a sentence— and it may be reiterated—as in these examples:

There was a time also when in the first fine flush of laundries and bakeries, milk deliveries and canned goods, ready-made clothes and dry-cleaning, it did look as if American life was being enormously simplified.

Margaret Mead

He had come not to make a scandal but to avoid it; not to raise a danger but to make one plain; not to oppose a truth but to offer it.

Giorgio de Santillana

Similarly, the same principle may be applied to larger units, such as sentences within a paragraph.

> In your statement you assert that our actions, even though peaceful, must be condemned because they precipitate violence. But is this a logical assertion? Isn't this like condemning a robbed man because his possession of money precipitated the evil act of robbery? Isn't this like condemning Socrates because his unswerving commitment to truth and his philosophical inquiries precipitated the act of a misguided populace in which they made him drink hemlock. Isn't this like condemning Jesus because his unique God-consciousness and never-ceasing devotion to God's will precipitated the evil act of crucifixion? We must come to see that, as the federal courts have consistently affirmed, it is wrong to urge the individual to cease his efforts to gain his basic constitutional rights because the quest may precipitate violence. Society must protect the robbed and punish the robber.
>
> MARTIN LUTHER KING

(For an analysis of this passage from King's "Letter from Birmingham Jail," see page 332.)

Parallelism is a powerful device, but it should be used with care. A balanced sentence in the wrong place can overly emphasize a minor point. You may also be tempted to crimp your intended meaning to fit a stylistic mold. The following sentence could be revised for sharper parallelism.

> The view that neurosis is a severe reaction to human trouble is as revolutionary in its implications for social practice as it is daring in formulation.
>
> JEROME BRUNER

Deleting the phrase, "for social practice," would improve the parallelism and enhance the impact; it would also delete part of what Bruner wanted to communicate. Once you lead readers to expect parallelism—as by using one of the pairs of conjunctions just listed above—you have made a commitment. If you lead readers to anticipate parallelism and then do not deliver, you may distort your intended meaning, disrupt their reading, and project an irresponsible or incompetent persona.

When you first study the balanced sentence, parallelism, or any new stylistic device, you may be tempted to overuse it. Remember, however, the reasons for studying sentence structure. It is not that certain sentence constructions are intrinsically good or bad. It is that competent writers know how to generate and consider alternative versions of the sentences they draft—and then choose the ones that best serve their creative and communicative purposes.

Table 5.3   Revision Heuristic: Sentence Structure*

Is each sentence as "tight" as possible? Can you shorten any sentences, either by deletion or by substitution, without losing any meaning that matters?

Does each sentence have the emphasis you want? Does any sentence sound "awkward"? Have you dangled any modifiers? Should any sentences be rearranged?

Is the grammatical subject of your sentences usually the real agent? Is the verb usually the real action? When this is not so, is there a good reason?

Are there any undesirable passive constructions? Any undesirable active constructions?

Is each sentence phrased in such a way as to flow smoothly out of the preceding sentence and into the following sentence?

Is the style "choppy"? If so, should that be solved by generating cumulative modifiers or by combining sentences?

Is each sentence phrased in such a way as to accurately indicate the interrelationships among the meanings it contains? Would the relationships among meanings be more clear if certain sentences were combined?

Have you avoided faulty parallelism? Have you used parallelism effectively for emphasis?

Remember: This is only a list of suggested questions. Choose from it only those questions that match your individual needs. Rephrase them more specifically, if possible, to focus your attention on your own particular weak points. Add any questions you need. Use this list to continue developing your own revision heuristic (see pages 133–35). And do not rely on this list alone: read the sections of the text that explain the concepts behind the questions.

You should, therefore, develop your ability to expand sentences—for example, along the lines suggested by the model of the cumulative sentence. You should also develop your ability to combine sentences, especially when a passage is choppy because it uses many short sentences or when relationships among ideas are not clearly indicated. You should develop your ability to deconstruct and reconstruct sentences in order to generate alternative versions of problematic sentences. You should develop your ability to transform sentences from one construction to another—for example, from passive to active, and vice versa. And you should develop your ability to use balanced sentences and other parallel structures when and where they will enhance the effect of your writing.

The questions in Table 5.3 should help call your attention to the sentence structure of your drafts. Add to your own revision heuristic any questions that pinpoint your own stylistic weaknesses.

As your ability to observe, think, and feel grows, you are likely to find yourself needing not only a better vocabulary, but also a greater variety of complex sentence structures to communicate the full subtlety of those observations, thoughts, and feelings. Similarly, although to a lesser extent, as you internalize a greater variety of complex sentence structures, you may be able to think and feel more subtly. Developing your style will help you communicate. It may also do more than that.

EXERCISE

1. Find some choppy passages in your own writings. Generate cumulative modifiers and combine sentences to eliminate the choppiness.

2. Explain, then fix, the following awkwardnesses:

No sharp distinction between a temporary halt and the final goal can be made, however.

An important new type, the upside-down spider which hangs from the filaments with tooth tarsal claws, arose thus.

Because of these papers (though few and far between), I know that I am capable of writing a worthwhile paper given the time I need. A set procedure outlining specific steps for producing this type of paper will help me achieve this each time.

I usually begin with writing the introduction—after much thought and reading and dreaming—and as the paper's direction becomes apparent, I jot down notes in minuscule writing in the margins that serve as reminders of where I want to go and what I want to say when I get there.

God's goodness is never a consideration with Satan and his rebels, as they are blind to what in others they themselves lack.

One person in five shows no alpha rhythm at all—only small, complex, irregular pulsations from all parts of the brain. In one in five also the alpha rhythms go on even when the eyes are open.

We have established a tentative classification of brain types in human beings on the basis of such personal differences. This system indicates differences in ways of thinking, rather than the relative success of people's thinking, as "intelligence tests" do.

3. Find some awkward sentences in your own writings (perhaps some which have been marked "AWK" by teachers in your past). Rearrange them to see if you can eliminate the awkwardness. Try this activity in a small group, and see if you can analyze and modify other writers' awkward sentences and passages more easily than your own.

4. Choose some good sentences you wrote. Rewrite them to shift the emphasis. (It may help to imagine new contexts that require new emphases.)

5. Search your writings for unnecessary passive constructions. Try to figure out why you used them. Transform them into active constructions.

6. Here are some rules commonly given to inexperienced writers. Evaluate three in terms of the writer's persona and readers' needs or expectations. Rewrite them in those terms.

a. Avoid the passive.

b. Put statements in positive form.

c. Omit needless words.

d. Keep related words together.

e. Place the emphatic words at the end of the sentence.

f. Express coordinate ideas in parallel form.

7. Add cumulative modifiers to the following kernel sentences, making up details as your imagination suggests:

The student sat down to start writing the assignment.

The professor burst into the room.

The waves thundered against the rocks.

Life is a highway.

The winger raced down the ice.

The dancer watched the rain.

Physicists define stress quite differently.

Form

Matter $\times$ *Form* $\longrightarrow$ ***Substance***

ARISTOTLE

C·H·A·P·T·E·R 6

Seeing and Writing

We can never break out of the circle of language and seize the object barehanded, as it were, or without some ideational operation.

RICHARD WEAVER

Even if any given terminology is a reflection *of reality, by its very nature as a terminology it must be a* selection *of reality; and to this extent it must also function as a* deflection *of reality.*

KENNETH BURKE

The community that genuine writing creates is one not only of ideas and attitudes, but of fundamental modes of perception, thought and feeling. . . . Experience, subtle shapechanger, is given form only by this or that set of conceptual habits, and each set of habits has its own patterns of linguistic expression, its own community.

HANS GUTH

G OOD writing begins with perceptive observation. And your purpose in writing is always, in at least one sense, to get readers to "see it your way." So this chapter begins "the grammar of perception." Used together with the invention techniques discussed in Chapter 2, an understanding of the complexities of human perception should help you become a more perceptive observer and a more sensitive writer. Because it is so important in academic and professional writing, you should also learn what it means to observe and write objectively.

The second section of this chapter is about description, a mode commonly used for reporting and persuading as well as in expressive writing. The main task for a descriptive writer is to discover, select, arrange, and verbalize information in order to re-create it for readers. This remains the case whether you are writing a literary description to evoke the grandeur of a storm in the mountains, a scientific description of the equipment used in an experiment, or a commercial description of a product you wish to sell. Directly or indirectly, you have experienced something your readers have not, and your immediate purpose is to communicate that experience.

The third section of the chapter is about narrative. Narration, like description, can be used for various purposes. It may be a story, as when you tell what happened the first time you drove a tractor. It may be part of a laboratory report, in which you tell what happened as you did the experiment. It may be a newspaper article, which tells what happened yesterday in San Juan, Puerto Rico. It may be a parable, a mythical story told to make a moral point.

Description rarely stands alone; descriptive passages are usually parts of longer pieces of writing that serve larger purposes. Narrative, too, can be subordinated, as when one tells a story to exemplify a point. This chapter closes with a section on using descriptive and narrative writing to serve other purposes, especially exemplification. These are important techniques for clarifying and convincing—for getting your readers to see your point clearly and to "see it your way."

Perception and Re-presentation _____

We don't take in the world like a camera or a set of recording devices. The mind is an agent, not a passive receiver; experience isn't poured into it. The active mind is a composer and everything we respond to, we compose.
ANN BERTHOFF

You can't depend on your eyes when your imagination is out of focus.
MARK TWAIN

In order to write about something, you must know about it. The quality of a piece of writing depends to a significant extent on the quality of the information it presents. The good writer is often the perceptive observer.

But observation is not simple, at least not for human beings. We very often look at something and fail to "see" it in any detail, especially if it is familiar. Different people, moreover, can look at (or feel, taste, smell, or hear) the same phenomenon quite differently. Indeed, the very purpose of a piece of writing is often to get other people to "see it your way." And as was emphasized in Chapter 5, how we name things when we verbalize our observations can significantly influence how we—and our readers—will perceive them.

Every academic or professional discipline demands the ability to observe rigorously for detail and to distinguish between relevant and irrelevant details. A rule generally applied to the writing done in academic and professional contexts is that you may hold any opinion you like—*if* you can support it with facts (see pages 124–29). Although the rule is occasionally broken by teachers, editors, and bosses who are biased in favor of their own opinions, it remains a generally accepted rule which will be enforced (especially if your opinions are unpopular). And all "facts" are observations, whether your own or someone else's.

Because observation is such a crucial aspect of the writing process, because it so greatly constrains what gets written and how, and because one of the most basic rules of academic and professional writing requires rigorous observation, it is useful for writers to understand how people perceive—to understand that *we compose our perceptions*, using a process in many ways parallel to that by which we compose writing. Understanding how people perceive also helps writers understand how *readers recompose* as they read (see page 157). And language—how we name as we perceive—matters because it exerts a critical influence on how both writers and readers compose their perceptions.

To understand human perception one must first realize that reality is much more detailed and complex than our observations of it. At this very instant, your eyes are picking up and transmitting to your brain thousands of "bits" of information. Since it would be impossible for a human mind to be conscious of that many "bits" of information, you unconsciously select those that seem most significant, because they form patterns. Then, still preconsciously, you compose those patterns into images, sounds, smells, tastes, and feelings.

This human ability to perceive meaningful patterns instead of individual stimuli is crucially important. It prevents us from being overwhelmed by masses of trivial information. It allows us to focus on what matters (or seems to matter) while ignoring what does not matter. Because there are many potential patterns in a batch of stimuli, different people will "see" different patterns. Even after a simple traffic accident, bystanders often give contradictory reports. Considering the nature and complexity of our perceptual processes, it is perhaps more amazing that people often agree about "what happened."

The terms we use to name things and events create conceptual contexts that influence, even shape our perceptions. A set of lines may mean nothing at all, or have various meanings for various people—until they are placed in context by being described. In such cases, to *de*-scribe is also to *circum*-scribe, or at least to constrain, perceptions. Figure 6.1, for example, usually does not signify much to most people. When *described* as a picture of a man wearing a bowtie who stood too close to an elevator door, however, it suddenly focuses into a meaningful perception.

If you stare at Figure 6.2 long enough, perhaps with a little help from your friends, you will probably see the image of a bearded man who resembles a late-medieval representation of Jesus Christ. The top border of the photograph cuts across his brow, his eyes, hair, beard, and the outline of his nose are dark areas; his cheeks, mouth, and lower lip are white. Although a few people

Figure 6.1 Man with bowtie.

see this Christ figure immediately and a few others never manage to perceive it, most people have to study the photograph for some time *under the influence of a verbal description* before the image emerges. Thus the words in this paragraph may have persuaded you to compose a mass of dark and light shapes into a image of Christ.

The differences in perception among people who view this photo have nothing whatsoever to do with eyesight. The retinal images and the optic nerve impulses to the brain are effectively the same for everyone with normal (or corrected) eyesight who looks at the photograph. To see the Christ figure, however, takes conceptualization—or to use another word, *imagination* (image–ination)—which can be significantly influenced by language. Paradoxically, the concept must be brought to mind *before* the image can be seen or named.

In Figure 6.3, a photograph of a dalmatian, most of the halftones have been lost (as in moonlight). And yet one can distinguish the spots that make up the dog's back from the similar spots in the background. A few of the

Figure 6.2 Christ-in-the-clouds.

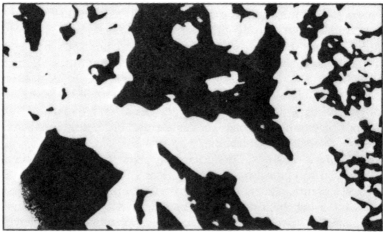

Figure 6.3 Dalmatian as if by moonlight.

lines that "outline" the dog do exist objectively in the picture, but most of them must be supplied by the perceiver. And in order to do that, the perceiver must have a mental image (i.e., concept) from which to work, must in effect think, "This is a dog." To someone who had never seen a dog or doglike animal, this photograph would be a meaningless blotch of spots (or perhaps something else altogether).

Often, as with this photograph of a dalmatian, the human perceiver must also *fill in* certain aspects of the perception that are not supplied by sensory stimuli. What happens is that *the stimuli trigger a process which locates a concept, and then that concept is used to focus a mass of sensations into a meaningful perception.* What a human being perceives is not determined entirely by sensory stimuli and is therefore not an exact copy of what is really "out there." Neither, however, is it entirely subjective, determined by the perceiver's preconceptions. Instead, a human being's conscious perception is a synthesis of the interaction of sensory stimuli with mental concepts. And that synthesis is significantly influenced by language.

Cognitive scientists disagree about the exact nature of our mental concepts. Some think we store them as abstract schema, much like definitions. Others think we store them as concrete images, much like archetypes or models. At any event, it is clear that, even when we are not thinking verbally, the concepts we use to focus our perceptions have usually themselves been shaped through language.

Since the sensory stimuli come from the real world, and since both our mental concepts and our languages were formed in response to our previous experiences with that same world, human perceptions are usually fairly accurate reflections of reality. Since the mental concepts are to some degree shaped by a person's socialization, including language experiences, however, human perceptions are not exact copies of reality and vary somewhat according to the person's cultural, linguistic, and personal background. The mental "lenses" that focus human perceptions also refract—thus they may reflect reality much in the same sense that a distorting carnival mirror does. An accurate perception is a reflection of reality, but it is also a selection—and thus inevitably a deflection of whichever aspects of reality are not selected.

Four Ways to Verify Observations

Since good writing is usually based on accurate and perceptive observations, would-be writers will do well to develop their abilities as observers. The various techniques for negative invention (pages 57–77) can help develop those abilities. Particular heuristics for positive invention (pages 78–98) can also develop abilities related to observing the particular circumstances for which they were devised—for example, the Pentad can help one to observe human behavior more insightfully. Perceptiveness can be learned.

However, it is not easy to evaluate one's own observations. Preconceptions and oversights that may have biased the observations are likely to bias the evaluation as well. Indeed, there is a kind of paradox here. In order to decide if one has observed all that is important and relevant, one must somehow see what one is not seeing!

What follows is a heuristic for evaluating the accuracy and fullness of observations. It does not entirely transcend the paradox, but it can help.

1. What preconceptions do I have about whatever I am observing? How do they influence my selection of "facts"? Is my observation suspiciously consistent with my ideas? If I specifically look for inconsistencies, can I find any? Does what I observe conflict with what I believe? If so, are my observations faulty or do I need to modify my beliefs? (See Exercise 2, page 271.)

2. What have I excluded? To which details have I (consciously or preconsciously) chosen not to pay attention?

3. If I "look again"—perhaps more carefully or more closely (or more widely) or from a distinct perspective or "through" a different heuristic— what do I observe that is different? How important is that difference?

4. Does my observation give me the information I need? How useful is it? How well does it serve my purposes (and the purposes of my prospective readers)?

Thus one checks for (1) *consistency* between particular observations and ideas, beliefs, and theories; (2) *exclusions*, what may have been overlooked or left out; (3) *correspondence* among observations made from various perspectives; and (4) *usefulness*, whether the information selected serves the purposes that motivated the observation in the first place.

No observation will ever be absolutely complete. The trick is not to see everything. The trick is to avoid leaving out information that matters (and to avoid distortion). The ultimate test of observations—and of reports written on the basis of those observations—is the fourth, *usefulness*. Except as an exercise, one observes not randomly, but purposively. Observations are made and reports are written to be used. The question is whether the report is accurate and complete *enough* to fulfill its purposes, to give readers the information they need to achieve insight and understanding, to make decisions and act correctly.

Being Objective

In practical terms, *objectivity* often means focusing on the "object" or event being described. It means excluding personal feelings, opinions, and beliefs that reveal more about the writer than about the reality being described. The guiding purpose behind an objective report is this: the readers want to know about what is being described, not about the writer's reaction to what is being described, not about the writer's feelings, opinions, or beliefs. This notion of objectivity became dominant with the growth of modern science. Its original function, during the European Renaissance, was to exclude Christian religious beliefs and preconceptions from scientific investigations.

Objectivity is often confused with neutrality. In practical terms that makes some sense. If one wants to know the truth about a matter being disputed by two or more interested parties, obviously one wants a chief investigator who is not initially biased toward one of those interested parties.

But absolute, pure neutrality is not humanly possible. What we perceive, even on the level of "fact," is not a simple copy of what is "out there." We compose sensory input into meaningful patterns, influenced by our conceptions, stereotypes, and various contexts. Moreover, as David Broder told the U.S. National Press Club in 1979:

All of us know as journalists that what we are mainly engaged in deciding is not what to put in [our reports] but what to leave out. . . . The process of selecting what the reader reads involves not just objective facts but subjective judgments, personal values, ideals and, yes, prejudices.

[In 1959,] Walter Lippmann said: "It is all very well to say that a reporter collects the news and that the news consists of facts. The truth is that in our world the facts are infinitely many, and that no reporter can collect them all, and that no newspaper could print them all—even if they were fit to print—and nobody could read them all. We have to select some facts rather than others, and in doing that, we are using not only our legs but our selective judgment of what is interesting or important or both."

Any report must be based on a *selection* of information, which is inevitably a *rejection* of other information that has been excluded from the report. The honesty of a piece of writing cannot be judged simply by asking if each assertion in the writing is true. No written communication can actually tell "the whole truth" because the whole truth includes masses of trivia that would just confuse the issue. Any report, moreover, must be written in words, and all words have connotations: there are no absolutely neutral words to use (see pages 211–13).

What then is objectivity?

First, objectivity means including all important and relevant information. In order to know what is important and relevant, we must know the purposes of both the writer and the intended readers. Only in terms of those mutual purposes can we decide what information matters. Although writers sometimes hide behind "objectivity" to exclude or disguise their feelings, opinions, or beliefs in contexts where those feelings, opinions, or beliefs are relevant, in many academic, scientific, and professional contexts, writers' feelings and moral beliefs are not important or relevant to objective reports. To judge objectivity, we must always consider the purposes of the writing and ask whether any important and relevant information has been left out or expressed only vaguely.

Second, objectivity means not manipulating. It means not manipulating your readers by presenting information favorable to your own conclusions or interest while excluding unfavorable information; it means giving readers all the information they need to make their own informed judgments. It means not manipulating your choice of words so as to disguise your value judgments. Thus objectivity goes hand in hand with stylistic honesty (see pages 220–23).

Third, being objective means revealing yourself. Since selection and exclusion of information is humanly inevitable, objectivity means revealing the criteria by which you made your selection. It is not dishonest or nonobjective to exclude information from a report or to use words with connotations. An honest, objective writer should exclude all irrelevant information. An honest writer should also choose words with connotations that accurately suggest the implications of whatever is being described. But since human beings inevitably observe from some perspective, being objective means allowing readers to be aware of your perspective and of the prejudices, biases, preconceptions, and interests that might influence it.

Objectivity is not easy. It requires insights not only into your subject but also into yourself. It is based on the Socratic dictum: "Know thyself." Ultimately, if you do not know yourself, you cannot be objective about your subject or fully honest with your readers.

The issue of honesty in writing is complex. Perhaps the most honest policy that writers can follow is to make their purposes and biases explicit so that readers can better judge their selections, exclusions, and emphases. In the words of the psychiatrist Erich Fromm, "Objectivity does not mean detachment, it means respect; that is, the ability not to distort and falsify things, persons, and oneself."

Language, Thought, and Culture

Linguist Edward Sapir argued that "we see and hear and otherwise experience very largely as we do because the language habits of our community predispose certain choices of interpretation." Since 1929 when Sapir made that assertion (later known as the Sapir-Whorf hypothesis), it has been much debated. The debate, however, turns not on whether language influences perception, but on *how* "very largely" it does so. There is little question that our perceptions are influenced by what Sapir called "social reality" and that "language is a guide to 'social reality.' " Language and culture significantly shape our perceptions. Most of our concepts—and especially the abstract concepts we use to understand and contextualize our concrete experiences—are learned, stored, and remembered through words. This is one of the important ways in which we differ from other organisms on this planet. It is also what allows us to adapt flexibly to a variety of environments and situations.

Figure 6.4 was drawn for a psychological experiment and intentionally violates stereotypes that were current at the time. In the experiment, people were shown the picture and then asked to describe it from memory. Very often they remembered seeing the stereotype even though the picture explicitly violates it. For example, many *white* observers remembered the knife as being held by the black man in the picture. As Mark Twain wrote in *A Connecticut*

Figure 6.4 Subway stereotype scene.

Yankee in King Arthur's Court, "You can't depend on your eyes when your imagination is out of focus."

The word *stereotype* was originally a printers' term for a block used to reproduce the same image time and time again. It has come to refer to a preconception that leads people toward the same perception time and time again—even when reality violates that preconception. Usually the word *stereotype* is used only for preconceptions that lead to harmful and erroneous conclusions.

The Horrors of Old Maidenship

Most people could describe the stereotype of the old maid aunt or school teacher and note in detail the particular attitudes and idiosyncracies of these women that love and life seem to have passed by. To be an old maid is something few women have aspired to, and generations of women have feared. To many women, the designation "old maid" has signified failure in the most important aspect of their lives—marriage. Traditionally women have feared and consciously avoided the horrors of old maidship.

An old maid is a woman who remains single considerably beyond the normal marrying age. The term "old maid" can also refer to anyone—including males—who exhibit priggish, finicky, overly "sensible" or sterile behavior. According to the Oxford English

Dictionary, the term first appears in the English language in the seventeenth century, at the same time that the word "spinster" became the legal designation for an unmarried woman. Literally, "old maid" refers to a maid who has grown older. The term "maid," unlike the term "old maid," has no negative connotations, for it refers to either something that is good and pure—such as the Virgin Mary or Joan of Arc—or something that is fresh and unused—such as the maiden voyage of a ship, or a maiden fortress. An old maid is presumably all of these things—unused, good, pure—but she is not fresh. A young maid who fails to marry when she is fresh becomes an old maid. All the qualities so attractive in a young maid apparently cease to be attractive with the onset of age.

"Old Maid" is also the name of a game of cards, still played by adults and children alike. The players sit around a table trading cards, matching pairs, carefully eyeing one another to determine who has the card designated as the "old maid." Eventually one player realizes with horror that he has been stuck with the "old maid" and as a result loses the game. To be stuck with the "old maid," in cards as in life, is obviously not considered an attractive proposition. Traditionally women who were not married by a certain age were likely to remain dependent on their families for the rest of their lives. Fathers and brothers, therefore, carefully calculated their moves, seeking an appropriate match for daughters and sisters, trying to avoid being stuck with an old maid. Women carefully monitored their own moves in order to acquire a suitable husband and avoid being a burden on their families.

In addition to being a burden to the family, an old maid has been considered a burden to society. The term "old maidenish" or "spinsterlike" was often used in Victorian England to refer to a general idleness and lack of moral responsibility. A woman who failed to marry, and therefore did not produce children, was considered negligent in her primary responsibility to society.

There is no term comparable to "old maid" to refer to men who have failed to marry and produce offspring. An old bachelor would hardly be pitied or condemned for his failure to marry. Rather, he might be congratulated or envied for his ability to escape marriage. His life, instead of being considered emotionally sterile, is considered carefree.

For generations the term "old maid" has convinced women that the only alternative to traditional marriage is a lonely and sterile existence. Women now know that they will not necessarily become a burden on their families and society if they do not get married. Women also know they can lead happy and fulfilling lives outside the bonds of marriage. The stereotype of the single woman as an "old

maid" is quickly disappearing, and women now consciously seek
single life rather than fear it.

Mary-Ellen Selby

As Mary-Ellen makes clear, the stereotype of an "old maid" once had a real basis in economic and social relations. Even though women's economic and social situation has changed considerably, the cliché and the stereotype it represents have not yet disappeared from our language, culture, or perceptions—it even survives in a card game played by children.

Human perception, although it has a basis in our hereditary makeup, is significantly shaped by language, education, and culture. We have evolved from instinctive animals, which respond largely by hereditary reflex, into learning animals, who respond more responsively to varied and variable environments. Our language both reflects and influences our perceptions and interpretations of our experiences.

Implications for Writers

The flexible, contextual, and language-influenced nature of human perception has at least five important implications for writers. The first is that you should strive to perceive whatever you are going to write about in various distinct contexts in order to discover as much as possible about it. Remember that your own perceptual habits, concepts, beliefs, and feelings significantly shape and limit your perceptions. Use the techniques discussed in Chapter 2 to broaden—and sharpen—your perceptions (see especially pages 57–77).

Second, remember that your readers do not necessarily have the same educational, cultural, or social backgrounds as you do. To communicate effectively with them, you should try to understand how they see things. In order to achieve stability, groups of people establish important perceptual values as cultural mores, reinforced by language, education, and other kinds of socialization. Use the techniques suggested in Chapter 4 to evaluate your audience.

Third, you should remember that human perceptions are composed in contexts—physical, social, linguistic, and emotional, among others. You have perceived your subject in contexts that make it meaningful for you. Your words should, at least by connotation, re-create enough of these contexts to make your subject meaningful for your readers—to make it *matter* to them.

Fourth, the forms you use to compose your writings also help shape the substance of what you discover and write about your subject. The choice of a form particularly influences the selection and arrangement of material—and thus emphasis. Part II of this textbook is designed to acquaint you with a variety of patterns of arrangement and other forms, so you can choose and use the most appropriate one in each case.

Fifth, remember that, even if you refrain from overtly expressing your opinions, the decisions you make about how to contextualize, what to emphasize, what to deemphasize, and what to leave out reflect your perspectives and biases. Your perceptions, however socialized, are generally functional; but on occasion they distort. Where objectivity is desired, it can be approached only if writers are clear about the bases for their decisions and honest about biases that may have influenced them.

EXERCISE

1. Sometimes when people disagree, they share the same perception but nonetheless have a *difference of opinion* about what it means or what should be done. Often, however, people disagree because of *a difference of perception:* although they are observing the same situation, they do not perceive it the same way. Write a paper about such a difference of perception. Your paper should include a report of each observer's perception and also an analysis explaining how their distinct preconceptions lead them toward distinct perceptions. You may write about a real situation or use characters from literature, cinema, or television. You may also use a situation in which *one* person has two distinct perceptions at two different times.

2. The paradoxes of perception apply to all five senses because they are not "in" the eye, but in the mind.

Perception Experiment 1: Pour a glass of water and take a sip. Then eat an ice cream cone or keep a strong solution of sugar-water in your mouth for one minute. Now that you have established a new taste context, immediately taste the glass of water again.

Perception Experiment 2: Prepare three containers of water: one hot, one lukewarm, and one cold. Place one hand in the hot water and the other in the cold water, and keep them immersed until acclimated (about three minutes). Now that you have established two distinct temperature contexts for your two hands, place both hands simultaneously in the lukewarm water.

If you do these experiments, you may find it difficult—in the second case, probably impossible—to believe the evidence of your senses. You will have perceived the lukewarm water in two distinct temperature contexts, and your mind will probably overrule the resulting contradictory perceptions. What does this demonstrate about human perception—and what implications has it for writers? After doing these experiments, use this experience and these questions to focus a freewriting or a journal entry.

3. Benjamin Lee Whorf was not only a linguist, but also an inspector for an insurance company. The following is one of seven cases in which he asserts that a fire was caused by language habits.

An electric glow heater on the wall was little used and for one workman had the meaning of a convenient coathanger. At night a watchman entered and snapped a switch, which action he verbalized as 'turning on the light.' No light appeared, and this result he verbalized as 'light is burned out.' He could not see the glow of the heater because of the old coat hung on it. Soon the heater ignited the coat, which set fire to the building.

Using this example as a touchstone, write your own short essay on the relationship between language and thought. (You might want to read some essays from Whorf's *Language, Thought and Reality* as well as some critiques of the Sapir-Whorf hypothesis that our perceptions and interpretations of reality are very largely shaped by language.)

4. Write a paper describing a stereotype, showing how it leads to distorted perceptions of reality and to socially harmful behaviors. Consider including a section on the virtues of nonstereotypical preconceptions and generalizations.

Description

A town or a countryside, seen from a distance, is a town or a countryside. But as one draws closer, they are houses, trees, tiles, leaves, grasses, plants, weeds, ants, legs of ants, ad infinitum. All this is enveloped in theme 'countryside.'
BLAISE PASCAL

Images of the world should yield a description that is useful to the viewer and not cluttered by irrelevant information.
HOWARD GARDNER

Purpose, Focus, and Selection

Description is a very common mode. Scientists reporting the observations made during an experiment, a poet reevoking emotions felt while watching a child sleep, a mail-order merchant advertising a commodity—are all describing. Because they serve distinct purposes, these descriptions will be written very differently; but the mode of discourse remains description.

The descriptive writer's main task is the selection and verbal representation of information. You must choose the details that matter—that are important to the purposes you share with your readers—as well as a pattern of arrangement relevant to those mutual purposes. Necessarily, these choices about what to include are also choices about what to exclude. Writers should be careful that what is excluded is not important to themselves or their readers.

Description can be an engineer describing the terrain where an embankment must be built, a novelist describing a farm where the novel will take place, a realtor describing a house and land for sale, a journalist describing a celebrity's birthplace, or a tourist describing a rural scene in a letter to friends back home. That engineer, novelist, realtor, journalist, and tourist may all be describing the very same place. If each is truthful, their descriptions will not contradict each other. But they will certainly include and emphasize different aspects. Because their purposes are widely divergent, they will use distinct principles of selection and patterns of arrangement.

> *Perception Experiment*: On a circle divided into quadrants (like the one below), draw as accurately as you can the dial of an ordinary dial telephone (of the sort that preceded the pushbutton phones). Do so before reading on.

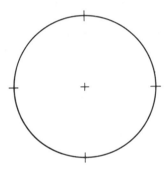

This experiment usually demonstrates two points. The first is that our perception is utilitarian, focused by our purposes. People who have looked at and touched dial telephones tens of thousands of times often cannot remember many details—details that are of no importance to a person dialing the telephone. For example, most people cannot remember which two letters of the alphabet do not appear. Many people cannot remember the proper orientation of the ten finger-holes or the details of the center disk.

The second, and more interesting point, is that our perception is conceptual. Many people draw the numbers in the finger holes. Conceptually, those holes do represent those numbers; so conceptually drawing the numbers in the holes is accurate representation. But only on very old-fashioned dial telephones are the numbers actually in the holes. More than three decades ago, on the basis of a quarter-of-a-million-dollar study, the telephone manufacturers moved the numbers out of the holes onto the rim and placed little dots in the holes. Because the number now remains visible even when the person's finger is in the hole, "wrong numbers" have been reduced and the telephone companies have saved millions of dollars every year. But because the holes continue to signify the numbers, many people continue to perceive the numbers as in the holes.

Here are two descriptions of tropical islands, one from a geography book, the other from a short story. The first makes little attempt to be vivid. For instance, it merely states that "the rainbow is a prominent feature of the tropical landscape" without making any attempt to evoke an image. Its purpose is to convey "geographic facts." The second description, though it does contain some geographic facts, serves a very different purpose: the writer uses description to set the mood for a story; he chooses his words and images to convey a sense of loneliness and desolation.

> The West Indies stand in a warm sea, and the trade winds, warmed and moistened by this sea, blow across all of them. These are the two great primary geographic facts about this group of islands whose area is but little larger than that of Great Britain.
>
> These trade winds, always warm, but nevertheless refreshing sea breezes, blow mostly from the east or northeast. Thus one side of every island is windward, and the other side is leeward. The third great geographical fact about these islands is that most of them are mountainous, giving to the windward sides much more rain than the leeward sides receive. This makes great differences in climate within short distances, a thing quite unknown in the eastern half of the United States, where our slowly whirling cyclonic winds blow in quick succession from all directions upon every spot of territory. Thus both sides of the Appalachian Mountains are nearly alike in their rainfall, forest growth, and productive possibilities. On the contrary, the West Indian mountains have different worlds on their different slopes. The eastern or windward side, cloud-bathed and eternally showered upon, is damp and dripping. There are jungles with velvety green ferns, and forests with huge trees. The rainbow is a prominent feature of the tropic landscape. On the windward side one receives a striking impression of lush vegetation. On the leeward side of the very same ridge and only a few miles distant there is another kind of world, the world of scanty rainfall, with all its devastating consequences to vegetation. A fourth great geographic fact is the division of these islands into two great arcs, an outer arc of limestone and an inner arc of volcanic islands. The limestone areas are low. The volcanic areas are from moderately high to very high. Some islands have both the limestone and the volcanic features.

J. Russell Smith and M. Ogden Phillips

> Take five-and-twenty heaps of cinders dumped here and there in an outside city lot; imagine some of them magnified into mountains, and the vacant lot the sea; and you will have a fit idea of the general aspect of the Encantadas, or Enchanted Isles. A group rather of extinct volcanoes than of isles; looking much as the world at large might, after a penal conflagration. . . .

It is to be doubted whether any spot on earth can, in desolation, furnish a parallel to this group. Abandoned cemeteries of long ago, old cities by piecemeal tumbling to their ruin, these are melancholy enough; but like all else which has once been associated with humanity they still awaken in us some thought of sympathy, however sad. Hence, even the Dead Sea, along with whatever other emotions it may at times inspire, does not fail to touch in the pilgrim some of his less unpleasurable feelings. . . .

In many places the coast is rock-bound, or more properly, clinker-bound; tumbled masses of blackish or greenish stuff like the dross of an iron furnace, forming dark clefts and caves here and there, into which a ceaseless sea pours a fury of foam; overhanging them with a swirl of grey, haggard mist, amidst which sail screaming flights of unearthly birds heightening the dismal din. However calm the sea without, there is no rest for these swells and those rocks, they lash and are lashed, even when the outer ocean is most at peace with itself. On the oppressive, clouded days such as are peculiar to this part of the watery Equator, the dark vitrified masses, many of which raise themselves among white whirlpools and breakers in detached and perilous places off the shore, present a most Plutonian sight. In no world but a fallen one could such lands exist.

HERMAN MELVILLE

For distinct purposes, even the same writer may write two very different descriptions of the same scene. As a journalist, Ernest Hemingway wrote

A Silent, Ghastly Procession

ADRIANOPLE.—In a never-ending staggering march the Christian population of Eastern Thrace is jamming the roads toward Macedonia. The main column crossing the Maritza River at Adrianople is twenty miles long. Twenty miles of carts drawn by cows, bullocks and muddy-flanked buffalo, with exhausted, staggering men, women and children, blankets over their heads, walking blindly along in the rain beside their worldly goods.

This main stream is being swelled from all the back country. They don't know where they are going. They left their farms, villages and ripe brown fields and joined the stream of refugees when they heard the Turk was coming. Now they can only keep their places in the ghastly procession while mud-splashed Greek cavalry herd them along like cowpunchers driving steers.

It is a silent procession. Nobody even grunts. It is all they can do to keep moving. Their brilliant peasant costumes are soaked and drag-gled. Chickens dangle by their feet from the carts. Calves nuzzle at the draught cattle wherever a jam halts the stream. An old man marches bent under a young pig, a scythe and a gun, with a chicken tied to his scythe. A husband spreads a blanket over a woman in labor in one of the carts to keep off the driving rain. Her little daughter looks at her in horror and begins to cry. And the procession keeps moving.

When Hemingway decided to reuse this description as a fictional vignette in *In Our Time* (Scribner's), he rewrote it like this:

Minarets stuck up in the rain out of Adrianople across the mud flats. The carts were jammed for thirty miles along the Karagatch road. Water buffalo and cattle were hauling carts through the mud. No end and no beginning. Just carts loaded with everything they owned. The old men and women, soaked through, walked along keeping the cattle moving. The Maritza was running yellow almost up to the bridge. Carts were jammed solid on the bridge with camels bobbing along through them. Greek cavalry herded along the procession. Women and kids were in the carts crouched with mattresses, mirrors, sewing machines, bundles. There was a woman having a kid with a young girl holding a blanket over her and crying. Scared sick looking at it. It rained all through the evacuation.

In the journalistic version Hemingway uses detail to give readers a concrete sense of the event; in the fictional version, he is more concerned with symbol (as when he juxtaposes the minarets with the mud flats) and structure (see below). Out of context, you may like the first version better and wonder why Hemingway discarded so much vivid detail, but the very compactness of the second version creates the kind of impact Hemingway sought for his vignette.

For fictional purposes Hemingway even falsified details, as when

A husband spreads a blanket over a woman in labor in one of the carts to keep off the driving rain. Her little daughter looks at her in horror and begins to cry.

became

There was a woman having a kid with a young girl holding a blanket over her and crying. Scared sick looking at it.

By compressing the husband and daughter into one fictional character and understating the ''horror,'' Hemingway retained the emotional essence and increased the impact. For a journalist, such compression would have been unethical; in fiction, it was both appropriate and effective.

Point of View and Arrangement

The arrangement of a description usually follows from the arrangement of reality. But more than one pattern can be observed in any particular reality, and the descriptive writer must choose. In reshaping his description of the refugees fleeing past Adrianople, Hemingway began with a wide view of the minarets above the mud flats and moved increasingly closer until he focused on the image of the girl holding the blanket.

The arrangement of descriptive writing suggests spatial metaphors and can be compared to the motion of a movie or video camera (with a zoom lens for close-ups, as well as medium- and long-range shots). As this metaphor suggests, the selection and arrangement of details depends on the observer's point of view.

The following piece, written by a first-year university student, starts from a center and expands outward. Presented from the point of view of a very young child, it is written almost as if she carried that camera mounted in her "rusty red wagon." As she moves through her world, she pauses at each important point and uses the zoom lens to bring details into focus. As she shows us these images, the writer acts as narrator, commenting sometimes from the perspective of a young girl immersed in the scene and sometimes from the perspective she has now. There is also some sense of motion in time as a secondary organizing principle. The motion from the center outward and from past to present is paralleled by a movement from simplicity to complexity. Thus there is also a thematic principle at work reflecting, reinforcing, and adding symbolic value to the spatial organizing principle.

I lived, for the first four years of my life, in North Bend, British Columbia. Its setting was significant—an obscure grouping of houses nestled snugly atop the canyon wall at the edge of the muddy brown Fraser River. North Bend was seldom placed on maps because its total area was only a half square mile. However, that little hole of a town did, as it does now, exist in B.C.'s interior land of dust and trees, blazing heat, and cruel winters. While I lived there that little hole was the world.

My world's focal point was my big white-with-pink-trim wooden house. From there I strayed in only two directions, forming a tightly closed triangular world. Slightly northwest of my house, on a small but pronounced hill, rested by best friend's yellow stucco home. It had a grey porch with majestic beams that supported the porch roof. I always stood and gazed at that house thinking it was the grand home of a great king. Yet I knew that, in reality, my friend's father was not a king. He did not even dress as a king.

The other point in my triangular world was directly west of my house. I remember it as the square pink general store at the end of the dusty dirt road. I used to go there often to buy a jaw breaker or maybe an orange popsicle to slurp on because of the scorching heat. Sometimes I would go back to my house and find my rusty red wagon abandoned beside my homemade wooden swing set, but usually my wagon was my source of transportation. It took me to my focus points, or perhaps I took it! I travelled to and from the three places, but I never found it necessary to visit any of the area in between them. There was nothing there except a few houses with neatly kept gardens.

What was beyond was, however, important because it seemed to threaten the static simplicity I had created in my world. Tall, thick-trunked, hanging-branched evergreens grew in an impenetrable mass not far behind my house. Their size and shape made them seem ominous and tough and frightening. Their existence fathered dreams of bears and wolves and other vicious animals attacking anyone who dared to walk into the forest.

Another feature outside my world also scared me. Small muddy-white cement homes, big enough to shelter perhaps three adults if they were standing upright, stood just by the edge of the canyon wall east of my house in a dusty, gravelly area. People of reddish-brown skin lived in these homes. I saw the houses only once, but the fear they instilled is with me even today. These houses were not right. They were not like my comfortable big house. Something about them was wrong. Therefore, both the mighty trees and the meagre homes I dismissed as not belonging to my world—I still knew they were there.

I realized, too, that the world might be a little bigger and more complex when I rode the cable for the first time. The cable was much like a basket box hanging from a tow line over the Fraser River. The box, like an article of clothing on a clothesline, was swung to the other side. The other side was a busy place. Cars whizzed by on the highway. Large stores, much bigger than my little pink store, were side by side along the shoulder of the street. I was troubled by the idea that my world was linked to this other world by a cable. That constituted a connection and I found it hard to see the relationship, for my world seemed not as complicated.

I feared aspects of North Bend that I could not easily understand fitting into my triangular setting. Perhaps the trees, the Indian homes and the buzzing little village across the river would have been less ominous had I not first of all created a simple setting. Yet I, as a child, wanted things to be simple, and I therefore resisted anything that seemed complex. North Bend was a town that I loved within my boundaries and feared in its entirety.

Susan-Ann Green

Note how Susan-Ann uses the "triangle" of her home, her friend's house, and the general store to help readers structure and visualize the details she presents. Note also how she selects certain points to emphasize while quickly passing over or even ignoring others. The assignment called on students to describe a place where they had grown up in such a way as to give strangers a sense of it. That became her principle of selection, and she did not need to attempt an objectively complete, physical description of North Bend.

It is also interesting how Susan-Ann uses sentence structure to reinforce perspective. When she writes most directly from the child's point of view, she uses childish sentence structures. Toward the end of the fourth paragraph, for example, she unnecessarily repeats *and*s as a child might. In other places, especially in the fifth and sixth paragraphs, she uses short, choppy sentences which contrast sharply with her normally complex style. She makes some use of comparison (e.g., "The box, like an article of clothing on a clothesline, was swung to the other side"). For the most part, however, she relies on the simple presentation of vivid detail and the contrasts produced by the juxtaposition of those details.

The following was written by another student in the same class for whom English is a second language.

> Thirty years ago, my parents left China during the beginning of the Communist revolution. They settled in a small town near Saskatoon, Saskatchewan, which had a meagre population of two hundred. My father owned a store which had a market of clients living within a radius of one mile. The opportunities which exist in cities beckoned too many families and consequently, the store's business suffered. The increasing drainage of people soon reduced the town's population to a mere fifty. In 1968, we moved to Vancouver, where my present life began.
>
> I dislike living in the typical slum neighbourhood of run-down houses, weed-covered lawns, and littered street curbs. On hot summer nights, it is not uncommon to hear the man and woman living on the second floor of the apartment adjacent to our home sobbing hysterically, screaming obscenities and threatening each other—with the rest of the boarders who live on either side of the couple joining in the slanderous match. The neighbor living across the street in his shabby, moss-covered house did little better. Two years ago, the police raided the house, arresting a girl on grounds of illegal possession of drugs while her father sat in a chair staring out his porch throughout the episode. It is very saddening to have such scenes blight an otherwise good day.
>
> We are not a close family. We seldom show physical affection towards one another. Instead, we are a group of individuals who struggle to solve their problems privately. The inability to voice

my conflicts has made my past life difficult, lonely and fiercely
independent.

Dovey Wong

Objectively, the description is again incomplete—only one of the three
paragraphs speaks directly to the assignment—but the passage fulfills its assigned
purpose effectively. We get not only a sense of the neighborhood, but also a
sense of the circumstances which are beyond the control of the writer and
her family. We are told, moreover, about the internal nature of the family,
which helps shape the response to the neighborhood. It is this context which
makes poignant sense of the egocentric final sentence of the second paragraph.

Such descriptions, given their assigned purpose, have much in common
with literary descriptions. They aim not at a scientifically accurate description
(which would demand an even-handed emphasis and an objective "completeness"); they aim rather to set mood, to give a sense of place. Such descriptions
succeed best when readers are *shown* rather than *told about* whatever is being
described.

A description is always a report of perceptions. But one makes observations
for a wide variety of reasons. A scientist, a salesperson, and a novelist may
write descriptions of the same piece of laboratory equipment; however, their
selections of information and words will vary as radically as their purposes
(and the purposes of their readers). Although the term *description* usually
suggests a concrete description of an object or scene, moreover, the descriptive
mode can also be used to represent ideas or even other reports (see pages
291–94). One could, for instance, describe René Descartes' theory of perception
(perhaps prior to criticizing it in terms of what has since been learned about
human perception).

The general principle is this: good description is based on the selection
and accurate verbal representation of information that is relevant to the purposes
that writing will serve. One need only contrast the descriptive styles of William
Faulkner and Ernest Hemingway—or Albert Einstein and Karl Marx—or Pablo
Neruda and George Eliot—or Jane Austen and Adrienne Rich to realize that
more specific rules about "good" description are either oversimplifications
or applicable only to certain particular types of description.

EXERCISE

1. Write a description of a place where you lived as a child. Write it in
such a way as to give a stranger a sense of what it would be like to grow up
there.

2. Write a description of a job you held, giving readers a sense of what
it would be like to work at that job.

3. The following description, excerpted from the novel *Bleak House*, serves to sct a mood.

> My Lady Dedlock's "place" has been extremely dreary. The weather, for many a day and night, has been so wet that the trees seem wet through, and the soft loppings and prunings of the woodsman's axe can make no crack or crackle as they fall. The deer, looking soaked, leave quagmires where they pass. The shot of a rifle loses its sharpness in the moist air, and its smoke moves in a tardy little cloud towards the green rise, coppice-topped, that makes a background for the falling rain. The view from my Lady Dedlock's own windows is alternately a lead-coloured view, and a view in Indian ink. The vases on the stone terrace in the foreground catch the rain all day; and the heavy drops fall, drip, drip, drip, upon the broad flagged pavement, called, from old time, the Ghost's Walk, all night. On Sundays, the little church in the park is mouldy; the oaken pulpit breaks out into a cold sweat; and there is a general smell and taste as of the ancient Dedlocks in their graves.

> CHARLES DICKENS

Analyze the passage to show how both the choice of details and the choice of words serve to create a sense of dampness and gloom. Imagine how this description of a nineteenth century English country mansion could be rewritten with a very different selection of details—say, roaring fires and steaming Christmas puddings—to create a very different mood. Then select an emotion, and write a description of a person or place which will evoke that emotion in readers.

4. Write a technical description of a piece of scientific apparatus which would allow a scientist who wished to replicate an experiment in which that apparatus was used to reconstruct it. (*Note*: Do not write instructions, just a description.)

Narration

We can perceive widely varying intentions in different narratives such as fictional story, a factual report of events, a scientific account of a sequence . . . , and a narrative contained within an advertisement . . . . It is no difficult matter to find narrative . . . which has as its dominant function calculated persuasion or highly didactic explanation.

JAMES BRITTON ET AL.

Through the work of women writers, women have been able to imagine themselves. . . . [Reading] has created a metaphysical community of like-minded women, reassuring these women that they are not alone. . . . The work of women writers has provided a context, a history, a mythology, a chart for their journey, empowering women with the courage to become the subject of their own narrative.

CAROL BECKER

Telling What Happened

Narratives are sometimes called *accounts*; writers of narratives are said to *recount* events. In Latinate languages, the very word for story derives from the Latin, *computare*, "to count" (e.g., Spanish, *cuento*; French, *conte*). This is a clue to the structure of narrative, which in a sense *counts* (or accounts for) the moments of time. In this sense, narration is the description of change: when the element of time is added to description, we have narrative.

Basic narratives start at the beginning and account for each significant moment until the end. More sophisticated narratives may start in the middle (or even at the end) and "flash back" to earlier moments. In any case, the underlying movement of narrative is progression through time. The essential order is chronological (from the Greek, *chronos* + *logos*; hence "following the logic of time").

If you tell some friends what happened on a television show they did not see, you are narrating. If you begin a literature paper by summarizing the plot of a novel, you are narrating (as was the author of the novel). If you recount something outrageous your boss did at work yesterday, or something bizarre that happened when your younger sister tried to join a Little League baseball team, or something funny that happened the first time you drove a tractor, . . . you are narrating.

As in description, so in narration the key task of the writer is selection. You must discover what happened—perhaps by searching your memory, perhaps by researching, perhaps also with the help of the journalists' 5Ws (see pages 79–80)—and you must select significant events to be *re*-presented verbally. Arrangement is relatively easy because it is essentially chronological. Explicit analysis is usually minimal because narration is generally most effective if you follow the rule, "Show, don't tell," and recreate events instead of telling about them.

The nature of the selection, of course, varies with the writers' purposes. A technical reporter, a newspaper journalist, and novelist may watch the same rocket launching, but their reports will be as distinct as their purposes.

Why Tell Stories?

Many narratives serve expressive purposes. The purpose of a personal narrative, for example, may be to express and share an emotion (e.g., your outrage at what your boss did). If readers understand what happened, feel the emotion and respond empathetically, the narrative has succeeded.

Here is a narrative that recaptures a memory of childhood romanticism.

Capturing the Pleasure of the Night

As a little girl I read a poem with a line that spoke of the joy you could feel "if you've ever dropped white, white stones into a moonlit pool." I puzzled over the poem for most of a winter, and that summer I found a quiet forest pool out behind the cabin where we slept. I collected a handful of very white stones, and stayed up till after two one brilliant, moonlit night.

I had marked the path to the pool during the day, but the moon was so bright I had no trouble finding my way. I squatted in the ferns at the water's edge, and one by one I dropped my stones into the water. I don't know what I expected, maybe some hidden understanding or revelation, or even a sense of joy, but there was nothing but the splash of the pebbles and a widening circle of ripples.

I was only a kid and I was disappointed, ready to go back to my cabin and comfortable bed. But as long as I had taken all this trouble I was reluctant to leave. Weren't my stones white enough? Had I missed some essential point about the verse?

Sitting there by the moonlit water, I became aware of the night sounds, the insect noises, and now and then the cry of a bird. I watched the water and the distinct, dark shape of the trees beyond it. On the far bank I saw a family of lilies--silver-white in the moonlight.

I looked up at the moon and watched a ragged edge of cloud pass across it. There was a momentary illusion that the moon itself was rushing through the sky. Now I noticed the sky for the first time, not quite black, but not blue--just a velvet combination of both. The stillness around me became more intense because of the night noises, the way a picture is enhanced by a frame. A white moth fluttered past, its wings glowing against the darkness and near the water's edge I heard a soft rustle in the grass--an animal came to drink.

Not all at once, but gradually, as I sat there, a deep sense of pleasure filled me. I had a sense of bodily well-being as if some quality in the night, part of the dark, was flowing into me. I leaned back and opened myself to it, letting it fill me with an absolute content.

Engulfed in the magic of the night, I sat there for over two hours unaware of time or the hard, damp ground or any physical discomfort, too overwhelmed by the strange joy I felt even to want to think clearly.

Was it only that night or did I ever feel that pleasure again? Yes, even though I never had a chance to go back to that spot, I was able to recapture that same feeling in other places at different times. I even found it one night on the roof of a highrise apartment house in a large city. There was only a silver moon, but the lights of the city softened the darkness of the sky, and the sounds of traffic filtered up muted. I sensed the stillness around me, behind the noise, but an intrinsic part of the night.

I have found the same pleasure on other nights in lonely places, often unfamiliar spots, but always with the same stillness and darkness, the same sense of being one with the earth.

Maya Kaplinowski

Although narrative is based on chronology, stories are often structured as situation, complication, and resolution. In Maya's narrative, the first paragraph presents the situation, the second and third paragraphs develop it into a complication, and the rest discovers a resolution. Although many narratives, like this one, begin with what happened first, narratives often start at the height of the complication, "flash back" to earlier events, and then end with the resolution.

Expressive narratives may be directed toward readers to whom the experience is foreign. One can read D. H. Lawrence's *Sons and Lovers* and Agnes Smedley's *Daughter of Earth* to gain some insight into what it was like to grow up in a mining town in the early years of this century. Such narratives allow readers vicariously to share experiences foreign to them.

Expressive narratives may also be directed toward readers who have had similar experiences. The function of the narrative may then create a sense of community. A personal narrative—originally written, perhaps, as self-expression because the writer needed to articulate and clarify an experience—can come to serve this function if other people identify with it. Much of the recently published literature of oppressed groups (women's literature, Black, Chicano, and Québecois literature) takes the form of personal narrative and serves that function. The power of such narratives comes from readers' recognition of the social validity of the personal experience. As Professor Hans Guth suggests (page 259), writing that genuinely reflects readers' "fundamental modes of perception, thought, and feeling" can create community. Indeed, a purely personal narrative that touches no social nerve is rarely published.

Such narratives, which express the shared experience of a group, also embody shared values. By expressing those shared values, they create a sense of community. That is the function of mythology in human societies. Any narratives that serve this function are, in the best sense of the word, *mythical*— whether they are stories about imaginary beings or ordinary people. The literal truth or falsity of such a myth is quite beside the point; the myth is essentially true if it embodies the right values.

The parable of the Good Samaritan is such a myth. The story is generally familiar to anyone from a predominantly Christian culture, even those who have not read the Bible. Almost everyone can identify with the conflict between selfishness and charity. And our culture upholds the latter as an ideal (and the former as "realism").

Though of less literary merit, frontier stories (e.g., "westerns") serve similar functions. Only on the most superficial levels are "westerns" about nineteenth-century cowboys (whom they depict with incredible inaccuracy). Science fiction, likewise, for all its intergalactic travel, is essentially a commentary on contemporary society. Both are really about the society that reads them.

Written to re-create one person's experience of working in a particular restaurant, "Sexual Initiation at $1.35 an Hour" is a character sketch that expresses an individual writer's feelings. It also presents an image with which many women workers can identify.

Sexual Initiation at $1.35 an Hour

The Lamas Restaurant was bleak, even at the noon hour when it was filled to capacity with hungry workers from the surrounding area. I am still not certain why anybody ate there at all. There was a loneliness about the place, and time passed slowly within its boundaries. Working there was like serving a prison sentence or being confined to hospital for a very long time. My shift lasted from eleven o'clock in the morning until eight o'clock in the evening, six days a week. Mr. Lamas preferred that I take all my meals in the restaurant and avoid walking the neighbourhood streets. He was afraid I might bring shame upon his establishment.

Lamas did all the cooking while his wife and I waited table. The only other staff member was an ancient Greek, who washed the dishes and scrubbed the floors. Toothless, humorless, nameless, he hobbled through the kitchen, cursing his life and coddling his dishes and brooms. When he cornered me in the basement with a wet mop in his hand, Lamas fired him and threw him off the premises. For the remainder of the summer, in addition to my waitress duties, I washed the dishes and scrubbed the floors. Lamas said it would be a lesson to me, but I knew that it really meant one fewer salary he had to pay out.

Lamas ran his meagre business as if he were putting on a show. Everything was said and done for the benefit of the customers. He treated them like rubes, paying fools whom he delighted in deceiving. Before them, he was magnanimous. As he stepped behind the kitchen door, his warmth would vanish. Only his wife and I would see the cruel stupidity that characterized the man.

The husband and wife gave no sense of being a couple or a partnership. She slept upstairs in her husband's bed at night and worked in his restaurant all day. He controlled—no, he hoarded—food, money and hardware. She used to steal special treats for us while he was out on business; like slaves, we would furtively gobble, and laugh at the mysterious motivation of Lamas and all tyrants.

It was Lamas who gave me my first lecture on sex education. He would not allow me to fraternize with the customers. It was simply forbidden. He treated me to a pathetic pantomime in which he illustrated the appropriate behaviour for a waitress to adopt toward her clientele. Pressed for a deeper explanation, he led me to the cash register and revealed the truth about men and women.

"Human beings," whispered Lamas, "are evil. They carry poisonous juices inside themselves. These juices can only be released through sex. Even I have these juices. When I need to get rid of them, I go to the street and find a woman. If you want to clean out your own poison, go to another neighbourhood. Never, never give it to a customer. You will infect the business. The business will become poisoned. Do you understand?"

I understood. The sickness of Lamas' philosophy had permeated the space around him. Life itself was a disease to be flushed out periodically into foreign territory. The restaurant, which he held sacred and struggled to protect from evil, embodied health. Its somberness, its sterility, reflected the imprisoned spirit of its confused owner.

Virginia Louise Clesse

Aside from the analogy in the fourth paragraph ("*like slaves*, we would furtively gobble, and laugh at the mysterious motivation of Lamas *and all tyrants*"), there is little in the text itself to suggest generalization. And yet, like good literature, it does suggest a contrast between *what is* (or was) and *what should be*. And insofar as readers are reminded of similar experiences, it serves to create a sense of community.

In this sense, expressive narratives can become persuasive. By telling stories that embody certain values, they may serve also to persuade readers to maintain or adopt those values. Even a narrative television commercial which has been impressed on the popular imagination is a "myth" in this sense. In addition to telling a story which is expressive enough to hold viewers' attention, and in addition to persuading them to purchase the advertiser's product, it also persuades them to maintain or adopt values it embodies (e.g., about the appropriate roles of men and women). As with any myth, each telling of such a narrative may have only slight persuasive power. But the repeated telling of that story, together with other stories embodying similar values, and in a social context which constrains people toward those values, can be powerfully persuasive.

Similarly, a story about your employer's outrageous behavior may be part of an attempt to convince fellow workers to unionize. Its moral may be left unstated, but the reiteration of that moral over time, through similar stories, may have a cumulative persuasive effect—at least if other workers recognize it as typical.

Narratives can also serve as examples in explanatory writings (see pages 294–97). That story about your younger sister's trying to join a Little League team may illustrate how perfectly ordinary people can behave bizarrely when their stereotypes are challenged.

Samuel Taylor Coleridge's "Prefatory Note to Kubla Khan" is a narrative that served and still serves a variety of purposes.

> The following fragment is here published at the request of a poet of great and deserved celebrity, and, as far as the Author's own opinions are concerned, rather as a psychological curiosity, than on the ground of any supposed *poetic* merits.
>
> In the summer of the year 1797, the Author, then in ill health, had retired to a lonely farm-house between Porlock and Linton, on the Exmoor confines of Somerset and Devonshire. In consequence of a slight indisposition, an anodyne had been prescribed, from the effects of which he fell asleep in his chair at the moment that he was reading the following sentence, or words of the same substance, in "Purchas's Pilgrimage": "Here the Khan Kubla commanded a palace to be built, and a stately garden thereunto. And thus ten miles of fertile ground were inclosed with a wall." The Author continued for about three hours in a profound sleep, at least of the external senses, during which time he has the most vivid confidence, that he could not have composed less than from two to three hundred lines; if that indeed can be called composition in which all the images rose up before him as *things,* with a parallel production of the correspondent expressions, without any sensation or consciousness of effort. On awaking he appeared to himself to have a distinct recollection of the whole, and taking his pen, ink, and paper, instantly and eagerly wrote down the lines that are here preserved. At this moment he was unfortunately called out

> by a person on business from Porlock, and detained by him above an hour, and on his return to his room, found, to his no small surprise and mortification, that though he still retained some vague and dim recollection of the general purport of the vision, yet, with the exception of some eight or ten scattered lines and images, all the rest had passed away like the images on the surface of a stream into which a stone has been cast, but alas! without the after restoration of the latter!

Coleridge recounts, in chronological order, the significant events which led to the creation and loss of several hundred lines of poetry. Some literary critics have accepted the account as accurate; others have doubted it to one degree or another. At any event, its original purpose was persuasive: it served, among other arguments, to justify the publication of a wonderfully rich but incomplete poem. In a sense, it has also since become part of the poem (with which it is usually published). And among those who study the creative process, it has also become a standard illustration (i.e., a "myth") of the importance of unconscious processes in human creation. Thus the narrative serves persuasive, expressive, and explanatory purposes.

Another statement by Coleridge summarizes the same information in a single sentence fragment:

> This fragment with a good deal more, not recoverable, composed in a sort of Reverie brought on by two grains of Opium, taken to check a dysentery, at a Farm House between Porlock and Linton, a quarter of a mile from Culbone Church, in the fall of the year 1797.

This version, probably earlier, lacks narrative form. It also lacks significant details and could not serve the persuasive, expressive, or explanatory purposes of the preface. Certainly, it could not stand as a myth representing the interaction of conscious and unconscious processes in human creation.

Like description, narrative should not attempt to recount everything that happened. It need only include those events that are significant. And it is only in terms of purposes that writers can distinguish significant from insignificant events.

Expressive narratives often stand on their own and are often read, as with novels, for the sheer pleasure of the story. Even in our efficient age, they are often quite lengthy. Narratives that serve persuasive or explanatory purposes, however, are likely to be subordinate parts of larger writings and are usually expected to be subordinated efficiently to their purposes.

When you think of narratives, you probably think of the sort of material represented by "Sexual Initiation at $1.35 an Hour." But any writing that reports what happened in a particular instance or set of instances is narration. Consider the following as narrative.

The method by which I wrote my first paper for this English course is typical of my writing process for most creative essays.

My first step was to consider briefly each of the topic choices as they were assigned, weighing the potential of each. Through the course of that day and the next, I thought of the topics from time to time. By the night after they had been assigned, I had a few ideas; and after re-examining them, I settled on one and mentally formed a rough draft of how I would describe my summer job. I was now ready to begin my second step: the actual writing.

Upon thinking of a thesis sentence, I began writing quickly. As I wrote, I was mentally a few sentences ahead of what I was actually writing, but I did not follow a concrete outline. As I wrote, I didn't pay a great deal of attention to spelling mistakes or punctuation. If I was at a loss for an appropriate word or phrase, I would pause briefly; but if I failed to think of the word, I would temporarily insert a synonym or a phrase which would convey the same meaning and continue writing. I wrote rapidly until I reached my concluding paragraph, at which point I stopped and re-read my essay, not for the sake of making corrections but rather to obtain an overall picture of what I had written. I then proceeded with the conclusion.

After having completed step two, I then progressed to the third stage in which I re-read the essay in order to correct any punctuation and spelling mistakes. With the aid of a thesaurus, I substituted appropriate words for those I was not satisfied with. Once this operation was finished, I waited one or two days before I commenced with the final stage.

This stage entails re-reading the paper to see if it flows smoothly and if what I had written made sense. Waiting a day or so increases my objectivity for this task. After making any further appropriate corrections or revisions, I copied the essay out neatly and the grueling process ground to a halt.

Fiona Barnott

Aside from the first sentence (and, perhaps, the beginning of the last paragraph), this is narration: it reports a particular happening in chronological order. Its first function was to make the writer articulate, and thus become more aware of, how she writes. In a writing class or workshop, a narrative of this kind could be shared, and sharing usually leads to a sense of "community" as members of the group realize that they are not alone in their difficulties. This particular narrative should perhaps have been more fully articulated: *How* did Fiona think of a thesis sentence? Aside from corrections, what sorts of revisions did she make? Those details could help readers understand just what Fiona did—and probably lead to some insights about why her writing came out as it did. Here, as so often, the quality of a narration results from the quality of detail, and what is left out can be as important as what is selected for inclusion.

Here is another narrative, this one from the methodology section of a scientific report.

> For three weeks in January and February 1986, I became an habituée of the Continental Billiard Room. I spent 9 periods of about one hour each observing the interactions and behavior of staff and patrons. I went there weekends and week days, morning, afternoon and evening. The sampling is a bit skewed in favor of early afternoon, as three observations were made during that period of time. I then interviewed a radio researcher and broadcaster who has been an habituée of the Continental for ten years. After having chosen my area of interest, made hypotheses and collected data, I went to two other local cafes for comparison. I spent two hours each at Calabria Bar, an Italian cafe, and La Quena, a cafe frequented by refugees from Central America.
>
> PAULE McNICOLL

Although it serves a very different purpose than "Capturing the Pleasure of the Night" or "Sexual Initiation at $1.35 an Hour," this, too, tells what happened and is organized chronologically. Its purpose is not to capture a mood or to encapsulate an experience, but to allow readers to evaluate the validity of the research procedures, perhaps even to test the results by repeating research. Nonetheless, it is narrative.

EXERCISE

1. Tell a story, or string together a series of incidents, that will give readers a sense of a place (e.g., where you grew up), a person (e.g., your mother), or an activity (e.g., a job you once had).

2. Select one of your important values or beliefs. Think of an event you witnessed that epitomizes that value or belief. Without actually stating your point, narrate the event in such a way that it communicates the value or belief. See if readers get the point.

3. Write about a recent frustrating experience as (a) an expression of your feelings addressed to a good friend, (b) an attempt to get someone in authority to do something about the situation, and (c) an illustration of a principle for a university class in psychology or sociology. How does the narrative change as your purpose changes?

4. Narrate everything that happened the last time you wrote something. Start from when you decided (or were assigned) to write. End when the piece of writing was ready for its readers. Share this narrative with other writers.

5. Select a contemporary popular narrative (e.g., a hit song, a best-selling novel, a television commercial). Analyze it as a "myth" which embodies and reinforces cultural values. Write a conclusion to this analysis that discusses the implications for writers and readers.

Summaries and Examples

The Example corresponds to the process of induction, and induction is the basis [of all reasoning]. . . . Examples function as witnesses—and there is always a tendency to believe a witness.

ARISTOTLE

A story which tells how a man through his work and talent climbs the social ladder, even if an explicit lesson is not drawn from it, is nonetheless a lesson in optimism and faith in a society which makes such success possible. . . . It is a matter of an argument aiming to move from a specific case toward a generalization.

CHAIM PERELMAN

Outside of literature, description and narrative are most commonly used in summaries and examples.

Summaries

The terms *description* and *narrative* usually suggest reporting observations of some object or event, but the process is essentially the same when you report what you have read or heard. Summarizing is different from other types of description or narrative only because the object or event is verbal. The writer's tasks remain essentially the same: observation (which in this instance means reading or listening), selection, arrangement, and verbalization. As in any description or narrative, the selection and arrangement is guided by your purposes.

A scientist or scholar who summarizes a published article, perhaps to support a new hypothesis or interpretation, is describing that article. Similarly, it is often necessary to describe or narrate the gist of what someone else has said prior to refuting it. In business and government bureaucracies, a report or proposal usually begins with a one-page "executive summary" to help busy bigshots decide whether to read all, part, or none of it—for such reports and proposals often contain much technical and financial detail that executives do not need. And writers frequently summarize their own arguments as thesis paragraphs or by way of conclusion (see pages 106–7 and 189–90).

Summaries come in various lengths, depending on their purposes. The longest type of summary, the *précis*, is approximately a third the length of the original text. A précis contains all the generalizations and a representative selection of the details from the original. The civil servants who administered the British Empire would commonly précis the reports of their subordinates before passing them up the bureaucratic hierarchy toward the colonial office in London.

The shortest type of summary is known as an *abstract*. An abstract briefly summarizes the main points of a text so potential readers (usually scientists or scholars) can decide whether to read it. The abstract of a book is usually 500–1,000 words, the abstract of an article merely 100–200 words. In at least one sense, the writer of an abstract is like the writer of a mail-order catalog description: both save prospective users the work of having to examine the item itself in order to decide whether they should acquire it. In the one case, we have a suasive description of a material object that is for sale. In the other, we have an objective description of the main ideas of an article. In both cases, the writer is using the descriptive mode.

> The lost wax process of making jewelry is the way the Indians of South and Central America worked with gold and silver. Greta Pack's *Jewelry Making by the Lost Wax Process* gives a very concise and informative account of the process and includes 14 projects of value. After the technique is learned, the myriad shapes of your imagination can be captured in gold or silver.

> In principle, a research paper gives students an opportunity to do independent work, apply what they have learned, think critically, and use research findings (primary or secondary) to draw and validate conclusions. In practice, a research paper often seems to have more to do with shuffling note cards, avoiding plagiarism and formatting footnotes correctly. This article describes our experience in a situation where inadequate library resources forced us to abandon the standard research paper and to devise an assignment that revived the basic purpose of assigning research papers. The assignment we describe here has particular relevance to teacher education, especially in English and language arts, but the broader implications have to do with the research paper in general.
>
> Irene Brosnahan et al.

Varying conceptual models of the relationship between reading and writing processes as parallel, interactive or transaction have influenced instructional practices. When reading and writing processes wcrc viewed as parallel, they were both emphasized but taught discretely or from an imitation perspective. When reading and writing were viewed as interactive processes, writers often focused on the role of reading during writing. From the most recent transactional perspective, meaning is composed by both readers and writers so that what emerges is a "new event, larger than the sum of its parts."

MARILYN S. STERNGLASS

As these examples suggest, there is an important distinction between abstracts that merely list topics discussed in a text and abstracts that actually reproduce the gist of the argument. The catalog description, in three sentences, tells enough about Pack's book so that you can decide whether you want to examine it more closely. The first abstract is like the catalog description in that it simply tells readers that they can find in the article a new type of research paper assignment—but does not describe the assignment. The second abstract actually narrates the gist of the argument, summarizing the three main points of the article. The second sort of abstract is somewhat more difficult to write, but often more useful (especially as a thesis paragraph or summary conclusion).

Summaries may include other information in addition to the gist of the original text. In psychology, for instance, the abstract of an empirical research report should, in 100–150 words, describe all of the following:

1. Problem investigated
2. Experimental subjects (specifying relevant characteristics, e.g., age, sex, species)
3. Experimental method (including apparatus, procedures for gathering data, names of tests and drugs used)
4. Findings (including statistical significance levels)
5. Conclusions and implications or applications

Psychology abstracts are also supposed to be clear, accurate, objective, coherent, and readable—no easy task with all that material to report in a maximum of 150 words.

Summaries do vary considerably according to purpose, subject, and length, but the following general heuristic can help you generate material for most sorts of summaries.

1. What is the text about (main subject)?
2. Why would someone want to read it (purpose)?
3. What is the main point? Is it the same as the stated thesis?
4. What are the underlying assumptions, the warrants upon which the major points depend?

5. What is the gist? How is the main point validated? What is the essence of the supporting evidence or reasoning? Is it convincing?

6. So what? What are the implications? What follows?

Examples

Examples are generally descriptions or narratives used in a larger text to support or illustrate a point. Examples can serve to convince, emphasize, clarify, or concretize.

Aristotle says an example is the rhetorical equivalent of inductive reasoning. The examples in a piece of writing rarely constitute statistically reliable proof. But they represent that proof. When you offer an example to support a generalization, you are implicitly asserting that it does *exemplify*, that it is typical, that it could be multiplied by enough examples to constitute empirical proof. Insofar as the purported example is not actually representative, it is invalid.

In the opening paragraph of his essay, "How to Grow Old," Bertrand Russell supports his two points almost entirely with examples.

In spite of the title, this article will really be on how not to grow old, which, at my time of life, is a much more important subject. My first advice would be to choose your ancestors carefully. Although both my parents died young, I have done well in this respect as regards my other ancestors. My maternal grandfather, it is true, was cut off in the flower of his youth, at the age of sixty-seven, but my other three grandparents all lived to be over eighty. Of remoter ancestors I can only discover one who did not live to a great age, and he died of a disease which is now rare, namely, having his head cut off. A great-grandmother of mine, who was a friend of Gibbon, lived to the age of ninety-two, and to her last day remained a terror to all her descendants. My maternal grandmother, after having nine children who survived, one who died in infancy, and many miscarriages, as soon as she became a widow devoted herself to women's higher education. She was one of the founders of Girton College, and worked hard at opening the medical profession to women. She used to relate how she met in Italy an elderly gentleman who was looking very sad. She inquired the cause of his melancholy and he said that he had just parted from his two grandchildren. "Good gracious," she exclaimed, "I have seventy-two grandchildren, and if I were sad each time I parted from one of them, I should have a dismal existence!" "Madre snaturale," he replied. But speaking as one of the seventy-two, I prefer her recipe. After the age of eighty she found she had some difficulty in getting to sleep, so she habitually spent the hours from midnight to 3 A.M. in reading popular science. I do not believe that she ever had time to notice that she was growing old. This, I think, is the proper recipe for remaining young. If you have wide and keen interests and activities in which you can still be effective, you will have no reason to think about the merely statistical fact of the number of years you have already lived, still less of the probable brevity of your future.

Examples are also the main support in the following passage from a student essay arguing that the English language needs a gender neutral pronoun.

> Proof of the need for third-person singular neutral pronouns is found in almost all textbooks and journals. Accounting textbook author, Ray Garrison, included an apologetic footnote in a 1982 text,
>
> > The English language lacks a generic singular pronoun signifying he or she. For this reason the masculine pronouns, he and his are used to some extent in this book for purposes of succinctness and to avoid repetition in wording.
>
> The quote indicates a practical need for expansion of the language.
>
> The precedent for successful expansion of the language (and attitudes) is the common use of chairperson, firefighter, mailcarrier and police officer. These nouns, at first perceived as radical and controversial, are now in common use. They have helped generate a new awareness and positive shift in the general public's attitude. The use of neutral pronouns will also require time to become commonly accepted, but precedent shows it will be successful.
>
> Shannon Willow DiBiasio

Examples are also used to clarify, concretize, and emphasize. Here the point is not so much to support a generalization as to make sure it is understood, that it has impact. One could delete the underlined passages from the following description without losing any ideas. But those examples serve to concretize and emphasize; without them, the passage would lose much of its impact.

> Many entering students are accustomed to getting by and "getting over the man." Their main objective is to find out what game is being run down so they can "psych" out those in charge. Knowledge about and appreciation for great ideas and accomplishments of civilization are not a top priority. What millions take for granted—

museums; music other than gospel, rock and soul; theatre (not
movies); world literature—is entirely foreign to the majority of
them. More than half have never been on a plane or a train and would
be frightened half to death of the subway. One student of mine had
never ridden an elevator until the summer after she graduated from
high school. The Pentagon, the Smithsonian Institute, Chase
Manhattan are as foreign as Olympus. In short, their world view is
limited to small towns and school buses.

Willease Sanders

The underlined words could be deleted. indeed, the passage could be cut by
half. But the details which could be cut make the description vivid and give
readers a concrete sense of the students. The details are more concrete than
the propositions they illustrate. By exemplifying the more abstract ideas, they
make the passage more convincing.

The following example was written specifically to illustrate a concept
readers might have trouble understanding in the abstract.

Wheeling & Dealing

Two individuals approach the drive—in window of a bank. One is
driving a late—model, shiny silver Rolls—Royce with a black top
and white—wall tires. The other person is driving a 1963 Volkswagen
sedan with three different colors of paint on it. What images
immediately come to mind? The person in the Rolls—Royce lives in a
twenty—room house with maids and butlers and talks with that certain
air of extravagance. He's always had an abundance of money right
at his fingertips. The guy in the beat—up little Volkswagen wears
jeans, knows the value of a dollar because he's had to sweat for
everything he's got and the biggest extravagance he can afford is
to take his family to McDonald's for dinner. Right? This is an example
of signifier/signified—the automobile being the signifier and the
image of status being the signified.

Cathy Stine

In practice, the distinction between supporting and illustrating is not
always precise. The following paragraph both supports and illustrates an argument that the same basic principle can have different implications in different
contexts. It was intended to help readers understand an abstract idea about
the relationship between rules and principles.

The principle of contextual relativity applies equally to the biological
ecosystem and to the ecosystem of ideas. The Boy Scout who twenty

years ago memorized the rule that one should always bury cans and other non-burnable garbage has had the environmental context shift out from under him. Most North American backpacking areas are so crowded these days that people would be burying cans faster than the earth could decompose them. Although the higher level value of preserving for other hikers an undamaged natural environment has remained the same, the specific rule has now been inverted—now a good Scout carries out her or his unburnable garbage. What this example illustrates is the tendency to memorize rules instead of understanding principles. This tendency leads to inappropriate behavior when the context shifts.

The main idea of the paragraph, about contextual relativity in ecosystems, is supported by the Boy Scout backpacking example. But the main point of the article in which the paragraph appeared was about the ecology of ideas. The entire paragraph serves only to illustrate and concretize the analogy.

Counterexamples

Examples can be used to counter, as well as to support an assertion. Sometimes even a single counterexample can devastate an argument. For millions of North Americans, according to public opinion polls, a single near-disaster at the Three Mile Island nuclear generator plant refuted volumes of statistics and expert testimony about the safety of such plants.

In some cases, a single counterexample is a logically valid refutation (especially if the original proposition contained absolutes like "all" or "never"). In other cases, the counterexample does not disprove, but only challenges the probability of original proposition. Perhaps the most effective counterexamples are created when you turn your opponents' statements against them and, as the saying goes, hoist them on their own petards.

Here are some counterexamples used by Professor Joseph Williams, who was refuting some of the simplistic generalizations that composition textbooks offer writing students. In every case, as indicated by the italics, the very reputable authors violate their own rules.

From *Simple & Direct* by Jacques Barzun:

In conclusion, I recommend using *that* [not *which*] with defining clauses except when stylistic reasons interpose. (p. 68)
Next is a typical situation *which* a practiced writer corrects for style virtually by simple reflex. . . . (p. 69)

From *The Elements of Style* (Macmillan) by William Strunk, Jr., and E. B. White:

> Express coordinate ideas in similar form. The principle, that of parallel construction, requires that expressions similar in context and function be outwardly similar. (p. 20)
>
> *That, which. That* is the defining or restrictive pronoun, *which* the non-defining or non-restrictive. (p. 47)

In "Death of a Pig," however, E. B. White writes:

> The premature expiration of a pig is, I soon discovered, a departure *which* the community marks solemnly on its calendar, a sorrow in which it feels fully involved. I have written this account *in penitence and in grief*, as a man who failed to raise his pig, *and to explain* my deviation from the classic course of so many raised pigs. The grave in the woods is unmarked, but Fred can direct the mourner to it *unerringly* and *with immense good will*, and I know he and I shall often revisit it. (Italics added)

From *Barnet & Stubbs Practical Guide to Writing* (Little, Brown):

> Negative constructions are often wordy and sometimes pretentious:
>
> 1. wordy: Housing for married students is not unworthy of consideration.
> 2. concise: Housing for married students is worthy of consideration. (p. 216)
>
> . . .
>
> The following example from a syndicated column is *not un*typical. (p. 216)

Williams' point is that handbook style rules are overgeneralized and imprecise, that they may be generally valid but even their advocates do not always follow them. Faulty parallelism *is* a stylistic problem, but E. B. White demonstrates in "Death of a Pig" that it is not always necessary (or even desirable) to represent "coordinate ideas in similar form."

A counterexample, even when it is not a logically airtight refutation, can persuasively deflate an authoritative statement, especially if that statement is overgeneralized. (To help yourself avoid being hoisted on your own petard by your opponents' counterexamples, see pages 112–15 on qualification.)

EXERCISE

1. Read an article in your area of special interest and write a 200-word abstract.

2. Read Antony's funeral speech in Shakespeare's *Julius Caesar*. Explain how he uses examples and counterexamples to convince his audience.

3. Pick an abstract concept from your area of specialization or special interest. Illustrate it with an example that would help nonspecialists understand the concept and its implications.

4. Use a counterexample to refute an argument with which you disagree.

C·H·A·P·T·E·R 7

Analytic Patterns

Perception takes whatever it perceives as a thing of a certain sort. All thinking from the lowest to the highest—whatever else it may be—is sorting. . . . We begin with the general abstract everything, split it, as the world makes us, into sorts and then arrive at concrete particulars.

I. A. RICHARDS

Through language we divide and organize experience in different ways.

FRANK D'ANGELO

Composing is like an organic process, not an assembly line on which some prefabricated parts are fitted together. . . . The task of the composer is to find the forms that find forms; the structures that guide and encourage growth; the limits by means of which development can be shaped. [Composing] is a way of making meanings by using the forms provided by language to re-present the relationships we see.

ANN BERTHOFF

Aristotle noted that the ability to detect likenesses is one of the sure signs of intelligence, and it is on this ability (which, of course, implies the ability to detect differences) that he based his system of classification and his theory of definition.

HAROLD MARTIN AND RICHARD OHMANN

WRITERS should remember that the word *compose* comes from the Latin *componere*, meaning "to put together, to make up." The goal of composition is the "putting together" of meaning. We start with questions about the whole, and we should end with an understanding of the whole. But in between we analyze, break a subject into its parts or aspects (*decomponere*).

People sometimes resist analysis. Beginning literature students, for instance, often complain that they lose the feeling of a poem while analyzing its symbols and structures. In one sense, these students are right: analysis serves no human purpose unless it leads to recomposition. Remember, however, it is precisely out of decomposition that life begins: *compost*, too, comes from *componere*. We analyze a poem in order to re-create the feeling more fully later. The end of analysis is synthesis (*recomponere*), understanding how the analyzed parts or aspects interrelate to form a whole.

This chapter is about rhetorical forms, abstracted from description, that are used for making distinctions, analyzing, explaining. To *explain*, as the etymology of the word suggests, is to *make plain*, literally by laying something out on a plain or flat surface. In keeping with this analogy, rhetoricians have sometimes called these the "spatial" patterns of development. Other rhetoricians have named these patterns "static" or "synchronic" to distinguish them from the progressive patterns, based on relationships in time (and abstracted from narration), that are the subject of Chapter 8. In any case, all the forms discussed in this chapter are founded in one basic mental process, what I. A. Richards calls "sorting."

In all our perceiving, thinking, feeling, and communicating, we sort or categorize. Though you may realize this textbook is unique, you still see it *as* a textbook. This means you have classified it with other textbooks, that you see it in relation to your expectations of textbooks. Even to see it as unique, as individual, you compare and contrast it with other textbooks. The same is true for any human being's perception of anything, from pomegranates to professors.

Comparison/contrast, classification and division, definition, and analogy are basic patterns of arrangement, ways of organizing written compositions (see Table 7.1). But they are also patterns of development, strategies for inquiry and articulation. They can be used to discover material as well as to arrange, it. If you describe your subject, define your terms, invent analogies, find examples, compare and contrast, classify and divide, you will generate material

Table 7.1   Basic Patterns of Development

	Analytic Patterns	Progressive Patterns
Report Patterns	Description	Narration
Explanatory Patterns	*Comparison/contrast* *Classification and Division* *Definition* *Analogy*	Process Analysis Causal Explanation Logical Progression

as well as organize it—indeed, you will probably generate insight, deepen your understanding. Think about these forms, therefore, not only as patterns of arrangement, but also as thought processes, as ways to generate and structure information.

Comparison/Contrast

The habit of creating order by comparison *and by* contrast *seems, as a matter of fact, to be almost as natural to [people] as thought itself. . . . [Comparisons] call attention to characteristics which might otherwise escape the eye. . . . Setting two objects or events against each other makes one into a touchstone or foil, a standard by which the other can be measured.*
HAROLD MARTIN AND RICHARD OHMANN

Perhaps *the* most basic mental act is to perceive similarities and differences. The rhetorical equivalent is comparison/contrast.

In description, writers often juxtapose two or more images, and readers then make the appropriate comparisons and contrasts. "Two years ago," reports Dovey Wong (page 279) "the police raided the house, arresting a girl on grounds of illegal possession of drugs while her father sat in a chair staring out his porch throughout the episode." Two images: the girl being arrested; the father sitting and staring. The juxtaposition is poignant in part because of the images, and in part because of a contrast between the father's reaction and readers' expectations about how a father should react to his daughter's arrest. As in most literature, there is an implicit contrast between *what is* and *what could or should be.*

Explanation, likewise, is often based on comparison and contrast. In explanation, however, the writer goes beyond simple juxtaposition and points out the similarities and differences. An explanation does not simply show; it tells. To *explain* is to *make plain* what readers might miss. You abstract similarities and differences for readers, try to make sure they notice the distinctions that matter.

The following passage, by the actor Ossie Davis, is one Black person's response to the way the word *black* is used in English.

The English Language Is My Enemy!

A superficial examination of *Roget's Thesaurus of the English Language* reveals the following facts: the word WHITENESS has 134 synonyms; 44 of which are favorable and pleasing to contemplate, i.e., purity, cleanness, immaculateness, bright, shining, ivory, fair, blonde, stainless, clean, clear, chaste, unblemished, unsullied, innocent, honorable, upright, just, straight-forward, fair, genuine, trustworthy. Only ten synonyms for WHITENESS appear to me to have negative implications—and these only in the mildest sense: gloss over, whitewash, gray, wan, pale, ashen, etc.

The word BLACKNESS has 120 synonyms, 60 of which are distinctly unfavorable, and none of them even mildly positive. Among the offenders were such words as: blot, blotch, smut, smudge, sully, begrime, soot, becloud, obscure, dingy, murky, low-toned, threatening, frowning, foreboding, forbidden, sinister, baneful, dismal, thundery, evil, wicked, malignant, deadly, unclean, dirty, unwashed, foul, etc. . . . not to mention 20 synonyms directly related to race, such as: Negro, Negress, nigger, darky, blackamoor, etc.

When you consider the fact that *thinking* itself is sub-vocal speech—in other words, one must use *words* in order to think at all—you will appreciate the enormous heritage of racial prejudgment that lies in wait for any child born into the English language. Any teacher, good or bad, white or black, Jew or Gentile, who uses the English language as a medium of communication is forced, willy-nilly, to teach the Negro child 60 ways to despise himself, and the white child 60 ways to aid and abet him in the crime.

Who speaks to me in my Mother Tongue damns me indeed! . . . the English language—in which I cannot conceive myself as a black man without, at the same time, debasing myself . . . [is] my enemy, with which to survive at all I must continually be at war.

The idea that thinking is always subvocal speech has recently been called into question, but that does not undermine Davis' main point. You can test Davis' response by going to a thesaurus yourself (see Exercise 4, page 309).

Of course, Ossie Davis presumably did not set out to write a comparison/ contrast essay; he set out to make a point about the "racial prejudgment" inherent in the connotations of certain English words. Outside of composition courses, few people sit down with the intention of writing comparison/contrast essays. The comparison/contrast essay *as such* is an exercise. But it is a useful exercise because it embodies the essence of a very basic thought process. No matter what type of writing you do—from a business proposal to a scientific report, from a diary entry to a literary critical essay—it is likely to include some comparing and contrasting.

Two Structures

The conceptual process that underlies comparison/contract can be represented by a grid (Figure 7.1). The number of characteristics you choose to

	Subject A	Subject B
Characteristic 1:		
Characteristic 2:		
Characteristic 3:		
Characteristic 4:		
Characteristic 5:		
Characteristic 6:		
. . .		
Characteristic N:		

Figure 7.1 Comparison/Contrast.

include depends, of course, on your subjects and your purposes. It is also possible to do comparison/contrast among three or more subjects, but two is most common. In any event, you can generate your material by filling in a grid like the one shown.

There are two basic ways to organize a comparison/contrast. Ossie Davis uses the divided or "half-and-half" structure. He makes all his points about *whiteness*; then he makes all his points about *blackness* (and then he moves to a higher level of generalization). The essential structure is this:

Introduction
Subject A (*whiteness*)
Subject B (*blackness*)
Conclusion

This is the easier comparison/contrast structure to compose and, since Davis' point is straightforward, there is no reason to do anything more complicated.

If the substance is more complex, readers may need more help—or they may miss some of the points. Then one uses the alternating characteristics structure:

Introduction
1st Characteristic
    Subject A
    Subject B

2nd Characteristic

    Subject A

    Subject B

3rd Characteristic

    Subject A

    Subject B

   . . . etc.

Conclusion

The alternating characteristics structure is a bit more work for writers. But it is also safer. First, it forces writers to be more rigorous (you are not likely to leave something out, as you might in an extended half-and-half comparison/contrast). And second, readers are not likely to miss any of your points. If the comparison/contrast is extended, therefore, the alternating characteristics structure is generally preferred, at least in academic and professional writing.

The following short piece of literary criticism was originally written with a half-and-half structure and then was rewritten with an alternating characteristics structure. Both versions begin with the same title and opening paragraph and make the same main point. The first version was easier to write, required fewer transitions, and seemed to have a more unified effect. But the alternating characteristics structure, because it tends to make writers (and readers) more aware of missing comparisons or weak support, often generates better evidence and tighter logic. Switching to the alternating characteristics structure led this writer to change one quotation and to add another—both of which support her point more strongly than anything in the first version.

Look What They've Done to My Song, Ma

The 1962 New Canadian Library edition of Susanna Moodie's Roughing It in the Bush omits certain portions of the 1852 London edition. The most significant of these omissions harm the reader's sense of the evolution of Moodie's response to the Canadian landscape and her poetic style.

The nature poems and songs in the first half of the original edition document Moodie's Wordsworthean response to nature, reflected in her choice of language and imagery:	Moodie's response to the Canadian landscape, for example, changes in the course of the text. Her early poems indicate that she has written from a decidedly European perspective—that of a Canadian immigrant trying to relate the Canadian landscape, the Canadian experience, in terms of her English experience:
The mighty river, as it onward rushes To pour its floods in ocean's dread abyss	

Checks at thy feet its fierce
  impetuous gushes.
And gently fawns thy rocky
  base to kiss.
Stern eagle of the crag! thy
  hold should be
The mountain home of heaven—
  born liberty!

Here Moodie's verse is imitative,
her rhyme is obtrusive, and her
imagery is clichéd. She has written
this poem from a decidedly European
perspective——that of a recent
Canadian immigrant trying to
relate to the Canadian landscape
the Canadian experience, in terms
of her English experience. In fact
when Moodie wrote this poem, she
had not yet set on foot on Canadian
soil; she was still on the ship that
brought her from England. How
Moodie's naive expectations of
life in the Canadian backwoods are
to be rudely fulfilled.

  The nature poems and songs in the
second half of the original text,
on the other hand, indicate that
Moodie has become more
realistically aware of and more
adjusted to the Canadian
landscape, and that she has found
a more appropriate imagery to
describe that landscape.

    Come, launch the light canoe;
      The breeze is fresh and
        strong;
    The summer skies are blue,
      And 'tis joy to float along,
        Away o'er the waters,
        The bright—glancing
          waters,
        The many—voiced waters,
    As they dance in light and
        song.

Queen of the West!——upon thy
  rocky throne,
  In solitary grandeur
    sternly placed;
In awful majesty thou sitt'st
  alone,
  By Nature's master—hand
    supremely graced.
The world has not thy
    counterpart, thy dower,
  Eternal beauty, strength, and
    matchless power!

How Moodie's romantic and naive
expectations of life in the
Canadian backwoods are to be rudely
fulfilled.

  The later poems, on the other
hand, indicate that Moodie has
become more realistically aware
of, more adjusted to the Canadian
landscape:

    Come launch the light canoe;
      The breeze is fresh and
        strong;
    The summer skies are blue,
      And 'tis joy to float along,
        Away o'er the waters,
        The bright—glancing
          waters,
        The many—voiced waters,
    As they dance in light and
        song.

Moodie has now come to terms with
the Canadian landscape——she can
appreciate the Canadian landscape
for what it is and without comparing
it to her beloved England.

  Secondly, Moodie's poetic style
evolves in the course of the text.
The nature poems and songs in the
first half of the original edition
document Moodie's Wordsworthean
response to nature, reflected in
her choice of language and imagery:

Here Moodie's style is much more simple and direct, and her language is less flowery and clichéd. The attitude toward nature revealed in her verse is more realistic, more loving. Moodie has now come to terms with the Canadian landscape; she can appreciate the Canadian landscape for what it is and without contrasting it to her beloved England.

"Stern eagle of the crag! thy hold should be/ The mountain home of heaven-born liberty!" Here Moodie's verse is imitative, her rhyme is obtrusive, and her imagery is clichéd.

The nature poems and songs in the second half of the original edition, on the other hand, indicate that Moodie has found a more appropriate language and imagery to describe the Canadian landscape. Her style is much more simple and direct, and her language is less flowery and clichéd:

> When the snows of winter are
>   melting fast,
>   And the sap begins to rise,
> And the biting breath of the
>   frozen blast
> Yields to the spring's
>   soft sighs,
> Then away to the wood
> For the maple, good,
> Shall unlock its honied
>   store.

In terms of the apprenticeship theme of the text, then, the omission of Moodie's nature poems and songs from the 1962 edition of Roughing It in the Bush harms the reader's sense of the structure, style and emphasis of the original text. The poems and songs of the original edition document Moodie's role as a precursor to the contemporary descriptions of the effect of the Canadian geography on the Canadian imagination, and document Moodie's concern for finding an appropriate language to describe that landscape. Look what they—the Canadian writers—have done with her song.

Mischelle Panagopoulos

The point is not that one or the other structure makes for better comparison/ contrast, but rather to demonstrate the effects of each. Which you should use will depend on what you are trying to accomplish.

The next example is an excerpt from an open letter in which a writer used comparison/contrast to serve a very different purpose: an alternating characteristics comparison/contrast was embedded in an extended persuasion. The writer hoped to convince sports fans to support public funding for ballet by demonstrating similarities between the sports they already support and the dance they misconceive. Thus an extended comparison became the major tactic in his persuasive strategy.

> . . . There happen to be quite a few similarities between dancers and athletes, some of which I would like to demonstrate. . . .
>
> Before any athlete is selected for the Olympic Games, you might agree that his body will have been prepared by a training program that will have commenced as far back as childhood. This proves that athletes and dancers begin with one basic thing in common: they both have to be trained very early in life. In fact, a dancer begins serious training at the age of eight or nine years. Obviously, athletic training and exercises have to be very specialized and specific to the particular sport in question. So does dance training, for example, "contemporary" or "modern" dancers will concentrate on exercises that develop different strengths than classical ballet dancers require. . . .
>
> Dancers have dedicated their lives to training their bodies, which have to have almost perfect physical proportions. Ballerinas train for at least four or five hours a day, doing strenuous exercises to sharpen their technique, in addition to performing. They are often called upon to dance allegro variations, that is, to dance full out for two minutes, which is equivalent to the 400 meter dash. The male dancer must be able to do the same, and *also* to perform high turning jumps and be capable of supporting the ballerina in high overhead lifts. This requires stamina to burn and great strength in both legs and arms.
>
> All athletes and dancers fear a common enemy, which is injury. Injury can result from a body contact or an accidental fall, however serious. Incapacitating injury can also result from a pulled muscle or snapped tendon or a strain. This kind of injury can often be avoided by stretching exercises in early training programs. These will lengthen the muscles, create greater elasticity in the tendons and develop greater suppleness in the body. They can also be used to "warm up" the body prior to competitions. Most athletic coaches today have learnt about the value of the stretching exercises that dancers are trained with, and with the Iron Curtain coaches leading the way, they are incorporating more and more of such exercises into their training programs. Today, athletes rigorously warm up before competitions with stretching exercises, just as dancers have been doing before performances for the last few hundred years.
>
> Many sports fans are not aware of the extent that athletes have borrowed exercises from the ballet curriculum. . . . Some college football coaches order their players to attend a ballet class once a week in the Dance Department to improve their footwork, balance and jumping. You will agree that gymnasts, whether performing on

the parallel bars or executing their floor routines, exhibit the highest degree of balance and grace. Their floor routines are, when analyzed, just a combination of dance and gymnastic tumbling. . . .

In Greece, where the Olympics began, the Grecian cities all had their sports arenas. However, in addition to their devotion to sport, the Greek democracies recognized that athletics were but one form of recreation and exercise, so they built amphitheaters to present dance and drama that were popular in those days.

Unfortunately, in our time, neither the athlete nor the dancer can exist without government support, especially when it comes to building sports arenas and opera houses. We can agree that both have their followers, and I put it to you that they should, therefore, both receive a fair share of the funds available.

I hope that this letter has made you change your mind a little and persuaded you that dancers should be regarded as athletes. Perhaps I can look forward to seeing you at the ballet one evening soon.

ANTHONY CLARKE

Comparison/contrast can be put to a variety of expressive, explanatory, and persuasive uses. Occasionally, especially in expressive writing, it stands on its own. More typically, it provides a basis on which writers can build explanations and persuasions.

EXERCISE

1. Write a short comparison/contrast essay using the half-and-half pattern. Rewrite it using the alternating characteristics pattern. How does the effect vary? (If at all possible use for this exercise part of a writing task with which you are already engaged, or at least a topic that already interests you, perhaps from another course you are taking or from your job.)

2. Reading in your area of special interest, find several passages that use comparison/contrast. For what purposes is it used?

3. Find two or more writers who have treated the same subject but with distinct purposes—for example, a journalist, a novelist, and an historian narrating the same event. Write a comparison/contrast in which you analyze and explain the differences. (See the Smith and Phillips, Melville, and Hemingway examples on pages 274–76.)

4. Divide a sheet of paper into four columns for (a) words with good connotations, (b) words with bad connotations, (c) words with neutral connotations, and (d) words you do not know well enough to classify. Then copy onto that sheet all the synonyms for black and white from an unabridged thesaurus published before 1970. Try the same exercise for two terms that define a crucial opposition in your area of specialization or special interest.

(Or paying particular attention to words that might be related to racism or sexism, compare and contrast a thesaurus published before 1970 with one published after 1980.)

5. Do a comparison/contrast of several pieces of literature with similar subjects—for example, D. H. Lawrence's *Sons and Lovers* and Agnes Smedley's *Daughter of the Earth* (both about growing up among coal miners) or the creation myths of the Hopis, Christians, and Taoists.

6. Compare and contrast two (or more) writers who have something important in common—for instance, two nineteenth-century English Romantic poets or two gothic novelists (perhaps Mary Shelley and Bram Stoker).

7. Compare and contrast several advertisements for similar products that seem to be aimed at distinct audiences.

8. Compare and contrast two analyses of the same war written by historians who sympathized with opposing sides—for example, a Canadian and a U.S. historian on the War of 1812.

Classification and Division

> *The categories developed in the humanities do not have the fixity and stability of objects and are not guaranteed by biological relationships . . . ; rather, they are constructions of the mind.*
>
> CHAIM PERELMAN
>
> *Our world divides into facts because we so divide it.*
>
> SUSANNE LANGER

To classify is to put your subject into a larger category or class. To divide is to break your subject down into smaller parts or aspects. The underlying thought process is crucially important. How we respond to an object or event often depends very much on how we classify it. How we divide a subject significantly influences subsequent analysis and interpretation.

When a writing student writes, "A major fault that runs consistently through my essays is the problem of fully developing themes and ideas," she is classifying. She has taken a number of specific flaws in a number of essays and generalized a single class that encompasses them all. She has reduced a number of flaws to a single problem and thus made an important step toward solving it.

Similarly, to get from "I don't know how to use commas properly" to "I misuse commas with coordinating conjunctions and with restrictive clauses," one must divide the use of commas so that the two problematic rules can be located. Here division is used to identify a vague problem more specifically, and thus an important step is taken toward solving it.

Real-world phenomena exist in overwhelming numbers and complexity. The ordinary human mind can handle approximately seven items (give or take two) in short-term memory. If you try to memorize the series "85490341," you will find it helpful to think of it as "854–903–41." Telephone numbers, credit card numbers, student identification numbers, and so forth, are usually so grouped.

Similarly, when you look at a rainbow, you probably see red, orange, yellow, green, blue, and purple. In other words, you probably divide the spectrum into six basic colors. The human eye is capable of discriminating about 7,500,000 colors; the human mind, however, is not capable of dealing with 7,500,000 distinct colors, so it groups them. Our culture happens, for most ordinary purposes, to classify those 7,500,000 colors into six groups. Some cultures have only two or three basic color words; others have more. Even within our culture, women tend to make more and finer color distinctions than men do (and to have a larger vocabulary of color words).

The concepts we use to classify and divide our experiences do not exist independently in the world; they are, rather, mental schema that we use to organize our experiences. We cannot perceive, think, feel, or communicate without such concepts, and one of the important functions of writing—especially academic writing—is to create and justify our concepts.

Classification and division are very basic and important patterns of development. How we "sort" the world can have very important pragmatic implications. When the United States government classified catsup as a vegetable and cupcakes as processed breakfast food, this affected meals served to millions of school children. Those people who make more and finer color distinctions have an advantage in thinking about interior design, fashion and other areas where color distinctions matter.

'Sorting' with a Purpose

One reason different people have distinct perceptions and interpretations of reality is because they classify and divide differently. As a writer, you should be aware of this, should classify and divide in ways that are relevant to your purposes. Just as we have various maps of the same terrain (e.g., road maps, hiking maps, nautical maps, aerial maps, geological maps), so we can use various schema for classifying and dividing a subject. Just as you would choose a road map for driving, a nautical map for sailing, an aerial map for flying, and a geological map for prospecting, so you can "sort" any subject about which you are writing in various ways. You should choose a way that is not only accurate but also serves your purposes.

There are, for instance, almost 200 countries in the world, too many for most of us to think about individually. So we classify them. To do so, we must choose a *salient feature*. If the salient feature is *location*, then Canada, the United States, and Mexico go in one class; Japan, China, Thailand, and

---

Table 7.2   Countries Classified by . . .

Location	Canada, Mexico, United States.	China, Japan, Thailand, Vietnam	
Population	Canada, Thailand, Vietnam	Japan, Mexico, United States	China
Size	Canada, China, Mexico, United States	Japan, Thailand, Vietnam	

Vietnam in another. If the salient feature is *population*, then Canada goes with Thailand and Vietnam, Japan with the United States and Mexico, and China in a class by itself. If the salient feature is *size*, however, then China goes with Canada, the United States, and Mexico. Major political issues and alliances turn on whether to classify the countries of the world East-West (i.e., procommunist or procapitalist) or North-South (i.e., developed or underdeveloped).

Our classifications and divisions are not totally arbitrary; they are based on real features of whatever is being categorized. Nonetheless, classifying schema are not "natural" or neutral; they are shaped by our purposes. When you classify and divide, you should think about the implications of using any particular schema. In order to make a point about literacy, for instance, a philosopher writes,

> People often speak of "literacy" as if it were . . . a skill, like being able to ride a bicycle or swim. I doubt whether any elements in reading and writing involve much skill in the strict sense, but in any case, the major elements certainly involve *understanding*, not just *doing* something. Computers can, in some sense, be programmed to read and write; but how thin this sense is—how much is missing from what we hope human beings do in their reading and writing—is, in general terms, clear enough. We want our children not just, like machines, to form strokes and letters, or to enunciate the syllables represented by "the cat is on the mat," but to express their thoughts and feelings in writing, and to understand those of others in reading. Literacy [is] far from being a single skill or even a set of skills.
>
> JOHN WILSON

Why does Wilson make a big deal out of such a distinction? Because classifications carry hidden assumptions, and those assumptions have implications. If writing were a skill, like typing or swimming, then one could presumably master it through training in a series of subskills. But Wilson favors humanistic rather than skills-based education. Depending on whether they perceive writing as a skill, craft, or art, people take radically different approaches to learning or teaching it. Because Wilson insists that *understanding* is a salient feature that must be considered when we classify reading and writing, he objects to classifying reading and writing as skills. Though the classification in and of itself may not matter, the unexamined assumptions it brings with it do matter.

The person choosing the salient feature on which to base a particular categorization does sometimes have considerable leeway. How much leeway varies from case to case. The following lists of synonyms for "masculinity" and "femininity" were selected from *Roget's International Thesaurus* (3rd edition):

MASCULINITY: manliness, manhood, mannishness, gentlemanliness, virility, potency, sexual power, manly vigor, manhood, homo, sire, fellow, chap, guy, bloke, gent, don, sahib, he-man, full-blooded, viripotent, ultramasculine, hoyden, he-manish, two-fisted, broadshouldered, hairy-chested, uneffeminate.

FEMININITY: womanliness, muliebrity, ladylikeness, matronliness, effeminacy, effeminateness, androgyny, sissiness, prissiness, milksopism, homosexuality, womankind, woman, calico, the distaff, the sex, the opposite sex, the fair sex, softer sex, weaker sex, "the lesser man," womanbody, weaker vessel, milady, gentlewoman, dame, dowager, squaw, girl, hen, biddy, petticoat, skirt, broad, curve, fem, frail, moll, "a rag a bone and a hank of hair," "God's second mistake," "one of Nature's agreeable blunders," "a necessary evil," "the female of the human species and not a different kind of animal," mollycoddle, old wife, henhussy, mother's darling, mamma's boy, muff, chicken, goody-goody, pantywaist, cream puff, powder puff, ladyfinger, lily, weak sister, softy, demasculinize, womanly, unmanly, womanish, chichi.

Perhaps the first question this list ought to bring to mind is why the editors of the thesaurus choose to classify under "femininity" words like "homosexuality," "demasculinize," "goody-goody," and "cream puff." In other words, what were the salient features by which the editors created this listing? (One might also wonder why there are quotations under "femininity," but no comparable quotations under "masculinity.")

Using Ossie Davis' "The English Language Is My Enemy!" (pages

302–3) and Mitchell Sulkers' essay (pages 73–76) as your models, consider how you would categorize these words. You will probably find that the synonyms for masculinity/femininity do not fit so neatly and easily into good/bad as did the synonyms for black/white; but you should be able to categorize them. What features of the traditional images of masculinity and femininity are implicit in the connotations of the words listed? What stereotypes (if any) of men and women are built into the English language?

Note how the preceding two questions provide a purpose that guides your categorization, leading you to select certain features as salient. The features are real: the words do have those connotations. But the words could be grouped in other ways (e.g., calico, petticoat, skirt, and pantywaist could be grouped as having to do with clothing; hen, biddy, henhussy, and chicken as having to do with poultry).

Like comparison/contrast, classification and division are patterns of arrangement that can serve various purposes and often are parts of larger writings. Classification, in particular, is often used to provide a context for the actual subject. Here, for instance, is a classifying paragraph which appeared near the beginning of a student's essay about the journal as a literary form.

> The memoir, autobiography, diary and journal may be grouped together as literature of personal revelation. In each form, the interest for the reader lies, to a larger extent, in the self-portrayal of the author. Memoirs usually give some prominence to personalities and activities other than the writer's own, and sometimes convey an historical event described from a personal viewpoint. Autobiographies are narratives of an author's life with stress on introspection, or upon the significance of their life against a wider background. Diaries and journals recount personal impressions while they are still fresh in the mind of the author and often provide reappraisals in the light of later experience. "What they lose in artistic shape and coherence, they [diaries and journals] gain in frankness and immediacy, many of the most famous having been kept with little if any thought of subsequent publication."[1] Although the two terms are identical in primary meaning, the journal has gained a slight differentiation as being a more reflective or detached record than the diary.
>
> Dianne Longson

---

[1] Joseph T. Shipley, ed., *Dictionary of World Literary Terms*, p. 23.

This classifying paragraph locates the writer's subject so readers will know where it fits into a larger body of knowledge. The journal is classified, along with three other forms, under the heading, "literature of personal revelation."

The paragraph is then developed by a comparison/contrast among the four genres. The first two sentences establish a basic similarity; the rest of the paragraph makes distinctions. The final emphasis falls on the most problematic distinction, between the diary and the journal.

Division

To write about any but the simplest subjects, you usually must divide it into its parts or aspects and arrange those parts or aspects in some order. And it is ordinarily useful to make the division explicit for readers (see pages 173–79).

Division is both a useful and a dangerous process. Using division can lead you inadvertently to imply that the whole is equal to the sum of its parts, that nothing essential gets lost in the process of discussing each part separately. You may not see the forest for the trees, not see the ecosystem because you are concentrating on the mosquitos. Nonetheless, we cannot ordinarily write without using division.

Obviously, division is more easily applied to some subjects than to others. You can take an automobile engine apart, study each part, and put it back together again without losing anything; but do not try to perform the same operation on someone's pet dog. Similarly, it is relatively easy to write about a machine part by part, but more difficult to write about an organic or social process one aspect at a time. Students who complain that their English teachers make them "dissect" poems are objecting because once they get the "parts" analyzed they cannot get the poem together again. The solution, however, is not to stop analyzing poems but to learn how to get them back together again.

When you use division, therefore, be careful to compensate for any mechanistic errors that may sneak into your analysis and distort what you are trying to communicate. Academic writers, in particular, often use thesis sentences to divide and order their papers (see pages 106–7). By careful use of framing paragraphs, transitions, and qualifiers, you can avoid mechanistic errors.

Like classification, division is purposive:

You may be surprised to learn, "There is no real majority in South Africa." The South African government demonstrated this in a *Globe and Mail* ad (19 March 1986) by dividing the South African population into Zulus, Whites, Xhosas, North Sothos, South Sothos, Shangaan-Tsongas, Tswanas, Venda Lembas, Swazis, Ndebeles, Coloureds, and Asians. The ad also demonstrated "that the Government of South Africa is clearly committed to power sharing and equal opportunity for all" by reporting such facts as that the "Wages Act of 1981 clearly established equality of payment for jobs irrespective of race, color or creed." (The ad did, however, neglect to mention that certain jobs are classified, restricted to people of a particular race—all of whom presumably enjoy "equality of pay.")

"DOUBLESPEAK UPDATE"
English Quarterly 20.3 (Fall 1987)

In the abstract, one division is as valid as another. In reality, however, divisions have implications. South Africa's apartheid laws divide people into just four categories—Black, Colored, Asian, and White—in which case the Blacks are clearly the majority. By choosing another division for its advertisement, the South African government was able to deny the existence of a Black majority.

Although the philosophical implications are complex, the practical applications often are not. Any subject can be divided in various ways. Reality is continuous—pick up anything and, as Thoreau said, you will find it attached to the rest of the universe. The divisions we make are the product of an interaction between our minds and that real world. These divisions, although they may correspond with certain features of the reality, do not exist objectively "in" the world. As a writer (and a thinker), you are responsible for choosing divisions that are accurate, to your purposes and appropriate to your audience.

EXERCISE

1. Do an "audience analysis" that classifies and divides the probable readers of something you intend to write.

2. Do an analysis of the types of writing that are common in your area of special interest. Classify writing in that area, relative to writing in general. Distinguish (divide) the various types of writing within the area. Do this classification and division in terms of both function (i.e., rhetorical context) and form (i.e., patterns of arrangement, format, conventions, etc.).

3. Write an essay analyzing a dispute that turns on how to categorize people (e.g., "Should principals be allowed to join a teachers' union?" "Can apartheid be justified in South Africa?" "Do girls have a right to play on Little League baseball teams?" "Should Haitians be allowed into the United States as political refugees?") Remember your primary purpose is to *explain* the dispute as an issue that turns on how people are categorized. If you want to use that explanation as a basis for asserting your opinion, do so. But be certain your essay includes the assigned analysis.

4. Whether one thinks of writing as a skill, art, or craft has implications for how one will go about learning or teaching it—that is why John Wilson asserts so strongly (page 312) that reading and writing should not be classified as a skill. His classification is asserted in order to make a point about how writing ought to be learned. Find another example where classification is used to set up an argument, and write a short analysis.

Definition

". . . and that shows that there are three hundred and sixty-four days when you might get un-birthday presents."

"Certainly," said Alice.

"And only one for birthday presents, you know. There's glory for you?"

"I don't know what you mean by 'glory,' " Alice said.

Humpty Dumpty smiled contemptuously. "Of course you don't—till I tell you. I meant 'there's a nice knock-down argument for you!' "

"But 'glory' doesn't mean 'a nice knock-down argument,' " Alice objected.

"When I use a word," Humpty Dumpty said in rather a scornful tone, "it means just what I choose it to mean— neither more nor less."

"The question is," said Alice, "whether you can make words mean so many different things."

"The question is," said Humpty Dumpty, "which is to be master—that's all."

LEWIS CARROLL

What Is a Definition?

Definition is a particularly important process. Defining your terms is often a good way to make sure you know (and can articulate) what you think you know. Definition of the central concept is often a good way to begin revising. And that same definition sometimes makes a good opening. Indeed, in certain types of writings, definition of key terms is mandatory.

The word *define* comes from the Latin *finire*, "to limit or end," which itself comes from *finis*, "boundary." To define is to establish limits, to make distinctions, to draw out-lines, to articulate boundaries. The function of a definition is to allow someone to distinguish the defined concept from all else. To define a concept we must both put it in a category (*classify* it, show what it is *similar* to) and also indicate how it is distinct from all else in that category (in-*divide*-ualize it). To define "yellow," for example, we classify it as a color and then create two boundaries that distinguish it from the two adjoining colors on the spectrum (orange and green). That is, we put it in a class ("color") and distinguish it from all other members of the class. Similarly, to define "yellow" in sense of cowardice, we put it in a class ("attitudes toward danger'') and distinguish it from all other members of the class, such as courage and caution.

The Importance of Definition

Words matter because they name concepts, and concepts matter because they influence our perceptions and interpretations. In and of themselves, words do not matter: "Sticks and stones will break my bones, but names will never harm me." But the words name concepts, and those concepts influence people's perceptions; and those perceptions may lead people to pick up "sticks and stones." So words do matter. It is not *"just* semantics." Our definitions matter because they are descriptions of our concepts.

Language is one of the social factors that influence the development of an individual's ideas. In this sense, our language to some degree defines us. Definition is a social process with which we live all the time. Formal definition is simply a verbal representation of that process.

Ordinarily, of course, when we want a definition, we do not become introspective and examine our concepts. We turn to a dictionary. Consequently, some people think definitions *come from* dictionaries. Indeed, the aura of absolute authority that surrounds "the dictionary" might lead you to suspect that the makers of dictionaries received their definitions from some omniscient deity.

In reality, however, a dictionary definition of a word is a generalized description of the way people use that word. A dictionary definition is, therefore, a sociological "fact" about how certain people use the word. Dictionary makers examine samples of language (usually with special emphasis on texts by noted authors, political leaders, and other such people). They isolate sentences using the word to be defined and then compose a definition (or set of definitions) that covers all those uses. Their task is easier when they are defining "desk" than when they are defining "pretty" or "tragedy." But the process remains the same. A dictionary definition is an abstracted and generalized description of how a certain word is actually used by certain people at a certain time in history.

Sometimes definitions are important because they are necessary preliminaries to the main point of a piece of writing. Often definitions are important because defining can be a form of hidden persuasion. Consider two social scientists arguing about whether apes can learn to use language: that is a very real question, but the answer (on one level at least) depends on your definition of language, and the scientist who gets to define language is likely to win the argument. That is why debaters have a slogan, "Define your terms," and often devote considerable time to debating those definitions.

How much poverty is there in the world? That, too, is a very real question; but it cannot be answered until *poverty* is defined. Is *Lady Chatterley's Lover* pornographic? Is *Ulysses*? That depends on your definition of pornographic. (Both of these novels have, incidentally, been classified as pornographic by agencies of various governments, including the government of the United States.) Whether a person goes to prison often depends on a definition: in the United States in the 1950s court cases turned on the definitions of *subversive* and *freedom of speech*; in the 1960s on the definition of *conspiracy*.

As a writer you are concerned with definition as a rhetorical form; always remember, however, that rhetorical form corresponds with a mental activity and relates significantly to events in the real world.

Formal Definition

Psychologically, we store concepts as prototypes: each of us has in our mind an image of the prototypical chair, and we decide whether a particular object is or is not a chair (or is "sort of" a chair) by comparing it with this prototypical image. Logic, however, demands more precision; logically, we define concepts by classification and division. The standard structure for formal definition is to state the *class* to which a term belongs and then show how it is *distinct* from all other members of that class.

Definition	=	**Class**	+	**Distinctions**
A chair is		a piece of furniture		that has a back and is used for seating one person

By putting *chair* in the class *furniture*, we distinguish it from most of the rest of the universe and reduce the task of defining it to manageable proportions. Had we said merely *a chair is a type of object*, completing the definition would be significantly more difficult. The phrase *used for seating* distinguishes chairs from most other furniture (bookshelves, television stands, dressers, china closets, etc.). *Has a back* rules out stools. *For one person* rules out couches and loveseats.

Thus we have a definition that can be used as a tool; one can go through the world armed with this definition and distinguish chairs from everything else, including other types of seats. This definition is not true or false—except in the sense that it matches fairly closely the way most English-speaking people do indeed use the word *chair*. Insofar as it does not match this usage (or perhaps even insofar as we decide this usage ought to change), we will have to revise our definition.

Yet all of this is not very interesting so long as we are defining *chair*. You probably already know what a chair is and are perfectly capable of distinguishing one from a stool, couch, or loveseat. But what if we define a term you are not so sure about, or a term whose definition is debatable, or a term that we wish to use in an unusual sense for some special reason? Suppose we define *tragedy* or *communism*.

Definition	= Class	+ Distinctions
A tragedy is	an imitation of an action that	(1) is serious, complete and of a certain magnitude, (2) in language embellished with artistic ornament, (3) in the form of action, not of narrative (4) through pity and fear purging these and similar emotions.
Communism is	a type of society	in which (1) the workers control the means of production and (2) goods are distributed according to need.

The definition of tragedy is Aristotle's, and it worked quite well for the tragic drama of classical Greece. Since then, however, a great deal of literature has been produced that many critics consider tragic, some of which is not drama and much of which would not meet Aristotle's other criteria. Considerable effort has been expended, therefore, on deciding which literary works should be considered tragedies—Is Milton's *Samson Agonistes* a tragedy? Is Dreiser's *An American Tragedy*? Is Miller's *Death of a Salesman*?—and on trying to redefine the term. The problem has been seen as how to broaden the term enough to include all of what the critic would consider tragedy without broadening it so much as to make any text with an unhappy ending a "tragedy." (See Chapter 10, pages 467–70, for an example of a term paper built around Aristotle's definition of tragedy and Milton's *Samson Agonistes*.)

The definition of communism is Marx's. If we accept it, none of the "Communist" countries in the world today would qualify, and many might not even qualify as "moving toward" communism. Indeed, if you hear such a definition of communism today, it is likely to be in the context of a discussion about whether the Soviet Union is really a communist country.

Essential and Operational Definitions

Aristotle's definition of tragedy by both form and function suggests a very important distinction between two types of definitions: the essential and the operational. An essential definition defines something in terms of what it *is* (essence); an operational definition in terms of what it *does* (function). An essential definition of a human being might be

A human being is an erect, bipedal, giant mammal relatively unspecialized in body form.

An operational definition of a human being might be

A human being is a social mammal that survives and produces by means of cooperation, typically uses tools and symbolic language, and whose nature is shaped more significantly by socialization than by heredity.

Note that both definitions use the same class (mammal), that both are accurate, and that there is no contradiction between them.

Similarly, we could define a screwdriver as a tool with a handle, a shaft, and a tip shaped to fit the head of a screw. For certain purposes that would be an effective definition (e.g., if you were sending someone to a hardware store to buy one). Now imagine that you are cross-country skiing and the screws have come out of your bindings somewhere in the wilderness. An operational—even tautological—definition would be more useful (e.g., a screwdriver is anything that might turn a screw) because such a definition might help you realize that a coin can be a screwdriver. Certainly if you were trying to invent a new type of screwdriver, an operational definition would be superior. Which type of definition you should use in any given case depends to some extent on the concept you are defining but more importantly on your purpose.

In the Western tradition, philosophy has typically been concerned with *essences*, with determining the "inner nature" of phenomena, with that which remains the same as more superficial "outer" characteristics change. Western philosophers have assumed that what we *are* determines what we *do*; that is why we reserve the phrase *essential definition* for definitions based on what something is, on its "inner" nature. More recently, certain philosophies (e.g., existentialism) have argued that what we do determines what we are—in effect, asking for an operational definition. Operational definitions have been more common in the sciences and technologies—generally in fields that are process-oriented and concerned with results. Here is an operational definition of work from an old Harvard University science syllabus:

We feel we have been doing more "work" when we have lifted 20 lb from the floor to a bench 1 ft high than if we had lifted only 10 lb; and we feel it takes more work to lift 10 lb from the floor to a table 2 ft high than to a bench 1 ft high. Such qualitative judgments may have been the starting point for the following quantitative definition:
The work done by a force F lb, constant in magnitude and direction, when it has moved its point of application a distance D ft along its own direction, is the product of F × D:

$$\text{Work} = \text{force} \times \text{distance.}$$

The unit of work is the foot-pound (ft-lb), a derived unit:

$$W \text{ (ft-lb)} = F \text{ (lb)} \times D \text{ (ft)}.$$

Note that this is a definition, not a physical law. Note also that it contradicts some of our experiences. If we lift 20 lb through 3 ft twenty times in succession, the definition says we are doing the same "work" each time, namely 60 ft-lb, whereas we know our work gets harder as the task progresses. The same would be true if we tried to climb the stairs in the Hancock Building. The fact is that physics uses some of the words of the English language, "work" for instance, in a new and specialized sense entirely its own.

PHILIPPE LECORBEILLER

Operational definitions are favored in science because they are often more concrete and revealing than essential definitions. In the following introductory paragraph, a constitutional lawyer uses an operational definition to discuss what democracy means, in practice, to the U.S. State Department.

For the past two centuries, the United States has defined democracy as representative government. For James Madison and the Federalists who drafted the US Constitution, direct participatory democracy was an evil, tantamount to mob rule. They favored representative democracy, based on large electoral districts and separation of powers, which they believed would make it difficult for the majority to enact what Madison termed "schemes of injustice," such as the renunciation of debts or violation of property rights. On the bicentennial of the Constitution's drafting, the United States government extols the virtues of a representative government and views the holding of national elections as the litmus test for democracy, at least where it approves of the results.

JULES LOBEL

Many grand slogans may be used to extol democracy, such as Abraham Lincoln's "government of the people, by the people, and for the people." In practice, however, says Lobel, the U.S. State Department generally defines democracy as existing wherever national elections are held. Discussion of whether a particular country is democratic, therefore, come down to whether its national government won power in a "free and fair" election.

Effective Definitions

In addition to the basic formula, there are certain rules we can state about *formal* logical definitions. (These rules do not necessarily apply in informal contexts.)

1. *A formal logical definition should not contain any* synonyms *or* derivatives *of the word being defined.* Do *not* say:

> A beautiful man is one who is unusually attractive.
>
> Communism is a form of government in which the Communist Party runs the country.
>
> Humor is a disposition caused by being exposed to something funny.

Synonyms can be useful for expanding formal definitions or for giving informal definitions; but from a logical point of view they are tautological (i.e., circular reasoning). Although it might be useful to a person learning English who happened to know the word *attractive* but not the word *beautiful*, the first definition essentially says merely that *beautiful* is a stronger synonym for *attractive*.

The second definition will not help a person who does not know what the words *communist* or *communism* mean. On the other hand, one might well want to use that definition in a statement like, "According to Marx, communism is a type of society in which the workers control the means of production and goods are distributed according to need; but in many so-called 'communist' countries, communism seems to be merely a form of government in which the Communist Party runs the country." Thus, although the latter definition is not a logical formal definition, it may still be a useful and meaningful statement (which we should probably classify as an ironic definition).

Note, moreover, that in defining a term like *root metaphor*, one might be able to assume readers who already understood the term *metaphor*. The defining purpose would then be to distinguish root metaphors from other metaphors. In such a case, therefore, the definition may begin, "A root metaphor is a metaphor that. . . ."

2. *A formal logical definition should not contain words that are ambiguous, figurative, or obscure.* Do *not* say:

> An immature person is one who is very sensitive.
>
> To be ironic is to speak with a forked tongue.
>
> A net is any reticulated fabric, decussated at regular intervals, with interstices at the intersections.

There are several problems with the first definition, one of which is that it begins to make sense only if the ambiguous word *sensitive* is construed in only one of several possible ways. The second definition is an insightful cross-cultural metaphor, which may possibly have broadened or sharpened your sense of the word *ironic*, if you already know what that word means. But it probably was not of much use if you did not understand the word to begin with. And the third definition, one of Samuel Johnson's most famous ironic definitions, would not be useful to people who did not know what *net* signified because such people would be highly unlikely to know half the other words in the definition.

3. *A formal logical definition should use the same parts of speech as the term you are defining.* (*Avoid using "is when" or "is where."*) Do *not* say:

> Swimming is when you propel yourself through the water with parts of your body.

> Women's liberation means they give women the right to crash men's clubs.

Definitions like these are not always wrong, but they tend to be. The first one needs merely syntactical revision: "Swimming is the act of propelling . . . ," etc. In the second one, however, the writer has given an example rather than a formal definition (and an inaccurate example at that).

4. *A formal logical definition should be positive.* Do *not* say:

> A whale is a big animal that lives in the ocean and is not a fish.

When one defines terms negatively, one tends to be imprecise. Precision, in this case, means saying "is a mammal" rather than "is not a fish."

5. *Generally, try to keep formal logical definitions as tight and precise as possible.*

The underlying principle here is the same as the general stylistic principle which calls for tight construction of most sentences.

Consider, for example, the following definition from a student's draft:

```
Boredom is that state in which an individual is, to different
degrees, uninterested in his present situation or the events at
hand.
```

Must boredom be individual? Could not a group (e.g., an audience) be bored? Must that which bores be present or at hand? Could one not be bored by the actions of a governmental body thousands of kilometers away? Is there any point in stipulating "to different degrees"—would one not assume that such a state could be experienced to different degrees unless the writer stated otherwise? Of course, the student who wrote it may well have drafted it in gobbledygook precisely to make it sound more impressive—not an unjustifiable response to a situation in which one is being judged, but not a useful way to reach the clearest possible definition of the term either. Gobbledygook removed, this definition reduces itself to the following:

```
Boredom is the state of being uninterested.
```

Having reduced it to that, are we not in a better position to consider just how useful a definition it is?

Another student wrote,

Child abuse shall be defined in this essay as intentional bodily
assault, sexual molestation or neglect causing bodily harm to any
person under seventeen years of age.

The style here is quite formal, but this is not gobbledygook; and the definition is quite precise.

Such definitions are called *stipulative definitions*, because the writer is saying, in effect, "For the purposes of this paper, I *stipulate* that child abuse will mean. . . ." A stipulative definition is often a one-sentence, formal definition set into a larger paper written for another purpose. This definition came from a causal explanation, the primary purpose of which was not to define child abuse, but to explain why it occurs. It was written by a young woman who was willing to admit that she was an abused child, and she wrote the paper in order to deepen her own understanding of what had happened to her.

Extending Definitions

Some pieces of writing are centrally and primarily *extended definitions*. An extended definition generally contains a precise formal definition, but it also goes beyond that definition in an attempt to give a fuller sense of an important concept. The techniques used for expanding definitions are also useful as definitions in less formal contexts; for example, if your husband looks up from the book he is reading and asks what a word means, you might respond most usefully and simply with a synonym or an example.

1. Definitions can be expanded by synonyms. One student, who was expanding her definition of anger as "the natural reflexive result of frustration— our reaction to having a goal blocked," turned to her thesaurus (often a dangerous turn, but one which she utilized effectively) and produced the following paragraphs (the middle paragraphs of a twelve-paragraph essay).

Anger is sometimes hidden even from ourselves because it hides
behind resentment, aggression, frustration, hate, fury,
indignation, outrage, wrath, antagonism, crossness, hostility,
bitterness, destructiveness, spite, rancor, ferocity, scorn,
disdain, enmity, malevolence, and defiance. Actually, no matter
how it is described, it still all means we are simply angry.

Our vocabulary has become very rich in describing other people
who are angry. We call people mad, bitter, frustrated, griped, fed
up, sore, excited, seething, annoyed, troubled, antagonistic, or

antagonized, exasperated, vexed, indignant, furious, provoked,
hurt, irked, irritated, sick, cross, hostile, ferocious, savage,
deadly, dangerous, and on the offensive. A lot of words, but they
often mean the same thing--angry.

What happens as a result of anger is behavior which prevents
communication. This kind of behavior, which is communication-
shattering, is described as, to hate, wound, damage, annihilate,
despise, scorn, disdain, loathe, vilify, curse, despoil, ruin,
demolish, abhor, abominate, desolate, ridicule, tease, kid, take
out spite on, rail at, scold, bawl out, humble, berate, beat up,
take for a ride, ostracize, fight, beat, vanquish, compete with,
brutalize, crush, offend or bully. We are angry--face the fact!

Janice Moulton

An entire essay written in this way would probably not work very well. But
these three paragraphs came in the context of a longer piece, one point of
which was that we too often try to deny and disguise our anger when we
would be better off if we accepted it and tried to direct it effectively (at least
when our goals are just and righteous). Note also that the synonyms were
used to expand, not to state the definition.

2. Definitions can be expanded by examples and analogies. A logical
definition is logically sufficient, but often we do not fully comprehend a concept
until it is concretized.

In the New Testament in the Book of Hebrews, it says that "to have
faith is to be sure of the things we hope for, to be certain of the
things we cannot see." Faith is what won man's approval to God in
ancient times. Faith lets us believe that God created the universe.
Faith made Abel sacrifice something better than Cain. Faith made
Noah hear God's warning. Faith made Abraham become a father way
past his age.

Janice Moulton

Note, incidentally, Janice's effective use of parallel structure in both this and
the preceding example.

**3. Definitions can be expanded by comparison and/or contrast, classifi-
cation and/or division.** Janice, defining "faith," suggests that it is very
similar to trust, except that trust is based on good reasons or evidence. Another
student in the same course extended a definition of "magic" by contrasting
it with scientific rationalism. Definitions can be clarified and sharpened by
using any of the basic patterns of development discussed in this chapter.

4. Definitions can be expanded by narration, process-analysis, causal analysis, or logical progression (see Chapter 8). You can tell a story that brings out the implications of a term or concept. You can explain how it might be used, why it came to exist, or what purposes it serves. You can relate it to processes or functions, to past and future.

Definitions can be expanded by discussing why's and wherefore's. A definition of water might be expanded by noting that it can be created by burning hydrogen in oxygen. It might also be expanded by listing the multitude of functions water has in an industrialized society. Kenneth Burke expands his definition of rhetoric explaining its function in a basic social process:

> [Rhetoric] is rooted in . . . the use of language as a symbolic means of inducing cooperation in beings that by nature respond to symbols.

Burke continues his definition, in the same section of *A Rhetoric of Motives* (California), by asserting that rhetoric is an ingredient in all socialization, that the manipulation of people's beliefs for political ends has been "a most characteristic concern of rhetoric, and [is] the use of words by human agents to form attitudes or to induce actions in other human agents."

5. Definitions can be expanded by giving the etymology of the term. Thus a student defining "political modernization" wrote,

> The Greek word <u>polis</u> is the root of the word 'political' and originally referred to the Greek city-state; it has come to refer to any organization of human beings in groups.

The authors of an article about error noted the derivation from the Latin *errare*, to wander, and then argued that,

> Just as wandering can be defined only in terms of a destination, so errors should be defined only in terms of goals.

The etymology and history of a word often tell a great deal about the concept it represents (and about the people who formed that concept). What can one infer from the fact that, according to the *Oxford English Dictionary*, the word *man* once referred to any adult and the word *girl* to any child?

Written to be distributed to undergraduate English majors, the following essay defines satire formally in its opening sentence, then expands the definition by division, etymology, examples, contrast, and analogy.

Satire: A Definition

In literature, satire is a poem or prose composition that mocks or ridicules prevailing human vices and follies, employing such methods as innuendo, burlesque, parody or irony. There are two types of satire: "Horatian satire is gentle, urbane, smiling; it aims to correct by gently and broadly sympathetic laughter"; "Juvenalian satire is biting, bitter, angry; it points with contempt and moral indignation at the corruption and evil of men and institutions" (Holman 473–75).

The word satire is derived from the Latin satira, a later form of satura, which according to ancient grammarians is elliptical for lanx satura, meaning "a dish filled with mixed fruits" or "food composed of many different ingredients." In its earliest use, satire was a "discursive composition in verse treating of [sic] a variety of subjects; in classical use a poem in which prevalent follies or vices are assailed with ridicule or with serious denunciation" (Oxford English Dictionary). The original meaning of the word suggests that the poem, like the bowl, is filled with a medley of follies and vices.

Satire existed in the literature of Rome and Greece and has survived with varying degrees of popularity to the present time. In eighteenth century England, satire reached its zenith with the essays, poetry, drama, and criticism of Dryden, Swift, Addison, Steele, Pope and Fielding. Jonathan Swift, a Juvenalian satirist, satirizes defective political, economic, and social institutions and man's moral nature in his well known Gulliver's Travels. Thus Swift pokes fun at Queen Anne whom he considered a royal prude when he describes the Lilliputian Empress's reaction to Gulliver putting out a fire in her apartment by urinating on it:

> And I was privately assured, that the Empress, conceiving the greatest abhorrence of what I had done, removed to the most distant side of the court, firmly resolved that those buildings should never be repaired for her use; and, in the presence of her chief confidants, could not forbear vowing revenge. (The Norton Anthology 1955)

An example of Horatian satire is Alexander Pope's long poem, "The Rape of the Lock," that gently makes fun of an actual quarrel between two families that was caused when Lord Peter cut off a lock of hair from the head of Anabella Fermor. Pope satirizes this quarrel by elaborating the trivial episode into a miniature epic complete with supernatural agents. Hence the "rape" of the lock. In the nineteenth century, Jane Austen's Horatian satire, Pride and Prejudice, satirizes the social manners of the day. In the twentieth century, Joseph Heller satirizes the absurdities of war in his novel, Catch 22, a Juvenalian satire.

Although satire might employ sarcasm, there is a clear distinction between the two. Sarcasm is the use of bitter irony with the intention of hurting someone's feelings whereas satire attempts through laughter to point out human flaws with the intention of inspiring improvement. In addition, sarcasm is often directed at individuals while satire is directed at a group or institution. It is, however, sarcasm's sneering bitterness and intention to hurt that distinguishes it from satire.

Like a surgeon with a scalpel, the satirist uses his wit to slice cleanly through the cancerous, rotting flesh of human vice and folly, scraping out the wound so that it can heal. The operation might be simple, an unsightly mole or wart that can be cut quickly off the surface. Or it might be a major operation that cuts deeply through the flesh to one of the vital organs. Whatever the disease, the satirist operates to heal the human condition.

Bonnie McComb

Works Cited

The Compact Edition of the Oxford English Dictionary. New York: Oxford UP, 1971.

Holman, Hugh. A Handbook to Literature. Indianapolis: Odysseys, 1960.

The Norton Anthology of English Literature, 3rd ed. Ed. M.H. Abrams. New York: Norton, 1974.

EXERCISE

1. Choose a term that names a socially significant group of people (e.g., "politician," "student," "jock," "gear," "parent," "feminist," "Vietnam veteran," "secretary"). Collect some sentences in which a particular group of people use the term. One way to get such a set of sentences is to select a particular group of people and ask them to complete a sentence beginning, "Being a _____ means . . ." Write a short paper analyzing what the term means to those people.

2. Choose a term that is important in your area of special interest. Construct two definitions, one essential and one operational. Check the derivation of the term in a historical or etymological dictionary (e.g., *The Oxford Dictionary of English Etymology*). Think of some synonyms and examples. Make up several analogies. Contrast the term with some similar terms. Think about how the term is used and why it is useful. Write an extended definition of the term for readers who are not familiar with your area of special interest.

3. Here are some student definitions of technical terms from rhetoric. How well do they achieve their defining purposes? Can you improve them?

Freewriting is a thought-generated process during which a person commits ideas to paper and is not concerned with using proper punctuation or grammar.

Freewriting involves self-determined, independent, unconstrained scribbling for the purposes of generating ideas and encouraging tolerance of chaotic composition processes.

Conceptual blockbusting is a discovery technique used to change old thinking patterns and generate new ideas by juxtaposing a statement and its contraries.

Conceptual blockbusting is a form of negative invention by which one explodes (or at least suspends) familiar concepts, attitudes, and perspectives—ideas that, inert and stereotypical, obstruct and prevent creative thinking.

A heuristic is a procedure to guide discovery of information and to prevent exclusion of relevant material. [*Heuristic*: seeking to find out, specifically applied to a system of education under which the pupil is trained to find out things for himself.]

A heuristic is a device providing systematic guidelines for inquiry, thus increasing the user's probability of discovering information he/she requires and decreasing the likelihood of the user overlooking relevant information. It does not lead mechanically and infallibly to a solution; it only increases the probability of discovery.

A root metaphor is a figure of speech based on some kind of comparison or juxtaposition that reflects people's assumptions, beliefs, and attitudes. It can function as a "hidden persuader." [From the Greek *metapherein*, "to transfer."]

Rhetorical context is a term used by writers to describe the circumstances of a particular piece of writing; these include purpose, audience, and occasion.

4. Choose a rhetorical term from this textbook (e.g., *heuristic*, *root metaphor*, *readability*, *gobbledygook*, *cumulative sentence*, *persona*). Write an extended operational definition for high school composition students.

5. Choose a term referring to a particular type of literary writing (e.g., *satire*, *haiku*, *epic*, *gothic fiction*, *Harlequin romance*, *proletarian novel*, *medieval English lyric*). Write an extended definition aimed at students in a university introduction to literature course.

6. Choose a current slang term. Write an essay that defines the term *and* explains how the term defines its users. Consider both how the term influences the perceptions of those who use it and how its use may label them.

Analogy

While it is true that argument by analogy always rests on shaky ground, it is possible for someone to become so niggling in his attitude toward all analogy that he is liable to strain at a gnat and swallow a camel. Perhaps we can avoid this carping habit by remembering that an analogy never proves anything; at best, it persuades someone on the grounds of probability.

EDWARD CORBETT

Bad analogies . . . tie us up if we take them too seriously. . . . These are wretchedly inconvenient metaphors [like the one] which makes language as a dress which thought puts on. We shall do better to think of meaning as though it were a plant that has grown—not a can that has been filled or a lump of clay that has been molded.

I. A. RICHARDS

In addition to supporting a point with logic, evidence or examples, writers often make analogies and use metaphors. Analogies and metaphors are often considered secondary support—not valid as proof, but powerful ways to emphasize and concretize, hence to help readers understand or to increase emotional impact.

Analogy is based on the logic of comparison. The word comes from the Greek *analogos*, originally a mathematical term, meaning "proportion" or "equality of ratios." When you make an analogy, you point out a similarity. You compare two situations and argue, implicitly or explicitly, that what is true for the first is also true for the second (at least to the degree to which the situations are similar). Usually you are comparing your subject with something more familiar or concrete.

In Chapter 2, the difficulty writers often have getting started was explained through the analogy of "mike fright":

Writers do not have the advantage of immediate feedback. Writing is, in this respect, very much like speaking into a radio microphone without the presence of a studio audience; and writer's block is very much like *mike fright*. When feedback is delayed, it is hard to continue verbalizing. But delayed feedback is in the very nature of writing: you write a sentence; then, before receiving any indication of whether that sentence has been understood, you have to write the next.

Writer's block is compared with mike fright; and on the basis of that comparison, something we know to be true for mike fright is asserted to be true also for writing. The analogy was intended to clarify and explain—and thus to convince you that a certain amount of difficulty generating words is to be expected when you are writing. If the analogy worked, it persuaded you to worry a little less about that difficulty.

Analogy, like enthymeme (see pages 131–33), is the rhetorical equivalent of deductive reasoning. If the comparison is valid, then what is true for the analog is also true for the subject. The logical syllogism would look like this:

> Writer's block is comparable to mike fright.
>
> Mike fright results from delayed feedback.
>
> Therefore, writer's block results from delayed feedback.

An analogy does not assert that the two terms are identical, just that they are similar in certain respects. The analogy is valid only if the compared features are actually equivalent.

The power of analogies is particularly apparent when they are used in refutations. In his letter from the Birmingham jail, Martin Luther King refutes the argument that peaceful demonstrations should be banned because they may precipitate a violent response:

> In your statement you assert that our actions, even though peaceful, must be condemned because they precipitate violence. But is this a logical assertion? Isn't this like condemning a robbed man because his possession of money precipitated the evil act of robbery? Isn't this like condemning Socrates because his unswerving commitment to truth and his philosophical inquiries precipitated the act by the misguided populace in which they made him drink hemlock? Isn't this like condemning Jesus because his unique God-consciousness and never-ceasing devotion to God's will precipitated the evil act of crucifixion? We must come to see that, as the federal courts have consistently affirmed, it is wrong to urge an individual to cease his efforts to gain his basic constitutional rights because the quest may precipitate violence. Society must protect the robbed and punish the robber.

King uses three analogies, each phrased as a rhetorical question. He arranges them in order of increasing power—how many Christians would blame Jesus for precipitating his own crucifixion? He makes a brief appeal to authority (the federal courts), and he closes with an implicit assertion that an injunction preventing peaceful demonstrations against racism is equivalent to a decision to protect thieves and punish their victims. (He also makes good use of repetitive sentence structure.)

Analogy as a Hidden Persuader

Analogies are much more common than is ordinarily thought, in part because many analogies are covert. We cannot think, or even perceive, without making comparisons. Whenever we attach familiar words to a new concept, we have the beginning of an analogy. Since the words carry connotations associated with the old concept, the very use of those words suggests an analogy between the old and new concepts. Any perception of similarity is an incipient analogy, and we cannot learn anything new without perceiving it as somehow similar to something we already understand.

In Chapter 2, the term "incubation" was used for a phase of the creative process that precedes inspiration. To incubate is to maintain something under conditions favorable for development, as when a hen sits on an egg. The very use of that word suggests an analogy between the biological creation of a new organism and the psychological creation of a new idea.

There is no problem with that metaphor in that context: it is apt; it makes a useful point about the creative process. It is, moreover, made explicit a few pages later when Gertrude Stein's analogy between writing and having a baby is quoted in full. The question, however, is this: when you read the word "incubation," did you stop to think critically about the implicit analogy it suggested? Presumably not. There are so many analogies implicit in the language we use that one simply cannot stop to think critically about them all.

For any subject, however, there are certain key analogies that manifest themselves as *root metaphors* (see pages 154–56). These analogies function as "hidden persuaders" and covertly persuade us to perceive that subject in certain ways. Insofar as they are accepted uncritically, these covert comparisons are as much a form of "subliminal seduction" as any advertising technique. They subliminally seduce us into perceiving in the ways they suggest.

Commonplace metaphors sometimes replace critical thinking and allow ideas to creep into our discourse unchallenged:

> Politics is often referred to as a game, especially by the media, though also in more "academic" discourses, and less so in everyday language. A cabinet is shuffled; a debate is a match; politicians gamble with their careers; issues are used as political footballs; an election is a "race for the crown." Though the game metaphor applied to politics has some validity, its connotations are not favorable in this context. A game is an act of competition, a sport or form of amusement with rules, usually involving more than one player. If politics is like a game, then an element of risk, chance, and luck is involved in decision-making; then images of amusement are attached to issues that are real and problematic; then politicians compete against each other rather than work in

cooperation for a similar cause: to represent the people.
Furthermore, the game metaphor is used to ridicule politics.

Nicole Duelli

The problem is not necessarily the analogy—which is often valid—but the covert and uncritical way it operates. Politics *is* in some ways like a game, but the political process can also be misconceived by someone who overrates this analogy.

In *The Art of Loving* (Harper & Row), psychiatrist Erich Fromm argues that we misconceive love through the root metaphor "*fall* in love." We will be more successful in loving, he says, if we change our metaphor. The analogy implicit in the phrase, "falling in love" constrains us toward impractical expectations by implying that love is easy (if dangerous), that all one need do is wait for the right person and then "fall." He tries to convince readers to perceive the "problem of love" as one of *how to love* rather than as finding the right person. He tries to persuade readers to approach love *as an art*, as an ability to be developed (like writing), rather than *as an experience*. He uses a series of analogies in an attempt to change the root metaphor that shapes many people's approach to love. Here is one of his more radical analogies, in which he tries to explain why two people "fall" in love with each other:

> Our whole culture is based on the appetite for buying, on the idea of a mutually favorable exchange. . . . [We look] at people in a similar way. For a man an attractive girl [sic]—and for the woman an attractive man—are the prizes they are after. . . . What specifically makes a person attractive depends on the fashion of the time, physically as well as mentally. . . . At any rate, the sense of falling in love develops usually only with regard to such human commodities as are within reach of one's own possibilities of exchange. I am out for a bargain. . . . Two persons thus fall in love when they feel they have found the best object available on the market, considering their own exchange values. Often, as in buying real estate, the hidden potentialities which can be developed play a considerable role in this bargain. In a culture in which the marketing orientation prevails, and in which material success is the outstanding value, there is little reason to be surprised that human love relations follow the same pattern of exchange which governs the commodity and the labor market.

Fromm is concerned, as a psychiatrist, with helping people to succeed in loving. In order to do so, however, he believes he must change their root metaphors, convince them to guide their perceptions and actions by more accurate analogies.

The Native American chief who said, "The earth—our mother—and I are of one mind," was similarly substituting one analogy for another. Though we commonly talk of "Mother Nature," the dominant modern Western metaphor makes the earth a resource to be exploited, a source of wealth given by God to Man for his use. The Native American's paradoxical analogy rhetorically denies the dichotomy between nature and people; it embodies instead the traditional assumption that people are part of the ecosystem.

Thomas Kuhn, who studies the history of science, argues in *The Structure of Scientific Revolutions* (Chicago) that the members of a scientific discipline share a set of "preferred or permissible analogies and metaphors." Physicists, for example, say that the molecules of a gas behave like tiny elastic billiard balls in random motion. These "standard analogies," Kuhn asserts, constrain the perceptions of the scientists and "help to determine what will be accepted as an explanation." Similar physical analogies underlie many popular arguments, as in these three short paragraphs from a newspaper feature article about sexually titillating magazines and advertisements:

> There is too much show and tell about sex these days. It is time the pendulum swung the other way. . . .
>
> I would like to be able to chat with my neighbor at the supermarket checkout without the magazines on display shouting: "Lookee here. All you wanted to know about orgasms and more, more." Or be able to buy a tube of toothpaste at the corner drugstore without a blatant Playboy model intruding on the transaction. . . .
>
> Granted there was too much puritanism at one time (that seems a very long time ago) and change often swings too far before a balance is obtained. Still, I look for the romance and find it missing when a sexpot coos me into buying a certain laxative.

People reading this ten-paragraph article in their afternoon newspapers probably did not stop to think about the commonplace analogy: social change is like a pendulum. To what extent is that analogy valid? A pendulum, as the writer suggests, swings regularly and predictably between two extremes before stopping in the center. Is that how social change works (and, if so, is there no such thing as progress)? Prior to the "puritanism" mentioned (note another implicit analogy), was there really a libertine period essentially comparable to the present in its tolerance for soft-core pornography?

There is no need to be overly picky. After all, this is a casual and commonplace analogy. And an analogy is only an assertion of similarity: it does not assert that the two terms (in this case, social change and a pendulum) are identical, just that they are similar in respect to certain salient features. But if the writer and readers of this article really want to do something about soft-core pornography in supermarkets and laxative advertisements, it matters whether they understand how and why it got to be there. Certainly, there is some similarity between social change and a pendulum, but is there enough to make it a valid analogy in this rhetorical context?

Here is a student essay that similarly analyzes a root metaphor. The writer's purpose here is to argue against the implications of the analogy.

No Cure for the Common Cold

As a child I was always unhappy with the fact that I was not allowed to take medication for a cold. All winter long, it seemed, I trudged over snow banks on my way to school, my ski jacket pockets stuffed with kleenex, feeling quite unloved as I thought of my friends who had colds sitting at home watching Bugs Bunny, taking pink cough syrup from a spoon, and swallowing candy coated aspirins. Inevitably, once I got to school, I would sniff and cough through silent reading while the teacher scowled down at me and asked why I didn't "take something." It wasn't until years later, after observing a roommate and the elaborate procedure she undertook to cure herself of a cold, that I realized the full extent to which people pamper themselves when they have colds.

One dreary January when I found myself with a cold, I decided to walk to a pharmacy, where I proceeded to fill my arms with the various cold remedies available——all designed to cure certain symptoms associated with a cold. When I got home, I felt like a junkie as I began to take my time-activated cold capsules, my pink lemonade cough suppressant, my special nose spray, and my adult aspirins. My cold did not go away any faster, but I did feel better temporarily, despite the fact that I had to contend with the guilt I felt about being such a gullible consumer.

At the time I attributed my behavior to the power of various forms of advertising which advocate taking cold medicine to relieve the symptoms of a cold. Television advertising, in particular, is very effective at convincing us that cold medicines will not only make us feel better, but improve our general outlook on life. Often we do feel better, simply because we are so convinced of the truth of what television advertising tells us. Also we feel better because we have bought ourselves something, and advertising recognizes that the act of buying goods is intrinsically tied up with our overall sense of contentment.

The advertising of cold medicine is effective only because it appeals to the belief, prevalent in our society, that when we are sick we should "take something." This myth is perpetuated by the immense pharmaceutical industry, whose very existence depends on our belief in the ability of their products to fix our ailments.

It is this belief that our bodies can be repaired that motivates us to visit a medical doctor when we have a cold. Doctors have led us to believe that by examining our bodies they can detect a specific

problem and then proceed to surgically remove or chemically combat
the problem. Doctors have encouraged us to think that our bodies
can be fixed just as machines can be fixed. Thus we have come to
regard our bodies as machines that break down from time to time.
When they do break down, or when one part begins to malfunction,
we seek an immediate answer to the problem. We may go to any one of
a number of specialists who have been assigned the task of keeping
different parts of our bodies in working order.

If a doctor doesn't fix our problem, we feel confused and angry,
just as we would if our mechanic failed to fix the brakes on our
car. We want a quick solution so we can get back on the road.

The fact that we have come to regard our bodies as machines is
indicative of the all pervasive influence of technology on our
lives. We believe that technology is constantly improving and
refining both ourselves and our environment. We don't question the
fact that someday science will provide us with a cure for the common
cold. In the meantime we will remain content with taking cough syrup,
nose spray and headache tablets to relive the symptoms of a cold,
and thus we will ignore the essential holistic approach to our minds
and bodies.

Mary-Ellen Selby

Let us bring the issue closer to home. I. A. Richards thinks that you
will have a clearer understanding of writing if you think of the composing
process by analogy to a plant growing. Gertrude Stein suggests the analogy
of a baby forming in a womb. Some contemporary rhetoricians, myself included,
have used the analogy of an evolving ecosystem. What all these analogies
have in common is this: they are consistent with Richards' assertion that language
processes should be understood *organically*, by analogy "with some patterns
of Biology." How will this set of analogies help you understand the writing
process?

Richards writes in *The Philosophy of Rhetoric* (Oxford) that we can
avoid "some traditional mistakes" by using organic analogies in place of
certain standard "bad analogies." He attacks the analogy that asserts "language
is a dress which thought puts on" because it implies that thinking is complete
before writing starts. He attacks analogies that assert meaning is "a can that
has been filled or a lump of clay that has been molded" because they imply
too rigid a relationship between "form and content." These analogies are
"bad" because they can lead you to take an overly rigid approach to the
composing process (thus interfering with your creative process) and to underestimate the importance of rhetorical contexts (thus interfering with your communicative process). It is these potential effects that make the analogies "bad."

It makes a difference whether writers think of revision as "polishing" or as "re-vision (re-seeing)." The two most common textbook analogies for the writing process are taking a journey and building a house. Both analogies overrate advance planning (maps, blueprints). Both analogies suggest that writing can be a linear, planned, and controlled process. If you think of writing, rather, as comparable to growing a plant—or a baby—these analogies guide you toward different writing strategies.

As a writer, you need to know that analogy, like exemplification, is an important technique you can use to clarify your explanations and convince your readers. To be honest, you should also understand the broader implications of the key analogies or root metaphors you use. Chapter 6 began with the thesis that we compose our perceptions (and that readers recompose writers' expressions) by juxtaposing sensory input with mental concepts. Verbal analogies epitomize that process. They embody all the advantages (and all the potential flaws) of the human mode of perception and communication. That is why analogy is such a powerful rhetorical form.

EXERCISE

1. Write an analysis of a conflict that occurred when two or more people perceived the same event differently because their perceptions were based on different analogies. Intercultural or intergenerational communications are good places to look for appropriate subjects. Be certain you are writing about a difference of perception, not just a difference of opinion (i.e., about a situation in which people "see" an event differently, not just one in which they make different value judgments about the event).

2. Read the short opening chapter, "Is Love an Art?" in Erich Fromm's *The Art of Loving* (Harper & Row). Analyze Fromm's use of both analogy and exemplification as persuasive techniques. Then write a short essay in which you use concrete examples to argue for or against Fromm's extended analogy.

3. Thomas Kuhn argues that standard analogies and examples, to which scientists were exposed as students, guide the perceptions of scientists and help determine what they will accept as a valid explanation. Select a standard analogy or example from your own field of special interest, and write an analysis of how it influences the perceptions of people in that field.

4. What analogies do you ordinarily use when thinking about writing? Can you remember how you acquired them? Write a short analysis of these analogies and their influence on your understanding and attitudes. By way of comparison and contrast, consider the many and varied analogies for writing cited in this book, among them those used by Andrew Crosse (pages 28–

29), Colin Grady (pages 29–30), Linda Flower (page 35), William Butler Yeats (page 37), Gertrude Stein (page 38), Monika Hilder (page 38), I. A. Richards (page 72), Adrienne Rich (page 108), Mary Stewart (page 110), Mina Shaughnessy (page 119), May Sarton (pages 119–20), Francis Christensen (page 170), W. H. Auden (page 210).

5. Pick any subject of particular interest to you and analyze the way in which standard analogies and examples influence people's perception of the subject. (Controversial social issues often make good subjects to analyze because people who take distinct positions usually use radically different analogies and examples.)

C·H·A·P·T·E·R 8

Progressive Patterns

The accelerated motion of a falling body, the cycle of a storm, the gradations of a sunrise, the stages of cholera epidemic, the ripening of crops—in all such instances we find the material of progressive form. . . . Syllogistic progression is the form of a perfectly conducted argument, advancing step by step. It is the form of a mystery story, where everything falls together, as in a story of ratiocination by Poe. It is the form of a demonstration in Euclid. To go from A to E through stages B, C, and D is to obtain such a form.

KENNETH BURKE

Narration (What happened? When did it happen?) is related to process (How did it happen? How does it work?); to cause and effect (Why did it happen? What caused or produced it? What are the results or consequences?); and to syllogistic progression (If certain things happen, then what must follow?).

FRANK D'ANGELO

How you broke open what sheathed you until this moment.

ADRIENNE RICH

THIS chapter is about rhetorical forms used to describe and explain *process and change*. Like all forms, they are not only structures for organizing writing, they are also modes of inquiry, strategies for generating material. Abstracted from narration, they are called the diachronic or *progressive patterns of arrangement* (see Table 8.1). They help writers think and write insightfully and logically about process and change.

In all our perceiving, thinking, feeling, and communicating, we make connections among events separated in time. We *see that* one event follows another. We *see that* one event is caused by another. We *see that* a conclusion follows logically from a fact or assumption. When you look at this textbook, for instance, you see that it was written, printed, and bound. You see that it may help you to develop your writing abilities.

Table 8.1   Basic Patterns of Development

	Analytic Patterns	Progressive Patterns
Report Patterns	Description	Narration
Explanatory Patterns	Comparison/contrast Classification and Division Definition Analogy	*Process Analysis Causal Explanation Logical Progression*

Narration is concerned with *what* happened. Process analysis explains *how* it happens (in general). Causal analysis explains *why*. The distinctions among the three forms are equivalent to the distinctions among the three questions: What? How? Why? An argument can also be considered a progressive pattern if it advances logically from one point to the next. It answers the question, "What follows logically?"

If you did the assignments in Chapter 1, you have already narrated (an account of what you did while producing a particular piece of writing) and generalized that narrative into a process analysis. When you tried to figure out why certain weaknesses recur in your writings, you did a causal analysis. The basics of providing evidence and being logical were discussed in Chapter 3 (pages 129–33). This chapter should help you develop a more sophisticated ability to use these patterns.

Like the sorting patterns discussed in Chapter 7, the progressive patterns are founded on the nature of human perception and thought. With the possible exception of dolphins, human beings are the only organisms on this planet that can communicate about events widely separated in time. Only human language has markers to indicate past and future. Only human language can communicate *if-then* propositions. (A dog's growl, for instance, can communicate, "I am about to attack," but a dog cannot communicate, "I will attack tomorrow.") A sophisticated ability to make connections among events separated in time is quintessentially human.

Process analysis, causal explanation, and logical progression are patterns of arrangement and modes of inquiry. By narrating what happened in a particular instance, generalizing that account into a process analysis of how it happens in general, and explaining why it happens, you are generating material as well as organizing it.

Process Analysis

Like narration, process suggests ongoing movement and continuous action. The emphasis in a process theme, however, is on the how, *rather than the* what.
FRANK D'ANGELO

Linear Processes

To move from narration to process analysis is to move to a higher level of generality, from *what happened in a particular instance* to *how it happens in general.* A process analysis can be an explanation of how something happens. It can also be instructions about how to make something happen.

Process analysis as you are familiar with it from school assignments probably meant writing compositions like, "How to Change a Flat Tire," "Baking Banana Bread," "The Life Cycle of the Butterfly," "Supply and Demand: How They Affect Prices," and so on. Such processes, at least as typically treated in school essays, are simple; their analysis is linear.

The general pattern is "*first* this, *then* that, . . . and *finally* the other"; the transitions are similar to those used in narrative writings.

First you take the spare tire, jack and tire-iron out of the trunk, *then* you loosen the lug-nuts, . . . *finally* you let the car down off the jack, tighten the lug-nuts and put everything back in the trunk.

First there is the egg, *then* the caterpillar, . . . *finally* the female butterfly lays her eggs and the cycle begins again.

The process may be described as a *straight* line, which ends at the last step or phase. Or it may be described as a *circle*, which begins anew at the last step or stage. Whether the line of development is straight or curved, the process may be accurately described step by step or phase by phase. Because it can be represented by a line, such a process is called linear.

The following recipe, like virtually all recipes, describes a real linear process. If followed step by step, it produces a lemon meringue pie.

Easy Lemon Meringue Pie

To make a quick and easy lemon meringue pie, first obtain the following ingredients:

1–1/2 cups graham cracker crumbs

2 tablespoons sugar (preferably brown)

1/4 cup butter or margarine

3 eggs

14 ounces condensed (*not* evaporated) milk

1/3 cup lemon juice (approximately 3 lemons)

grated rind from 1 lemon

6 tablespoons of white sugar

Begin with the crust. Preheat oven to approximately 190°C (375°F). Mix graham cracker crumbs with sugar in a 9-inch pie plate. Melt butter or margarine and mix thoroughly with crumb-and-sugar mixture. Press against bottom and sides of pie plate with back of spoon. Bake for seven minutes. Set aside to cool. Leave oven on.

Next make the filling. Separate the egg yolks from the egg whites. Put the whites aside. Mix the yolks with the condensed milk and lemon rind. Beat in lemon juice until the filling sets. Pour into crust.

Next make the meringue. Meringue sets up best if everything— egg whites, bowl and beater—is at room temperature or slightly warmer. In a ceramic bowl, beat the egg whites until frothy. Then slowly add white sugar while continuing to beat rapidly. After the meringue holds stiff peaks when you lift the beater, spread over pie. Be certain to seal the edges.

Bake for 15 minutes at 190°C (375°F). Cool. Enjoy.

Some recipes are difficult to follow, but that has more to do with subtlety or number of steps than with intrinsic complexity. In this recipe, for example, the filling may not set if the lemon juice is not measured precisely, and the meringue may not stiffen if there is yolk in the egg whites. Nonetheless, the process itself is linear and may be accurately presented in this step-by-step format. In the end, the test is in the pie: if the typical reader can follow the instructions and produce a tasty lemon meringue pie, the writing was successful.

The methodology section of a scientific report is very like a recipe. Scientific and technical reports include a section explaining how the experiment was done. If readers want to evaluate the validity of an experiment, they need to understand how it was conducted. If other scientists decide to repeat the experiment—and one of the basic principles of science is that experimental findings are valid only if they can be replicated—the methodology section should tell them all they need to know. The following methodology explains how census data were analyzed statistically. It will allow social scientists both to evaluate the validity of the procedure (hence of the conclusions) and to do parallel studies on other data (e.g., the next census).

In this study, we analyze three clusters of independent variables. One important *economic* variable is the maximum benefit for a family of three from Aid to Families with Dependent Children (AFDC) and food stamps. We adjusted this welfare guarantee (GUAR in our tables) for differences in state cost of living using an index developed by Fournier and Rasmussen (1986). We expect GUAR to vary directly with the percentage of female family heads. A second important variable is a dummy indicating the presence of a state AFDC program for unemployed fathers (AFDC-U); we hypothesize that there will be fewer single mothers where such a program exists. Labor market opportunities are measured by the ratio of women's to men's earnings (RELEARN), or by separate variables for women's and men's earnings (FEARN, MEARN). These earnings measures were adjusted by the state cost of living index. We expect RELEARN and FEARN to positively affect female headship, and MEARN to show a negative effect.

The *cultural* variables were the percentage of women who had finished high school (EDUC), the metropolitan area (SMSA) population size (POP), the number of women aged 15–34 divided by the number of employed men aged 16–39 (RATIO) and dummy variables to indicate regions (SO, NC, W). We thought that more educated women would be generally more cognizant of various social resources including work opportunities, would earn more and would be more likely to head their own families. There may be less social stigma against single motherhood in larger SMSAs. To test this hypothesis, we included the population size. RATIO is meant to measure the availability of marriageable men for women of the same race: it takes into account local male mortality and employment (hence breadwinning capability), which have been found relevant especially for the black population (Aponte, Neckerman and Wilson, 1985). We expect that women who have lower opportunities to marry employed males will more likely become single heads of family. Regional dummies are proxies for cultural differences. Based on past results, we expect the South to have a lower incidence of female family heads, other things being equal.

We examined three *legal* variables. All three represent new hypotheses on the determinants of female headship and have not been tested before. One indicates whether restrictions on public funding for abortion had been implemented in the state by 1980 (ABORT80). The same variable was created for 1982 (ABORT82). Obviously, adding restrictions in 1982 would not have prevented poor women from getting an abortion in 1980. We interpret ABORT82 instead as an indicator of state conservatism on issues related to family matters. The number of restrictive state laws regarding sexual education, contraception and abortions, LAWS, is the third variable. The 1980 abortion variable and the number of restrictive laws are expected to vary directly with female family headship; conservatism is expected to reinforce the traditional family model.

Previous studies on the subject used data from the 1960 or 1970 U.S. Census, or from other data collected in the mid 1970s, and did not incorporate our legal and some of our cultural variables. We drew data from the 1980 Census on the 56 SMSAs with a population of over 100,000 for which black and white data were compiled separately. We ran linear and logarithmic regressions. Since results are similar, we only report the linear estimates.

PAULE MCNICOLL

This methodology section, like the preceding pie recipe, represents an ideal of process analysis: one step at a time, in chronological order, it tells how the data was analyzed. Whenever it will not distort your subject, *organize process analyses linearly, step-by-step or phase-by-phase* because linear structure is easiest for readers to follow.

Not all processes are linear, however. The process by which we interpret a poem, for instance, will be misunderstood if we try to describe it linearly. The depth and multiplicity of connotations is often part of what makes a poem poetic; the simultaneous experience of several levels of meaning is part of what makes reading poems wonderful. A linear process analysis will not help us understand what happens when people read poems.

Nonetheless, in literary criticism and especially in teaching people how to read poems, we often do reduce the poem's multiple meanings to a series of linear representations. Since reading a poem is a *supralinear* process, such literary critical and pedagogical representations do distort the poem. But the distortion is usually intentional, part of the pedagogy; and the unstated assumption is that readers will go back to the poem, that they will reread it in light of what they have learned, and that the rereading will restore the unity of the poem by recreating the simultaneity, depth, and multiplicity of meaning. Without this assumption, the distortion would not be justifiable.

Complex Processes

Sometimes the various aspects or subprocesses of a process intertwine, interact, occur simultaneously on various levels, and ebb and flow instead of following discretely one after another. We *can* treat such a process *as if* it were linear by focusing on the subprocess or aspect that predominates at any given point in time. When and to what extent are we justified in presenting complex processes as if they were linear? What are our other options?

When we say, "the writing process has three stages: prewriting, drafting, and revision," we are representing the writing process as linear. Although a distortion, this statement is justifiable in certain contexts. When it was originally put forth, for instance, it served to focus attention on an aspect of the writing process that had been neglected for more than a century: the means by which writers invent or generate material for their writings. Even now, it can be a useful simplification for guiding young or inexperienced writers.

Many processes, of course, are linear and may be so represented without distortion. This is especially true of mechanistic and organized processes, such as those that predominate in certain areas of the hard sciences and in their applications in engineering. As we start to deal with living systems, processes become less and less linear. By the time we get to what we consider quintessentially human, whether we are concerned with aesthetics or psychology, we are usually involved with supralinear processes. Social and ecological processes are even more typically supralinear. If we try to analyze these processes by analogy to "How to Change a Flat Tire," we often distort them and sometimes end up in a mess.

The writing process is an apt example. It is a quintessentially human creative (psychological) and communicative (social) process. Empirical studies of experienced writers clearly show that linear representations seriously distort what writers actually do when they write. A more accurate representation was suggested in Chapter 3 (page 116).

> Writing consists of two contradictory subprocesses: on the one hand, we must generate or discover material; on the other, we must select and order that material. The first subprocess usually predominates in the early phases, the second in the late phases of writing.

This statement represents writing as the interaction of two contradictory tendencies, either of which may occur at almost any time during the process. It orders the process conceptually without reducing it to discrete chronological stages.

Within the framework provided by such a statement (and with appropriate reiteration to keep the framework in readers' minds), one can go on to discuss first the generation of material and second the selection and ordering of that material. Within a framework which asserts that the process is supralinear, one can discuss various aspects of that process in a linear order. To use I.A. Richards' term, it is the interinanimation of the framework with the more linear parts of the analysis that communicates the supralinear complexity.

Part One of this textbook is a process analysis of a complex supralinear process: writing. The subject—how to write—is distorted if represented linearly. Here is an example of a student's attempt to write an analysis of a supralinear process.

My Supralineal Writing Process
Told in a Lineal Way

My writing process, from initial assignment to final completion, roughly follows three basic stages. I name these stages with the acknowledgement that the thinking process involved in writing does not follow neat, orderly stages of development, but rather that thought processes are haphazard and that, consequently, writing is a supralineal process. Naming stages allows me to simplify a normally complex process in reality. The stages are procrastination, thought and actual writing.

When I have been given an assignment, the majority of my time (from assignment to completion) is spent procrastinating; I never do today what I can do tomorrow. I generally avoid thinking about the project and do nothing towards its completion.

But when the due-date of any particular essay creeps uncomfortably close, small beads of sweat form above my brow and I end my thought stage: I consider just what I should do. Generally, no writing is attempted. If the assignment is a research essay, I choose a topic (if I have a choice), gather relevant books and begin reading. If the assignment is like the first essay of this class, I merely think about how I should tackle the essay because I already have the knowledge and no research is necessary. This thought stage prepares me for the third stage, actual writing.

I seldom know exactly what my essay will say until I begin writing. I must write to clarify my ideas; my thoughts are too fleeting to possibly organize and write an essay in my head, so I must capture those elusive ideas and ground them on paper. Once I have written many ideas down, my thesis statement or controlling idea begins to show itself. With such a controlling idea, the purpose of my paper becomes clear and further reading, thinking and writing that I do becomes focussed; the essay begins to become organized.

Yet, even with such an organizer as a controlling idea, my writing process is far from the accepted methodology for writing essays. For example, I constantly revise as I write, not after I have finished. Also, I generally write the body of the essay first; and as I mentioned previously, I seldom come up with a controlling idea until I have written much of this body. After I have the controlling idea and have finished the body of the essay, I write the introduction, making it suit the body. Then comes a conclusion, a title, and a rewrite. Because I procrastinate so much, I have little time for the actual writing and therefore revise only once. I do this revision as I am making the good draft. Consequently, though, my final draft is seldom as polished as it could be.

Despite my haphazard ways of completing an essay, the essay does get finished. This lineal process analysis can capture only some of the complexities of my supralineal writing process.

Brad Lloyd

Brad makes good use of the framework—title, opening, and ending—to state explicitly that his writing process is supralinear, that he is "naming stages" only "to simplify a normally complex process." Since clarity often demands that the aspects of a process be discussed individually, using the framework to emphasize the actual complexity of the process is a very important technique.

Brad also emphasizes the supralinear complexity in the body of his process analysis. About his "actual writing stage" he states, "Procrastination, thinking, reading, agony and writing all play roles in this stage—with no particular order." In his penultimate paragraph, he makes use of readers' contextual knowledge when he contrasts his process with "the accepted methodology." Referring to contexts of various sorts is another important technique for communicating the supralinear nature of a process.

Brad's process analysis is characterized by a certain guilt, manifested first on the level of word choice. "Haphazard" is something of a snarl-word for a process that loops back upon itself, repeating procedures that were initiated in earlier phases, as when Brad returns to thinking and reading after he has already begun "actual writing." "Procrastination" is also a snarl-word, which may or may not be appropriate. Insofar as Brad's first stage is essentially stalling and results in his not having enough time to revise adequately, the connotations of "procrastination" are correct. Insofar as this reluctance to get started actually includes some creative incubation, it may be more functional than Brad realizes.

There is order to Brad's process. It just is not the linear order of "the accepted methodology." It moves from thinking to unstructured writing, finds a center of gravity (i.e., a controlling idea), and then is organized; the body is finished, and an introduction, title, and ending are written (in that order); the essay is polished and recopied. Revision recurs throughout this process. Although the "actual writing" starts too late and structural revision is probably slighted, the process is not haphazard. Like most writers' creative processes, it just has an order distinctly different from "the accepted methodology." If Brad could just get started a bit sooner, thus allowing time for an additional phase of revision between his first draft and final drafts, the process he describes might be just fine.

Brad's "problem" is that what he has read and heard about how people should write represented writing as a linear process. Consequently, he feels guilty about the messiness of his "haphazard" process. In truth, however, writing is often a somewhat chaotic process. Writing often must pass through chaos on its way to creating order. The real problem is how to describe the writing process without implying that it should proceed in neat, orderly stages from start to finish.

This is a common problem. There are many psychological, social, economic and ecological processes we misunderstand because we squash their supralinear complexities into the form of a linear process analysis. Though linear process analysis is easier to read (and to write), there are times when we should use a more complex form.

Exercise

1. Do a process analysis of your own writing process. (See pages 7–14, and Exercise 4, page 291.)

2. Consider the process analyses you have written in the past. If you had a choice, what type of processes did you choose to write about? Did you represent the processes as linear? To what extent was this representation accurate?

3. Select any supralinear process (e.g., the interaction around your family's dinner table, the process by which someone gets to be a political leader in the United States, Canada, New Zealand, Australia, or Great Britain, the evolutionary development of a complex species of organism). Be sure to select a process you know well. Analyze it carefully. Write a process analysis that accurately represents the process.

4. Try to write an analysis of the mental processes of a person reading a complex poem.

5. In the science section of a newspaper or newsmagazine, find a summary of a process analysis originally presented as a scientific paper or article. Obtain the original. Compare and contrast the two versions.

6. Find an instance in which a linear process analysis led to a social or ecological blunder because a choice was made or a policy chosen on the basis of a simplistic analysis. Write a critique.

Causal Explanation

It is very remarkable how often a symptom is determined in several ways, is "overdetermined."

SIGMUND FREUD

We are especially arbitrary in picking out the cause from among the whole group, or context, of conditions—of prior and subsequent events which hang together.

I. A. RICHARDS

Correlation and Causation

Scientists make a useful distinction between causation and correlation. *Correlation* means two events regularly occur together. Demonstrating a correlation does not necessarily mean there is a causal connection between the events.

Almost every morning, my father makes a pot of coffee and then takes a shower.

The correlation is close to 100%, but it seems highly unlikely that the shower is caused by the making of the coffee.

According to a scientific study, juvenile delinquents drink four times as much milk as teenagers who do not commit crimes.

Does drinking a gallon of milk a day cause criminal behavior? Can we reduce teenage crime by rationing milk?

Scientific reports are often reports of correlations. A correlation is much easier to demonstrate than a causal relationship: if events occur in conjunction more frequently than can be explained by chance, there is a correlation. Scientists (or for that matter, literary critics) often demonstrate a correlation first and only second attempt a causal analysis to explain that correlation. The correlation between smoking cigarettes and contracting lung cancer, for example, was demonstrated long before any causal relationship was scientifically established. The parallels between Dickens' *Dombey and Son* and Lawrence's "A Rocking-horse Winner" are more easily established than Dickens' influence on Lawrence's story.

It is easy to jump to the conclusion that because two events regularly occur one after the other, the first must be causing the second. But this is a fallacy: correlation is actually no more than grounds for suspicion that a causal relationship may exist. Even if a causal relationship is discovered, the first

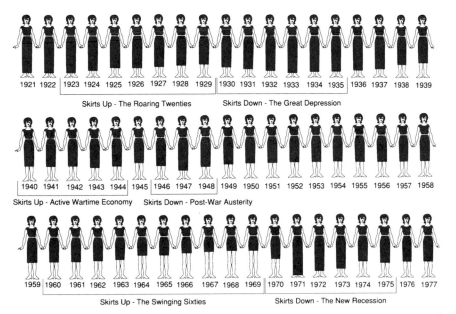

Skirts Up - The Roaring Twenties   Skirts Down - The Great Depression

Skirts Up - Active Wartime Economy   Skirts Down - Post-War Austerity

Skirts Up - The Swinging Sixties   Skirts Down - The New Recession

Figure 8.1   For most of this century, one can easily demonstrate an extraordinarily direct correlation between fashionable hemlines and the state of the economy. A causal explanation is, however, more difficult and complex.

event may not have caused the second: it is possible, for instance, that both events result from a third factor not originally considered.

> In order to help himself wake up, my father takes a shower and drinks coffee.
>
> The sort of teenager who finds it difficult to sit down for a proper meal is likely to grab a pint of milk and a donut instead. Whatever is causing that restlessness may also contribute to criminal behavior.

For most of this century, women's skirts have gotten shorter during economic prosperity and gotten longer during hard times (see Figure 8.1). Do fashion designers check the major economic indicators before designing next year's hemline? Do investors reduce their investments when deprived of the sight of women's knees? Unlikely. But perhaps there is a rough causal relationship between people's economic well-being and their confidence—and perhaps women who are feeling optimistic and self-confident tend to take more risks when they choose their clothing. Correlation does imply some sort of causal relation, but often not a simple, linear cause-effect relationship.

Causal explanation is one of the most common and most important types of writing. We are asking for a causal explanation whenever we ask, "*Why* did such-and-such happen?'' Questions about meaning, too, are essentially requests for causal explanation: ''Why is a reader justified in taking this meaning from the text?'' or ''How are readers constrained to see this meaning in the text?'' In human affairs, causation becomes a question of motivation, *''Why did so-and-so do such-and-such?''* (see Burke's Pentad, pages 82–86).

Different types of societies seem to rely on distinct types of causal explanation. Though we all tend to consider our own ways of thinking ''natural,'' historical and cross-cultural studies indicate that there are at least four basic types of causal explanation, any one of which may be predominant in a given culture or subculture.

Authoritarian societies often rely on *explanation by authority* (which is really a form of nonexplanation). ''Why should I obey the Queen?'' ''Because God said so.'' (Or ''Because we'll cut your head off if you don't.'')

Traditional societies tend to rely primarily, though not exclusively, on explanation by analogy. Indeed, explanation by authority may be a special case of *explanation by analogy*. If asked, ''Why should I obey the Queen?'' some people in Elizabethan England would have replied, ''Because the universe is arranged in a Great Chain of Being with God on top, then the angels, the Queen, the aristocrats, the freemen, the serfs, the animals, and so on; just as the angels should obey God and the animals should obey people, so ordinary people should obey the Queen and the aristocrats.'' (See pages 331–39 on analogy.)

This type of explanation has predominated in most human societies for most of the time human beings have been on this planet. It operates by establishing analogical parallels (sometimes called *myths*). These parallels may be, for instance, between past and present or between the behavior of nature (or the gods) and the behavior of people. But there is usually no attempt to demonstrate a cause-effect relationship between, say, God's authority over the angels and the Queen's authority over her subjects. Although people in such cultures are certainly aware that physical actions produce physical reactions, another form of explanation predominates.

A third type of explanation, *cause-to-effect* reasoning, becomes dominant in industrial societies. Indeed, when third world countries that are trying to industrialize quickly import technology from the industrialized countries, people often have difficulty thinking along the lines required to run imported machinery. The kind of linear cause-to-effect reasoning required to repair a broken machine does not come naturally.

A fourth type of causal analysis explains events in relation to contexts. As we move from an age dominated by machines to an age dominated by computers, and as our social and ecological systems grow ever more complexly interrelated, this type of causal explanation becomes increasingly important. It is increasingly widely used in such fields as computer science, ecology, linguistics, the social sciences, and biology. *Contextual explanation* is particularly useful for explaining complex systems and choices.

Cause-Effect Patterns

Because it is the type of reasoning that gave rise to machines and that best explains their internal workings, mechanical cause-to-effect reasoning predominates in industrial societies. If you learned a structure for writing about causation from a previous writing textbook or course, it was almost undoubtedly cause-to-effect.

Philosophers sometimes talk about cause-effect thinking as "the billiard ball model of the universe." In cause-effect reasoning, events are explained in much the same way as motion on the billiard table. The physical analogy is apt because this type of cause-effect reasoning become dominant first in physics, where it is called *action-reaction* (i.e., Newton's third law of motion). Cause-effect reasoning was so effective in physics (especially in mechanics) that it has since been applied in the other sciences. In psychology, for example, it becomes *stimulus-response*.

The terms "cause" and "effect" are labels we attach to events to represent our explanations of *why* those events happen. One billiard ball ("the cause") strikes another, which moves ("the effect"). But if the second ball also strikes something, it becomes a cause and the reaction of that something becomes an effect. Likewise, the motion of the first ball was itself was an effect (caused by the motion of the billiard cue), and the motion of the cue was caused by a person.

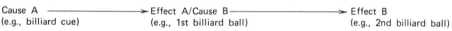

Cause A   ⟶ Effect A/Cause B ⟶ Effect B
(e.g., billiard cue)   (e.g., 1st billiard ball)   (e.g., 2nd billiard ball)

Figure 8.2 Simple linear cause-effect.

The result of cause-effect reasoning is a causal chain, such as the one epitomized by this old nursery rhyme:

> For want of a nail the shoe was lost,
>
> For want of a shoe the horse was lost,
>
> For want of a horse the rider was lost,
>
> For want of a rider the battle was lost,
>
> For want of a battle the kingdom was lost,
>
> And all for the want of a horseshoe nail.

A causal chain can branch, for example, if the second billiard ball strikes two or three others. And naturally, if the chain is broken at any point—for example, if the billiard cue misses the fist ball—all subsequent effects disappear.

In an industrialized culture, the most common response to the question, "Why?" is a causal chain.

"Why were you late to class?"

"Because it takes nine minutes to walk here from my previous class, and the instructor didn't let us out until three minutes ago."

A *full* explanation would be more complex—"Why couldn't you interrupt or leave before you were 'let out?' "—but the causal chain is accepted as a *sufficient* explanation in most social contexts.

Causal chains flow from cause to effect. But explanations based on them can flow in either direction. One may reason from *effect to cause*. In human terms, this involves explaining, though not necessarily justifying, the means in terms of the ends. ("I couldn't interrupt or leave before my instructor let us out because I was afraid that might affect my grade.") In terms of Burke's Pentad (pages 82–86), we would say the *act* is explained by the *purpose* (i.e., by the purpose-act ratio).

Thus the anticipated effect explains the act. In an essay about mugging, for instance, a writer might argue that such crimes are common because they so often go unpunished. The anticipated effect (lack of punishment) is offered as an explanation of the crime, even though the mugging occurs first and the lack of punishment later.

As this example suggests, explanations often must be multiple. The anticipated lack of punishment could not by itself explain a mugging. There must be at least one other anticipated effect, such as financial gain or the pleasure of being in a position of relative power. Writers using cause-effect reasoning must be careful not to oversimplify by leaving out important parts of an explanation. Consider, for instance, the following problem-example:

A student is studying late on the last night of finals week because he has three examinations on the last day. He runs out of cigarettes. Tired and groggy, he goes downstairs to buy some more. He cuts across an alley to an all-night store. A car with one headlight and bad brakes comes down the alley. The driver had taken his last examination that day and had been drinking. He tries to stop quickly, but cannot. The police form, which must be filled out, asks, "What was the cause of the accident?"

Remove almost any single element from the story and the accident probably does not occur—for example, if the student did not smoke cigarettes or if examinations had been scheduled so that no one had more than one test on any given day. That raises another level of questions, such as why people smoke cigarettes and why university examination schedules are structured as they are. But the police are not looking for a full explanation. "Defective vehicle and intoxicated driver" is a sufficient explanation for police purposes. As Figs. 8.2–8.4 suggest, linear cause-effect patterns are comparable to linear

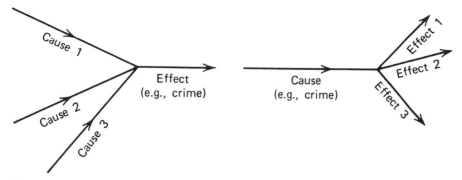

Figure 8.3 Multiple cause-effect.

processes. Indeed, linear processes are most accurately explained by cause-effect reasoning.

Just as processes can be cyclical (see page 342), so cause-effect chains can be circular. When the cause-effect pattern is circular, as in an ongoing cycle, distinguishing cause from effect can be problematic (or irrelevant). "Which came first—the chicken or the egg?" is a misleading and paradoxical question. As the following examples suggest, accurate causal explanation must take this additional complexity into account.

> Hudson's Bay Company records from certain areas of northern Canada demonstrate a cyclical relationship between the lynx population and the snowshoe hare population. The cycle typically runs four years, during which the lynx population rises to a peak and abruptly drops off to near extinction. Meanwhile the snowshoe hare population slowly declines and then starts to rise rapidly. The explanation is as follows: as there get to be more and more lynx in this simple ecosystem, they eat more hares until there are so few hares that the lynx have little to eat and most of them die off; this allows a rapid rise in the hare population, which allows the lynx population to grow again until the system once more reaches its limit. This sort of oscillation, incidentally, is typical of simple, not complex ecosystems.

> Scientists (and therapists) investigating couple relationships among human beings have often discovered cyclical patterns. Imagine a stereotypical married couple in which he tends to criticize and she tends to withdraw. The correlation is undenied. But her explanation is that she withdraws *because* he nags her. And his explanation is that he criticizes her because she is so withdrawn that he has to do something aggressive to get any response whatsoever. In other words, both agree about the ongoing causal chain, but each blames the other; each says "My undesirable behavior is an *effect*; yours is the *cause*."

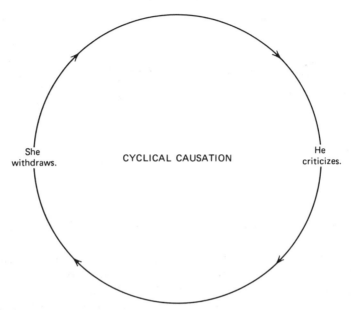

She
withdraws.   CYCLICAL CAUSATION   He
criticizes.

Figure 8.4 Cyclical causation.

The cause-effect distinction tends to break down when a causal chain is cyclical. Either we must say that each event is *both cause and effect* or we must say that the distinction is not relevant. Even if we wish to assign blame, when a cycle has been going on long enough, the appropriate question changes from "Who started it?" to "What is keeping it going?" An investigation aimed at finding out whether, many years ago, he criticized before the first time she withdrew, or vice versa, is probably futile and almost certainly irrelevant. Indeed, such couples typically do spend a lot of time arguing about who started it—which allows each to blame the other and also allows the cycle to continue.

The futility of trying to impose cause-effect distinctions onto ongoing cycles has interesting implications in practical situations. One standard example of a cyclical relationship is the Cold War arms race: the U.S. government said, in effect, "We must increase our military strength *because* the Soviet Union is increasing its military strength"; the U.S.S.R. government said, in effect, "We must increase our military strength *because* the United States is increasing its military strength." Each government claimed that its armaments were defensive, that it was increasing its military might only in reaction to the threat from the other; and, for a variety of reasons, the cycle continued to escalate for four decades.

The distinction between "cause" and "effect" is difficult to make in cyclical systems. Fortunately, it is often also unimportant—because events are shaped not so much by initial conditions as by the structure of the ongoing process.

Causes and Contexts

Certain situations are so complex that any sort of cause-effect analysis (even multiple or cyclical) oversimplifies them. To use a cause-effect pattern when you are writing about such situations will likely distort reality and lead you into errors. At best, it will leave you with a partial and simplistic explanation.

This danger is especially great when important causal factors are contextual, i.e., features of the environment. If we ask why a company markets a particular type of product, the most important causal factors may lie not within the company, but in its environment (a.k.a. the market). Similarly, if we ask why Hollywood produces certain types of movies but not others, contextual factors may be more significant than the personal motives of individual movie producers and directors.

The word *overdetermination* was coined by Freud to describe situations where cause-effect reasoning is inadequate. Freud used the word first in speaking of psychological symptoms. Later he applied it to dream symbolism (which suggests why the concept is also usefully applied to literary criticism). I. A. Richards took up the word to explain his context theory of meaning, which treats discourse "as overdetermined, as having multiplicity of meaning." It was, in part, Richards' literary critical background that led him to assert in *The Philosophy of Rhetoric* (Oxford),

> we are especially arbitrary in picking out the cause from among the whole group, or context, of conditions—of prior and subsequent events which change together.

When using cause-effect reasoning to write analysis, writers tend to stop when they have provided sufficient "cause" to explain the event. They have answered the question implicit in the cause-effect pattern—the poem, incident, decision, or whatever has been "explained." The writing formally achieves closure (see page 182) and feels complete. So the writer stops.

But the most interesting and important levels of explanation may not have been reached. One of the greatest virtues of contextual explanation is that it encourages writers to delve more deeply and readers to consider more fully. The following paper is an analysis of why people eat popcorn in movie theaters. On the most immediate level, the explanation is obvious (and boring). But by delving more deeply, the writer comes up with an interesting and significant theory.

Popcorn Goes to the Movies

People go to the movies for various reasons. They like to enjoy themselves, learn something new, edify themselves, etc. In short, they are in search of illusions, dreams, entertainment, magic.

Having equipped themselves with a box of popcorn and a cup of Seven-Up, and having occupied their comfortable seats, they are ready to be amused. Popcorn and Seven-Up only heighten and add to their enjoyment of a movie.

The factors which influence this widespread and unique ritual seem quite obvious. One of them is simply the fact that popcorn tastes good. Going to a movie is, therefore, a perfect occasion for buying a box of it. Another constraint is the traditional association of popcorn with movie-going. For some people movie-going is just inseparable from popcorn-eating. At the movies, the odor of popcorn and the fizzing of Seven-Up and Coke mixes with their joyful expectations of something new and enjoyable that will start unreeling before their eyes in a few moments. It has, therefore, become a habit to eat popcorn at the movies. This habit is also reinforced by parents who are quick to oblige their little ones with a bucket of popcorn. For others who are also being initiated into movie-going, this atmosphere at the movies can be contagious, and the odor of popcorn so attractive that they quickly line up to get their own box of epicurean pleasure.

These are the factors that lend themselves easily to the apparent and superficial explanation of the eating habits at the movies. There are, however, several other factors which also influence popcorn consumption at the movies. Since people usually go to the movies after a week of hard work, they are feeling relaxed and free. Their thoughts are not only tuned to the atmosphere at the cinema, but are also motivated by the steep admission price. The four or five dollars should entitle them to get their money's worth of entertainment and for a few cents more also a box of popcorn. Complete enjoyment, of course, means not only a "good" movie, but lots of popcorn along with it. In this narrow sense, money also functions as a constraint. If they are going to spend money, they might just as well spend it in a proper way.

Eating and watching a movie could, however, be considered two actions which are quite incompatible. Usually a movie should demand a certain degree of commitment to its message and, of course, its artistic qualities. It seems that, by drinking and eating while watching it, the viewers interfere with the communication between the movie and themselves. Consequently, these eating habits point to the most important constraint: the attitude of viewers towards movies in general.

This attitude is quite simple. An average movie-goer pays his five dollars, buys his popcorn and a drink, sits in the back row and waits to be entertained. Indeed, the very use of the word "cinema" and the word "movie" seems to point at the underlying difference in approach to the cinematic art. While "movie" is a popular word denoting something entertaining, "cinema" implies something more serious. What with the influence of television and the impact of Hollywood's movie industry, films have in a sense degenerated into movies pure entertainment. As people go to the movies mostly to enjoy themselves, the pleasure of eating becomes extremely compatible with watching a movie. Like sitting in front of a TV set, for some people watching a movie is not complete if they are not gorging on popcorn while Dudley Moore is falling in love with Bo Derek. Ironically, it is not so much the attitude towards food in general that constrains the eating habits of some movie-goers, but primarily their attitude towards movie-theaters as places of entertainment.

This attitude has been promoted largely by the consumerist nature of North American society. Not only does this society dispose of diapers and paper cups, but also of works of art: films. The prevailing getting-your-money's-worth mentality of this society functions as a kind of underlying constraint. This mentality can be seen in the attitude of movie-goers. Parallel with the change in the social significance of the movies, the public has also changed its attitude towards them. The movie-theater, an enchanting place of entertainment, edification, and even an occasional catharsis, has, therefore, degenerated into a supermarket of amusement and a feast of popcorn.

To summarize, the constraints that influence the eating habits of some movie-goers are the following:

Constraint 1: popcorn tastes good

Constraint 2: association of popcorn with movie-going

Constraint 3: atmosphere at the movies

Constraint 4: money

Constraint 5: attitude towards movies

Constraint 6: consumer society

Although each of the constraints separately determines popcorn eating at the movies, no one can singly explain the complex pattern of motivation. Only by demonstrating how and why these factors mutually constrain popcorn eaters can an adequate explanation of the habit be provided. In terms of these constraints, movies are viewed as an integral part of the North American consumer society, which sheds additional light on this facet of the North American way of life. However, if you happen to agree with the quotation of Orson Welles—"All the good movies have already been made"—it might not be unreasonable to contend that some people chew richly

buttered popcorn and chase it down with a huge cup of Coke because
they are inclined to agree with Mr. Welles.

Branka Ozbolt

In a sense, this essay could have ended after the second paragraph. Had it been structured in a cause-effect pattern, it might well have, for the second paragraph contains sufficient "causes" to explain the widespread eating of popcorn in movie theaters. But the interesting part of the essay—the writer's theory that eating popcorn at the movies is a symptom of a consumer society—would have been lost. Looking beyond the immediate event to its contexts encourages writers to develop explanation beyond the obvious minimum.

Note also that this explanation has several levels. The most basic, encompassing causal factor is the consumer society, which promotes the relevant attitudes toward both films and money. These attitudes then allow and encourage the association of popcorn with movies. The association of popcorn with movies and the good taste of the popcorn lead some people to buy it, thus creating an atmosphere that encourages other people. It is important in a contextual analysis, especially in the introduction or conclusion, to indicate what the relationships are among the various factors. Only then has one produced a logically rigorous explanation.

Fortunately, there is an ancient rhetorical pattern that is admirably suited for discussing situations where contextual factors are an important part of the causal explanation.

Look again at the nursery rhyme on page 353. The moral is quite clear: be painstakingly careful about every detail. The rhyme fulfills its rhetorical purpose—to convince little children that extreme carefulness is a virtue. But it is not very informative about why kingdoms fall (nor, for that matter, is it seriously intended to be). Just as no straw ever broke a camel's back unless the camel was overloaded to begin with, so no kingdom ever fell for want of a horseshoe nail unless it was already in dire peril. Although it might have been the immediate cause, "all for the want of a horseshoe nail" is hardly an adequate answer to, "Why was the kingdom lost?" Pushing this nursery rhyme beyond its intended purpose suggests the limitations of the cause-effect "billiard ball model."

To clarify the point, let us return to the billiard table. Suppose we take up the same billiard cue and make the identical stroke—but strike a person instead of a billiard ball. We are no longer dealing with merely physical motion. To predict or explain subsequent events, we must analyze a person's interpretive response to a symbolic action. And such human "reactions" cannot be explained adequately by analogy to physical motion.

The nature of the response will depend on how the person who is struck interprets the event. And that we cannot predict without knowing a lot of *contextual* information. Is this person an acquaintance, a friend, a stranger, an enemy? Are we in a billiard parlor, a bar, a friend's gameroom? What memories and interpretations does this person have of comparable events? What analogies come into her or his mind? Is this person presently sober, slightly intoxicated, drunk, or stimulated?

Of course, we could call all these contexts "causes." We could say, for example, "Because we were in a bar and the person was a drunken stranger who had recently been poked by a police officer's nightstick (which reminded him of the times he used to be poked by his father as a child), his response to being struck by a billiard cue was to throw a punch." But this is a different level of explanation from one based on the momentum and direction of the billiard cue. On the billiard table we are concerned with the mechanical transfer of physical energy. When we become involved with meaning (that is, with the transfer and interpretation of information), various contextual factors become more important than the immediate physical "cause."

Consider the following example:

> Konrad Lorenz, the Nobel-prize winning ethologist, was crouching in the tall grass outside his country house, moving about in figure-eights, glancing regularly over his shoulders and quacking constantly. He looked up to see a group of tourists standing at the garden fence, staring horrified in his direction.

From the tourists' perspective, Lorenz' behavior was inexplicable, if not insane (indeed, we often use the word *insane* precisely when we have failed to explain an action). However, hidden in the tall grass was a line of ducklings; Lorenz had substituted himself for their mother, and he was at that moment congratulating himself "on the obedience and exactitude with which my ducklings came waddling after me." The tourists could not explain the event because they could not see the ducklings *and* because they did not know Lorenz was a scientist doing an experiment. Even if they had seen the ducklings, they still might have judged Lorenz insane if they did not understand the scientific context.

Contextual explanation is increasingly common in various disciplines, from biology to psychology, from linguistics to computer science. Often it is used to explain decision-making processes. Contextual explanation often evades errors or solves mysteries created by the limitations of cause-effect thinking. Paleontologist Stephen Jay Gould, for instance, uses contextual explanation in *The Flamingo's Smile* (Norton) when he proposes "a new kind of explanation for the oldest chestnut of the hot stove league—the most widely discussed trend in the history of baseball statistics: the extinction of the .400 hitter." The crux of his argument is that you cannot explain the failure of any player since Ted Williams to hit .400 by looking at hitters and hitting; the explanation is not that hitters have changed, but that the context in which they hit has changed. Here, in summary, is his explanation:

There have been tremendous improvements in relief pitching and fielding. Today's players are also handicapped by a longer, more tiring schedule and by more games played at night, when the ball is harder to see.

But even these factors constitute "an incomplete explanation, expressed from an inadequate perspective. . . . As with most persistent puzzles, we probably need a new *kind* of explanation, not merely a recycling or refinement of old arguments." To understand why Mantle, Minoso, Kaline, Carew, and Brett never hit .400, we need to look also at the worst players. The extinction of the .400 hitter is a symptom of a more general extinction of extremes. What we have, in fact, is a decrease in variation, a common phenomenon in the evolution of many systems.

The greatness of the great hitters is not produced by careful management and training, but good managers and training methods can make the lesser players better. Though the great players of yesteryear sometimes faced each other, they often played inferior opposition. What needs to be explained is not what happened to the .400 hitters, but what happened to the inferior opposition. And that we can explain, for managing and training baseball players has become a science, and the worst major league players of today consequently perform better than the worst players of yesteryear.

It is tempting to treat contextual factors as if they were just another set of causes and then to explain such situations as if we were dealing with multiple cause-effect. Sometimes that can be done without distorting meanings. Other times, especially when the matters are psychological, social, aesthetic, or ecological, such analyses oversimplify actual events and lead toward erroneous conclusions.

In the example of the student struck by the automobile (page 354), all of the factors mentioned in the narrative function on the same level. But suppose we need a deeper explanation. We might argue, for example, that the incident occurred because the city in which it happened lacked an inexpensive and efficient system of public transport, which the second student might have used instead of driving while drunk. Or because automobile safety inspections were not required. This is another level of explanation. It does not contradict the level called for by the police form. The immediate causes still include bad brakes and slowed reflexes. But the contextual factors are a different sort.

Suppose we were to ask what motivated the first student to smoke despite clear evidence that tobacco fumes are harmful to his health. Suppose we discover that he smoked cigarettes because (1) they were available, (2) he could afford them, (3) having been raised by a father who smoked, he associated cigarettes with masculinity and maturity, (4) having been exposed to advertising, he associated cigarettes with sensuality and independence, and (5) nicotine physiologically reduces tension in mammals who are habituated to it. How do these factors mix with bad brakes, slowed reflexes, and the absence of an inexpensive, efficient public transport system?

A *full* causal analysis of any such event is complex and involves many levels of explanation. For the police, this is not a problem. Given their practical purposes, they can ignore all but one level. Writers can sometimes do the same. In scientific, academic, or professional contexts, however, writers' purposes are often such that a simplistic explanation will not do.

Levels of Explanation

Historians try to deal with such complexities by creating a distinction between *immediate* and *basic* causation. Thus World War I may be explained like this:

> The largest war the world had yet seen was immediately precipitated by the assassination of Archduke Francis Ferdinand of Austria-Hungary by a Serbian nationalist in 1914. There were, however, many factors that had led toward war. Prominent causes were the imperialistic, territorial and economic rivalries that had been intensifying from the late nineteenth century, particularly among Germany, France, Great Britain, Russian, and Austria-Hungary. Of equal importance was the rampant spirit of nationalism, especially unsettling in the empire of Austria-Hungary and perhaps also in France.
>
> THE NEW COLUMBIA ENCYCLOPEDIA

This distinction creates an explanation with two levels. The basic causes create a *basis* for the event; the immediate causes spark the event. The assassination of Archduke Ferdinand could no more have caused a war by itself than a straw could break the back of a lightly loaded camel. If asked whether World War I was caused by the assassination of the Archduke or by "imperialistic territorial and economic rivalries," one should answer, "Both," and then go on to explain the relationship between the two levels of explanation.

Just as a poem may have more than two levels of meaning, so a causal analysis may require more than two levels of explanation. The writing process is also a good example. Suppose, for instance, we want to explain a writer's choice of the last word of the following sentence:

By 1910, Kansas City was definitely _____ .

To simplify the example, let us imagine that the writer has come up with the following possibilities: *metropolitan, citified, urban, suburban, oppidan, civic*.

The most basic constraint—that the word match the intended meaning—rules out *suburban* and *civic*. Then the writer is constrained not to choose *oppidan* because most of the intended readers would not know the word. The writer happens not to remember how to spell *metropolitan* (and does not want to make a bad impression with a misspelling). *Citified* does not "sound" quite right because it has slightly negative connotations, and the writer does not want to create a judgmental persona. Thus, by a process of elimination, the sentence becomes

By 1910, Kansas City was definitely urban.

The advantage of this sort of contextual explanation by constraints or parameters is flexibility. Cause-effect reasoning is rigid: if a particular cause of combination of causes is present, then a particular effect must follow. Contextual explanation allows for individual differences. Though somewhat constrained, our writer is free to choose *any* word that meets all relevant criteria. Contextual considerations do not force a writer to choose a particular word. Various options are possible, as long as they meet all the constraints present in the situation.

Contextual explanation accounts for an event by explaining why other possible events did not occur. The writer's choice of a particular word is explained by listing the constraints that ruled out other words. In a sense the question is changed from *why?* to *why not?* Because it is formally negative, explanation by constraints is equivalent to what classical rhetoricians called argument by *reductio ad absurdum*. In this type of argument, one first states all the possibilities, and then eliminates them one by one until only a single possibility remains.

Any of the six people in the house could have committed the murder. The husband was too frail to lift the murder weapon. The gardener, the maid, the cook and the valet were playing poker together at the time of the crime. Therefore, the butler did it.

Indeed, this is how both Arthur Conan Doyle's Sherlock Holmes and Agatha Christie's Hercules Poirot say they solve mysteries: each begins by considering all possibilities, and then gathers information that eliminate possibilities. Having ruled out the impossible, he then accepts the remaining possibility, however improbable.

Contextual explanation is more difficult than cause-effect explanation. Since simpler patterns are to be preferred, all else being equal, contextual explanation should be used only when cause-effect reasoning is inadequate. For better and for worse, however, this means you usually should use contextual explanation when you want to give a reasonably full explanation of almost any human, ecological, or aesthetic event.

Something Is Missing in Our Lives

Very rarely do you see two teenage girls—and never two teenage boys—holding hands while walking down the street. It is not that these actions are disgusting or outrageous—in fact, people who can express their affections openly are often looked at with envy—it is just that in our society the constraints against this type of expression we grow up with are constantly reinforced through oneself, family and friends.

The dominating constraint against someone being able to show their affection physically is within that person himself. As adults, we have built up our own personal space that usually can only be penetrated by a lover or a child, a lover because the relationship is sexual and a child because the relationship is nonsexual. With any other person that we might touch the innocent gesture could be considered sexual and if it taken as such we find ourselves in a very awkward situation. The longer it is left the more secure our personal space becomes; friends and associates do not expect any more affection than we have previously shown them. Another fear for a person in this situation is how the receiver of new affectionate gestures will react. Though I have never known anyone to shake off a hold, or push away from a hug, when it is done affectionately at the right time by a friend, we seem to think it is highly possible for this to happen. So we just stay safely inside our space and do not bother to try to establish new relations.

The family is the first and most influential aspect of a person's life in shaping his character and habits. As a child I was hugged and cuddled by my parents, but once I reached adolescence the touching ceased. Initially, it was that I did not want to be baited in public, or in front of schoolmates, but this soon infiltrated the privacy of home. There was no longer the hug hello or the kiss goodbye, I learned to associate physical affection or comfort with very special occasions.

Also missing in the family arena was physical affection between my parents. I never saw them hold hands or hug; there was never any chance of us kids walking in on "something." Though they did love each other, there were no affectionate physical gestures; this became my first model of how a married couple acts, only to be re-affirmed through the examples of my friend's parents. I think it is so nice to see an elderly couple walking through a park holding hands, the point being that it is so unusual that I consciously notice it.

Growing up in the suburbs was an isolating experience. People were constantly moving around, faces at school were always changing.

In my area if a family moved more than one mile away the children would have to change schools. Just as you would start to form a strong friendship, the family would move and the friendship immediately dissolved. This led to more casual and distant associations with classmates, and friendships were formed within groups.

Our role models and influences reinforced the isolation. We, both boys and girls, idolized the characters that were tough, independent, and loners. Television and theatre characters of John Wayne, Clint Eastwood and Charles Bronson became the ideals that boys were to live up to. The music we listened to was hard, driving rock and roll; concerts were big and rowdy, always with a few fights— you had to be tough to endure it.

There were a lot of expectations, physically, emotionally and sexually, to meet when one was trying to become tough. There was a real hangup about homosexuality: two boys would never touch each other, or even sit on the same seat on the bus, or else they would be labelled "faggots." They were considered weak and often spent weeks getting terrorized and abused until the "tough" kids got bored with them. Their only claim to difference was that they usually had a very close friend and they were more open with their affections and emotions.

Once the barrier is built up around oneself, it is hard to let it down. Our families show us how to act, our friends, during childhood and adolescence, insist that we act as they do, and once all has been said and done, we have become adults and find it very hard to change. To have the possibility of enhancing our relationships with physical gestures of affection and love we must consciously make an effort to change. It can be done slowly so that the only thing people may notice is that they feel closer to you than they used to. Eventually those touches and hugs will be readily returned.

In many instances, no single factor is an adequate explanation. A writer's word choice, for example, can usually be explained adequately only in terms of a number of overlapping factors. This is also often the case when a number of individuals are noticed acting in remarkably similar ways. You must then explain what about the context constrains individuals toward that particular sort of behavior. The following paper attempts to explain why some—but not all—people get depressed and disoriented when they move into an old age home. The explanation is not simple because individuals vary and similar behavior may be motivated by different factors in different individuals.

Just Filed Away . . .

An elderly person who has just moved into a nursing home is often depressed, disoriented and dissatisfied with this change in his life. Because of certain constraints, the senior citizen may decide to run away from the home, refuse to get up and eat in the morning, or even commit suicide. The reasons for his depression and his inability to adapt to the new surroundings are complex.

Constraint 1: Although a nursing home is generally viewed as a place which offers adequate to excellent care and opportunities for the resident, some people find it difficult to adjust to the home. When he enters a home, the new resident is astounded by how different the surroundings are from his apartment or son's home (for example). The nursing home could also be as far away as five hundred miles from his family or friends. The nursing home can be impersonal in decor and furniture. The colours of the walls are often quite dull. There may also be many wings to the home, making it difficult for the new resident to find his way from his room to the dining-hall. Although he may not be ill, he is confronted by nurses in white uniforms many times during the day. The lounge, t.v. room, and identical bedrooms combine to give the home an institutional atmosphere.

Constraint 2: The daily routine of the home can also make the resident feel as if he is just another patient in the home—even if the nurses are kind and caring. (And often the nurses are too busy to give a resident the type of emotional support or attention that he may need.) Although independence is encouraged in most "good" homes, a resident may feel that he is no longer in control of his life. In fact, he must wake up at a precise hour and have his meals in the dining hall at a certain hour. He must also eat what the particular menu for that day might be. In addition to this, he must exercise in the exercise room at 11:00 a.m. He is given/allowed only one bath on a certain day once a week. Also, if he leaves the home for an afternoon of shopping downtown, he must notify the nursing station. If he does not notify them of his return, they will search for him and perhaps call the police for assistance.

Constraint 3: Other residents in the home can also contribute to the dissatisfaction of life in a home. Because most residents and their families can afford only double rooms, a resident must usually share his room with someone else. Often personality-clashes arise because one might be tidy or messy, loud or quiet. They may even end up fist-fighting with one another or spreading malicious gossip about each other.

Constraint 4: Often a new resident has trouble adjusting to the home because he is too introverted or confused about his new surroundings to participate in the craftroom activities, excursions, and card games with the other residents. At times, other residents do not welcome a new resident into their "clique."

Constraint 5: The feelings of alienation are compounded by the fact that children and family often do not visit, phone, or write. When a resident is not invited for Christmas by his family, he can feel quite depressed and lonely. At these holiday times, he is most vulnerable to depression and the consequent actions of withdrawing from the routine of the home, running away, or attempting suicide.

Constraint 6: Society is to blame for the frustrating, serious, demoralizing condition of the senior citizen in a nursing home. Once someone who is used to being independent enters a home, he soon feels useless and depressed. He feels as if he has been "filed" away by the rest of society. The nursing home is viewed by society as a suitable place to leave the aged, for they no longer play a productive role in society. Yet society, on the whole, does not realize that this attitude only makes a resident feel ignored, unwanted and forgotten.

These six constraints—(1) the impersonal environment, (2) the daily routine, (3) the other residents, (4) his own inability to adapt to a new situation, (5) family and friends who do not call, and (6) an uncaring society—all contribute to the confusion and depression a resident may feel when he enters a nursing home. Society is ultimately to blame for the depression and uselessness felt by a new resident of a nursing home. Although this constraint is most out of the resident's control, it is responsible in the long-run for his condition in the nursing home. The negative attitudes towards aging and the aged must change for the new resident's condition to improve within a nursing home.

Claudia Moryn

In this case, social attitudes toward the elderly are presented as the basic constraint, the encompassing factor that should be changed to allow the other constraints to be modified.

Contextual explanation allows writers to explain causation flexibly. If you say that someone is *constrained toward* some action, you avoid the deterministic implication that he or she has no free will. You are able to discuss causation without implying a rigid determinism, without suggesting that *either* people have free will or their actions are biologically and socially predetermined. Contextual causal explanation allows writers to assume that people have *both* a significant degree of free will *and* are constrained in various ways.

Each constraint *underdetermines* the event. For instance, a person's preconceptions and the perceptual context *underdetermine* what that person will perceive. Only the combination of sensory stimuli, preconceptions, and perceptual context can explain the perception.

Perhaps the most basic and important example of contextual explanation is the theory of evolution. That theory is important here because, essentially, it is a theory about *change*, and causal explanation aims to explain change. As a theory about change, the theory of evolution is applicable, by analogy, to virtually any subject that might be treated using the progressive patterns of arrangement discussed in this chapter. It is especially relevant to linguistics, which is concerned with the "survival" of words, and to rhetoric, which is concerned with the "survival" of verbal messages and the ideas they represent.

In biology, the theory of evolution begins with the assumption that any organism could evolve and that, all else being equal, only chance explains the existing plants and animals. But many existing species do not seem very probable—some seem downright strange. Darwin's explanation was that all else is not equal, that environmental constraints prevented other variants from surviving.

Thus an organism that is fit to survive in one ecosystem may be unfit in another. In an environment with few predators and little food, an organism that is small, slow, and efficient might be more fit than an organism that is strong, fast, and expends a great deal of energy. The biologists' term for a set of ecological constraints is niche. To survive, an organism must fit into a niche in the environment.

Like any explanation by constraints, the theory of evolution is formally negative. As Konrad Lorenz writes in *On Aggression* (Harcourt), "In nature we find . . . everything which is not so inexpedient as to endanger the existence of the species." In other words, the theory of evolution explains not so much "the survival of the fittest" as the extinction of species that do not fit their environment. Similarly, a piece of writing does not need to be perfect; it need only be good enough to meet all the semantic, rhetorical, and linguistic constraints imposed by its context. Consequently, there is no one right way to write (although there are many wrong ways).

In situations defined by linear cause-effect, there is no freedom or flexibility; events are determined; actions are forced. Such situations are not uncommon. In most social, ecological, and aesthetic contexts, however, choices are constrained, not forced. Which type of reasoning and which pattern of arrangement is best for a particular piece of writing will depend on the subject and the purpose of the piece. As a writer, you should learn how to use both patterns because the wrong choice can lead you either to oversimplify or to overly complicate your explanations.

EXERCISE

1. Choose a novel or play that you understand well. Select one character. Write an analysis of the constraints within which that character acts. For example, what are the constraints which lead Hamlet not to avenge his father's murder sooner than he does? See Burke's Pentad, especially the scene-act ratio (pages 82–86).

2. Read several samples of a particular type of writing (e.g., scientific research reports, Harlequin romances, literary critical articles interpreting a single text and published in a particular journal, advertisements in a particular magazine.) Analyze the constraints that explain any consistencies of style, structure, or substance (see pages 418–37).

3. Write an analysis of the readers of a particular piece of writing you intend to do, showing how they constrain the choices you will make.

4. Choose any topic in your area of special interest. Write two short explanations, one using cause-effect reasoning, the other using contextual explanation. Compare and contrast the results.

5. Choose any situation in which large numbers of individuals act similarly (e.g., a rock concert, football game, a classroom). Write an analysis of the constraints that explain the similarity within this group.

6. Choose a situation in which you acted strangely. Write a causal explanation of your unusual behavior.

Logical Progression

We reason deeply when we forcibly feel.

MARY WOLLSTONECRAFT

Thinking and Writing

The quality of a piece of writing depends very much on the quality of thinking that goes into it. Though bad wording may obscure good thinking and clever wording may fool some readers sometimes, thinking well is one key to writing well. And though there is more to thinking well than just being logical, logical progression is a crucially important rhetorical strategy. That is why the basics of writing logically were discussed in Chapter 3. What follows is a fuller and more formal treatment, beginning with some of the same examples.

Logical proof is structured as are the other progressive patterns. The similarity is emphasized when the logical progression is represented in *if-then* statements:

If we plant in April, *then* we should have fresh corn in September.

If Socrates is human, *then* he is mortal.

If whales are warm-blooded and nurse their young, *then* they must be mammals.

In the first case, there is actually a progression in time, from June to September; but the logical progression is from general to particular. The unstated generalization is, "This type of corn takes five months to grow." The thought process moves from that generalization to a particular conclusion.

In the second case, the unstated generalization is, "All human beings are mortal." If Socrates is a particular instance of human being, it follows that he must be mortal. In the third case, the unstated generalization is the definition of mammal, which includes being warm-blooded and nursing young.

The term *logical progression* emphasizes that logical structures reflect thought processes, which do progress in time. Fully stated, the progression could be written as follows:

If you admit that all human beings are mortal and I demonstrate that Socrates is human, then you must logically admit that Socrates is mortal.

Thus stated, it clearly represents a thought process. It also suggests a causal connection:

Because you are a logical person who admits that all human beings are mortal and *because* I will demonstrate that Socrates is human, you will admit that Socrates is mortal.

A logical progression thus can be a causal explanation of why someone believes (or should believe) something.

Toulmin Logic

A complete logical proof has three basic and three optional components. The basic components are *claim*, *evidence*, and *warrant*.

The claim is the statement to be proven; in a piece of writing it may be called a thesis or topic sentence. The evidence is whatever specifics support the claim, sometimes called data or "facts." Warrants are generalizations that link the evidence to the claim; in effect, they assert, "This evidence supports this claim because . . . ." Warrants are often obvious, hence sometimes left unstated, but they are part of any logically complete proof.

In the fable, "Chicken Little," a chick claims "the sky is falling." She supports this claim with empirical evidence, a bump on the top of her

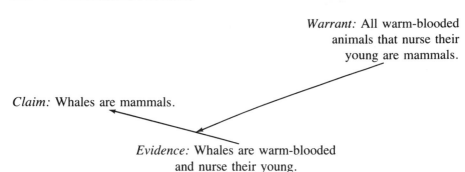

Figure 8.5. Toulmin logic.

head; and, with this evidence, she convinces the hen, rooster, duck, and turkey. The implicit warrant is that "a bump on top of a head must have been caused by something falling from above—namely, the sky." The owl exposes Chicken Little's error not by refuting her evidence, but by demonstrating that things other than the sky, in this case an acorn, can fall from above. The owl, in short, refutes the unstated warrant, thereby giving the chick, the hen, the rooster, the duck and all the children who grow up with this story a lesson in logic.

Warrants can be crucial components in logical progressions. In the following excerpt, one student writer based her claim on two warrants: (1) individuals should be free to do anything which does not harm others, and (2) one of the main purposes of marriage is "to provide a stable family environment for children."

> Perhaps the single biggest reason why polygamy is feared is because it is unfamiliar in our society, and subsequently believed to be generally uncommon, practiced only by a small minority—probably uncivilized "pagans." This, however, is not totally true. The Mormons, for example, whom most observers would agree are very devout and pious people, at one time condoned polygamy. Many Moslems still practice polygamy today, and in their society it is not seen as "immoral" or "harmful." In both cases, polygamy as a marriage alternative is meant to provide a stable family environment, not a "free love" arrangement.
>
> The effects of polygamy, then, need not necessarily be negative. Polygamy could perhaps reduce jealousy and possessiveness—both of which are to a large extent conditioned responses and not particularly desirable characteristics. It could also provide another child-rearing model for those who need an alternative to the existing one(s).

It is perhaps an illusion to think that humans are monogamous by nature; one need only look at the rising divorce rate to see that the choice of a mate is no longer an irreversible decision. If, for whatever reasons, a marriage fails, the effects on all concerned (and especially the children) can be painful and even detrimental. Polygamy could perhaps replace divorce as an alternative in those cases where one of the marriage partners has a need that their spouse cannot fill. Furthermore, it is certainly no less moral an alternative than an extramarital relationship. A stable household could perhaps be maintained if polygamy were possible.

It should be realized that the world and the nature of our society are continually evolving. It seems unrealistic to think that the canons of the past will not require readjusting to suit today's realities. We can see, for example, through softening attitudes toward divorce, that the beliefs underlying our laws are slowly evolving and becoming better attuned to individual needs. . . .

Should it not be up to individuals to decide how they want to conduct their private lives? This does not mean that everyone must agree with the practice of polygamy or approve of it; but it is an option which, in all fairness, should be available to those who want to consider it.

Pat Baitz

In addition to claim, evidence and warrant, a logical proof may also include *backing*, *rebuttal* and *qualification*. Backing is argument that validates the warrant. If the audience is likely to disagree with the warrant or if the warrant is the main component of the argument, one may need to *back up* the warrant as well as the claim.

To be logically convincing, one often must rebut contrary arguments that have been put forward by an opponent or that are already in readers' minds. Since many of her readers associate polygamy with promiscuousness, Pat must rebut that assumption if she wants her argument to be considered. Similarly, because many of her readers believe that certain acts are simply "right" or "wrong," Pat argues that basic ethical principles have different implications in different contexts.

Both to avoid false overgeneralization and to be convincing, one often must qualify one's claim or make concessions to other opinions. Thus Pat does not claim polygamy is better than monogamy or right for everyone, just that it could be a good option for some individuals and that it should not be illegal.

The essence of a complete logical proof is claim, evidence, and warrant, but backing, rebuttal, and qualification are also often necessary.

The Genetic Fallacy

The very process of logical progression sometimes leads to the *genetic fallacy*. This fallacy occurs when someone argues that whatever came first *must* be the explanation of whatever comes later. Although it is typically taught first when children learn to write, penmanship is not the basis of good writing.

Perhaps the best-known example of the genetic fallacy is the psychoanalytic assertion that people's adult behavior is determined by childhood traumas. That assertion may be somewhat true—certainly childhood experiences have some influence on one's adult character. But it is illogical to presume that *just because* they came first, early childhood experiences *must be* the explanation for later development.

A particular version of the genetic fallacy, *the intentional fallacy*, was criticized by the school of literary criticism that was dominant in North America during the mid-twentieth century. The critics of that school asserted that it is fallacious to determine the meaning of a literary text by asking its author what she or he *intended* it to mean. To be sure, those intentions did motivate the author; they were, in a sense, the seed from which the text grew. But we cannot deduce the meaning of the finished text from those intentions.

The meaning, and even the wording, of a literary text is influenced by a variety of factors. Since we know that essential parts of the human creative process are unconscious, we know that the author was not fully aware of how and why the text took the form it did. We also know that writers work in social contexts, and that they choose words, images, and even concepts from among—or in reaction against—those available in their culture at the time. Furthermore, we know that some of the meaning of a literary text results from what readers bring to it, that the meaning of the text emerges in the transaction between text and reader (which also occurs in a social context).

Given these complexities, we most move carefully from process analysis to logical or causal explanation. And the more complex the process, the more wary we must be of the genetic fallacy.

Other Fallacies

In formal logic, one version of the genetic fallacy is sometimes called *post hoc, ergo prompter hoc* (after the fact, therefore because of it).

Both major European revolutions of the modern era—the French Revolution of 1789 and the Russian Revolution of 1917—were followed by periods of literary rebellion. The political revolutions must have caused these literary rebellions and we can expect future revolutions to inspire other literary innovations.

There are other logical fallacies of which writers should be wary because they can lead to invalid or unconvincing logical progressions. Among the most common are the following.

Division: inferring that whatever is true for the whole is true for the parts.

Average income increased faster than inflation last year, so we are all financially better off.

Composition: assuming that whatever is true for all the parts must be true for the whole.

Each member of the commission represents an interest group; since each member is biased, the commission's recommendations must be biased.

Begging the Question/Circular Reasoning: assuming what should be proven (often by asserting it in other words).

He had an antipathy for ballet because he did not like it.

Antibiotics cure bacterial infections because they have a therapeutic effect.

Science students should not be required to study literature because that would waste their time.

We should encourage people to drive to work because without the money from gasoline taxes we could not pay for our highways.

Reification: treating an abstract concept or a process as if it were a real entity or object.

Destiny made him great.

The economy failed to perform.

Hasty Generalization: drawing a broad conclusion from limited evidence.

Abraham Lincoln did not really care about slavery—otherwise he would have issued the Emancipation Proclamation in 1861, not 1863.

Non Sequitur: drawing a conclusion beyond what the premises logically prove.

By law, each person is responsible for the consequences of any illegal act, so anyone who has a collision while driving faster than the speed limit should be held legally and morally responsible.

Smuggled Connotation: shifting from one word to a cognate that does not actually have the same meaning.

> Never a day passes when this candidate does not drink wine. Do we want to elect a wino?

Ipse Dixit: using the testimony of an unqualified "expert."

> Many great athletes drink this beer; it must be a good beer.

Ad Hominem: attacking one's opponents rather than their ideas.

> No one but a traitor would oppose my patriotic proposal.

Damning the Source: discrediting a position or argument because of its origin.

> Remember that the first modern politician to make "law and order" a cornerstone of his political program was Adolf Hitler.
>
> Of course, the union president thinks the corporation oppresses the workers. There is no need to investigate her charges.

Straw Man: attacking a simplistic or false version of an opposing position.

> How could Thomas Jefferson have written that "all men are created equal"? People are obviously born with differing abilities and differing needs. It would be wrong to treat everyone the same. [*Note*: In context, Jefferson clearly meant that all men were born with equal *rights*; *equal*, moreover, does not mean the *same*.]

Oversimplification

Many logical errors, not all of them fallacies as defined by formal logic, result from oversimplification. For instance, writers sometimes present a single cause as the full explanation for a complex phenomenon.

> No one would be less than functionally literate if schoolteachers spent more time drilling grammar and usage.
>
> We could eliminate crime if we just stopped insisting that the police obey the law when apprehending possible criminals.

And sometimes writers simply leave out all evidence that does not support their assertions. Obviously, such errors of omission can lead to false conclusions.

A less obvious form of oversimplification occurs when writers present a complex situation as an either/or, two-sided dilemma.

> Anyone who is not with us is against us.

> Coleridge's "Kubla Khan" must be explained either as a reflection of his personal neuroses or as a reflection of his society.

There are some issues with only two sides, but many issues are many sided. And sometimes writers claim or imply that there is only one side to an issue:

> Anyone who disagrees with me is wrong.

> Abhorrence of terrorism and its perpetrators is a universal dictum.

> > BERT SNELGROVE

Closely related to either/or thinking is a confusion between equality and sameness, called symmetrizing. Perhaps this error begins in elementary school, where we learn that equality means giving each child the same number of cookies (which is true enough in that case). But if one person has two healthy legs and another is confined to a wheelchair, equality may mean treating them differently, giving one special treatment so that they each end up with equal access. Similarly, if two drivers, one a billionaire and the other impoverished, both exceed the speed limit, fining each $50 will not deter them equally from speeding again.

To update Anatole France's parody of this error, vagrancy laws are said to apply "equally" to both the homeless and to those who have no need to sleep on heating grates or park benches. If two situations are not equivalent, especially if they involve people who do not have equal opportunities or power, equality is not sameness—and many erroneous conclusions are drawn by those who confuse equality and sameness, who insist on symmetrical responses to unsymmetrical situations. (In the early 1970s, for instance, it was commonly and seriously argued that women's equality would logically mean letting women and men use the same public toilets.)

A conclusion is not necessarily false just because it was reached by fallacious reasoning—indeed, it is a fallacy to conclude that a statement is false just because the arguments offered in its support have been discredited. Similarly, if one starts from false premises, a valid logical progression may well lead to false conclusions. But thinking well is a key to writing well, and the ability to present a clear logical progression, devoid of fallacies, is crucially important in many types of writing.

Exercise

1. One way to describe logical relationships is in terms of patterns of inference. (And the ability to recognize and evaluate inferences has been found to correlate significantly with college grade point averages.)

Assume the statements in each of the following passages to be true. Then mark each suggested inference as correct (C), probably correct (PC), false (F), probably false (PF) or impossible to determine from the reading (I). Worry less about getting the answers right than about grasping principles of inference.

Rhetoric has been defined as the study of the symbols which we manipulate and which manipulate us. Rhetoricians are often more concerned with the effects of communications, with the meanings that reach an audience, than with the objective content of statements. First-year university and college rhetoric courses often focus on the communications abilities needed by students in their academic work.

_____ 1. Nine out of ten rhetoricians teach first-year university students.

_____ 2. A rhetorician might study advertising.

_____ 3. First-year rhetoric courses have a different focus than graduate rhetoric courses.

_____ 4. Many rhetoricians believe that our behavior can be manipulated by the symbols we use.

"North Americans All Look Alike"

HAMILTON, Ont., June 27, 1973 (AP).—A visiting Chinese said today that all North Americans look alike. "We can't tell them apart from the faces," said Zhu Muzhe, director of the New China News Agency. [*Note*: In proper international usage, "American" can signify anyone from North or South America; "North American" signifies someone from Canada or the United States.]

_____ 1. The facial features of the Chinese are more diverse than those of North Americans.

_____ 2. Zhu Muzhe is a woman.

_____ 3. Zhu visited Canada in June 1973.

_____ 4. Zhu had not spent much time in North America.

Unlike cattle, sheep or goats, pigs do not eat grasses. They live, instead, on roots and grains—foods which are in short supply in the desert and which are eaten also by *Homo sapiens*. Pigs, therefore, are in ecological competition with people in a way which is significant in the desert. The cultures which became dominant in the Middle East were not burdened with pigs.

Insofar as *why?* is a question about psychological motives, the reason neither Moslems nor Jews eat pork is because they believe Allah and Yahweh told them not to (and because those beliefs were enforced by social pressures within certain communities). But when *why?* is a question about survival or dominance, the taboo on pork must be explained as an adaptation to the environment.

_____ 1. Pigs will eat wheat.

_____ 2. Sheep will not eat wheat.

_____ 3. Roots and grains are important in the diet of human beings.

_____ 4. The Hindu taboo on beef can be explained as an adaptation to the Indian environment.

2. Find an example of the genetic fallacy. Write a critique.

3. Study a textbook of formal logic, preferably one oriented toward writers' needs (e.g., Howard Kahane's *Logic & Contemporary Rhetoric*). What can you learn from it that might help you as a writer?

4. Go back to something you wrote recently that included logical progression. Analyze the components of your proof into claim, evidence, warrant, backing, rebuttal, and qualification. Does that analysis help you see how you could have developed your argument more effectively?

C·H·A·P·T·E·R 9

Persuasion

Rhetoric may be defined as the faculty of observing in any given case the available means of persuasion.

ARISTOTLE

In order to persuade, there are two things which must be carefully studied by the orator. The first is to excite some desire or passion in the hearers; the second is to satisfy their judgement that there is a connection between the action to which he would persuade them and the gratification of the desire or passion he excites.

GEORGE CAMPBELL

Rhetoric as such is . . . rooted in an essential function of language itself, . . . the use of language as a symbolic means of inducing cooperation in beings that by nature respond to symbols.

KENNETH BURKE

HUMAN society is founded on cooperation. Perhaps the most basic function of language is to induce and facilitate that cooperation. Directly and indirectly, we all use language to induce people to adopt attitudes and perform actions.

Where Chapter 8 focused on using words to explain change, this chapter will focus on using words to *produce* change. Persuasion—like representation and explanation—is a basic *purpose* of discourse. All of the patterns of arrangement discussed in the preceding two chapters—description, narration, comparison/contrast, classification and division, definition, analogy and exemplification, process analysis, causal explanation and logical progression—may be used in the service of that primal purpose, persuasion.

The formal study of rhetoric began in the fifth century B.C.E. as a guide to effective persuasion. This chapter will begin with some of the insights of classical and traditional rhetoric. Various types of appeals will be discussed and the formal structure of a classical persuasion explained. A modern structure—Rogerian persuasion—which is appropriate to different sorts of persuasive tasks, will also be presented. The chapter will conclude with a short section on two persuasive techniques, constructive criticism and consensus, which are especially important to writers and writing students.

As you read this chapter, you should try to master several distinct persuasive strategies and structures. You should work on your ability to evaluate rhetorical contexts (see Chapter 4), so you can select the appropriate strategy and structure for any given persuasion. Specifically, you should learn how to do both classical and Rogerian persuasions. You should also learn how to give constructive criticism (i.e., how to persuade people to accept your criticisms) and to create consensus (i.e., how to persuade people to cooperate with each other). This chapter contains a number of formulas for persuasion. As you practice them, remember that the formulas are just guidelines. Master the underlying principles of persuasion, and you will be able to modify the formulas to match particular situations.

Traditional Argument

Mere knowledge of the truth will not give you the art of persuasion.

PLATO

Of the modes of persuasion furnished by the spoken word there are three kinds. The first kind depends on the personal character of the speaker; the second on putting the audience into a certain frame of mind; the third on the proof, or apparent proof, provided by the words of the speech itself.

ARISTOTLE

Human beings have undoubtedly used verbal persuasion ever since we evolved language, but the formal study of rhetoric began in Classical Greece.

Some 466 years B.C.E., in Syracuse, a Greek city on the island of Sicily, the people revolted against Thrasybulus, the last of a series of dictators, and reestablished democracy. Thereafter the courts were flooded with litigation from citizens claiming their property had been confiscated by the despots and distributed among various followers. In circumstances where definite proof was often unavailable, hundreds of citizens needed to present persuasive arguments substantiating their claims. Responding to this need, Corax is said to have formalized a strategy for presenting arguments effectively in courts of law. For the succeeding two and a half millennia, this formal structure, slightly amplified by Corax's Greek and Roman successors, has been taught as the standard way to organize an argument.

We can learn a lot from these rhetorical principles, which have certainly stood the test of time.

Three Types of Appeal

According to Aristotle, who summed up and systematized the insights of several generations of Greek rhetoricians, there are basically three ways to appeal to people and thus to induce them to agree with you. The Greek terms for the three types of appeal are *ethos*, *pathos*, and *logos*, usually translated as ethical, emotional, and logical, although the Greek words have somewhat different connotations than the English ones.

> Persuasion by *ethos* is based on persona, on the image of yourself that is projected by your speech or writing. Audiences that perceive you as wise, knowledgeable, and trustworthy is more likely to be persuaded by you.

> Persuasion by *pathos* is based on the feelings and desires of audiences. Not only do emotions aroused in audiences affect the ease with which they are persuaded, but all successful persuasion must ultimately identify itself with something its audiences desire, be that truth, justice or a larger slice of pie.

> Persuasion by *logos* is based on evidence and reasoning. If what you present at least seems to be well-founded and logical, that should help persuade.

In certain contexts—such as writing for university courses—you are concerned mainly with *logos*. Your primary interest is in reaching truth and your readers are in a highly rational mode, hence most likely to be convinced by logic and evidence. However emotional you may feel about the topic, therefore, you confine yourself to logical and empirical argument.

But persuasive writing aims through understanding to belief—and ultimately to acting on that belief. That is why Augustine, when he adapted classical rhetoric to Christian purposes, told would-be preachers that no matter how well they explicated the scriptures, no matter how well they convinced their hearers to believe, the sermon had failed to persuade unless the parishioners were also moved to live a Christian life. Taken more generally, Augustine's point is that all persuasion, though it may include explanation and argumentation, is ultimately a matter of motivation. Any complete discussion of persuasion must, therefore, include all three types of appeal.

Ethical Appeal. The first type of appeal is called *ethical* because it turns on the ethical judgment readers make about the character of the writer.

Readers who trust you may be persuaded even by unsupported assertion. That trust may be based on the persona you project or on readers' previous knowledge of you. Thus a recognized authority, such as a certified expert or a leader who is perceived as having been right often in the past, may be able to persuade people without providing much detailed argumentation. On the other hand, those who are perceived as having been wrong often in the past may fail to persuade even when they have good evidence and make a logical case. The ethical appeal opens readers' minds, prepares them to consider and perhaps accept a writer's evidence and arguments. According to the classical rhetoricians, therefore, the place to emphasize the ethical appeal is generally toward the beginning of a speech or writing.

Aristotle says that the ethical appeal is based on your ability to project yourself

1. as a sensible person who understands the subject,
2. as a good and forthright person who would not lie to your readers, and
3. as an unselfish and benevolent person who has the readers' best interests at heart.

On a trivial level, this might mean that poor spelling could convince some readers that you are not intelligent, a minor inconsistency that you are being dishonest, and a few unfortunate word choices that you do not understand them. On the most exalted level, this means that effective persuasion is honest, truthful, and loving.

Emotional Appeal. Our culture emphasizes the virtues of empiricism and rationality. We tend, therefore, to feel there is something wrong with appealing to emotions. But as the eighteenth-century Scottish rhetorician George Campbell asserted in his *The Philosophy of Rhetoric*, "So far . . . is it from being an unfair method of persuasion to move the passions, that there is no persuasions without moving them." As human beings, we always choose our ultimate goals passionately (be those passions large or small, loving or selfish). We must and should set our ultimate aims on the basis of what we disparagingly call "emotions"; it is the means to those ends that should be chosen rationally and empirically.

Thus it is as proper to use emotional appeals to motivate people as it is improper (though not necessarily ineffective) to continue using emotional appeals when the focus shifts from ends to means. In part for this reason, according to the classical rhetoricians, the place to emphasize the emotional appeal is generally toward the end of a speech or writing, when you hope that your readers have been convinced and now need to be motivated to do something about it. In certain contexts, as Adolf Hitler so devastatingly demonstrated, judgment may be warped by emotional appeals. But it is not degrading to appeal to someone's love of freedom or unselfish caring about other people. Nor is it necessarily improper to supplement statistics on malnutrition with a vivid description of one starving child.

Logical Appeal. The third type of appeal is *logical*. Aristotle reminds us that what persuades is not logic, but apparent logic, the verbal representation of logic. To an honest writer, this distinction ordinarily makes little difference, except as a reminder that the logic *must be made apparent* to readers. Still, since even the best of writers may have occasion to lie—perhaps to protect innocent people from violence—you should remember that it is *the appearance of logic* which persuades. (See pages 370–79 for a discussion of logical progression.)

Aristotle, moreover, used the Greek word *logos*, which has a considerably broader range of meaning than does the modern English *logic*. To take full advantage of what the Greek rhetoricians taught their students about using logical appeals, we should remember that *logos* meant using words to make logical statements about reality. It referred to the structures of what we would now call language, logic, *and* reality. It was thus more closely related to both language and reality than modern formal logic.

Rhetoric and Ethics

Any and all of these three basic types of appeal may be used or abused. The ethical appeal, despite its name, is often abused for unethical purposes, notably in commercial advertising and political propaganda (e.g., when a celebrity who has no relevant expertise endorses a product or candidate). Emotional appeals have an obvious potential for abuse. And history is replete with cases in which logical arguments were used to abuse and oppress "illogical" peoples.

Rhetoric shows us the tools of persuasion and teaches us how to use them effectively. Rhetoric cannot tell us whether a particular use is ethical. The same rhetorical technique may be used honestly in one case and deviously in another. For example, when speaking to someone recently bereaved, it is a kindness to use the euphemism *passed away*, in order to avoid direct reference to death. But the very same rhetorical figure, euphemism, may be abused when a hospital report refers euphemistically to a "terminal episode" or "negative patient outcome" in order to avoid saying directly that a patient died under questionable circumstances. Similarly, when someone in the U.S. State Department decided to instruct employees not to use the word *kill* in reports on human rights abuse—in State Department reports, death squads no longer kill anybody; officially what happens is the "unlawful or arbitrary deprivation of life"—rhetoric was used to evade.

Rhetoric teaches us how to use language as a means to motivate people, but any rhetorical technique may be used honestly or dishonestly, for good or evil ends. Aristotle's classification of appeals into three types can help you both to invent and to analyze persuasive discourse. But judgments about whether you *should* use any particular appeal depend on how it is used, to what ends, and in what contexts. Ultimately, persuasive tactics can be evaluated morally only in real contexts.

Evaluate the Rhetorical Context

Persuasive writing is oriented toward its readers. It aims to induce them to act in a certain way or, at least, to adopt certain attitudes. More than other types of writing, persuasion is purposive, a strategy, a means to an end. More than other types of writing, it is properly judged by its effects on readers. Even more than other types of writing, therefore, persuasion must be adapted to its rhetorical contexts. The first section of Chapter 4 is, therefore, particularly relevant to persuasive writing.

As a persuasive writer, your goal is not just to make your statement, "to have your say." Your goal is to change your readers' minds, to motivate them where they were not motivated before. It is useful to have a very clear sense of purpose, of what you want them to believe or do. An explicit statement of purpose helps distinguish what you mean to communicate (subject matter) from what you want your readers to believe and do after they have finished reading.

To achieve your persuasive purposes, you should evaluate both your intended readers and the circumstances in which they will be reading what you write. Since you want to move them to a particular belief or action, it is useful to know where you will have to move them from. An awareness of your readers' knowledge, attitudes, beliefs, and vested interests and of any distinctions between primary and secondary audiences is particularly important. You should ask what frameworks or root metaphors your readers have for your subject. You might well use the Pentad to analyze your readers and decide how best to motivate them. And you certainly want to be writing reader-based prose that appeals to a mutual purpose, is focused according to readers' needs, and is organized to facilitate readers' discovery processes (see pages 151–59).

> I wish to address students who advocate economic boycott of South African products as a means of changing the policy of apartheid practiced in that country. I assume this audience will have a reading ability above high school level, will be generally well informed, mostly middle class, and will be more critically concerned with the intellectual rather than the emotional content of an argument.
>
> Their values, I believe, are encompassed by liberal–democratic politics and a Christian ethical code. According to Burke's Pentad,

> a liberal and idealistic audience such as this would most easily
> be motivated by appeals which emphasize scene and purpose. Some
> key terms that highlight this group's beliefs are "liberation
> struggle," "self-determination," and "democratic freedoms."
>
> As middle-class intellectuals, they have vested interests in
> social cohesion and international political stability. They
> believe these interests are best served when all members of the
> international community are democratic, consumerist (in the sense
> of having rising material expectations), and share a general set
> of morals. They are committed to benevolence, charity, and
> fraternity.
>
> The group I am targeting is largely center-left on the political
> spectrum but not far left. . . . My purpose is entirely subversive:
> to create doubt, thereby lessening their will to spread their
> opinions and stifling their enthusiasm for political activity.

This writer's purpose is not to convince everybody ("the general reader") that he is right; his purpose is to weaken the antiapartheid movement's push for an economic boycott of South African products. So he has focused on a particular group (liberal, not far left) he believes is relatively vulnerable to persuasion. And at least for this particular piece of writing, his goal is not to convince them, just to weaken their commitment, reduce their level of activity. To that end, he has made a rather detailed analysis of their values and interests.

Writing with this sort of purpose is, of course, commonplace is business, politics, and other arenas where the primary concern is to change readers' behavior. The advertiser's purpose is to write something that will increase sales. The politician's purpose is to write something that will motivate voters. Logical argument supported by full and fair presentation of facts may not be the best way to achieve such purposes. Again rhetorical strategy leads to ethical considerations. It makes sense to be clear with yourself about your purposes, and it makes sense to consider your audience. Ethically, however, such considerations should be accompanied by consideration of the moral relationship between ends and means.

Logical Argument

There are circumstances in which the only or predominant appeal should be to logic. In such cases, persuasion comes down essentially to presenting logical arguments. Ethical appeal is reduced to maintaining a persona which seems fairminded and rational. Emotional appeal is minimized because it tends to undercut that persona, thus to reduce the effectiveness of the argument.

The conventions of academic and professional discourse, for example, generally demand that writers assume—or at least pretend to assume—an ideal audience of rational readers. Of course, real academics, scientists, and professionals are human beings and, therefore, are less than perfectly rational. Scientific studies of scientists clearly demonstrate, moreover, that factors such as the status of the experimenters or of the journal that publishes their results have a great deal to do with whether a scientific article actually convinces its readers. And even the most objective and academic writing ultimately has some persuasive purpose—if only to enhance the reputation of the writer and to persuade granting institutions to give financial support for further research. Nonetheless, overt ethical or emotional appeals are not permitted in this sort of discourse. One may not write, "Believe me because I'm an expert." One may not write, "This had better be true or else everybody around here will end up losing their jobs." The persuasive persona the writer must project is one of disinterested and dispassionate objectivity.

But logical argument is still not quite the same as the philosophers' formal logic. Important practical arguments often involve making predictions or arguing probabilities in real-world situations where formal logical proof and definite knowledge is impossible. In this sense, logical argument must do more than formal logic. Indeed, for Aristotle, the primary function of rhetoric is to help people make decisions in situations where formal analytic logic by itself is inadequate.

Because your purpose is not to state the logic but to make the logic apparent to your audience, moreover, you need not necessarily restate what the audience already knows and believes. In this sense, logical argument is less rigorous—and also less tedious—than formal logic. Thus one writes,

> Since Socrates is human, he is mortal.
>
> or
>
> We must cut costs or increase sales because otherwise the company will fail to make a profit.
>
> or
>
> This type of corn takes five months to grow, so if we plant it in April we can harvest it in September.

The philosopher may say these assertions are logically incomplete. The first is missing its major premise ("All human beings are mortal"). The second similarly fails to state explicitly that the primary purpose of a capitalist enterprise is to make profits. The third is not only missing its minor premise ("September is five months after April") but also is only generally true (after all, corn worms may kill the plants in August). Formally the philosopher is right. But if your audience already knows about corn worms (and how many months there are between May and September), the shorter version of the argument will be less tedious and more effective.

For a discussion of what makes an argument logically valid, see Chapter 3, pages 129–33, on generalization and Chapter 8, pages 370–79, on logic.

The Arrangement of a Classical Persuasion

Classical rhetoric offers a standard structure for arranging persuasions. Although this structure has not been widely studied in recent decades, analyses of many speeches and writings show that it is still used and still works. That is because the parts of a classical persuasion represent basic functions of persuasive discourse. Although the structure was (and is) intended more as a guideline than as a hard-and-fast formula, it remains one very effective way to structure a persuasive speech or writing.

The structure is as follows:

Introduction. The Latin term is *exordium*, which is related to the English *exhort* and means "beginning a web," as in weaving. Here one makes contact with the audience, indicates one's subject (and perhaps even one's thesis), and tries to dispose the audience favorably to what one is going to say. Here is a place for ethical appeal.

Narration and Explication. The facts are set forth, key terms and issues defined. In a legal case, this might include literally *narrating* the events which judge and jury will have to evaluate (hence the term, *narration*). In a funeral oration, it might mean telling the story of the dead person's life. In a political context, it might mean describing the present situation. Aristotle, at least, makes clear that this is not usually a "neutral" statement of facts: ethical and emotional appeals, he asserts, should be implicit here.

Proposition and Partition. The main proposition—i.e., the thesis—is explicitly stated here. Then one prepares the audience for what will follow by mentioning, in order, the various proofs (and perhaps refutations), the *parts* of the argument.

Proofs. Called *confirmatio* in Latin, this part is devoted to confirming the proposition. Here one offers arguments in support of one's thesis statement, proves that the defendant could not possibly have committed the crime, demonstrates that the deceased lived an exemplary life, argues for a particular course of action. Often this is the bulk of the speech or writing. (See pages 89–96, on the *topoi*, the heuristic Aristotle recommends for inventing arguments.)

Refutation. Other viewpoints are criticized and their flaws demonstrated. One pokes holes in the prosecution's case, attacks evil people who spread false rumors about the deceased, demonstrates the disadvantages of the alternative policies suggested by others.

Digression. Some versions of the classical structure allowed for the possibility that one might have reason to say something that does not strictly fit, usually just before the conclusion.

Conclusion. This may be a summary of proofs and refutations. It may also be a renewal of ethical and, especially, emotional appeals. It serves to emphasize what you want your audience to remember and also to motivate them. (See pages 189–92 on endings.)

It will be worth your while to practice this structure rigorously. After you have mastered it, however, you can change the order, combine or eliminate parts, so long as the functions are accomplished. Even classical rhetoricians, such as Cicero, emphasized the need to apply the formula flexibly. If the opposing case is strong and has already been argued, it may be best to put the refutation before the proofs—or even to begin with the refutation. If the narration of events will serve as an introduction, there may be no need for a separate *exordium*. If the facts are well known, there may be no need for a full narration. If the thesis has already been made clear in the introduction, there may be no need to restate it before the partition. It is even possible to imagine situations in which the proofs might be left out (e.g., a defense attorney might say no more than, "Your honor, the prosecution has failed to make a case, my client is innocent until proven guilty, so I move that all charges be immediately dismissed.")

Consider the following persuasion, addressed to the management and executive committee of a private club. Though the writer's ultimate desire is to outlaw smoking in the club's dining room, she here confines herself to arguing only that the membership should be allowed to vote on the issue. Note how carefully the persuasion is adapted to its audience, those with responsibility for managing the club. In particular note how much of her argument is not about smoking but about the efficacy of administering a dining room where smoking would be prohibited.

A New Majority: Let Us Vote

As you are no doubt aware, a growing number of club members are now nonsmokers. As one such member, I have noted that many of us no longer wish to dine in our club's smoky atmosphere. Though the staff, service, food and ambience all combine to create a delightful dining experience, staff members have told me that many members and their guests have expressed dissatisfaction with the smoky air even in the nonsmoking section. Because I personally know several disgruntled members, I can only surmise that this dislike for our dining facilities is becoming widespread.

Every time I arrive for meals I have a difficult time getting a table in the popular though small nonsmoking section of the dining room. Many of my friends report similar difficulties, and all agree that making reservations has not proven to be a solution. Fortunately the staff are always willing to make an extra effort to provide smokefree space in the smoking section when times are really tough, but frustrated members are not likely to keep tolerating makeshift arrangements indefinitely.

I propose that we club members be offered the chance to register our preference for a smokefree dining room through a formal vote. In my opinion a strong majority will indicate our desire for complete freedom from smoky dining. As our elected representatives and employees, you will have only to carry out the wishes of the majority, but I do have some suggestions you may wish to examine in consideration of those members least likely to agree. I have thought of some options we can make available to them, just as options were available to nonsmokers when we were in the minority. I know my proposal can be successful, just as I know the present situation is no longer viable.

I have noted a trend in the dining room that has perhaps been noted by the staff also. Many smokers dining with nonsmokers already considerately refrain from smoking until after everyone at their table has finished dinner. The staff could easily take this tendency one step further by inviting diners into the smoking lounge for after dinner drinks and desserts. Given the probable popularity of my proposal, I doubt many members would request dinner service in the lounge, but I trust the dining staff could easily satisfy those few who did so.

In general, I believe that nonsmoking sections are too small to accommodate all who desire a smokefree dining experience. Furthermore, a nonsmoker cannot depend on enjoying a smokefree dinner if his fellow diners are mixed smokers and nonsmokers. Despite claims that tradition must be given its due, even smokers in our club have indicated a desire to eat in a nonsmoking section on occasion. This club must endeavor to serve all its members as they prefer or risk decaying into a smokers–only, member–poor club. Without sacrificing comfort for tradition, the bottom line is that we prefer a smokefree atmosphere in the dining room.

The key point of my proposal rests on the fairness of allowing all members of this club an equal opportunity to express an opinion. Thus the only responsibility assumed by you, the club management and executive board, will be to provide us with an opportunity to vote on the issue. I have always believed that, thanks to you, this club creates a welcoming sense of privacy, comfort and quality for its members. I only want to see this standard of excellence upheld.

Kari Killy

In this piece, the writer is quite understated. She subtly works the democratic connotations of *majority/minority* to her advantage and appeals quite directly to the self-interests of the club management. Is that an effective strategy? Does she overdo the flattery? Would a stronger statement about the harmfulness of smoking have worked better?

The structure of classical persuasion, like Aristotle's three types of appeal, has stood the test of time and changing contexts. It may be used to organize a written persuasion in the late twentieth century quite as effectively as it was used to organize spoken persuasions more than two millennia ago. Flexible though it is, however, it is not always the most effective structure. The next section of this chapter will present an alternative structure as well as criteria for deciding which structure to use in which rhetorical contexts.

EXERCISE

1. Choose an appropriate topic, thesis, and rhetorical context, and write a persuasion that follows the classical structure as outlined in this section. Your readers obviously must not be people who agree with you from the start (or there will be no reason for addressing them with a Classical persuasion). If you choose a controversial and emotional topic, however, you should probably not select an audience strongly committed to the opposing view. For instance, if you want to write about abortion, you might address an audience of young women still in the process of making up their minds rather than an audience of committed pro-choice or anti-abortion activists.

2. Select several short, published persuasions from recent newspapers, magazines, and journals. Analyze each in terms of ethical, emotional, and logical appeals.

3. Select a short, published persuasion written some years ago (perhaps a newspaper editorial from the day you were born). Judging by the writer's persuasive strategy, construct a statement of rhetorical context (see pages 146–53) as the writer probably saw it.

4. Select a persuasive writing that you did at least a year ago. Create a statement of rhetorical context for it, and consider how well it was adapted to that context.

5. Read the following excerpts from Aristotle's *Rhetoric*:

Book I: Chapters 1, 2, 9, and 10

Book II: Chapters 1, 19, 20, and 25

Book III: Chapters 1, 7, 12, 13, 14, 16, 17, and 19

6. Compare and contrast Antony's funeral speech in *Julius Caesar* with the speech by Brutus that precedes it. Brutus' speech has succeeded largely because of ethical appeal, for all Rome knows that Brutus is honorable. How is his speech structured to fit its rhetorical context?

Antony addresses a hostile audience, which has just been convinced by Brutus that Caesar had to be killed because he was ambitious (to become dictator of Rome). He moves quickly from an *exordium* to careful refutation. He skips the narration of facts. He offers no partition. He begins with his weakest refutation and works toward his strongest. Why do you think he thus varies from the standard structure of classical persuasion? Is Antony correct when he calls himself a "plain blunt man" and Brutus an "orator"? Why do you think Shakespeare wrote Brutus' speech in prose and Antony's in verse?

See Kenneth Burke's discussion of Antony's funeral oration, "Antony in Behalf of the Play," in *The Philosophy of Literary Form* (University of California Press).

7. Consider the following persuasion, aimed at education majors who are about to graduate and become teachers, which seems to follow the classical structure quite strictly. Its purpose is to convince prospective teachers to concern themselves with marijuana use among their students.

Teenagers and Marijuana

As a parent of two teenagers and a teacher/counsellor for several years, I am all too aware of the problems young people face today. The world I knew as a teenager is not the one my teenagers face today, and I worry about them—about them and the many others in our schools. They have so many choices to make, so many pressures with which to cope. Now as never before, the use of drugs has become one of the choices, the pressures. As you near the end of your teacher training and look with apprehension and eagerness at your new world, the world of young people, included in that world will be the problem of drugs. How will you deal with this problem? Should it concern you at all? Is this a problem area for teachers?

A recent survey showed that about one-quarter of teenagers aged 12 to 19 had tried cannabis (marijuana or hashish). About 2% were using cannabis daily. Marijuana and hashish have been known and used for 5000 years, but little is understood about their chemistry in the body. Today they are used solely for their mood-changing effects. Some of these changes may be harmless or temporary while others may pose real dangers. Research into cannabis use suggests that someone who uses cannabis is taking some very real risks. These include health risks (damage to the immune system, lungs and throat, reproductive system), learning and psychological risks, and safety and legal risks.

As teachers, it makes sense for us to take the cannabis issue seriously, especially the learning risks, shortterm and longterm.

Cannabis intoxication interferes with shortterm memory and logical thinking. There is no doubt that when you're stoned you can't concentrate for very long and you can't remember very much, so people display unusual absentmindedness while on the drug. A student whose memory and concentration are impaired during class because of cannabis use is obviously not in a good position to learn. People who sit through class stoned on marijuana may think they're getting great insights at the time, but more often than not they can't remember much the next day. Any activity requiring concentration, good judgment, coordination, timing, or fast reactions may be potentially dangerous for people high on pot. While this has particular relevance to safety, e.g., driving a car, it is also relevant to learning.

Unfortunately, because so many of the effects show up only in the long term, the facts can be all too easy to ignore. Some scientists are beginning to think that heavy, longterm cannabis use may cause changes in brain cell connections and in brain wave patterns. Does longterm use have an effect on personality? Does it dull intelligence? While there are no conclusive scientific answers to these questions, it is safe to say that a person who is stoned much of the time is, to some degree or another, cut off from normal experience. The more time a person spends stoned, the more the attitudes, perceptions, and experiences during those times may begin to affect his or her reality.

Because of the widespread use of cannabis, the taboos against it have weakened. Pot has developed a positive image among many young people. It is associated with pleasant sensation, a good time, with feeling "high." The fact that so many people use it and talk about it means that it has achieved a degree of social acceptability. As a result, kids today face a situation and a temptation unlike previous generations. There is a certain excitement to the cops—and—robbers game, with the high stakes of arrest and jail only adding to the excitement. The rebellious, or simply curious, adolescents can identify with this lifestyle and may be tempted to partake in what they feel is the recreational use of marijuana. Authority figures who point out the risk of jail, etc. are missing the point: part of the excitement and reason for using the drug is this participation in the rebellious act of using pot. Programs geared to challenging adolescents to take risks of a positive nature probably have more anti—marijuana impact than any "Reefer Madness" anti—marijuana film could have.

To summarize, we know that cannabis affects shortterm memory and that while intoxicated the user may have difficulty remembering

```
how to do simple tasks or maintaining a train of thought. It has an
impairing effect, even in small doses, on the ability to perform
complex tasks such as driving a car, as it distorts visual
perception, reaction time and judgment. Although research on the
longterm use of cannabis has not been conclusive, investigations
indicate the possibility of a variety of harmful effects, e.g.,
chromosome alterations, impairment of the body's immune system,
reduced male hormones, and brain and liver damage. As teachers,
we should take the cannabis issue seriously.
                                                         Pat Dale
```

Although the central argument is that marijuana interferes with learning, the writer assumes that many in her audience do not categorize marijuana with hard drugs, may even use it recreationally themselves. Some of her emphasis consequently shifts toward a more general argument that marijuana is bad for people. Her refutation is an attack on the social acceptability of marijuana and an explanation of adolescent motives for using it. Her summary conclusion emphasizes evidence that marijuana may be physically harmful. Was this good persuasive strategy? Should the refutation have focused not on students' motives for using marijuana but on teachers' reasons for not concerning themselves seriously with such use (including perhaps not believing it is their responsibility to do so)? Should the conclusion have come back to the central argument about marijuana and learning or was it more persuasive to emphasize the general harmfulness of marijuana? In short, the writer could have focused more sharply on the incompatibility of marijuana and education, perhaps restricting herself to an argument that teachers should be concerned if students use marijuana in school or while studying. Would such a focus have been better, or did the broader focus make the piece more persuasive?

Rogerian Persuasion ───────────────

You persuade a man only insofar as you can talk his language . . . , identifying your ways with his. . . . True, the rhetorician may have to change an audience's opinion in one respect; but he can succeed only insofar as he yields to that audience's opinions in other respects.

KENNETH BURKE

Carefully reasoned logical arguments . . . may be totally ineffectual when employed in a rhetorical situation where the audience feels its beliefs or values are being threatened.

PAUL BATOR

Antagonistic and Nonantagonistic Rhetorical Contexts

Traditional advice about persuasion generally presumes an antagonistic rhetorical context—basically a speaker or writer to represent each side of the issue and an audience to judge who is right. The word *antagonistic* comes from the Greek *agonia*, meaning a "contest," such as a wrestling match, in which athletes contend for a prize; and that is essentially the sort of context rhetoricians have traditionally assumed when discussing persuasion.

The epitome of this type of antagonistic context is found in an English or North American courtroom. There is an issue: Is the defendant guilty as charged? There are representatives of both viewpoints: the prosecuting and defense attorneys. There is an audience to decide who is right: the judge and jury. There is a complete separation of functions: no one represents more than one point of view; and those who will pass judgment are supposed to be neutral, disinterested (i.e., they represent no point of view, have no vested interest in the outcome). Everyone would be shocked if the defense attorney were to announce, "Your Honor, after hearing the prosecution's case, I am convinced of my clients' guilt, so I will say nothing in their defense," because attorneys are supposed to represent, not to judge.

The key point about the separation of functions is this: *the opponents who are arguing against each other are not trying to convince each other.* The prosecutor does not expect to convince the defense attorney, just the judge and jury. Debating politicians, likewise, are not trying to change each other's minds; they argue against each other in order to convince the voters. They are trying to defeat, not to convince, their opponents.

Similarly, when a writer produces an article that takes a position on a controversial issue, that writer is usually trying to convince a relatively uncommitted readership, not partisans of an opposing view. The writer may argue overtly against the author of a previous article, but the persuasion is ordinarily aimed at other readers who are, in effect, a third party judging the debate.

Under these circumstances, the appropriate strategy is to present your position as strongly as you can. Depending on the nature of the issue, opponents, and audience, this strategy may include criticizing, refuting, or even ridiculing opposing viewpoints and their representatives. Though the ultimate purpose of such persuasion may be a social good—such as determining truth or responsibility, choosing an effective course of action or the best candidate—the rhetorical means is antagonistic, as I. A. Richards puts it in *The Philosophy of Rhetoric* (Oxford), "an offspring of dispute" and "dominated by the combative impulse."

If, however, you are arguing with somebody *and trying to convince that same person*, the rhetorical context is radically different and demands a distinct persuasive strategy. Suppose you are writing a private letter to the author of that article you disagree with. Suppose that your rhetorical purpose is to change that author's mind, perhaps even to convince that author to publish a retraction. Under this sort of circumstance, where the "opponent" and the audience are the same person, the antagonistic strategy is often entirely ineffective.

To present your case strongly is to strongly attack the position with which your reader or readers identify. When attacked, people feel threatened. When people feel threatened, they get defensive and "stick to their guns." So if your purpose is to persuade people to change, the last thing you want is for them to feel defensive. For you may win "the battle of words" and still not win over your opponent.

People do sometimes manage not to take arguments personally. They manage not to react defensively even though their beliefs and/or statements are being criticized. And even if they do react defensively at first, people often manage to hear the argument and may well change later, after the threat is gone—often without even remembering when and by whom they were persuaded.

But to use a persuasive strategy that threatens your readers is not the best way to achieve your persuasive purposes. In a three-way situation, you can attack your opponent's position with impunity because that will not threaten your readers (after all, except insofar as they identify with your opponent, it is not *their* position being attacked). A two-way situation, however, usually calls for a less aggressive strategy. As Anatol Rapoport puts it, you want not a strategy that will threaten, but a strategy that "dilute the threat," thus making it easier for your readers to consider your points. As Kenneth Burke writes in *The Philosophy of Literary Form* (Vintage), "humaneness is the soundest implement of persuasion."

There is an apparent contradiction in all of this. You are attempting persuasion because you disagree with your readers. You want to explain why your position is correct. But to present your position strongly is to attack theirs, which is not a good way to encourage them to change. How then can you state your case persuasively without threatening your readers?

The Rogerian Way

There is a form of persuasion, identified with the humanistic psychologist Carl Rogers, that is appropriate to rhetorical contexts where you should avoid threatening those who hold opposing views. It is especially appropriate to conflicts that seem to be antagonistic but really are not because you actually share significant common ground with your "opponents." Although it can be used manipulatively to win arguments, Rogerian persuasion basically aims at achieving consensus around a correct position. The objective is truth, not victory.

In Rogerian persuasion, you convince your "opponents" that you understand their position before stating your own. You do this by restating their position so fairly that they recognize your restatement as an accurate representation of their position. What is more, you next validate their position by explaining the senses or contexts in which you see that position as correct.

This may seem an odd way to begin to persuade them to change their minds. But note what you have done. You have demonstrated that you are a fair-minded person who can understand your readers—and who cares enough to try to. You have indicated that, at least in some sense or some context, you can see some validity in their position. Although you disagree, you do not think they are totally stupid. In a situation where they probably expected to be attacked, they feel understood and valued. As Anatol Rapoport puts it in *Fights, Games, and Debates* (Michigan), you have shown them the limits inside of which they are right and thus induced them to enlarge their vision, to consider new information and broader contexts in which their opinion may not hold.

In other words, you have done what Aristotle says to do when he discusses emotional and ethical appeals: you have put your readers "in the right frame of mind" and convinced them that you are at least somewhat empathetic, fair-minded, and sensible. You have not done so in quite the way Aristotle had in mind, but that is because you are dealing with a sort of rhetorical context with which the Greek rhetoricians did not much concern themselves.

The logical appeal comes next, after your readers have been prepared to consider it. The transition from representing your readers' position empathetically to presenting your own convincingly is the fulcrum on which successful Rogerian persuasion turns: if it is too abrupt or rings false, you may lose your fair-minded persona and your readers. Be careful here: many writers unintentionally slip into a classically antagonistic mode as they move to state their own opinions. Try instead to avoid exaggerated claims and what may sound to your readers like biased language, while making a fair statement of your position. Then demonstrate the contexts in which you believe your position is valid. Presumably at least one of these contexts closely resembles the actual context with which the persuasion is concerned.

Finally, instead of restating your case, explain how your readers would benefit by adopting your position (or at least some aspects of it). In other words, you explicitly state what in Chapter 4 was called the *mutual purpose* you share with your readers.

The formal structure of an ideal written Rogerian persuasion looks something like this:

Introduction. Here, of course, you are trying to introduce the subject in such a way that your readers will read on. That may be difficult because most people try to avoid reading material with which they radically disagree. Try presenting it as a *problem* to be solved rather than as an *issue* that divides. Thus you can begin with agreement—that a problem exists. Though somewhat comparable to the Classical introduction and narration, the Rogerian introduction weaves a very different kind of web.

Fair Statement of the Opposing Position. The goal here is to convince your readers that you understand their perspective by stating their position in a way they will recognize as fair and accurate.

Statement of Contexts in Which that Position May Be Valid. Here you are trying to convince your readers that you understand how they could hold their position by suggesting that in certain contexts it has some validity.

Fair Statement of Your Own Position. You want here to state your position convincingly while maintaining your image as a fair-minded person. Your immediate goal is to get your readers to reciprocate, to understand your position as fairly and thoroughly as you have understood theirs. So you must *make a smooth transition and maintain a Rogerian tone* while presenting your opinion fairly and convincingly. Though this part of a Rogerian persuasion contains material that might go into the Classical proposition, partition, and proof, the tone is very different.

Statement of Contexts in Which Your Position Is Valid. Here you are trying to induce your readers to look at the problem from new perspectives and hence to see it in contexts they may previously have ignored.

Statement of How Readers Would Benefit by at Least Moving Toward Your Position. Here you are appealing to your readers' self-interests, at least in the broader, long-term sense. You are trying to transform your position from a *threat* to a *promise*. The Rogerian ending is not a summary and usually does not emphasize appeals to the readers' emotions.

Rogerian persuasion is especially appropriate for dealing with touchy subjects or hostile readers. It should be used when logic alone will not work because readers feel angry, scared, or threatened.

Broadly conceived, Rogerian persuasion is an application of the ancient ethical principle, "Do unto others as you would have others do unto you"; that is, demonstrate that you have considered and understood their position as carefully as you want them to consider yours. The Rogerian combination of ethical and emotional appeals minimizes the threat that is usually implicit in any change. Thus it allows the logical appeal to be more rationally considered. That, not the precise formal structure, is what makes it Rogerian and humanistic.

The success of a Rogerian persuasion depends first and foremost on how well the writer understands the readers. If readers are to feel understood, they must recognize their own opinions and reasons in the first part of the essay. Word choice is also crucial. An inappropriate purr-word or snarl-word (see pages 211 – 12), a bit of overstatement at the wrong spot, or an awkward transition can ruin the effect.

Consider the following persuasion, in which the management of a restaurant tries to convince the smokers among its regular patrons to accept a new policy that excludes smoking in the dining area. Note the effort to understand both the smokers' motives and the context in which smoking may be considered a pleasurable and valid personal preference.

Dear Patron,

Attending to your personal preferences is our greatest concern, and the appreciation expressed by a satisfied diner is our greatest reward. We try for the 'extra touch' that can make the difference between a pleasant evening and a memorable one. Satisfying some patrons' preference to smoke in the dining area, however, is not so straightforward. Because smoke cannot be confined to one table, nonsmoking patrons must also be considered.

Many people feel smoking before and after a meal contributes immensely to the full enjoyment of dining out. While waiting for the meal to arrive at the table or during coffee afterwards, they may anticipate the cigarette that accompanies conversation among friends. As dining itself is a leisurely activity, so smoking may be viewed as one aspect of it. As dining out is a well deserved luxury, so smoking may be viewed as a satisfying act of indulgence to be included. After choosing a restaurant that suits their personal tastes and standards, patrons rightfully expect to be accommodated in every way possible in order to make the evening most enjoyable.

Thus smokers will wish to have the cigarette they are accustomed to. And when smokers are seated next to patrons who share their preference or when other patrons are seated far enough away that the smoke does not reach them, smoking is fully acceptable because no one is unwillingly subjected to it.

Nonsmokers share the same sentiments towards their evening out and have the same expectations of quality, service and atmosphere. They too expect to be accommodated in every way possible in order to make the evening most comfortable and enjoyable. A smoke–free environment contributes immensely to their full enjoyment of dining. Smoke can be as irritating to a nonsmoker as excessive noise is to most everyone except those who make it. When a diner sits next to someone who is smoking, the effect is the same as smoking and eating at the same time. This is something even smokers do not do because it interferes with the taste of the meal and the smell can be unpleasant even if one is accustomed to it. Regardless of the duration, moreover, nonsmokers may view exposure to smoke as a disregard for the right to protect one's health.

Thus nonsmokers may rightfully desire the absence of smoke in the dining area. When the dining area is crowded, many nonsmokers may feel some degree of discomfort. In this sense, smoking, though a personal preference, is not an individual act that can always be dealt with on an individual basis. As a public act, it sometimes has to be dealt with in the spirit of compromise.

The management believes that pleasing results can be accomplished for both smokers and nonsmokers. We can all agree that every action has its appropriate time and place. As a pastime before and after eating, smoking is not necessary to the enjoyment of the meal itself and, therefore, is not a priority in the dining area. In fact, separating the two activities, eating and smoking, should make each more enjoyable for both smokers and nonsmokers. Nonsmokers will enjoy the smoke–free environment and smokers will be accommodated through the extended services of the staff. The hostesses and servers will make a conscious effort to seat or move smokers into the lounge before and after the meal. In the lounge smoking will be a priority and socializing will be uninterrupted by waiters cleaning tables, attending tables and delivering food. Through such compromise, not smoking in the dining room may be an indirect means to improved quality, service and comfort for all.

Kathy Fansega

Assuming that a restaurant's customers were willing to read such a letter, how well would this persuasion work? To what extent do you think the opening paragraph succeeds in presenting the subject as a problem rather than an issue? Would it work better if the last two sentences were moved down to the third or fourth paragraph? How well does the writer minimize threat and make smokers feel understood while approaching this touchy subject? How smoothly does she handle the transition to her point of view? How well does she maintain a Rogerian tone in the second half? To what extent does the ending succeed in presenting the conclusion as a promise?

The formal structure of Rogerian persuasion, like any other rhetorical pattern, should be treated as a guideline. When you are first learning it, you will probably do well to follow it explicitly. Once you have mastered it, however, you should adapt it to suit your purposes and your readers. The original version of the preceding persuasion used the contrast between contexts in which smoking is fully acceptable and those in which it may not be acceptable as the transition to the writer's opinion.

> Thus smokers will wish to have the cigarette they are accustomed to. And when smokers are seated next to patrons who share their preference or when other patrons are seated far enough away that the smoke does not reach them, smoking is fully acceptable because no one is unwillingly subjected to it. When the dining area is crowded, many nonsmokers may feel some degree of discomfort. In this sense, smoking, though a personal preference, is not an individual act that can always be dealt with on an individual basis. As a public act, it sometimes has to be dealt with in the spirit of compromise.

Which version do you think would be more effective?

The traditional and Rogerian approaches to persuasion are quite distinct (although the classical notions of ethical and emotional appeals do provide a link between the two). You will do well to learn both and to use each where appropriate. There is also a larger lesson to be learned from the juxtaposition of these two approaches: the rhetorical forms you use to give shape to your ideas are very important. If you do not believe that, try doing a traditional and a Rogerian version of the same argument. One writer (pages 402–5) tried to do just that in response to a paper on world starvation which had argued,

> The problem is this: our meat industry uses scarce, rich agricultural land to grow grain for cattle—high quality grain that could be eaten directly by humans. . . . As individuals, we can be part of the solution to feeding the world's hungry and malnourished by reducing the amount of meat we eat and thereby releasing grain for human consumption instead of feed for cattle.

The Classical persuasion is addressed to those who read and were perhaps convinced by the original article; the Rogerian persuasion is addressed to the author of the original article. The tone, of course, is radically different, as is the order in which certain arguments appear. Note also how the fact that the entire piece is essentially a refutation blurs the distinction between the proofs and refutation sections of the Classical version. Note how successfully the Rogerian version ends with a promise—because the basis of the whole piece is *agreement* that we should do something about world hunger—rather than a put-down.

To the Editor:

Here's the beef. I think JW is full of granola when she says in her article, "Thought for Food," that if we all ate more grain the world would be a fatter place. Specifically, she claims that meat eaters contribute to world hunger because the animals they eat are fattened on rich grain that could have fed many more people than the meat does. She says, "we can all be part of the solution to feeding the world's hungry and malnourished by reducing the amount of meat we eat and thereby releasing grain for human consumption instead of feed for cattle." Unfortunately, the suggestion is a gross oversimplification of a very complex and difficult problem.

The problem is important, too important to be defined so narrowly. The Ethiopian famine of the summer of '86 illustrates the tragic consequences of food shortages in disadvantaged countries. Thousands died tragically, and perhaps needlessly. Surely, given the choice, we would all want to be "part of the solution." The real difficulty, though, comes in identifying the solution and, perhaps more importantly, in implementing it. JW's simplistic solution--giving up meat, and eating more grain and legumes-- ignores the far more important political and economic aspects of the problem, and naively proposes to remedy the inequities of the world's complex economic

Dear Ms. JW:

I read with interest your recent article, "Thought for Food." The solution to the world food shortage you propose in that article deserves consideration--perhaps we should all try to "do our part" right here by adopting a grain-based diet. This, as you say, would be a more efficient use of agricultural resources than using grain to fatten cattle. You will get no argument from me--the problem of world hunger is serious, and every possible solution should be explored.

You say that our preference for meat over grain as a primary source of protein leads to inefficient food production practices, because it takes twenty pounds of grain to produce one pound of meat, and that this inefficiency contributes to the problem of feeding the world's hungry. It follows then that lowering the demand for meat should free scarce agricultural land for the production of grain for people instead of grain for cattle, and that this arrangement could feed more people.

infrastructure with a few granola
and soybean recipes for gout—
afflicted Westerners.

In short, JW chooses to ignore the
social context of the problem and
focuses too narrowly on the
simplistic equation that feed
cattle must eat twenty pounds of
grain to produce one pound of
protein. Though there are other
flaws in JW's argument, the main
criticisms I have are these: (1) she
fails to show how the grain would
get to the hungry; (2) she ignores
the costs that an effective
distribution system would entail;
and most importantly, (3) she
ignores the problem of mustering
the necessary political will at
home when unemployment is high and
people line up for government
assistance of every kind.

The first thing to consider then
is how does more grain at home
translate into more food in places
like Africa? The answer is that it
doesn't. Not unless we are willing
to pay the costs of harvesting,
shipping and distribution in the
areas of need. More grain at home
will help feed the world only if this
new supply of food is indeed
diverted to the needy. A more likely
outcome is that farmers would
simply stop producing the crops
altogether, unless they were
assured a paying market.

Your argument, based as it is on
the relative efficiencies of these
two food sources, certainly holds
well in a situation where the grain
can readily be passed on to the
hungry. For example, if farmers are
fattening cattle in a region where
the grain supply is inadequate to
feed the hungry, say in Ethiopia
itself, then it is fairly clear that
such a strategy could prove
helpful. In such a situation, where
the grain source is relatively
close to the point of consumption,
more grain should translate into
less malnutrition and starvation.
There would be more food around, and
this could conceivably make it more
affordable for those of meager
means. And this, of course, is
another necessary assumption: that
those in need have at least the
minimal means to compensate the
producers and also access to
essential implements for food
preparation, such as water and
containers.

I do agree that meat appears to be
a wasteful method for obtaining
protein. I wonder, however, if you
have considered the other
variables that may play an equally
important part in the problem. It
is not clear that a greater grain
supply will necessarily lead to a
more equitable distribution of
agricultural output. I wonder, for
example, who will pay our farmers
(who already struggle to meet their
own obligations) to ship their
wheat across the oceans and

The issue is whether or not the developed nations want to accept financial responsibility for feeding the world. Supposing that we did increase the global grain supply through a large-scale change in diet, who would pay for the distribution, and what would the costs be? Indeed, is this not the situation today? Countries like Canada, the USA and Australia produce grain far in excess of their own requirements, but their first interest is to get it to paying markets. And even if excess grain remains, it is cheaper and simpler to "dump" the surplus output than to attempt a costly distribution program to the scattered and unorganized nations in need. Governments in developed countries have for years been paying farmers not to produce crops they could not sell.

This last statement gets to the heart of the problem—political will. For even if the costs and distribution problem were manageable, the problem of the politician's need to satisfy fickle voters at home remains. Yes, we do "give generously" when asked. But for the most part, charity is not a matter of ongoing policy; it is frequently a matter of responding to particular crises, and often motivated by guilt or tax considerations. So in this kind of social environment, and given the political realities of elections and budget deficits, it seems doubtful that many governments could commit the resources required to make JW's "recipe"

continents? And who will build, organize and pay for the transportation system in the countries that receive the food? It has been widely reported, for example, that the most unfortunate aspect of the Ethiopian relief project was that much of the goods donated never reached their destinations within the country for a lack of adequate roads and vehicles. The problem is not really a "world food shortage"; it is an uneven distribution of resources and population. It is a complicated geographic, economic and political problem that goes well beyond diet management.

The crux of the matter then revolves around the question of physical distances and economic inequalities that separate meat-producing regions and those nations we awkwardly call "underdeveloped." If the physical or economic barriers are great, then finding the economic resources and political will necessary to redistribute the lifegiving food is clearly the biggest problem and the most important priority. We must also admit that the "charity begins at home" mentality cannot easily be discounted in periods of high unemployment and huge government deficits. When governments cannot find the resources to solve work, at least on a longterm basis. It is an economic and moral problem, not simply a matter of diet choice, and even this is an oversimplification: after all, would it not be a better use of resources to supply the needy with the means to help themselves?

Are twenty pounds of grain better than one pound of animal protein? Unfortunately, JW's argument cannot be evaluated in a political and economic vacuum. Her assumption that the freed—up grain would automatically flow to the needy is simply untenable. (If everyone in Vancouver were to fast today, would that make anyone in Bangladesh less hungry tomorrow?) As is invariably the case in a "free market" society, resources will typically be allocated on the basis of power or ability to pay, and only a small residual will flow to the less fortunate—and that only given the right political and economic conditions.

Dominique Lecasse

domestic problems, they may be hard—pressed to maintain, let alone increase, expenditures abroad. In these circumstances, economic and political variables are likely to seriously overshadow the relative efficiencies of diet.

It is an axiom of all problem—solving strategies that the most important step is to identify the problem accurately and completely. For it is only through identifying the relative importance of the various factors involved, while recognizing the complexity of their interrelationships, that we can start toward a usable solution. This holds for finding an equitable solution to global food production and distribution. For though an efficient mix of nutritional sources may be part of the "food solution," it will solve nothing if the economic and political dimensions of the problem are not first recognized and addressed. Yes, we may eventually substitute much grain for a little meat. But first we will have to make financial sacrifices and tough political decisions to move that grain and, ultimately, to help the less fortunate acquire the resources and knowledge necessary to feed themselves. For now, though, the question is not really what food do we eat, but rather who should eat it? That is where the solution lies— not so much in a change of diet as in a more equitably "balanced diet."

Dominique Lecasse

Rogerian persuasion, as Paul Bator says, is especially appropriate in situations where "carefully reasoned, logical arguments" by themselves will not work because "the audience feels its beliefs or values are being threatened." Indeed, in such cases, arguments are often doomed to failure if they are not founded on careful analysis of readers' underlying beliefs and values.

Consider, for example, arguments about abortion. The overt discussion typically turns on such issues as whether a fetus should be considered a person (in which case abortion becomes homicide, legally justifiable only in cases of self-defense), whether the pregnant woman's well-being should take priority over the well-being of the fetus, whether the individual woman or society should make the decision. But research in both the United States and Canada shows that the disagreement is often founded upon much more basic differences.

This research shows that people who strongly oppose abortion and people who strongly support the individual woman's right to choose disagree on a whole range of fundamental values. For instance, anti-abortion activists generally believe (1) that men and women have different roles (and that what makes women special is their natural ability to nurture), (2) that the availability of abortion (like the availability of highly effective contraception) worsens women's position because it makes it easier for men to be irresponsible and to treat women as sexual objects, (3) that the universe is guided by a greater purpose to which human beings should subordinate themselves. Pro-choice activists make very different assumptions: (1) that one's role in life should not be determined by gender (and that *involuntary* motherhood oppresses women), (2) that women should try to better their position not so much by holding men more responsible as by taking more responsibility for themselves, (3) that the ultimate purpose of human society is to enable individuals to actualize their potential. Anti-abortion activists, moreover, are generally moral absolutists who presume clear rules, an absolute moral code such as the biblical ten commandments, by which human conduct can be judged. Pro-choice activists, by contrast, generally believe the actual implications of ethical principles vary from one situation to another and that people must use moral judgment because absolutely clear-cut rules do not exist.

Because the disagreements are so basic, the usual arguments about whether a fetus is a person or about what might be best for either the pregnant woman or the fetus are not likely to move these activists. Even with less committed readers, to discuss abortion is often to call into question their basic assumptions about men and women, the purpose of human life and the moral nature of the universe. Only an approach that minimizes threat and considers these assumptions is likely to move readers who do not already share the writer's underlying assumptions.

Similarly basic disagreements underlie many controversial issues and touchy subjects. If the audience is not yet firmly committed and already makes or is open to the right assumptions, then a Classical persuasion emphasizing logical appeal may work well. But if an audience is firmly committed or already holds contrary underlying values, then Rogerian persuasion is a better strategy. Though no single communication is likely to transform a strongly committed opinion rooted in a person's basic values, a Rogerian strategy is more likely to open a mind, begin a process of reconsideration.

The Ethics of Rogerian Persuasion

Rogerian persuasion raises a number of ethical issues. Rogerian persuasion may seem morally superior to Classical persuasion because it is founded on empathy and works toward common ground, whereas Classical persuasion is founded on conflict and works toward winning. As envisioned by Rogers and those who adapted his concept to written communication, Rogerian persuasion means to understand those who oppose you and work with them toward the best possible resolution. Occasionally writers using the Rogerian structure actually convince themselves and change their minds while writing the first half. But the Rogerian structure can also be used deviously by writers who want only to win and only pretend to empathize and respect. Like any rhetorical technique, Rogerian persuasion can be used or abused.

There are those who believe that the assertiveness of traditional argument constitutes verbal violence, lack of empathy, lack of respect and consideration for others. There are also those who believe that traditional argument is more honest because more direct. Rogerian persuasion does involve what a combative debater might call "pulling your punches." In moving from Classical to Rogerian persuasion, Dominique Lecasse had to delete such strong (and clever) statements as these:

```
Here's the beef. I think JW is full of granola when she says . . .
that if we all ate more grain the world would be a fatter place.
. . . JW's simplistic solution . . . ignores the far more important
political and economic aspects of the problem, and naively proposes
to remedy the inequities of the world's complex economic
infrastructure with a few granola and soybean recipes for gout-
afflicted Westerners.
```

Rogerian persuasion also usually means that you do not fully reveal your own position until after the turning point. And even then you often do not assert it as strongly as you feel it.

There are rhetorical contexts in which Classical persuasion offers a more effective structure and rhetorical contexts in which Rogerian persuasion offers a more effective structure. There are contexts in which it seems ethically most important to be direct and out front; there are contexts in which it seems ethically most important to be gentle and empathetic. There are even extreme contexts in which it seems ethical to lie. Either structure, moreover, can be used or abused. For better and for worse, there is no simple rule. Whether Classical or Rogerian persuasion is superior, ethically or rhetorically, depends on the context. Writers who wish to be persuasive in various contexts are well advised to master both the Classical and the Rogerian modes.

EXERCISE

1. Carl Rogers' original use of the principles behind Rogerian persuasion was in oral communication. The basic rule was this: no one may speak without first summarizing what the last speaker said accurately enough to satisfy that speaker. Next time you have an argumentative discussion, try following this rule. How does it affect the discussion? What does this exercise teach you that might be useful when you are writing Rogerian persuasion?

2. In *A Rhetoric of Motives*, Kenneth Burke asserts that "you persuade a man only insofar as you can talk his language by speech, gesture, tonality, order, image, attitude, idea—*identifying* your ways with his." Explain how both Rogerian and traditional persuasive strategies encourage such identification.

3. Choose a thesis statement you believe in, imagine an appropriate rhetorical context, and write a Rogerian persuasion that follows the Rogerian format.

4. Pair yourself with someone with whom you can agree on a thesis for a persuasive writing. Working together, brainstorming, using Aristotle's *topoi* or whatever other invention techniques you wish, invent as many arguments as you can in support of that thesis. Then one of you should choose an appropriate audience for a Classical persuasion, the other for a Rogerian persuasion. Do an audience analysis, select your arguments and write your persuasion. Compare and contrast what you produced with what your partner produced from the same materials. Consider how audience and form have affected the tone and substance of the writings. (See the discussion of collaborative writing, pages 137–40, and Exercise 5, below.)

5. Select a controversial and touchy issue, such as abortion, on which you have a strong position. Select an audience that holds a similarly strong but contrary position, an audience that would likely feel its beliefs or values are being threatened. Research that audience and devise a Rogerian strategy that might at least open them to an understanding of your beliefs or move them a bit toward your position. (If you choose to write about abortion, for instance, you might look at Chapters 5 and 6 of Kristin Luker's *Abortion and the Politics of Motherhood*, University of California Press.)

6. The following open letter was addressed to parents of pupils in a school that had just instituted sex education classes for seventh-graders. Though generally Rogerian, it makes several tactical errors. Evaluate its effectiveness, note what works well, and make suggestions about how the letter might be improved.

Should We Have Sex Education Classes
in the Seventh Grade?

Many parents of children in this school have expressed their disapproval of our recent decision to implement sex education classes in the seventh grade. A number of you feel that the material presented in these classes could—and should—be discussed only in the home. As concerned parents many of you feel that some of the children simply are not ready to learn the facts of life. In many instances, you are correct. Even at the seventh grade level, many children are not mature enough to be told about sex. It is something they may not be concerned with personally for a good many years.

We can sympathize with the difficulties faced by today's parents. It is indeed frightening to consider that there is a need to educate children about the "facts of life" at such an early age. For many of you, it is also upsetting that the people imparting this information are relative strangers. In addition, because the information is being relayed in a classroom situation, many of you feel that sex will become the number one topic of conversation outside the classroom as well. We can certainly see why you would prefer to have something as personal as sex discussed in the home rather than in the school. We can agree with you that the ideal situation for children to learn about sex is in the home, with clear and concise information being given. However, it is almost impossible to ensure that every child is being informed about sex in this manner.

If sex education is the responsibility of the school, the material is presented clearly. The teachers lose a great deal of emotional bias which is felt by a parent protecting his or her child from the realities of life. Questions which many parents would feel uncomfortable dealing with are dealt with much more easily in the classroom. Topics such as homosexuality, on which many parents have very biased opinions, are discussed openly. Many of you question the wisdom of presenting such advanced topics in the classroom. However, unless your children do not watch television or look at newspapers, it is very unlikely that we are telling them about anything they do not already worry and wonder about. It has also been our experience that when all children are equally informed

about sex, the clandestine street—corner discussions usually
disappear, and the topic of sex loses its allure. It is these secret
teaching sessions that promote sexual ignorance, and sexual
ignorance can only lead to tragedy.

7.   The purpose of the following Rogerian persuasion is to persuade government office workers to use cumulative sentences. Look back at the discussion
of cumulative sentences (pages 239–44) and then consider how effective this
persuasion might be.

The Long and the Short of It

Many office workers in your industry do a variety of writing in
the course of their jobs: drafting letters, filing reports, or
issuing newsletters. While these forms of writing differ, they all
must use the sentence in order to communicate effectively. The
sentence, however, also differs—in length, structure, and ability
to convey meaning. It is often difficult to choose the appropriate
sentence type for each piece of work, some writers preferring long
sentences, others using short sentences.

In your experience as an office worker, you find that short
sentences are easier to read and understand. They are
uncomplicated, compact, and are extremely effective in expressing
your subject. You are able to make clear the importance of your ideas
by using short sentences, and you find that your readers are easily
able to remember what you have written.

It is true that short sentences can be easier to read and
understand, particularly if your writing style is smooth and
flowing. When writing for an audience with low or mixed reading
abilities, as you often do in your work, shorter sentences may be
a better choice. They are also useful in writing articles, such as
inter—office memos or newsletters, where several points are made
in a limited space and must stand out to be remembered. They also
enable you to be concise in such instances.

Cumulative sentences, however, although long, are exceptionally
useful. A cumulative sentence is simply a main clause to which
modifiers have been added. These modifiers give additional meaning
to sentences, making them more detailed, allowing for better
understanding. Cumulative sentences are very effective because
they are more concrete than kernel sentences, painting a more
detailed picture for the reader. The use of cumulative sentences
make a writing seem more mature, creating a sophisticated persona
for the writer.

Cumulative sentences can be very powerful and are particularly
useful when writing narrative or descriptive passages. They are

used to make a writing concrete, rather than abstract, producing a more vivid account. Concrete writing has a greater effect on the readers—they become more involved in interpreting the writing and the conclusions are additionally convincing. Cumulative sentences are also effective in making the writer's persona evident.

In many instances, the use of cumulative sentences would benefit you in your work. If you used this sentence structure you would encounter fewer misunderstandings—your writing would be more precise with the additional details. Also your persona would be that of a more mature and skillful writer and you would gain the trust of your readers, a valuable asset in your field of work. Often you require a narrative or descriptive style of writing, such as when you file reports, and the cumulative sentence would be particularly useful to you in these instances. The use of cumulative sentences would make your writing more convincing as well, an especially useful trait when you are communicating with the government bureaucracy.

Willow Tegart

C·H·A·P·T·E·R 10

Special Discourses

Genuine speech is the expression of genuine personality. Because it takes pain to make itself intelligible, it assumes that the hearer is a genuine personality too—in other words, wherever it is spoken it creates a community.

NORTHRUP FRYE

In order to participate in the community and its changes, however, one must first master its language using practices.

PATRICIA BIZZELL

The only test a writer applies to a page is the craftsman's question, "Does it work?"

DONALD MURRAY

GOOD writers know how to apply the general principles of composition to particular writing tasks and contexts. They understand that what works in one rhetorical context will not necessarily work in another, that good journalism is not good business writing, that literature and literary criticism use radically different rhetorical structures, that the style which succeeds in a sales proposal could be disastrous in an academic grant application.

The people who write and read any particular sort of writing share certain assumptions about what is appropriate in that type of writing. Because their community can be defined by this shared discourse, we call them a *discourse community*. If you want to communicate with these readers, you should learn the standard features of the discourse.

Engineers, for instance, spend an estimated 40% of their work time writing, and the quality of this writing is crucial to their professional success. Professional engineers share certain general assumptions about their professional discourse and also particular assumptions about particular *genres* within that discourse—project proposals do not have the same structure as project reports.

These assumptions, moreover, may vary somewhat between electrical and mechanical engineering—or from one country to another. An engineering proposal that does not contain the appropriate subject matter, is not organized in the standard way, or does not follow the professional style may be perceived as unprofessional. Engineers who read it are likely to doubt the professional competence of those who produced it—often with good reason.

A discourse community is, in effect, a kind of ongoing discussion. If you want to join—and influence—that ongoing discussion, you should normally write in a way that fits into the discussion. Your new interpretation of the opening scene of *Hamlet* will take taken more seriously if you establish your authority as a literary critic not only by using an appropriate structure and style, but also by making clear your awareness of what other literary critics have been saying about that scene.

This chapter begins with Metaheur, a heuristic for analyzing any particular type of writing. Metaheur, like the heuristics discussed in Chapter 2, will focus your attention, guide your investigation in fruitful directions. Metaheur, however, is based on general principles of composition; it helps you investigate not your subject matter, but how to write within the conventions of a particular discourse or genre.

After introducing Metaheur, this chapter presents examples from students' analyses of various particular types of writing and then discusses academic writing at length. As you read about the characteristics of each specialized genre, try to see how they relate to the general principles of composition. Then see if you can apply Metaheur to a type of writing task that is of special importance to you. If you can do that, you have taken a big step toward being able to teach yourself how to do whatever types of writing you may wish to do.

A Heuristic for Analyzing Writing Tasks _____

Imagine that you enter a parlor. You come late. When you arrive, others have long preceded you, and they are engaged in a heated discussion, a discussion too heated for them to pause and tell you exactly what it is about. In fact, the discussion had already begun long before any of them got there, so that no one present is qualified to retrace for you all the steps that had gone before. You listen for a while, until you decide that you have caught the tenor of the argument; then you put in your oar. Someone answers; you answer him; another comes to your defense; another aligns himself against you, to either the embarrassment or the gratification of your opponent, depending upon the quality of your ally's assistance. However, the discussion is interminable. The hour grows late, you must depart. And you do depart, with the discussion still vigorously in progress.

KENNETH BURKE

Clearly, the structure of anything limits the uses to which it may be put.

JAMES KINNEAVY

Over time, particular communities—be they journalists, technical writers, or postmodernist poets—evolve effective strategies for achieving their communicative purposes and communicating the particular substance that concerns them. These strategies are embodied in rhetorical structures that become standard ways of writing for that community. As the common etymology of *communicate* and *community* suggests, part of what makes a community is shared ways of communicating.

Successful writers understand the parameters within which they work. Millie McCavour, who has won 28 prizes in recipe contests, claims no special talent as a cook; but she does admit to a knack for picking recipes that appeal to recipe contest judges. Recipes that win prizes, she says, tend to have relatively few ingredients, all readily available. But she also slips in a unusual ingredient or two, such as sour cream in her country scones recipe. To invent winning recipes, she certainly exercises her individual creativity—but within these parameters.

Individual pieces of writing often stand alone. We can understand them better, however, as discourse, as part of an ongoing discussion among a community of people. To do any particular type of writing is to address such a community, to participate in its discussion. The members of such a community—be they research physicists, readers of detective novels, or government bureaucrats—have evolved conventional expectations about how writing should be structured. Even if one intends to violate some of those conventions, it is useful to know what they are.

You can learn how to write for a particular discourse community by becoming a member of that community, by serving an apprenticeship or novitiate and, over time, developing a feeling for how that community communicates. Or, especially if you have less time, you can analyze the discourse and thereby discover the principles that make it work.

What follows is a procedure for investigating and analyzing almost any particular type of writing to discover its assumptions and describe its standard structures. This analysis is, in effect, a kind of literary criticism, although the types of writing you analyze probably will not be literary. Literary critics have, albeit for somewhat different purposes, applied this sort of analysis to literary texts for millennia. So, too, rhetoricians have analyzed persuasive texts and philosophers certain types of logical texts. Writers do this sort of analysis in order to learn how to produce specific types of writing.

The approach is two-pronged. Because there is little point in starting from scratch, in rediscovering what other people have already explained, you should search the library for guides or manuals. But manuals do not exist for all types of writing—and when they do exist, they are sometimes inaccurate and often focus on superficial features (e.g., the precise format of bibliographic references). So it is important also to look empirically at real instances of the type of writing you want to master.

Style Guides

Style guides are often published by professional organizations. The Modern Language Association (MLA), for example, publishes the style guide generally used by North American literary critics. The American Psychological Association (APA) publishes the guide generally used by social scientists. The Institute of Electrical and Electronics Engineers (IEEE) publishes one guide widely used by engineers. When in doubt, a good general guide is the *Chicago Manual of Style*.

Popular book and magazine publishers often provide freelance writers with similar guides. If you want to write a romance novel, for instance, Harlequin Books will send you a very detailed description of what they want. Many magazines will do the same. And at least one university press has a pamphlet explaining how to transform a dissertation into a scholarly book. These publishers are trying to save themselves time by encouraging writers to submit the sorts of manuscripts they seek. Any government agency, private foundation, or corporation to which you might be submitting a proposal is likely to offer similar advice. Such advice can save writers considerable wasted time and effort.

The main function of a professional style guide is to assure that all the writers in a particular profession or organization use a standardized format and style. You may learn, for example, that it is usual in your field to begin journal articles with a statement of the problem being investigated and a review of previous studies. You may be told that your manuscript should have a left-hand margin of $1\frac{1}{4}$ inches (3 cm). If there is a style guide for the type of writing you are trying to master, you should obtain it and follow it. If you are a student, your professors will probably expect you to follow the style guide that is standard in their field.

Manuals often give more substantive advice. The following excerpt is a student's summary of what she learned about the structure and style of news articles by consulting several journalism manuals.

> The news story is strictly governed by a prescribed format which can be visualized as an inverted pyramid: the most important facts are placed at the beginning, with the less important following. This enables the reader to get the "gist" of the story by scanning the first paragraph. It also makes it easier for the copy editor to shorten a story—he starts "cutting" from the bottom, knowing he is eliminating the least important facts.
>
> The beginning of a story is called its lead. The lead can run from a few words to two or more "grafs," and how its information is presented can make or break the story. The readers read the lead before anything else, apart from the headline, and if they don't like it, they won't continue. The lead sets the tone for the story and contains the most important information. The traditional "5Ws and H" (who? what? where? why? when? and how?) are usually contained in the lead.
>
> Following the lead is the body of the story. The body elaborates on the facts represented in the lead, as well as introducing new ones. Tight, concise writing is important in news stories for two reasons: one, because it makes it easier for the reporter to keep his audience interested; and two, because as far as publishers are concerned, space is money.
>
> Short words and compact phrases are the keys to good, tight journalistic writing. The reporter is taught to substitute "suddenly" for "all of a sudden," to write "soon" instead of "in the near future," and that "now" is preferably to "at the present time." Newspaper-writing style manuals contain long lists of words and phrases with their more succinct equivalents.
>
> Fiona Barnett

The constraints within which a writer must work may be peculiar to a particular discourse or genre. As Fiona found, for instance, modern newspaper journalists do not use standard paragraphs but indent very frequently, creating *grafs* which are often only a single sentence and rarely over 75 words. In other discourses (as occasionally in journalism) various sorts of numbered or bulleted lists may sometimes be substituted for paragraphs. And storybooks for very young children rarely use paragraphs or any such structure at all.

The general principles of paragraphing are generally valid, but unusual contexts may call for unusual applications of any principle.

Because writing can hardly be separated from thinking, descriptions of the sort of thinking required in the field are also likely to be helpful. The structure and style of a piece of writing often follow from the structure of the thinking processes which underlie it. If you are trying to figure out how to do research reports in sociology, an article by a philosopher of science analyzing the method of contemporary sociology may prove very useful. In academic and professional writing, it is often particularly important to understand just what "objectivity" means in the particular field and what you must *do* to achieve it (see pages 264–67).

Analyzing a Sample

Though style guides and manuals are useful, looking at actual writing of the sort you want to learn is more important. Begin by choosing some examples of successful writing of that type. In an academic or professional field, articles published in the most reputable journals are good choices. Thus if you are trying to learn how to write scholarly literary criticism, you might select ten articles from recent issues of *PMLA*, *American Literature*, *College English*, *Modern Drama*, and *Victorian Studies*. If, on the other hand, you are trying to learn how to write popular film reviews, you might turn to *Time*, *Cosmopolitan*, *Maclean's*, *McCall's*, and *Variety*.

As you read the pieces of writing you have selected, you will be doing an unusual type of reading. Although you will pay some attention to what the writers are saying, your focus will be on how they approach their subject matter, which sorts of material they choose to include, how they structure it, what they seem to assume about their rhetorical contexts, and what sort of persona and style they adopt.

In the following discussion you will find a list of questions to guide your analysis. The questions are derived from the principles of composition discussed in previous chapters of this textbook. Taken together, they constitute Metaheur, a heuristic for analyzing a particular discourse or genre of writing. Certain questions will, of course, prove more important than others for the particular type of writing you are investigating. Focus your effort on those questions that help you understand the defining features of the particular type of writing. Pass over questions that prove unimportant or irrelevant.

By answering these questions (and others which may arise as you analyze your sample and review your secondary sources), you should reach an understanding of the particular type of writing that concerns you. Try then to write out your answers as contextual constraints (see pages 367–70) within which writers must work to produce this type of writing. In particular, try to create:

1. a heuristic that will help generate the material,
2. an outline of any common format or structure, and
3. an analysis of the rhetorical context (purpose, audience, and occasion).

By doing these things, you will produce your own writer's manual and be well on your way toward teaching yourself to do the particular type of writing successfully and efficiently.

The constraints within which writers must work are often quite specific and sometimes rather rigid. A journalist often must write to a very specific length because the article must fill a certain space in the newspaper or magazine. Some scientific journals still refuse to publish first- or second-person pronouns. After analyzing storybooks for very young children, a writing student reports the following quantitative constraints:

> These books must not be too long because the young child has a
> short attention span. Forty—eight pages is usually cited as the
> maximum length for picture books (with a maximum of five hundred
> words per book). Sentence length must also be monitored. Most
> sentences have a maximum of eight words. Any longer than this and
> the child will lose the sense of the words. There are usually no
> paragraphs, and seldom are there more than eight or ten lines per
> page.
>
> Mischelle Panagopoulos

Subject Matter

It is often useful to begin by examining constraints on subject matter itself.

1. What kind of material is usually treated? Does there seem to be a shared heuristic that some or all of the writers use to generate their material? Could you invent such a heuristic? What sort of material, if any, is noticeably avoided? (For a discussion of heuristics, see pages 78–98.)
2. Do the writers seem to share approaches, methods, or techniques for handling the material? How are writings focused in this discourse? Are there certain key terms, root metaphors, or standard analogies that recur in this discourse? Are there "buzz words"? (See pages 103–6 on focus, pages 154–56 and 210–12 on key terms and root metaphors, pages 331–39 on analogy.)

Mischelle reached the following conclusions about the subject matter of storybooks for very young children:

To be successful, the story must deal with the needs and common
experiences of the wee tots. For this reason, many children's
writers use tiny children as their central characters. Kids will
identify with other kids who share their problems and
interests. . . .

   The picture books are quite short; therefore, the characters are
never fully developed. Although they are uncomplicated and flat,
they must still arouse interest and excitement. Maggie Scraggles
is a stereotyped witch, but her magical actions make her lively,
and this holds the attention. Character names are important because
they snag the child's attention. . . .

   Most picture stories have an element of humour in them, whether
it is presented in the comic illustrations or within the story.
The humour is always obvious and direct; this is no place for adult
wit or complex word plays. In these books, laughter is initiated
by the juxtaposition of incompatible elements or by the reversal
of common expectation.

Mischelle Panagopoulos

Another student writer, a sailor, wanted to learn how to write narratives
for sailing magazines like *Pacific Yachting*. Here is her analysis of the normal
subject matter of such articles:

The material is informative and entertaining, and usually describes
a specific cruise . . . . Details of navigation, tides, charts and
coastal scenery are included, and interspersed with specialized
information about the boat itself—the size and make, the type of
hull and engine, the standing and running rigging, and the overall
condition of the vessel. . . . Weather conditions are stressed.
Amusing anecdotes and minor incidents are included. For example,
Chettleburgh writes, "Chunks of kiln-processed stone lay in sorry
looking heaps along the waterfront. We tossed several pieces into
the saltchuck; they bobbed pumice-like back to shore."

Anne Jackson

Three other students investigated journalistic movie reviews. Here, slightly
abridged, is what they discovered about the substance of such reviews. (See
also the heuristic they devised, Chapter 2, pages 80–81.)

Writing Movie Reviews

<u>Movies</u>: Open the newspaper to the section that is current, where
first run movie ads are displayed and you will see the catalogue

from which all of the reviewers in our sample selected their material. The film that you review will be above all <u>news</u>: an event of the moment, the current hit, the talk of the town. Advance publicity will have appeared on television and magazines. Often this amounts to a total saturation, a blitz of ads, interviews, and gossip.

Readers expect what they consider to be informed, imaginative and, above all, relevant response to the movies. They know the other reviewers, they keep up with the controversies and they expect you to keep your opinions within the context of the existing debate. They don't want to hear about the latest controversy in deconstructive criticism. This is not an issue with them. On the other hand, the pros and cons of movie sequels as these apply, for example, to "Friday, the 13th, Part Umpteen," fall within the limits of what your audience considers the relevant opinion. So, even before you see the film you are going to review, you need to have some idea of what the other reviewers will be saying and how they will focus their reviews.

<u>Press Kit</u>: The way any given movie is described is usually very much the same from review to review. Do reviewers get together and collaborate? Are they psychic? How could this happen? After much research and a lot of thinking, we found our answer, an answer which is of great importance in determining which movies are reviewed and how. When you become a movie reviewer for a newspaper or a magazine, one of the materials you will use to write your review is a press kit. The kit includes a plot summary, a summary of the director's achievements, a list of actors, producers and special effects persons and also a list of the songs heard throughout the movie.

Reading the plot summary, you will realize—as we did—that the way a reviewer refers to a character or an action seems to be almost exactly the way film company refers to these things. Film companies want to promote their movies. To do so, they send biased information to magazines and newspapers that may well feel compelled to use much of this information because film companies are such a major source of financial support for both newspapers and magazines.

<u>Shared Approach</u>: The fact that all the reviewers work with the same material should not be construed to mean that they lack judgement or resourcefulness. Good writers write to an audience; the boundaries of their subject matter correspond to the interests of a specific group of readers and to the occasion and purpose of their reading. To go outside these boundaries in a review would mean losing some of that audience. Granted that's a risk some writers

take, but usually only when they feel they have enough power or control over their audience to take that audience along with them.

On the whole reviewers approach their material from the point of view of mainstream values. They assume there is a shared agreement on what is beautiful or bizarre, wholesome or funny. Along with this assumed agreement goes an implied acceptance of diversity. This attitude is established in the good-natured, sophisticated approach adopted by the reviewers. They supply commentary, not analysis. They balance the good with the bad. Their treatment is glib, ironic and knowing, conveying a worldly tolerance of freedom of expression.

Reviewers share one very important attitude: they treat movies exclusively as entertainment. From what we were able to observe newspaper reviewers rarely attempt to educate or persuade their audience. In fact they rarely presume to explicate or interpret the "meaning" of a film. Instead, they concentrate on the entertainment value. The only rating that counts is the satisfaction rating. If the audience likes blood, kisses and puppies, the reviewer tells them if the blood is red, the kisses hot or the puppies cute.

Reviewers construct the frame of Hollywood reality using the sensational aspects of the production—particularly expensive special effects and location shooting or infighting against producer and director. The lives of all the stars, their scandals or heartbreaks, any human interest angle to the original story or local connection are material the reviewer uses to center the film in its Hollywood context. The attitudes, ideas, lifestyles of the stars off the scene are discussed with enthusiasm and this scandalized interest is carried over into the discussion of their films.

The Hollywood of the reviewer is more than a geographic place. It is the world view within which writer and audience do their business. Questions about the social value of the film are never raised; movies are presented as in a world of their own. Reviewers only discuss the "long-suffering wife", the "faithful black butler", the "rogue policeman" with reference to their movie type, bringing in comparisons from film history or from other current films, commenting on what is exceptional, innovative or contrary to type. They rarely, if ever, discuss the social ramifications. Constructive social analysis plays no part in the reviewer's art.

Vikki Coupland, Tim Shireman, Rebecca Soles

Rhetorical Context

It is not enough, of course, to define the subject matter of the genre you wish to master. To present that subject matter appropriately and effectively, you need a sense of the rhetorical context:

3. What basic purposes does the writing serve? Is it primarily expressive, explanatory, persuasive, or literary? Is there a ''hidden agenda'' beyond the overt purposes? Are distinct purposes emphasized in different parts? What specific functions does this type of writing serve within its discourse community?

4. Who reads this type of writing? Why? What do you know—and what assumptions do the writers seem to be making—about the knowledge, attitudes, beliefs, and vested interests of the readers? (See pages 150–52.)

5. Where is this type of writing usually published? Is it likely to be read casually or seriously, for entertainment or for use? If the writing must be accepted by one or more editors before it reaches its readers, what can you surmise about these editors' motives and criteria? How would you name and describe the discourse community that reads this type of writing? (See pages 152–54.)

6. Is there a common persona that the writers adopt? Can you detect shared values? Do the writers take a particular stance and, if so, what does it imply about readers' expectations? How formal is the word choice and usage? (See Chapter 5, especially pages 207–12 and 220–23 on persona and word choice.)

One can often deduce a great deal about the rhetorical context by examining the publication in which the writing appears. A rock climber who wished to make some extra money by writing profiles of famous mountaineers for popular outdoors magazines analyzed that rhetorical context like this:

> As far as the editors are concerned, your article will be judged
> on whether or not it can help sell the magazine, based on the editors'
> concept of audience appeal. This form of article has been published
> most often in Outside magazine . . . . With a readability level
> ranging generally between Grades 10 and 12, this magazine is meant
> to be read along a scale from casual to serious, for both
> entertainment and serious use; articles of the type you will be
> writing should be thought-provoking enough to provoke discussion
> but casual enough to be read for entertainment. Outside's market
> is a competitive one, its chief competitor being Backpacker . . . .
> Their shared audience (determined by an analysis of advertisements,
> article appearance, and content) is invariably outdoors-oriented

and focussed on adventure and risk activities. Everyone pictured
in the ads is young (25—35 years), white, and apparently upwardly
mobile and/or affluent. There is a decidedly macho—oriented,
dominant—male ethic portrayed in the ads, though overall there are
probably more women represented. (This may explain why, although
there are numerous female climbers who fulfill all criteria for
this kind of article, all published articles so far have been about
men.) . . . The writers assume an educated audience with little
geographical knowledge and little informed understanding of the
significance of specific mountaineering achievements. . . . The
readers are assumed to be interested in climbing, but probably from
a spectator's point—of—view. What they are really interested in
is personalities, motivation, achievements and conflict.

Mitchell Sulkers

The students who investigated journalistic movie reviews went a step
further. In addition to analyzing reviews in context, they gained some inside
information by interviewing the movie critic of a big-city newspaper.

The Media

Daily Newspapers: The daily newspaper is a major source of up—
to—date reviews of current popular films. Occasion here refers to
the frequency of the reviews, their inclusion in a section with
other forms of entertainment, and their immediate proximity to
full—page ad spreads. Readers have probably turned specifically
to this section. Accompanying ads contribute to the sense of urgency
of consumer choice. Perhaps it is a mere hour before showtime. Or
the readers may want to be able to talk about the film knowledgeably
and critique it through borrowing or assuming the authority of the
reviewer. Newspapers are of particular use to those parents who
wish to decide which movie they will allow their children to see.
If the review mentions coarse language or sexual intimacy, they
may decide the movie is not appropriate for their children to see.
On such occasions the movie review serves as a quick guide for
immediate consumer choice.

Weekly Magazines: Reviews in Time, Maclean's, and Newsweek are
generally geared toward more liberal readers who might well
regularly read the reviews without seeing the films. These people
are looking for a different angle or interpretation and expect some
amount of depth or critical acumen when they read the review. They
also expect their reviewer to use outside sources of information,
preferably from esteemed critics, to form a critical analysis. And
that is just what you will find: a deeper analysis of the movies

with a higher degree of literacy than that of the newspapers. The
language is often more abstract and words indicative of a liberal
postsecondary arts education—such as allegory, microcosm, and
sociopathic—are frequently evident.

Audience

A movie review is an event—actually it is several kinds of events.
It is one kind of event for the editor, another for the advertiser,
and another for the reader, all of whom bring expectations to their
reading of the review.

The Editor: Through our interview with newspaper film reviewer
Marke Andrews, we found that the editor has a great deal of control
concerning the way movie reviews are presented. Editors exercise
their right to chop an article as they see fit. Reading a review,
you sometimes wonder why an article seems to be short, or why it
does not come to an adequate conclusion. On closer examination you
can see the raw edges where sentences or even whole paragraphs have
been cut out. The editor's purpose is to attract as many readers
as possible: therefore s/he wants to be as inoffensive as possible
to whomever might read the review. . . . The editor mediates the
competing interests of the newspaper's audience. Certain radical
concepts must be avoided while societal norms must be reinforced.
Certain words, such as adulterer, should not be used.

The Advertisers: All of these publications are in the business
of advertising. While they may have political or social purposes,
the principal reason they print what they print is to attract readers
for their ads. The more readers they attract, the more they can charge
for their ad space. Lose readers and you lose your job. However this
doesn't keep reviewers from trashing movies. A third of the reviews
we read were devastatingly critical. This establishes the
credibility of the reviewer and helps define the public perception
of their critical style. A controversial review is always good for
business. The consumer guide approach that characterizes newspaper
reviews reflects the extent to which the 'occasion' is defined by
the immediate consumer activity. Movies themselves, of course,
cater to consumer fantasy and reviews of movies further indulge
the infatuations of the readers. Here you have the reinforcement
of the expectations of society: consumption of commodities, heroism
of the underdog, heterosexuality as normal and natural, life as
drama, racial and fe/male (gender) stereotypical roles.

The General Public: The general audience reflected in the reviews
we examined is approximately 16 to 45 years old. Films for children
are rarely reviewed. Neither did we find reviews aimed at an older

audience, one that we would consider critically sophisticated. The audience was mostly middle class, liberal, and interested in topical social issues and human interest stories. Reviewers addressed the concerns of parents—somewhat obliquely—by detailing kinds and amounts of sex and violence presumably to help parents decide what kinds of films are acceptable or entertaining for their children. The reviewer acts as an consumer guide in other respects also by giving information about the nationality of films and their quality, with special attention to distinguishing between highbrow and intellectually demanding films on the one hand and lowbrow and amusing films on the other. The audience as we found it reflected in their reviews is white and decidedly male. Particulars of plot, for example, that might be of special interest to women are rarely identified, and the norm by which most humour, romance, adventure, and ideas are measured is Male. . . . The authoritative, audacious tone of the reviews, the hip language and the specialized knowledge in them all help female and male readers keep on top of the culture scene.

Every review participates in an ongoing community of discussion. Reviewers must imagine themselves present when people are talking about movies.

Persona: The persona of the reviewer is an important device used to tie the elements of material and purpose together with those of structure and style. Persona is a unifying presence, a fabrication of attitude, delivery and voice used to convey authority and personality. At times the reviewer is the Snob and at other times the reviewer is the Clown.

Expressions of snob range from lofty, bored dismissals of low-brow material ("In the end, the wafer-thin script capitulates to the routine horror-movie conventions it's been battling against") to brash know-it-all putdowns of prizewinning performances ("In an earlier life Shirley MacLaine was a splendid actress. Not so in her current reincarnation as the Aunt Mame of films and chat shows"). The snob review is like cocktail party banter by a fluent, somewhat outrageous egotist with a flair for anarchy.

Every critic is a performer. When you write, you will find numerous occasions when the film will serve as the stage upon which you will carry out your own comic performance. Humour is valuable to reviewers in a purely practical way: it allows them to point out faults in a film—readers do want an opinion—and at the same time it leaves readers feeling good and not necessarily discouraged about the movie.

Vikki Coupland, Tim Shireman, Rebecca Soles

Structure and Style

Many genres of writing use standard structures. These structures are rarely arbitrary; they have usually evolved to serve substantive or rhetorical functions. From the perspective of an individual writer, however, they are predetermined. A scientific research report, for instance, is almost always structured something like this:

1. Introduction to the *problem*, *review of previous research*, and statement of specific *hypotheses* investigated.
2. Explanation of the *methodology* used to test these hypotheses.
3. Report of *findings* (i.e., experimental results).
4. Discussion of *implications*, including recommendations for future research.

Even though you may not always want to follow them exactly, it is useful to know such structures. Here are some heuristic questions about structure and style:

7. Is there a standard format or typical structure for the whole writing or any part of it? Which of the basic patterns of development are used regularly? Are different patterns used in different parts? How do the writings begin? How do the writings end? What sorts of transitions predominate? How long are the paragraphs and how are they typically structured? Do most paragraphs have topic sentences (and if so, where)? What is the relationship among levels of generality within typical paragraphs and for whole pieces of writing? (See pages 124–29 on levels of generality, pages 170–93 on beginnings, endings, transitions, and paragraphing, pages 300–302 and 340–41 on the basic patterns of development.)
8. How long are most of the writings in your sample? How long and difficult are the words and sentences? What is the level of readability? Do any particular sentence patterns stand out? How many sentences are ten or more words longer than the average sentence? How many or five or more words shorter than average? Does the text have texture (i.e., many cumulative or embedded modifiers)? (See pages 159–63 on readability, pages 235–55 on sentence structure.)
9. Is the style nominalized or is more meaning carried by verbs and adverbs? To what extent are there overt figures of speech? Is there a standard jargon? How formal is the usage and diction? How would you rate this writing on a scale of abstraction? (See pages 223–35.)

10. What is missing? Are there any structures that are noticeably avoided? What unique features does this discourse have which were not elicited by the preceding questions?

Mischelle reached the following generalizations about the appropriate structure and style for young children's storybooks:

> These stories are meant to be read aloud, and this means that narration is emphasized. The style of writing is very informal, precisely because the writer uses language in an attempt to create a story-telling atmosphere. There is limited description because the vivid illustrations usually fulfill this function. . . .
>
> The plot consists of a very simple progression: one central idea is presented and carried clearly throughout the story. . . . Picture stories start with an inciting incident, which grabs the young reader's attention and then leads to further action within the story. . . . Frequently the plot is circular: by the end of the story the character and conditions have often returned to their original condition. Most of the action usually occurs in the middle of the book.
>
> The ending must be satisfying and pleasant for the youngster. . . . By the end of the book the tiny tot has usually had an adventure, learned to accomplish something, overcome a fear, or learned a lesson. . . .
>
> The writer must always be conscious of the sound of his words because the story will be read aloud. Often key words of phrases (for example, "everybody said no!") are repeated throughout the story. This repetition will create pleasing, friendly landmarks for a child. Kids react strongly to the colors, shapes, sizes, sounds, and smells of their world, and they will respond to such elements within a story. A children's writer should strive to use textural, rhythmic and onomatopoeic words.
>
> Mischelle Panagopoulos

By contrast, a student who wanted to write Christian children's stories, such as those by C. S. Lewis and Madeleine L'Engle, discovered that such stories follow quite a rigid outline based on a journey motif:

> (1) The children stumble into the supernatural world as if by chance. . . . Once they are in a different world, it becomes obvious that they were called for a purpose.
>
> (2) The children are confronted with an evil so great that it threatens the annihilation of themselves and the given world. . . .

In every case the children realize that they have been called to avert disaster.

(3) Much of the plot consists of the children learning how to combat and overcome evil. . . . The training period is no carefree game and the battle is deadly serious.

(4) Once the victory is won, the children participate in its glories. The personal joy of winning is surpassed by an appreciation of the greater glories of a universe restored. . . .

(5) Finally, the children return to their own world, recognizing that the fantasy was much more than an idle dream. . . . Children learn that thoughts and actions always count, and that they must overcome less-than-moral tendencies within themselves before they can overcome any larger evil.

Monika Hilder

Note that a standard structure can often be used, in effect, as a heuristic to help generate material.

A student who wanted to write feature articles for ski magazines came to these conclusions about the standard structure:

The title draws the reader to the story's first lines, and the first paragraph should, likewise, lead the reader on to the body of the story. Ski writers often start with an analogy or a suggestion of interesting material to follow:

> Some people just can't stand success. Show me a guy who has the world on a string and I'll show you a guy searching for a pair of scissors. When the ski run of life becomes smooth and effortless, some people go off looking for a mogul field.

Skiers are notorious story-tellers and certainly this enticing little item is more likely to lead us onward than an outline of the story written in essay form. . . .

A sense of action is also created by composing paragraphs which rarely exceed two or three sentences. . . . Usually the first sentence introduces an idea and the following ones expand on it: facts, descriptions, implications . . . . One idea soon gives way to another, and in this manner interest is sustained. Take this example from a recent issue of Powder, for instance:

> At times there is a melding of man with mountain across impossible terrain. A smooth give and take between the two which spills over defined boundaries to become one. "Like pouring 30-wt. oil over a sea of ball-bearings." This accomplished, it is said to take one to a higher state of consciousness.

This short, four-sentence paragraph uses analogy, quotation, and
humour to amplify the "melding of man with mountain," and it
exemplifies the blending of detail with brevity . . . .

Like the sentences and paragraphs from which they are made,
articles are quite short, typically ranging in length from one
thousand to two thousand words. . . . Usually writers have an
"angle" which they develop . . . . The last paragraph always sums
up the story in some way. This can mean anything from reiterating
the main points to extending the story's implications, to involving
the audience in one last personal note, but it always rounds out
the article—as any final paragraph should.

Peter Vogler

In the ski magazines he examined, Peter found that "sentences are usually
short and interest is generated by packing in modifiers." But preferred style
can vary radically from one genre to another, sometimes even violating what
might generally be considered good style. A student who wanted to sell freelance
articles to upscale city magazines discovered a preference for "long, informa-
tion-packed cumulative sentences":

Meanwhile, after graduating third in his 1956 law-school class of
60 (class-mate Bob Guile: "He was serious. Gawd, he was serious."),
Berger was making a name for himself with Shulman, Tupper and
Company, a feisty, anti-Establishment law firm, representing
workers up and down the coast.

The format, structure, and style of a genre can usually be explained in
functional relation to its substance, purpose, audience, and occasion. Here is
part of what Vikki, Tim, and Rebecca concluded about journalistic movie
reviews.

Photographs: Because film reviews are written for an audience
attracted to a visual medium, virtually all of them include
photographs, which convey important information to the audience
about the contents of the review, so you should scrutinize the
photographs you receive in the press kit with this in mind.

1. If you plan to focus on the film as a whole, choose a photograph
   of two or more people. Your audience will wonder about the
   relationship between these people and look to your review for
   an answer.

2. If, on the other hand, you plan to focus on a particular star,
   choose a picture of that star to highlight your piece. In that
   way, those familiar with the star will instantly be drawn to

your review and those not familiar with that star also—— especially if the picture itself intrigues them or the cutline below the picture mentions a familiar name.

Headlines: The editor will probably write your headline for you. Clearly, editors put layout considerations first, but they also consider that if a headline doesn't catch the attention of the reader, that reader will move on to something else. It does no harm for you to write your own headlines and submit them. Such an exercise will help to focus your review, and sometimes, it would appear, reviewer's headlines actually survive the editorial cut and lend some sense of coherence to the review as a whole. If the editorial policy requires that you mention the name of the film you are reviewing in your headline it might go something like THIS DRONING FLY DESERVES A FULL SWAT ("the Fly II") or HEAVY METAL FILM IS HEADBANG ON ("The Metal Years: The Decline of Western Civilization, Part II"). If the editorial policy does not require you to do this, you might try writing a catchy alliterative title like MANHATTAN MAYHEM ("The January Man") or THE VICTIM OF THE VERDICT ("The Accused"). As a general rule, you will use the first approach when your audience reads reviews to decide whether or not to go to a movie, and the second when your audience reads reviews more for their entertainment value.

Length: Film reviews are very short, from 250 words or so in the smallest newspaper to 500—700 words in magazines. From time to time reviews may even stretch to 1000 words or more, but then only if the review is considering two or more films, and even then the maximum per film is usually 500 or so words. You should learn what you have to say in 250—500 words——which is not a lot of room, you will find. You must learn to make every paragraph, every sentence, every word——yes even every punctuation mark——convey the maximum amount of information and evaluation.

Functional Elements of Structure: Since reviews are short, very active pieces of writing, these functional elements are usually distinct, concise units on the page——usually in single paragraphs that often consist of a single sentence. In the more unified and developed reviews characteristic of the weekly magazines, however, these elements can interrelate with considerable complexity and produce patterns of organization that are subtle and quite seamless.

Opening: The Hook. The reviewer poses a dilemma, sets up an expectation, or establishes some provocative relationship between reviewer and reader. Always at the beginning.
Opinion: What the Reader is Waiting For. The reviewer

evaluates the movie. Often the first few words of the piece.
Sometimes in a series of well-developed paragraphs. It is a
rare, and usually a mutilated review that comes without an
opinion.

Plot: The Storyline. Some reviewers withhold most of it;
others tell every gory detail. But every review has it—it
is crucial consumer information. Essential.

Development: Extra Gravy. The reviewer goes beyond a sentence
on any one of the preceding. Usually written so that it can
be cut—and often it is. A bonus.

Narrative: An Action Device. The reviewer includes scenes
from the film, episodes in her viewing experience, or just
the story of her thoughts to set up a fast-paced narrative.
Very common.

Digression: A Grab Bag. The reviewer plugs in disconnected
information: interjections, asides, afterthoughts, or
anything that might appeal to local audiences. A catch-all.

Conclusion: The Wind-up. The reviewer usually attempts the
obligatory connection to the rest of the piece. But often
this, like the plot, falls victim to the editorial knife.
Here really witty reviewers show their stuff, pulling
ingenious conclusions out of the air. The climax.

Patterns of Organization: Reviewers structure these functional
elements according to two basic patterns: a linear one and a circular
one.

If the purpose of your review is to give your audience enough
information to decide whether or not to see the film (and to entertain
them while you do so), you will probably use a linear structure.
Here your review will move from opening, to opinion, to evaluation,
to plot, back to opinion, on to more plot, and then right to a
conclusion. There is no development. The point is to cover as much
territory as quickly and as entertainingly as you can. The
digression and narrative characteristic of the linear pattern often
suggests the action editing of free-association sequences in the
film.

If the purpose of your review is not only to offer your audience
information and evaluation, but to stimulate them to think about
larger issues in the movies, you will probably adopt a more circular
structure, a structure in which the introduction and conclusion
are closely connected. Here your review will move from an opening,
through as series of relatively well-developed paragraphs that
focus on particular aspects of the movie, to a conclusion that echoes

the introduction in some way. The connection between introduction and conclusion can occur through the repetition of a concept, a series of words or a single word. In Richard Schickel's review of "Pelle, the Conqueror," for instance, the repetition of concepts—imaginary and scenic—draws the introduction and conclusion of the review together:

> Whiteness: the perfect whiteness of an enveloping fog. Muted sounds: voices, creaks of sails and rigging. Very slowly, the outlines of a 20th century sailing ship begin to take shape from the brume. The great image that opens "Pelle, the Conqueror" turns out to be the perfect emblem for the long, entirely absorbing work that unfolds: very simple yet powerfully, mysteriously absorbing. . . .
>
> These little lives, spun out in a time and place far distant to us, would be easy to ignore. But they are all vividly played, and Bill August's gift for austere, striking imagery and for the short, perfectly shaped scene impart to this film an epic richness, range and energy.

The intimate connection of introduction and conclusion in this structure gives it a polished air that more sophisticated readers prefer and less sophisticated ones can appreciate.

Oral Style: In a review it is essential to use the first person singular. The personal presence of the reviewer—complete with her big ego—is the essence of this style. You can use single words and phrases as sentences, use slang, compound adjectives, alliteration, puns, mixed metaphors—anything goes. Reviewers cultivate a gushy, delirious oral style. Reviews read like radio commentary on a wrestling match. It's a feeding frenzy technique. Hyperbole. Use plenty of hyperbole. Compare and contrast and let the parallels fall where they may.

Narrative Style: This style is very much associated with the linear pattern of organization and is geared towards the audience most attracted by that structure, one looking for information and generally speaking has a lower reading level than the more sophisticated audience. As the name suggests the narrative style employs a time frame as a structural device. This time frame may be plot time ("Years later, when Gerald returns to town . . .") or viewing time ("We are halfway through the movie before Brando makes his appearance") or real time, as when the writer refers to coming out of the theatre ("It was months before I could tolerate a Buñuel film.")

Paragraphs: Generally the more local the publication, the shorter
and more general the paragraphs will be. In many of the publications
we looked at, however, paragraphs became longer towards the end
of the review, as did sentences—the assumption being that better
readers will read further into the article. A first sentence will
often be a topic sentence, the second a reassertion of that topic
sentence—perhaps referring to a single character or scene that
exemplifies the assertion, often in the form of quoted dialogue.
Often first paragraphs consist of a single sentence.

Sentences: The sentences within these paragraphs are also often
very simple. Sentence fragments, parenthetical inclusions and
split compounds abound and build a sense of urgency, tinged with
familarity.

Words: Word play and alliteration run rampant in this genre,
effectively associating what might otherwise be considered
disparate concepts. And on the grammatical level, virtually no noun
is ever used without at least one adjective—often whole strings
of them—preceding it. Verbs are usually in the active voice to
help convey a sense of immediacy to the narrative, and many of these
are associated with the movie itself to reinforce this function.
For example, in Brian Johnson's review of "Mafia Moll" he says that
"jokes are fired deadpan from the hip" giving us an immediate sense
of the violence associated with the mafia, if not with the movie
itself. Adverbs, specifically comparative adverbs such as more,
less, better, and worse, are indispensable: they epitomize the
union of evaluation and comparison, the very purpose that you, the
reviewer, are trying to serve.

Vikki Coupland, Tim Shireman, Rebecca Soles

Virtually any type of writing you may wish to master can be analyzed
similarly. The rest of this chapter is devoted to academic discourse because
that is likely the immediate concern of most of the people using this textbook.
Learn how to do your own analysis, however, and you can apply the basic
principles of composition to whatever type of writing you want or need to
master.

EXERCISE

1. Make a list of the various types of writing that are done in your area
of special interest. Using the procedures discussed above, analyze one such
type of writing. Write a short manual based on your results. (If possible,

work together with others from your field, and do the manual as a collaborative writing project.)

2. Using specific examples of one particular type of writing, explain James Kinneavy's assertion that "the structure of anything limits the uses to which it may be put." Demonstrate and discuss the extent to which the structure of that type of writing constrains writers. Does the structure encourage them to generate certain sorts of material and not other sorts? Does it constrain them toward certain approaches? In other words, does the form constrain the substance? If so, does it do so in ways that are helpful?

3. The following essay analyzes the material and structure of a particular brand of popular fiction, the Harlequin Romance.

A Harlequin Romance: The Final Frontier

Rowena, the shy, but unusually intelligent, librarian, could not look away. She stood still, spellbound by the glints in the publisher's dark, flashing eyes. He winked and grinned his approval. He came down the steps toward her, triumphantly brandishing a paperback. Suddenly, she found herself running, running away from a fate she knew she could never escape!

Bookstores, newstands, and libraries everywhere are filled with a distinct brand of paperback love story bearing the emblem "Harlequin Romance." Once opened, these stories transport the reader to an exotic land where true love predictably conquers all. In a larger sense, these stories possibly represent the biggest money-makers in the publishing industry.

What are Harlequin Romances? Some people call them "junky novels." Others call them "a form of relaxation," while others prefer the term "escape." In order to understand more fully just what Harlequin Romances are and the reasons behind their phenomenal success, one should first investigate the range of characters, settings, and narrative sequences typical in this genre.

The principal characters of a Harlequin Romance conform to four easily recognizable stereotypes: the heroine, the hero, the side characters, and the friendly adviser.

The heroine: The heroine is usually young and attractive, possessing high intelligence and even higher morals. During the course of the story, she is revealed to have some special ability which elevates her from the more ordinary characters. The following charts her special ability as it occurs with a variety of roles:

ROLE	ABILITY
governess	—She has the ability to get along with vicious, hateful brats. Generosity, fairness, and honesty are her virtues.
secretary	—She whips the office into better shape than it has ever been in before. Organization, tidiness, and a keen eye for business are her special traits.
journalist	—She usually possesses a superior writing ability accompanied with a remarkable intuition for scoops.
doctor or nurse	—She is unappreciated and overworked, but she always has the time to care for people. She is generous in spirit and loving in heart.

The hero: The hero is usually older, more sophisticated and sexually experienced than the heroine. He is either bored with an all-too-wearisome world or a bitter cynic, more hurt by an uncaring world than he will ever let on. He is introduced to the reader with a description of his lean, weathered good looks, his stubborn jaw, and his intense, steely eyes. At the beginning, he is ruggedly independent, but as the story progresses, he, first grudgingly, then wholeheartedly, admits his need for the heroine.

Side characters: These characters play an important role in the story by providing most of the conflicts. They are more colorful in personality and action than the hero and heroine but lack the strong moral values of the latter. The side characters are as follows:

The "other woman": This woman is beautiful, sophisticated, and very much a woman of the world. Secure in her claim for the hero, she is rather condescending to the heroine.

The "other man": There are two distinct types of the "other man." The first is older and lecherous, forever drooling after Harlequin heroines. The second is young and klutzy, but is sweet.

The friendly adviser to the hero and/or heroine: This is usually a friend who acts as a fairy godmother. The adviser knows that the hero and heroine are meant for each other and is determined to remedy Fate's procrastination.

The exotic Harlequin settings provide the perfect backdrop for the characters. Whether it is the beach, a ranch in the back country of Australia, or a castle amid the moors, the surroundings are guaranteed to provide the romance and mystique necessary for the readers escape to the world of Harlequin.

Though not as exotic as the scenery the storylines maintain the Harlequin tradition or formula. Twelve different stories come out each month, but there seems to be a common structure to the narrative sequence that identifies them as Harlequins. This common structure can be depicted in this way.

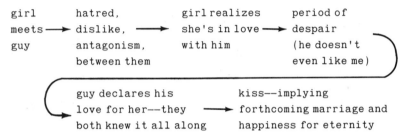

girl meets guy → hatred, dislike, antagonism, between them → girl realizes she's in love with him → period of despair (he doesn't even like me) → guy declares his love for her——they both knew it all along → kiss——implying forthcoming marriage and happiness for eternity

With this one formula, hundreds of variations can be generated. For many readers, the entertainment that the book provides lies in guessing which variation the author will use. I asked one woman why she reads Harlequin Romances and she replied, "I know that the girl is going to get the guy. I read them to find out <u>how</u> she's going to get him."

However, these books can hardly be called intellectual exercises. Even their advertisements acknowledge this by emphasizing their relaxing qualities. These books offer more than just escape and relaxation. They are fantasies where traditional values, attitudes, and roles are re-evaluated and tested against the picture of modern society. Life is rewritten and changed. The stereotypes and predictability of these novels, which some "discriminating" readers describe as disgusting, give meaning and a sense of order to this otherwise chaotic world where roles and values are hopelessly ambiguous. Perhaps Harlequin Romance readers are looking for stability in an unstable world.

Margaret Coe

In this short essay, Margaret captures the essence of the Harlequin Romance by analyzing the basic structure of character and plot and discussing social function and rhetorical context. What else would you need to know in order to write and publish a Harlequin Romance? What would you have to add if you wanted to transform this essay into a sociological or literary analysis?

[Margaret Coe, incidentally, is a former student, but not a relative of the author of this textbook.]

4. Do an analysis of another genre of popular fiction, perhaps a certain type of bestseller or the popular "western" novel epitomized by Louis L'Amour. (Assuming Harlequin Romances do really represent a certain socially typical female fantasy and Louis L'Amour westerns represent a certain socially typical male fantasy, how do you think the women and men who enjoy these fantasies would get along?)

Academic Discourse

Research is a way of learning, important in formal study, which we can use for the rest of our lives: we can research the voting records of congressmen, recipes, genealogy, precedents in zoning for the neighborhood, or types of schooling for information of the PTA. Research is a method. The research paper is a particular embodiment of the general method.

DONALD HALL

[Students] must learn to try on a variety of voices and interpretative schemes— to write, for example, as a literary critic one day and an experimental psychologist the next . . . . What [they] need to learn is to extend themselves into the commonplaces, set phrases, rituals, gestures, habits of mind, tricks of persuasion, obligatory conclusions, and necessary connections that . . . constitute knowledge within the various branches of our academic community.

DAVID BARTHOLOMAE

Why Students Write

Writing helps students learn and develop independence. Even a simple research report requires students to find, select, and organize information. This may be the same sort of information that the instructor has presented in class, but the students must discover it themselves. Thus they learn how to acquire that sort of information without depending on the instructor to give it to them.

A critical paper requires students to make inferences and draw their own conclusions. They use the concepts and methods of interpretation that were taught in the course, but they apply those concepts and methods to new material. Thus they learn to think critically instead of depending on the instructor to interpret for them.

Professors also require such related tasks as annotated bibliographies, summaries of readings, responses to readings, reports on experiments or other assigned experiences, case studies, and so forth. Each of these tasks has some relationship to how knowledge is created, tested, and communicated in academia.

An objective examination can measure how well students have learned the material the instructor gave them. A paper can develop and evaluate students' abilities to acquire information and think critically on their own—which is what education and graduation are ultimately about. It is in this rhetorical context that papers make sense.

What Academic Discourse Does

People at universities write (and read and talk and listen) in a special way, which we call academic. This academic discourse is a particular version of the way all professionals in our society write, read, talk, and listen. When students learn academic writing, they learn the basic principles of all technical and professional discourse. In a sense, students are like apprentices or immigrants, who have entered a special community and need to learn that community's customary ways of doing.

Academic discourse does vary from one field to another. Chemists, historians, and anthropologists do not talk and write the same way. Even within a particular discipline, there are various distinct writing tasks, each of which follows its own particular structures and conventions. There may also be significant differences between different schools within a discipline. Nonetheless, there are basic principles that guide academic discourse in general. Though the "research paper" as practiced in composition courses is something of an artificial exercise, it is also an opportunity to master the general principles that guide all professional discourse. As Professor Donald Hall reminds us, research is essentially a method, a way of knowing, and the research paper embodies that method.

The primary function of academic discourse is to create, test, and communicate certain kinds of knowledge. This is true of articles scholars publish in academic journals; it is also true of papers and essay tests written by undergraduates. Though students' paper topics and theses are normally less ambitious, looking at the journal articles professors read and write can help university students understand what they are supposed to do when they write papers.

Student papers are modeled upon the sorts of scholarly articles professors write. In professional contexts, this kind of writing serves to keep members of the profession up to date on new research results and their implications, new or modified theories, innovative procedures, and so forth. The intended readers are specialists in the same field, who can be presumed to share certain concepts, knowledge, and methodological values.

Student papers do have special characteristics that reflect students' status as unproven apprentices. With student papers the balance between creating and testing knowledge leans more heavily toward testing—both of the ideas and of the student. Students are, consequently, expected to make their arguments and detail their evidence more explicitly than are established scholars.

Published scholarly articles are, of course, end products. They have a formality and a polished rigor which has evolved as the original concept was developed through a more informal discourse. An article may have begun as a comment in a discussion, perhaps at a scholarly conference. It may have started to take shape in a letter to a colleague or in the process of drafting an application for research funds. It usually was presented orally at a conference or seminar and revised on the basis of subsequent discussion and criticism. The published articles represent an ideal, finalized version of academic discourse.

Rigor and Clarity

Because the primary function of academic discourse is to create, test, and communicate knowledge, the primary quality that defines academic discourse is *rigor*. Many of the standard structures and most of the conventions of academic discourse were designed to encourage rigorous precision.

A scientist or a lawyer or a literary critic would rather communicate a concept exactly than approximately. Though clarity is desired, precision is more important. Thus a precise technical term will often be chosen over an ordinary word that represents roughly the same idea. Translating the discourse of specialists into something ordinary literate people can understand often means achieving clarity by deleting the technicalities and complexities, i.e., settling for a reasonable approximation. When a concept—and the aspect of reality it represents—is complex, academic discourse aims to describe that complexity. Writing rigorously for an audience of specialists can be very different from writing clearly for a popular audience.

To be sure, specialists often get caught up in their jargon, use technical terms and complex sentence structure even when it is possible to communicate the same idea or information in straightforward ordinary language (see pages 217–18). At times it seems they write academese—or legalese or bureaucratese—only to make their ideas seem more complex and sophisticated than they really are. Students sometimes do the same thing, with various degrees of success, in an attempt to get higher grades. Despite such abuses, academic and professional writers are in principle right to choose rigorous and precise description of complexities over simpler and clearer approximations.

Applying the Heuristic

The heuristic discussed in the first part of the chapter was designed for analyzing specific types of writing within specific communities or disciplines. It can be used to discover the general principles of academic writing. But after reading the following general discussion, you should apply the heuristic specifically to the particular types of academic or professional discourse that you expect to write.

There are various general guides to writing and publishing academic and professional discourse, such as Kate Turabian's *A Manual for Writers of Term Papers, Theses and Dissertations*, the *Chicago Manual of Style*, and the U.S. Government Printing Office's *Style Manual*. There are also style guides for specific disciplines and professions (see Table 10.1). Social scientists generally follow the guidelines published by the American Psychology Association (APA). Literary critics use the one published by the Modern Language Association (MLA). Engineers generally use the ones published by the Institute of Electrical and Electronics Engineers (IEEE) or Engineers Joint Council. These manuals are excellently precise and detailed guides to appropriate format and conventions, especially referencing. They can be reasonably good guides to appropriate style and standard structure. Some, like the APA *Publication Manual*, provide extremely detailed instructions about what to include in various types of articles. But many manuals offer little such substantive guidance. There are also more subtle—but often crucial—standard communicative strategies that the manuals cannot cover.

One psychology graduate student, for instance, drafted the beginning of her "Results" section like this:

Phase 1. The immune responses of the nursery-reared monkeys were compared to those of the socially-reared. No sex differences were found in the analyses, and therefore, males and females are combined in the following results.

The NK activity (Figure 1), as measured by the percent of cell lysis produced by the effector cells, was not statistically significant between groups for any of the three effector-to-target cell ratios. However, there was a strong suggestion of increased activity in the nursery group.

The tendency toward increased immune activity in the nursery-reared subjects reached statistical significance in the mitogen assays. As illustrated in Figure 2, the lymphocytes from the nursery subjects proliferated to a greater extent than those of the socially-reared subjects.

Her professor responded,

It was a mistake to begin with a passive opening sentence. Worse yet, you began with negative findings. While the "Results" is technically an objective statement of the "facts," I have found that it is best to lead with a sentence that biases the reader to accept the "facts."

Table 10.1   Academic Style Manuals

Every scholarly field has its preferred format or ''style.'' MLA style is widely accepted in the humanities. APA style is widely accepted in the social sciences. The following manuals describe the styles of some major disciplines:

Biology

Council of Biology Editors. Style Manual Committee. *CBE Style Manual: A Guide for Authors, Editors, and Publishers in the Biological Sciences.* Bethesda: Council of Biology Editors.

Chemistry

American Chemical Society. *Handbook for Authors of Papers in American Chemical Society Publications.* Washington: American Chemical Soc.

English

Modern Language Association of America. *MLA Handbook for Writers of Research Papers.* New York: MLA.

Geology

United States Geological Survey. *Suggestions to Authors of the Reports of the United States Geological Survey.* Washington: GPO.

Linguistics

Linguistic Society of America. *LSA Bulletin*, Dec. issue, annually.

Mathematics

American Mathematical Society. *A Manual for Authors of Mathematical Papers.* Providence: American Mathematical Soc.

Medicine

International Steering Committee of Medical Editors. ''Uniform Requirements for Manuscripts Submitted to Biomedical Journals.'' *Annals of Internal Medicine* 90 (Jan. 1979): 95–99.

Physics

American Institute of Physics Publications Board. *Style Manual for Guidance in the Preparation of Papers.* New York: American Inst. of Physics.

Psychology

American Psychological Association. *Publication Manual of the American Psychological Association.* Washington: American Psychological Assn., 1983.

For other style manuals and authors' guides, see John Bruce Howell, *Style Manuals of the English-Speaking World* (Phoenix: Oryx, 1983).

> Also it is better to state negative findings
> parenthetically, instead of as primary findings. Otherwise
> there is a chance the critical reviewer will think this is
> not an important article or was done sloppily. You also
> reported secondary findings as importantly as the primary
> finding. We found that the length of time an infant spends
> with its mother will determine the nature of its immune
> responses later in life. This has tremendous implications;
> one would never know it from your version.

The student could not have learned this from the APA *Publication Manual* or any other guide. Indeed, the suggestion that effective scientific writers may need to prepare readers to "accept the 'facts' " contradicts a traditional stereotype of scientific readers.

It is sometimes possible to obtain computer software, usually attached to a word processing program, that automatically formats text and references. Many universities provide software, often through their mainframe computers, that formats theses and dissertations. This software can be used for shorter papers too.

Though students frequently find referencing and format requirements mysterious, cumbersome, and even oppressive, it is very useful for a disciplinary community to have standard ways of communicating. These structures assure that information readers may need is included and can be found where those readers expect to find it. The fact that all members of the community do it the *same* way is probably more important than *which* way they do it.

Subject Matter

Good academic writing is not only rigorous but relevant, original, informed, objective, sharply focused, and sophisticated in its treatment of complex subject matter.

The subject matter of a piece of academic writing must be relevant to an intellectual problem the particular discipline or subdiscipline is trying to solve. Academic journals often reject manuscripts because of "inappropriate" subject matter or approach. Students generally must choose a paper topic that fits within the subject of the course for which they are writing. The question the paper tries to answer, moreover, should be related to the course material.

Because the purpose of academic discourse is to generate knowledge, academic writing should be "original." Synthesizing and summarizing previously published ideas (or ideas from the course) is not normally sufficient—unless those ideas are treated critically. Indeed, academic articles often challenge previously published ideas. And professors often encourage students to challenge ideas in their papers.

The challenge must, however, be carried out in a particular way. You are allowed to express any opinion you like, but—and this can be a big "but"—you must express and support that opinion in the proper way. As Professor Keith Fort put it, "Teachers give A's to diverse interpretations. Editors accept works with opposing conclusions. But while freedom is permitted in content, formal conformity is rigidly demanded."

Opinions must be "informed." This means they should be both based on the relevant facts and grounded in knowledge of what has previously been said about the subject. Indeed, the right to express an opinion within the academic community is often contingent on its being in this sense an informed opinion. This is because academics share a methodological bias in favor of inductive empiricism: academic writing is generally based on the assumption that generalizations should be supported with specifics, opinions based on facts.

For this reason, academic discourse generally avoids personal, subjective material—or reframes it so that it ceases to be *merely* personal or subjective. Personal experience is relevant only if it is reframed as an example or a representative anecdote, used to illustrate a point also supported in other ways. This is part of what academics mean by objectivity.

Certain key terms, such as *objectivity*, represent values generally shared by the academic community. It is important to find out precisely what *objectivity* means, in practice, in your particular field (see pages 320–22 on operational definition).

Like almost all specialized discourses, academic writing is characterized by technical terms. This is not just a matter of style or diction. Those technical terms often represent key concepts that shape the substance of the writing. Such terms are usually specific to particular disciplines or approaches. One way to write a paper is to take a term that represents a key concept and apply it to a particular text or set of data.

Academic writing usually has a sharp and narrow focus. Digression is frowned upon and transitions are often more explicit than in some other types of writing. Topics can be extremely narrow, but their relation to larger issues is usually explicit. A literary critic may analyze the symbolism of clerical collars in D. H. Lawrence's short stories. But this analysis will normally be related to an assertion about how best to interpret those stories. Although academic papers often deal with narrow and specialized topics, the conclusions should be related to larger issues.

Academic discourse tends to concern itself with complexities. Consequently, one of the values of academia is a preference for complex views that take into account various perspectives. Students learning and practicing this kind of writing should be careful to choose topics with sufficient complexity to reward sophisticated analysis. Otherwise they may find themselves embellishing and obscuring a simple insight with excessive jargon and verbal complexity.

Rhetorical Context

To understand the papers students write, one should consider their unusual rhetorical purposes, audience, and occasion. Some of the characteristics of these papers can be understood only by remembering they are modeled after scholarly articles. But other characteristics make sense only if one remembers that students write papers mainly as exercise: the papers serve primarily to help students develop, practice, and demonstrate certain abilities.

Because its function is to generate and test knowledge, academic discourse usually begins with an intellectual problem. The purpose is not to write "on a topic," but to answer a question. Perhaps no one has yet provided a fully satisfactory explanation for some text, event, or phenomenon. Perhaps the writer thinks a generally accepted explanation is false or inadequate. Perhaps a general theory seems to be contradicted by a particular event.

A paper for a university course usually takes a concept or method that has been taught in the course and applies it to new material. Although your effort is focused on explaining that material, you are more importantly developing and demonstrating your ability to use the concepts and methods of the discipline. Through readings, lectures, demonstrations, class discussions, and guided experiences, you have learned certain concepts and ways to approach certain types of material. On tests, you have shown that you understand those concepts and methods well enough to define and exemplify them, and even to apply them in limited ways. The paper is your opportunity to develop your ability to think critically and utilize independently the concepts and approaches you have been learning.

Suppose you take an anthropology course in which you study and analyze the kinship structures of various societies. Do you understand the concept and method well enough to apply it to societies you did not study? Suppose you take a literature course in which you study and interpret five of Shakespeare's tragedies. Could you, on your own, interpret one you did not study? Writing a paper is a good way to find out. To write it, you must go beyond passive understanding and actively use what you have learned in the course.

Students should imagine themselves writing not for the so-called "general reader," but for a community of specialists. They should imagine that their purpose is to present original contributions to that community. These readers are extremely knowledgeable, critical, and interested in furthering their own understanding of the subject (and hence their own research). At the same time, students must remember that the real audience is a grader, who will be looking for proof of competence. Thus students must, for instance, include a lot of information and explanation that both the imagined readers and the real reader already understand. Like most discourse communities, academic disciplines are hierarchical: members considered to have proven themselves may skip steps or bend rules that writers with less status must follow rigorously.

Most student papers are primarily explanatory, but the real reader (the instructor) usually does not need the explanation. This audience is usually a single reader, an expert who presumably knows more about the subject than the writer does. The occasion is valuative: students receive grades and comments indicating how well they have learned and how they need to improve.

A professor, moreover, is not only evaluating papers, but also certifying students as competent (or not) in the subject matter of the particular course. And after a student collects certifications of competence (in the form of passing grades) from enough professors, the university certifies the student to society by granting a degree.

Academic articles are usually published in journals, and academic books by university presses, as part of an ongoing search for knowledge. As such, they are subject to peer review: editors, who may themselves not be entirely competent in a specific specialty, send manuscripts to specialists, who advise them whether to publish. The reviewers are not supposed to know who wrote the manuscript, thus insuring they make their decisions without considering the status or authority of the author. A professor reading a student paper is, in effect, editor, peer reviewer, and grader rolled into one.

The academic community normally expects writers to present an unbiased, objective, rational persona. Of course, academics and other professionals are really human beings, hence less than perfectly objective, disinterested, and rational. Scientific studies of scientists demonstrate clearly that extrinsic factors have a great deal to do with whether a scientific article actually convinces its readers. Some of these factors have to do with the status of the authors and of the journal that published the article. Others have to do with the presentation itself, with the persona created by the structure, style, and format of the article: competent writing that follows the accepted conventions of the discipline is taken as an indication of the authors' more general and substantive competence. The writer's persona is important: to be persuasive, academic writers usually must project a persona of disinterested and dispassionate objectivity.

Such a persona is created in part by avoiding overt emotional or ethical appeals (see pages 382–84). Even the most objective and academic writing does ultimately have some persuasive purpose—if only to enhance the reputation of the writers (i.e., to persuade readers to respect the writers) or to persuade granting institutions to give financial support for further research. And virtually all academic writing seeks to persuade readers that what it says is true. Nonetheless, academic writing is generally presented as explanation, and persuasion by any means other than evidence and logical reasoning is not normally overt.

The academic persona is created also by relatively formal usage, including distinctions that most popular writers have given up on (e.g., between *disinterested* and *uninterested*). Technical terms, especially, must be used with precision. Following the conventions of the discipline exactly (e.g., formatting the bibliography precisely as per the style guide) creates a persona of competence, suggesting that the writers are experienced members of the community. Established members of the community are often impatient with writers who make reading more difficult because they have not bothered to learn the conventions.

Structure and Style

The structure, style, and format of papers and published academic discourse reflect the formality of the professional occasions and the specialized purposes and knowledge of the audiences.

Academic writing is generally analytic and explanatory. There is an element of persuasion in its attempt to convince readers that the explanation is valid. And the paper almost inevitably reports research results, expert opinions, and other information in support of its analysis. But the ultimate function is to present an interpretation and draw conclusions. The dominant purpose is explanation.

Academic writing often begins with the statement of a problem and a review of what is already known; it often ends with an assertion of significance or implications. Academic writing may use any of the patterns of arrangement discussed in Chapters 6, 7, and 8. Narrative, description, summary, exemplification, and comparison/contrast, however, are likely to be subordinated to definition, classification and division, process analysis, and, especially, causal explanation. In the end, academic discourse usually serves to answer a *why*? "Why does such-and-such happen?" "Why is thus-and-such a correct interpretation of this poem?"

In order to allow readers most easily to evaluate the logic and evidence, academic writing generally states the main point near the beginning. For the same reason, a summary of the supporting arguments is usefully presented near the beginning. This is the function of thesis paragraphs, which are common in academic writing.

Paragraphs tend to be quite long, typically 150–250 words, though they rarely run to a full double-spaced typewritten page. Paragraphs typically contain explicit topic sentences, often as the first sentence. Most paragraphs are not simply topic sentence + support; they typically have three or four levels of generality (see pages 124–29).

Overall length for a student paper is often assigned. Journal editors, too, often have "preferred" lengths, and it can sometimes be hard to publish a manuscript that is "too short" or "too long." These length requirements, however, are deceptive. Professors typically say a paper should be a certain number of words long. What they are really saying, though, is that students should choose a topic that can be fully and appropriately treated in approximately that number of words. Thus an instructor who says a paper should be 5000 words long is really saying something about what sort of topic students should select. Students who pick a "3000-word topic" and then discuss it in the required 5000 words are usually criticized for wordiness or "padding." Students who pick a ''10,000-word topic'' but stop after 5000 words are usually criticized for failure to develop the topic adequately.

Because academic readers are assumed to be highly literate, academic prose often has long sentences and uses an extended vocabulary. The long sentences allow writers to qualify assertions and explain interrelationships. The style is highly nominalized, sometimes excessively so (see pages 227–34). Though sometimes abused, the freedom to use ''big words'' allows academic writers to be precise. Academic prose is highly textured, with lots of embedded modifiers (see pages 240–47), but overt figures of speech and ambiguity are generally eschewed. Though academic writing is often abstract, generalizations are normally supported by specifics (or statistics).

Although details vary from from discipline to discipline, academic manuscripts should generally be formatted as indicated in Table 10.2. Many of these requirements make sense only if one thinks of the paper not as completely finished, but as a manuscript to be edited and later published. A manuscript that follows the required format makes the editor's job that much easier. Authors' names appear only on the title page, for instance, so editors can easily remove that page before sending the manuscript to reviewers (who are not supposed to know who wrote it). The title appears both on the title page and the first text page so the editor can reconnect them after the reviewers return the manu-

---

Table 10.2   Academic Manuscripts

1. All but the shortest manuscripts have a title page, which not only gives the title but also identifies the author(s). For student papers, this usually means title, instructor's name, course number, date, student's name and number. The author's name normally appears nowhere else on the manuscript.
2. Academic manuscripts are typed, doublespaced, on unlined white paper. The paper should be standard size ($8\frac{1}{2}'' \times 11''$). The typing should be dark (which means the typewriter or printer should have a relatively new ribbon).
3. Standard margins are one inch (2.5 cm), except the lefthand margin is $\frac{1}{4}$ or $\frac{1}{2}$ inch wider (3–4 cm).
4. The title appears not only on the title page, but also at the top of the first page. It is neither underlined, nor typed in all capital letters.
5. Pages are numbered. This numbering may appear in a header or footer together with a short version of the title. Because the full title already occupies the top of the first page of text, that page is either not numbered or numbered at the bottom.
6. If required, an abstract appears either on a separate page following the title page or just below the title on the first page of text.
7. The standard system of the particular discipline is followed exactly for headings, notes, and references. Usually this means that the manuscript ends with a bibliography (often called ''List of References'' or ''Works Cited'').

script. Although this convention, which requires typing the title twice, may seem arbitrary to a student writing a paper for a course, it does have a real function.

The following paper was written collaboratively by two students trying to figure out how to write literary critical papers that would get A's from English professors at their university. They used Metaheur, the heuristic explained in this chapter, and supplemented it with interviews and analysis of professors' comments. Although their conclusions apply only to one university and their sample was too small for those conclusions to be definitive, their findings are intriguingly suggestive.

A Leap from 'B' to 'A':
Some Rules for the English Paper Game

When you think about it, an English essay assignment or term paper is an odd type of writing: it is most often read by just one person, a marker, and generally it is not something you might have chosen to do. Term papers are usually assigned as an exercise to find out how much you know, how well you can think, how well you can research, and how well you can say what you want to say.

If you add up the purpose of your writing, and the audience and occasion for which you write, you are defining your "rhetorical context". Your understanding of rhetorical context is important when writing term papers. It can give you clues to help you approach your work. For example, a student's academic writing is usually not published, so the student writer can generally ignore the stylistic conventions required by the publishing industry. And, although a term paper can be a self-improvement exercise, it is also written to be graded. So, it can be useful to remember that as you write you are arguing not only for your thesis but also for your grade.

In particular, it can be useful to consider just who will be reading and marking your paper. As far as their ability goes, markers and professors are generally well-educated and have no trouble with long or uncommon words. They are also usually familiar with works of literature or criticism that you may refer to. In general, a marker is someone you must prove things to. If whatever you choose to discuss cannot be proven, you should consider changing your position. It may be better to make such a change than to wander off your topic or produce a weak argument.

Persuading your marker is important, so consider the attitude you adopt. If you give the impression that you are right, your marker will be more likely to believe what you say. And, if you remember that markers do not read for enjoyment, then it is easier to see why your paper does not have to be enjoyable. Although it may seem kind to write a humorous or satirical paper—in sympathy with the marker who must go through stacks of papers—comic abilities will not usually improve your grade. On the other hand, if you think you know what your instructor prefers or expects, keep that in mind when you write: with "insider" knowledge, you may be able to include something he or she will be particularly impressed with. By considering your rhetorical context, you'll be better prepared to satisfy the "who", "what", "when", "where", and "why's" of your assignments.

Starting at the End: What Markers Like in "A" Papers and What Markers Don't Like about "B+" and "A−" Papers. If you've never had a chance to read what markers say on the last page of an "A" paper, then here's a summary of some we looked at:

> Comprehensive, carefully presented, well-developed or well-researched discussions. Good writing. Effectiveness in the handling of sophisticated topics. Conformity to the standards of the English-paper genre. Good style. Evidence of effort and "committed curiosity." Illumination—a new light on a much-discussed topic.

And, from another sample, we found that while markers don't actually hate "B+" or "A−" papers, there are things about them which they certainly don't like:

> Contradictions. Uneven development. A lack of a conclusion, or a conclusion which doesn't assert any implications of the discussion. Off-topic writing.

What do the markers' comments tell you? How ideas are handled is important. When such handling is seen to be deficient, papers seem doomed to a maximum of "A−". In contrast, "A" papers are ordinarily free of flaws such as contradictions or uneven development. Although few "A" papers are deemed by their markers to be "excellent," all that we looked at had been commended as being "well developed."

Sometimes, defects in the construction of "A" papers—spelling, footnoting, sentence or paragraph construction—are compensated for by virtuosity in other areas: research, originality, or insight. Sometimes the defects are overlooked and require no such compensation. "A" papers are not structurally perfect, nor,

according to their markers, are they required to be. "A" papers
are just as likely as "B's" to contain awkward sentences or
redundancies.

By remembering what separates "A" from "B" work in the final
analysis—how ideas are handled—one gets a clue about how
priorities should be placed in writing. For instance, when making
a choice of theses to write on, always choose one which is challenging
enough for both you and your marker. A simple thesis may be easier
to research and prove, but, on the other hand, it may be difficult
to say anything new about it. And further, don't overlook the
importance of developing complexity and sophistication in your
work! When drafting and revising, especially when time is limited,
remember to pay the most attention to the development of <u>content</u>,
rather than to perfecting any points of <u>form</u> in your paper. By
considering what markers praise and what they pan, one can move
closer to performing a "B" to "A" leap with precision.

<u>And Now, Back to the Beginning: The Thesis Statement</u>. A thesis
is the most crucial part of your paper—without it, you have no
position to argue from. And, without it, your reader can
misinterpret your work. Keeping in mind what you've learned of your
rhetorical context and of what markers look for, your thesis should
be sophisticated and complex. To this list, we would now add
"understandable." We didn't find any examples where obscurity was
praised in the statement of a thesis.

In an English essay "understandable" does not mean "undeveloped"
or "artless". So, despite what you may have considered to be a general
rule, if you make a habit of focusing your subject by putting your
whole argument into one sentence, you may be causing yourself
problems. If that sentence is not long enough to show the "art" and
"development" of your ideas, you're probably limiting your reader's
expectations of the whole paper. In fact, an "A" paper may not have
a thesis sentence at all. If it does, the sentence is usually long
and complicated. Here is a particularly long thesis sentence from
our sample:

> Fantasy is a genre through which authors commonly write about
> changes children undergo, but the ways in which they use
> fantasy and fantastic elements vary as widely as the changes
> they describe: in The Princess and the Goblin George Macdonald
> describes a very specific stage one girl goes through as she
> gains a strong sense of personal identity and as she develops
> a private life, all of which she does with the aid of a very
> private fantasy; in Charlotte's Web, E.B. White deals more
> generally with the concept of change as it relates to a child's

changing needs, and the truly fantastic elements in this story
are to be found in the wonders of the world and the magic of
nature--in those "realities" which are accessible to
everyone. [130 words.]

If you do not have a thesis sentence, then your thesis must be
stated in some other way. About half of the papers we looked at
followed a tacit method of development in which their theses were
developed over the course of one or several paragraphs. For an
example, consider the development of one thesis in its extended
introduction:

> Modern industrialized society is at war with the individual.
> . . . One's own personal context in fact creates, and is
> inextricable from [the peculiar insights, ideas or range of
> possibilities one perceives.] Thus, one cannot passively
> receive profound knowledge because one is actively involved
> in creating the profound potential. . . . The society that
> is at war with the individual is inherently at war also with
> the profound. . . . Art has the potential for profundity when
> it does not try to be exhaustive or conclusive, but rather
> attempts to open up possibilities. . . . Thus, a film might
> undermine the societal forces that would deny us the capacity
> to think profoundly, for ourselves. [These excerpts were taken
> from the first four pages of an eight page paper.]

So, a thesis sentence is a thesis statement but a thesis statement
is not always a thesis sentence. What else is a thesis? A good thesis
does not partition, or set up the framework, for the ensuing
discussion. None of the "A" papers we looked at had partitions
associated with their theses. So, a "proceed with caution" for
English students. Keep your thesis and partitioning statements
separate. And, avoid a common partitioning pitfall: do not make a
list part of your thesis. A "list", rightly or wrongly can lead a
reader to expect that the discussion to follow will proceed in a
rather unsophisticated manner. Such lists are underlined in the
following:

> [Phyllis Webb's] is a poetics of motion; its jumps occur
> intellectually, symbolically, temporally, emotionally.

> The phenomena suggested by the terms "public" and "private"
> embrace much of the entire contents of culture, society,
> personality and social character.

If you notice a "list" in your thesis statement, it may be a sign for you to spend more time sorting out your ideas. Although a thesis with a list may be understandable, the ideas it contains may not be complex or sophisticated enough to merit an "A".

An English term paper can be an immense assignment. However, if you understand what to write and how to write it, it may not seem quite so ominous. Consider who you are writing for and why you are writing. Spend enough time on your thesis to make it complex yet understandable. Above all, keep thinking. As you will see in the next section, "thinking" is what "A" students give the most credit to in developing their best ideas.

Beyond the Beginning: An Interview on the Process of Writing. Our manual has up to now focused on the final product. To satisfy the curiosity you may have developed about how "A" paper writers actually "do it", we'll give the last word to those "A" writers we had a chance to meet with:

When do you begin working on your paper?

I begin working and generating ideas as soon as possible. It isn't easy to get started or to get the ideas flowing but the best thing to do is to write things down. Start thinking on paper. Usually I have a general idea of what my thesis will be before I start—what I want to say, what to prove. Pre-writing, getting my first thoughts down on paper is generally an efficient way to form ideas.

How do you arrive at a thesis?

I think out several before choosing one. It's difficult to get an original idea, I just have to keep thinking. I don't like to start into my paper until I feel I can approach the material with some new insight or angle. Sometimes, my choice of thesis is affected by the demands, or what I know to be the expectations, of the course or instructor. I try to keep my ideas focused and verifiable according to my sources.

How do you do research for an English paper?

Mostly, I use the text to generate and support my ideas. I sometimes use secondary sources if the topic demands it, if an idea needs more support, or if I'm stuck for an angle. Although I used to write almost exclusively from the primary text, I find that now I refer to the critics more. Sometimes I use information that I've picked up in other courses such as Psychology, Philosophy, or Communications. I don't like to go to the critics unless my thesis is secure— otherwise my reading tends to be unfocused and time-wasting.

What do you do with your first draft?

I try to leave it for at least couple of days so I can look back at it objectively. If I can, I get someone else to read it. After that I may save most of it or completely change the whole thing. Usually it's something in between, although lately, with my style and approach becoming more formal, I find my early drafts more closely resemble my finished ones. My marks are better now too, but it really isn't any easier to write my papers.

How do you revise?

Ruthlessly. I slash whatever doesn't immediately fit, and it's usually gone forever. I'm not afraid to change things around. I ask myself, on every point, "Why am I saying this?" "Where is it leading me?" "What is the purpose of this?" Sometimes, when I'm revising I use negative invention: by considering how my ideas might be disproved I can see where to strengthen my arguments or where I might develop another point. The closer I get to the finished form, the more I prefer to do my revisions in ink, even if I use a word processor. The word processor is great for early, major revisions. I save my marked essays and generally keep the marker's comments in mind when I write my next paper. For me, the hardest draft to write is the final one because that's the one you have to hand in.

Robyn Fox and Leanne Woolsey

Research

Research is a discovery process. To research is to search for information that can help you solve the intellectual problem you are investigating and help you convince readers to accept your solution.

Research often begins with a review of previous analyses and explanations of the same or similar problems. Reviewing this material not only helps you avoid reinventing the wheel, it also helps you formulate your research questions precisely and usefully. Then research becomes a search for information that will help you answer those questions. Once you have found your answers, research can help you discover evidence and arguments to validate your explanation.

There are two types of research, primary and secondary. If you do an experiment, that is primary research. If you interview a person you will be writing about, that is primary research. If you read and reread a literary text to find details which support an interpretation, that is primary research. In short, whenever you yourself investigate a subject directly, you are doing primary research.

When you consult the reports and analyses of other investigators, you are doing secondary research. If you read a report about an experiment someone else did, that is secondary research. If you read someone else's interpretation of a literary text, that is secondary research. If you consult a computerized database, that is secondary research. When university professors ask for "a research paper," they are usually asking for one based on secondary research.

In what is sometimes called an "opinion" paper, you support your conclusions with your own observations (i.e., primary research, however informal) and with general knowledge (i.e., information and theories that you may presume your readers share). In a typical research paper, you put your opinion in the context of prior discussion and you support your conclusions with secondary research, (i.e., with information reported by other investigators and with the critical judgments of experts). The paper is built around your own thesis statement, but you use secondary research findings to support for that thesis.

Logically, research findings are subordinate to the critical thinking process they serve. Research findings are meaningless unless somebody generalizes and interprets them, thereby building a theory, answering a question or solving a problem. However you get your information, when you analyze it, evaluate it, and draw conclusions from it, you are doing critical thinking.

Within a corporate or government bureaucracy, or even an academic research team, however, there may be a division of labor. One person or group may be assigned to collect and summarize relevant information in a research report; and then another person or group may analyze, evaluate, and draw conclusions. Because this division of labor is common, students are sometimes asked to practice writing *research reports*, which simply present and summarize findings without drawing further implications. It is important to remember that such a research report is only one intermediate step in the problem-solving process. Ultimately, a research report is significant only when someone uses it to develop theoretical explanations, define implications, or make recommendations or decisions.

The "Results" section of a scientific article is, in effect, a research report. It presents and summarizes research findings, thus answering *what*? or *how*? But ultimately we want to know *why*? And perhaps even *so what*? So a scientific article usually ends with a "Discussion" section, which attempts to explain, evaluate, and draw implications.

An academic paper may also synthesize research findings from a number of investigations and suggest a single, consistent interpretation. Or it may juxtapose a number of interpretations and suggest one general theory that encompasses them all.

One reader may, for example, point out that snow (frozen water) is a symbol of spiritual paralysis in James Joyce's "The Dead." Other readers may find other symbols. To interpret the story, however, a literary critic must show how the symbols cluster—how snow is associated with darkness and fire with light—and then, by weight of evidence, show that the many clusters can be explained by a theme that contrasts paralysis (spiritual death) with motion (resurrection). Then this interpretation can be linked with interpretations of other stories in the collection, and with various sorts of contexts, to reach a more general theory of the meaning of Joyce's *Dubliners*. Only then do we understand why the recurrent symbol patterns exist in that text.

In practice, critical analysis and explanation often come after the research, to make sense of the findings (and suggest promising directions for further research). But an "opinion" paper can become a critical research paper if its empirical assumptions are researched and its interpretations supported with expert testimony—if one asks "How do I know this is true?" and "How does my opinion fit with what others have said, especially recognized authorities on the subject?" What matters is the logical relationship between information and explanation, between your opinion and the ongoing discussion.

Research Questions

Students often consider research papers onerous assignments—necessary (or perhaps unnecessary) evils involving a lot of drudgery, such as note cards, precisely formatted footnotes, bibliographies, and so forth. But research is not meaningless to someone who needs the information. Research is not meaningless to the lawyer who later uses it to get a client acquitted. Research is not meaningless to the television journalist who later uses it to expose the lies being told by a politician. Research is not meaningless to the scholar who later uses it as evidence to resolve a critical issue or to reach the definitive interpretation of a text. Research is not meaningless to the teacher who later uses it to teach more successfully. Research is not meaningless to the scientist who later builds an explanatory theory from it.

Perhaps you notice in the novels of George Eliot a recurring symbol that you think has never been analyzed. Through research you can make sure your discovery is original and also define its significance in relation to the main themes of the novels. Perhaps you believe that human behavior is primarily the result of socialization, and you arguing with a sociobiologist who says human nature is genetically determined. Through research you can find evidence and arguments to support your opinion. Perhaps a political theory tells you that all wars are based on economic conflicts, but your newspaper tells you about a war being fought over religious differences. To resolve this contradiction, you must reinterpret the particular instance or modify the theory. Research can provide facts about the particular instance and help you be sure you understand the theory correctly.

Research answers empirical questions, such as the following:

What percentage of paragraphs in published modern prose begin with topic sentences?

How do experienced writers work?

How has the symbolism of the lighthouse in Virginia Woolf's *To the Lighthouse* been interpreted by critical authorities?

Is there any historical connection between the word *niggardly* and the racial epithet *nigger*? Between *Gypsy* and *gyp*? Between *Welsh* and *welsh*?

Is there any correlation between diet and juvenile delinquency?

What happens to the divorce rate among contemporary North American married couples as the husband's earnings increase? As the wife's earnings increase?

What is the correlation between scores on scholastic aptitude tests and school grades? Between test scores and fathers' occupational status?

What is the correlation between the state of the economy and the length of fashionable women's skirts?

What at present is the authoritative explanation among geophysicists for the aurora borealis?

Each of these questions can, in principle, be answered by empirical investigation.

Depending on the nature of the question, the research may have to be conducted in the library, the laboratory, or the world. It may be very difficult and expensive to discover the required information. In the case of an historical question, like the relationship between *Welsh* and *welsh*, the information needed to provide an empirical answer may be irretrievably lost. And pure research generally demonstrates only correlations, not causal relationships (see pages 350–51). Nonetheless, all of the above are *research questions*, and every reasonable attempt should be made to answer them empirically rather than speculatively.

There are two other types of questions that, in principle, cannot be answered by research alone. The first type tends to go beyond correlation and to inquire about causal and meaningful relationships. For example:

Does the way experienced writers work explain the relatively high quality of their writing?

Did contemporary male critics correctly interpret the symbolism of the lighthouse in Virginia Woolf's *To the Lighthouse*?

Are dietary inadequacies among the factors that contribute to juvenile delinquency?

To what extent do economic factors affect the stability of contemporary North American marriages? the fashionable length of women's skirts?

Although research findings can provide an informed basis for answering such questions, the answers depend on interpretation and critical judgment. That is why Aristotle said that the answers to such questions are never definite, but only probable. Even physical explanations, such as the causes of the aurora borealis, sometimes change when scientists reinterpret old research results in the light of new theories.

The second type of question that cannot be answered by research alone is ethical (or aesthetic). These questions have to do with relationships among means and ends, with effects (and affects). They are characterized by the word *should* and value-laden terms like "fair" or "great."

Should writers begin paragraphs with topic sentences?

Is *To the Lighthouse* a great work of literature?

Should we stop using *gyp*? If so, should we substitute *cheat*?

Should we restrict juvenile delinquents to two quarts of milk per day?

To what extent should married couples be discouraged from separating?

Is it fair to use scholastic aptitude test scores when determining university admissions?

If the aurora borealis becomes endangered by pollution, what is the maximum amount of money that ought to be spent to protect it?

At best, research can provide information about the effectiveness of means; it cannot, by itself, be the basis for choosing ends. Research cannot guarantee you a valid interpretation of *To the Lighthouse*, let alone a judgment as to its greatness. What research can do, however, is provide an informed basis for interpretations, judgments, and decisions.

Writing a Research Paper

There is a standard procedure for writing research papers. It is modeled after processes developed by scholars for major library-research projects, such as theses and dissertations, scientific and scholarly books. The research papers students write to practice this standard procedure are much shorter; the procedure, therefore, seems artificial and students are often tempted to take shortcuts. But one of the points of an undergraduate research paper, especially in a writing course, is to master the procedure. If one remembers both the educational purposes for writing research papers and the academic models on which they are based, then the standard procedure should make some sense.

1. Finding a Topic. Finding a topic for a research paper is much like discovering a topic for any writing. In the real world, a piece of writing often begins because a question has presented itself and you lack the information to answer it reliably. For the student, however, the topic more often has to be discovered. Since a research paper is often a somewhat lengthy project involving considerable drudgery, you should find a topic that will sustain your interest, either because you find it intrinsically interesting or because it is a matter of some importance. It should also be do-able with the time and resources available to you.

You could start with a critical problem, with a contradiction that has come to your attention during the course for which you are writing the paper. Perhaps there is a question that arose in a class discussion but was never answered. Perhaps an interpretation was put forth with which you disagree. Perhaps two or more assertions were made which seem to contradict each other. Perhaps a few particulars seem to contradict a general theory. Any such contradiction could be a starting point for a research paper. The advantage of starting with such a critical problem is that your research efforts are clearly focused right from the beginning.

Another good starting point could be an opinion. Opinions usually have a basis in beliefs about reality. Finding out if those beliefs are true and if you can prove them might make a good and interesting research project. Imagine that you have written an opinion paper about marriage (or that you will draft one as a starting point for this research project). Perhaps you attempted to persuade readers that the structure of the traditional Western marriage is superior to any of the alternatives that have been tried. In asserting that opinion, you have inevitably made a number of empirical assumptions, probably based on your own experiences and observations. Investigating, if necessary correcting, and proving those assumptions could produce a good, critical research paper. All you have to do is go through your ''opinion'' paper, stop at each factual statement or implicit assumption, and ask, ''How do I know this is true? How can I prove it? What do the recognized authorities say?'' That might lead to a list of questions like these.

> Is the traditional Western marriage really like my image of it?
>
> Am I really aware of all the alternatives that have been tried? How did they work out?
>
> What are the social functions of marriage in modern Western societies? What is marriage expected to do for the individuals involved?
>
> What alternatives are possible within the structure of modern Western societies? How well would they fulfill the social and personal functions of marriage?

Go to the library, find the answers to the questions you have discovered, insert them at appropriate places in your paper, revise as necessary, add footnotes and bibliography—and you have turned an "opinion" paper into a research paper.

If neither of these methods produces a topic, choose some rather general area and do some introductory reading. Go to the library, find some materials related to the area you picked, and read until you discover a more focused topic that interests you. There is no need to take notes during such introductory reading. Just read quickly and broadly, getting a general background for your paper and watching for a critical problem or researchable question. Since what you want at this stage is an overview, useful sources might include (1) review articles that summarize major books and articles on the topic, (2) a general textbook that includes some discussion of the topic, (3) a good encyclopedia, and (4) the *Book Review Digest*.

Whichever method you use, you want to focus your topic as soon as possible. Not too soon, because you usually need to have some background in order to focus on a good research topic, and you do not want to be stuck with a dull topic or one which is excessively difficult to research. But not too late, because research can be a time-consuming process, and you want to focus soon enough to leave yourself plenty of time for the rest of the project.

In order to use your time efficiently, you also want to distinguish between *preliminary research*, which locates information resources and helps define the research problem, and more focused later research, which selects and organizes information to help solve the problem. Preliminary research involves a lot of quick general reading, skimming and scanning; you take notes only to help yourself remember where certain types of information can be found. Once the problem is defined and the research focused, you should read more carefully and take more thorough notes.

You also want to make sure that the topic you choose can be researched. Are the empirical questions substantial enough? Will the information you need be available when you need it? Does your university library have enough material on the topic, or will you have to resort to interlibrary loans?

2. Finding Information.   If you do not know your way around a library very well, you will probably head straight for the card catalog. Inexperienced university students turn to the card catalog as automatically as high school students turn to the encyclopedia. The card catalog is useful; it will lead you to books on your topic. But much of the information you want will probably be located in journal articles, and those are not listed in the card catalog. You can, moreover, often get a better overview by reviewing ten or fifteen articles than by reading the same number of pages in a single book.

Ask a librarian. Most university libraries have research librarians with graduate degrees in library science. They are experts on finding information in libraries, and one of their functions is to help people find information. They know how to find and consult computer databases as well as books and periodicals. If you know, even roughly, what you are looking for, a research librarian may save you a lot of time.

More and more university libraries also offer guided tours. Such tours are devoted primarily to telling people how to find information in the library. You may have been bored by such an orientation tour at some time when you did not have a research project to do. But you may well want to take one now if it is available.

If you are new at library research, perhaps the most important advice is to look at indexes and bibliographies as well as at the card catalog. You may be familiar with *The Readers' Guide to Periodical Literature*, which lists articles published in over a hundred U.S. magazines since 1900. This is an index of *popular* magazines, however; much of what it lists will not be considered sufficiently reliable for the sort of research done at the university level. The *Social Sciences and Humanities Index* lists more scholarly sources. The *Essay and General Literature Index* is a good place to look for articles that were published in collections rather than in journals. There are also restricted indexes on such subjects as agriculture, art, education, industrial arts, and Catholic publications. Both the *New York Times* and the *London Times* publish annual indexes.

Bibliographies are lists of books and articles on given subjects. Some bibliographies cover rather broad fields. Many of them are published annually by major scholarly journals or professional organizations. Your main problem is to find the bibliography or bibliographies that will cover your topic. In some fields, especially the sciences, bibliographies have been computerized, and you can do a computer search on your topic. Ask a librarian how.

There are also works like *A World Bibliography of Bibliographies*. Your best bet, however, would be to ask a research librarian or a professor who specializes in the field. Any active scholar or scientist should be aware of the standard bibliographies in her or his field.

For English literary studies, for example, the standard bibliography is published annually by the Modern Language Association. There are also journals that publish annual bibliographies for particular literary periods and for the literatures of various countries or regions. If you were looking for critical articles about some works of English literature, these would be the bibliographies in which to look.

In addition to indexes and bibliographies, you can sometimes find listings like *Psychological Abstracts* and *Abstracts of English Studies*. Like bibliographies, these give the title, author, and facts of publication for articles on certain general topics. As their titles imply, moreover, they also include abstracts, that is, very brief summaries of each article. By reading the abstracts, you can save yourself the trouble of having to check articles which, judging by title alone, you might have thought relevant to your research. Two other important resources, which many researchers overlook, are the *Book Review Digest* and *Dissertation Abstracts*.

Computerized databases may contain the same material as bibliographies and abstracts, but they often include other information as well, such as statistical information collected by government agencies. In some cases, they contain otherwise unpublished research, as does *Educational Resources Information Clearinghouse* (ERIC).

The card catalog, indexes, bibliographies, abstracts, computerized databases, and other reference works should provide enough sources for you to begin your research. You will ordinarily discover other sources as you work: the books and articles you read will refer to others (either in the texts themselves, in footnotes, or possibly in selected bibliographies). Eliminating the less important references may become more of a problem than finding enough information to answer your research questions.

Each time you find a potentially useful reference, copy it onto a bibliography card—or enter it into your computer. A bibliography card is usually 3" x 5" or 4" x 6". Whether you use cards or a computer, you should copy all the information you might need later for your footnotes or bibliography: full name(s) of the author(s), full title, and the facts of publication (e.g., for a book, publisher, date, and place of publication). Add whatever information you may need to locate the reference, usually a library call number. You may also wish to write yourself a brief note indicating what can be found in this source. Some researchers also code their bibliography entries for reasons which will be discussed below.

If you are using cards, put only one reference on each card. What you are assembling is a *working bibliography*. As you work with it, you will be discarding items that turn out not to contain useful information. You will be adding new items as you find them. And you will want to keep the bibliography alphabetized. If the bibliography is on cards, with only one item to a card, it will be easy to add and discard items while maintaining alphabetical order. If

Figure 10.1 Bibliography card.

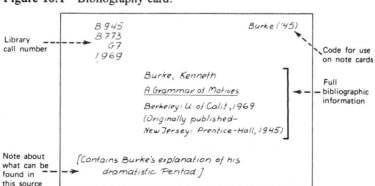

the bibliography is in your computer, it will be relatively easy to add and discard items and to keep or create alphabetical order. But if you try to keep the bibliography in a notebook, it will get very messy and may need to be recopied several times.

3. Collecting Information. After you have done your background reading and found at least the beginnings of your working bibliography, you usually begin a period of intensive reading. At this point you have enough sense of what information you are seeking that you can start taking notes.

Your intensive reading should be critical reading. You are now collecting the evidence on which your paper will be based. You want that evidence to be valid. Beware of unsupported or sweeping generalizations. Watch out for statistics that are slanted or that leave out relevant information (e.g., "50% of all voters surveyed" sounds impressive, but what if only twenty voters were surveyed?) Take note of any conflicting assertions, whether within one source or among several sources. Be sensitive to apparent biases.

You will be collecting information as you happen to discover it. Later, you will want to reorder that information to reflect your understanding of the subject and to support your thesis. Therefore, whether you use a photocopier or write notes on cards (usually 4″ x 6″ or 5″ x 7″), you want to end up with each bit of information on a separate card or piece of paper. Otherwise reordering as you organize becomes chaotic. (You could also take notes directly on a word processor, but you will waste a lot of paper printing each note on a separate sheet of paper.)

The first thing to put on each note card is a code for the exact source of the information. Typically, that might be the author's last name and the year of publication. The rest of what you will need is already on the bibliography card, which you can easily locate because it is filed alphabetically by the author's last name. If the author's name is inordinately long or if you are using several sources written by the same author, you may wish to invent a code. You might, for example, refer to Edward Corbett's *Classical Rhetoric for the Modern Student* as "Cor(65)"—the first three letters of the author's name plus the last two numbers of the year of publication. If you do invent such a code, be sure to copy it on the bibliography card.

The second thing to put on each note card is the information you are noting. This may be an exact quotation (in which case be sure to put it in quotation marks). Or it may be a paraphrase, the author's information rephrased in your words. Either way it will have to be footnoted or referenced, but you will need to distinguish exact quotations from paraphrases when you are writing your paper. Under the quote or paraphrase write the page number(s) you will need for your footnote or reference.

If the quotation or paraphrase is very long, you may also wish to title it with a short phrase that will allow you later to identify its content at a glance.

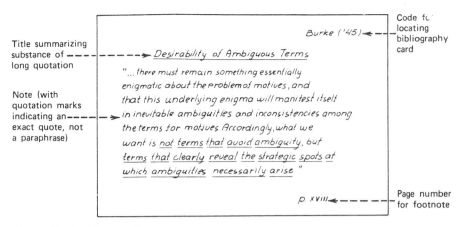

Figure 10.2. Note card.

4. Organizing Your Information. Having collected a mass of information in whatever order you happened to find it, you now must rearrange it into a meaningful pattern. This is done by sorting the note cards into smaller piles which constitute subtopics and may become sections of your paper.

If you have a pretty good idea of what you are going to say, the sorting is relatively easy. If you can write out a tentative thesis statement and outline for your paper, you can sort the note cards into piles that correspond to the major divisions of your outline. You may even be able to subdivide each pile, perhaps even assigning each note card to a particular line on the outline. Or you may leave the subdividing until you are ready to draft that section of the paper.

On the other hand, you may not yet know what the main point of the paper will be or how it will be organized. In that case, you might try to sort the cards into piles without having any predetermined divisions in mind. Just look for related bits of information. The sorting process could well organize the paper for you.

Or it may be that you have a pretty clear sense of one section of the paper. For example, you may have decided that the paper will include (and probably will begin with) a chronological review of previous positions on the issue. If so, pull out the cards related to that one section. Go ahead and draft that section, hoping that the rest of the paper will become clearer as you work. If it does, you will be able to start on a second section of the paper. This is the system I most commonly use, and it works rather well. I sometimes feel a little guilty about not knowing how the parts will hang together until I have drafted most of the paper. But what I finally end up writing is often a lot better than what I would have thought I wanted to say if I had been forced to come up with a thesis statement and outline immediately after collecting all my information. It is how you interrelate your information that makes or breaks a research paper.

5. Supplementing Your Information.   As you organize, you will often realize that you do not have all the information you need. When you sort your note cards, for example, you may realize that you have very little supporting evidence for one of the points you wish to make. Or you may realize that, to be complete, the paper will need to include a whole section you had not originally planned. Fortunately, you have been managing your time efficiently (of course!). So you still have time to go back to the library to collect this additional information.

Supplementary research of this sort does not take much time. It is usually directed by very specific questions. You know what information you need and can go straight to it. Nonetheless, it is hard to do while the library is closed the night before the paper is due. It is even hard to do the day before the paper is due if a book you need happens to be checked out. So it is important to work well ahead of your deadline.

6. Drafting the Paper.   You draft a research paper pretty much the way you draft any other paper. Some people work from memory, write out their own interpretations and opinions, and then insert supporting evidence from their note cards. Other people work from the note cards, building their own assertions from the evidence. Which way you work does not much matter, so long as the evidence, interpretations, and opinions all come together in the end.

It is important to work quotations and other evidence into the paper smoothly. In part, this depends on the skillful use of transition words and phrases. In part, it is a matter of making good stylistic choices about when to use direct quotations, indirect quotations, and paraphrases. Short quotations should be indirect, i.e., woven into your own sentences in such a way that nothing more than the quotation marks interrupts the flow of the writing. If a quotation does not fit smoothly, try paraphrasing all or part of it.

In certain fields there are standard formats for research papers. Those formats make it easier for readers to anticipate and absorb information. If such a format is available, you should usually use it. It will help you to organize and draft the paper, and it will help readers to understand it. Even when there is no standard format, it remains your responsibility to frame and integrate your information into a meaningful and readable whole. A research paper is not a list of findings; it is the coherent communication of a meaningful pattern of information. Readers must be able to perceive structure.

7. Documenting Your Evidence.   Most people's least favorite part of writing a research paper is adding the notes and references. Even as a typing chore, it can be painful. The details of doing it properly can also get quite complicated. Fortunately, sophisticated word processors, perhaps supplemented by special bibliographic software, can now take over much of the drudgery.

To help preserve your sanity, remember the purpose of documentation. In writing a research paper you have used a great deal of evidence for which you cannot personally vouch. By the time it appears in your paper, this is secondhand information (or even further removed from the original source). Your readers have a right to know where it came from. They may wish to go back to the original source in order to verify your accuracy or to evaluate the information in its original context. You should also give credit where credit is due: if you took an idea or phrase from someone else's work that person deserves credit.

A real research paper (as opposed to one done primarily as a school exercise) is usually part of a larger, ongoing search for knowledge. It is important that readers, who may be participating in the continuation of that search, be able to go to your sources. Otherwise they will work from your secondhand evidence, which will be thirdhand by the time it appears in their writings. As other people work from their papers, it will become fourthhand, fifthhand, and so forth. An inquiry which gets further and further from its firsthand evidence is more and more likely to make errors. Thus documentation is important because it allows readers the option of verifying and reevaluating your evidence, it gives credit where credit is due, and it helps keep other researchers in touch with the original sources.

The format of documentation can get confusing. That is in part because it varies considerably from discipline to discipline. What varies, however, is only the arrangement of information. The information itself is determined by the purposes documentation serves. Readers need enough information so that they can readily find and refer to your sources. Essentially that means they need *author, title, and facts of publication.*

Giving the full names of all authors and full titles allows readers to identify your sources precisely. Giving the facts of publication allows readers to locate the volume in which the information appears. And, of course, for each citation, you must indicate the page(s) on which the particular information or quotation can be located. Your readers do not want to look through the entire volume.

The facts of publication for a book include the date and place of publication and, in almost all systems, also the name of the publisher. You should also indicate which edition you used (if you did not use the first) and the names of any translators or editors. If you are referring to an article, the facts of publication include the name of the periodical, the volume number, and the issue number and/or date.

Depending on which system is used in your discipline, you may have to give some or all of this information twice. Generally, it appears in a complete form at the end of the paper as a *list of references*, list of *works cited*, or *bibliography*. In some fields, this *may* be optional if you are using a footnote system that already contains complete bibliographic information.

Some or all of the same information also appears as a footnote each time you make a references. The term *footnote* came into being because the citation was a *note* at the *foot* of the page. Nowadays, the note may be found at the foot of the page, at the end of the paper, or parenthetically in the text itself.

In most fields, the note is foreshortened. It appears in parentheses in the text, usually at the end of a clause, sentence or paragraph. It consists of a code, which allows readers to locate the item in the list of references. In the standard social science system, for instance, the parentheses contain an author's surname, the year of publication, and, if needed, the page number of the citation. Readers who want the rest of the bibliographic information turn to the back of the paper.

In more traditional systems, all the documenting information is supposed to appear in a note the first time each source is cited. This means that the bibliography is largely a duplication of information from the footnotes (slightly rearranged). In short papers, therefore, it is sometimes permissible to omit the bibliography. Some journals, in fact, are reluctant to publish bibliographies, but students are often required to include them, if only to practice the conventional format.

Since the format of documentation varies so considerably from field to field, you need to locate instructions for the particular discipline in which you are writing. Most journals indicate which style guide they wish contributors to follow. Course instructors will do likewise, especially if asked. These style guides should be available in your library or university bookstore. If not, they are available from the professional organizations. When you have chosen an academic or professional specialization, you should acquire your own copy of the appropriate style sheet. Keep it with your dictionary, handbook, and other reference works.

What is most important is that you include all the documenting information readers may need. To make things easy for your readers, you should also use the standard format. At first that may seem like drudgery, but in the long run a standard format facilitates effective communication. In this, as in all writing, a clear sense of purpose, audience, and occasion will enable you to make sense of what you are doing.

What follows is a short critical research paper on a specialized subject. The topic was chosen precisely because you probably know little or nothing about it: you most probably have not read Milton's *Samson Agonistes* and very likely have not read Aristotle's *Poetics* either. As you read the following paper, notice how it gives you the information you need about those two texts without going into a long summary of either. The writer is presuming that most readers are somewhat familiar with both, but is writing nonetheless in such a way that you can understand the paper even if you are not.

Notice also the fourth reference, which demonstrates the usual way of avoiding excessive repetition of what has been well established by previous research. The writer could have gone on for pages showing the parallels between *Samson Agonistes* and various classical Greek tragedies. Instead, one long note sends readers who might doubt those parallels to previous research that establishes them. The sixth reference similarly demonstrates the usual way of avoiding excessive summaries of previous research on the topic: refer readers to a published summary of that research.

Notice also the structure of the paper. The title and introductory paragraphs explain the critical problem. The last two sentences of the second paragraph state the writer's thesis and, by partition (see page 388), summarize the substance of the body of the paper. The body consists of five paragraphs that discuss the five critical elements mentioned in the partition sentence. The concluding paragraph restates the thesis more strongly, generalizes it with a comparison to another play, and suggests its implications.

Finally, notice that this is basically a critical paper. Most of the quotations and footnotes provide expert testimony in support of the writer's judgments. Although thoroughly researched, this paper is organized around the writer's thesis.

Is Samson Agonistes *a Tragedy?*

John Milton consciously imitated Classical Greek tragedy when he composed Samson Agonistes. Even without Milton's explicit introductory essay, Samson Agonistes clearly "agrees with classical theory and practice" in its plot and structure, in its use of the chorus, in the ways it limits the scope of the action and confines itself to a single place and day, and in making hubris (excessive pride) "the ultimate cause of the tragedy" (Epps). Equally apparent is the intent of Milton's closing lines,

> His servants he with new aquist
>
> Of true experience from this great event
>
> With peace and consolation hath dismist
>
> And calm of mind, all passion spent (ll. 1755–58),

to conform to Aristotle's definition of the purpose of tragedy as "through pity and fear effecting the proper purgation of these emotions" (34). The parallels with Aeschylus' Prometheus Bound and Sophocles' Oedipus at Colonus are clear, and the indebtedness to other Classical tragedies can be argued (Brewer 913, Baum 363, Bowra 114 ff., and Timberlake.) Since 1751, however, when Samuel Johnson charged in The Rambler that Samson Agonistes "must be allowed to want a middle since nothing passes between the first act and the last that either hastens or delays the death of Samson," there has been considerable debate about whether Samson Agonistes is essentially tragic (cf. Krouse 3–21 for a review of the relevant criticism).

Milton clearly modelled his drama on classical Greek tragedy. He clearly intended it to meet Aristotle's definition. He used the forms prescribed by classical theory and practice. Because of his Puritan religious beliefs, however, he articulated those forms in ways that undercut their tragic impact. Five critical elements in Milton's drama are qualitatively different from their equivalents in classical Greek tragedy: the hero's weakness, the reversal of fortune, the catastrophe, the clear causal relation of each event to the catastrophe, and the evocation of pity and fear.

According to Aristotle, the error or frailty that brings about the hero's downfall should be a weakness, not a vice (41). As Milton's drama opens, we see Samson fallen to the "lowest pitch of abject fortune" (1. 169), having been betrayed by Delila, captured and blinded by the Philistines. In an apparent parallel to the most common weakness of the heroes of Greek tragedy, Milton portrays Samson as having been "swoll'n with pride" (1. 532) prior to his downfall and now as on the brink of despair. In a Judeo–Christian context, however, pride and the despair that follows from it are serious sins; a true believer should know that the glory is God's and that whatever occurs is God's will. Thus Samson's misfortune is not "unmerited," as Aristotle would have it (41); it is a lack of "virtue" (1. 174) that casts him down, not fate, error or frailty. He himself realizes he was the "prime cause" (1. 234) of his own misfortune. From a Protestant point of view, he has taken the first step towards a restoration faith in God, but his full responsibility for his own misfortune is not compatible with the Greek conception.

Aristotle states, moreover, that the reversal of fortune in a tragedy "should be not bad to good, but . . . from good to bad" (47). True, at the beginning of Oedipus at Colonus, the hero is persecuted and miserable, and in the end he dies mystically illuminated, having achieved sainthood and transcended misery through death. Oedipus at Colonus is not only atypical, however, it also ends with an awareness of misery pending for Oedipus' family and city. Samson, by contrast, repents his sins, regains his faith, revenges himself on his enemies, and is reunited with God. Samson Agonistes presents a "steady psychological progression from despair through heroic conflict upwards to an exultation and the final assumption of beatitude" (Ellis–Fermor 32). Samson "becomes a knight of God, a saint, distinguished by his faith and obedience" (Wesley 208).

Samson's pulling down of the Philistine temple is catastrophic for the Philistines and their God, Dagon, but hardly for himself. True, Samson dies along with his enemies, but the blinded Samson has five times announced his preference to be dead (11. 548–550, 575–576, 590–598, 629–630, 1262–63). He has been "restored to harmony with God's will" (Whiting 216), and his act is the "vindication of Jehovah . . . over Dagon" (Tupper 377). Even his father admits there is little cause for lamentation (11. 1708–9).

Another objection to classifying Milton's drama as a tragedy has its roots in Johnson's charge that "the action does not precipitate the catastrophe" (cited by Woodhouse 460). Johnson's point, which does not lack supporters (cf., e.g., Knowlton and Tupper), is that Samson Agonistes lacks unity of action because the events of the play do not all function as causes or motives for the catastrophe, as they should according to classical theory. The scenes with Delila and the Philistine captain, Harapha, could be deleted without undercutting the main action of the play. The scene with Delila allows Samson to "demonstrate by Delila's powerlessness to reassert her sway the completeness of [his] repentance" (Woodhouse 453); it does not bring about that repentance or bring him closer to his revenge. The scene with Harapha likewise allows Samson to demonstrate his regeneration; it does not move him closer to either God or revenge.

The strongest objection to accepting *Samson Agonistes* as a tragedy is that Milton fails to meet Aristotle's central criterion, that the tragic incident and the play as whole should evoke pity and fear. As Bowra points out, "Samson's fault is stressed so strongly that we hardly pity him, and if we feel any fear it is for the Philistine" (128). Where Oedipus' misfortune was excessive and his death mysterious, Samson's misfortune is just and his death is happy. Samson sacrifices himself to expiate both his own sin and Israel's sins. Samson Agonistes is "concerned essentially with the fallen Samson's recovery of friendship with God" (Clare 33) and restoration to "harmony with God's will" (Whiting 216). There is no reason why this conclusion should evoke pity or fear.

Samson Agonistes falls into the same category of religious drama as T.S. Eliot's Murder in the Cathedral, which is also heavily indebted to Greek forms (Fell, 152). It is a religious drama that portrays a hero's passage through temptation. The hero avoids sin, rises above human frailty, and achieves union with God. The hero's death, like Christ's, is an expiatory sacrifice, an offering made for the salvation of his people. Whatever else this type of drama may be, it is not tragic—neither in the Greek, nor in any other sense. To read it as a tragedy is to miss its essence.

Works Cited

Aristotle. Poetics. Trans. S. H. Butcher. Rpt. The Great Critics, 3rd ed. Ed. J. H. Smith and E. W. Parks. New York: Norton, 1951. 25–61.

Baum, Paul F. "Samson Agonistes Again." PMLA 36 (1921): 201–16.

Brewer, William. "Two Athenian Models for Samson Agonistes." PMLA 42 (1927): 151–64.

Bowra, C. M. Inspiration and Poetry. Folcroft, PA: Folcroft, 1955.

Clare, Miriam. Samson Agonistes: A Study in Contrast. New York: Pageant, 1964.

Ellis-Fermor, Una Mary. The Frontiers of Drama. London: Methuen, 1945.

Epps, P. H. "Two Notes on English Classicism." Studies in Philology 13 (1916): 196.

Fell, K. "From Myth to Martyrdom: Towards a View of Samson Agonistes." English Studies 34 (1953): 145–55.

The Rambler 3.139 (July 16, 1751).

Knowlton, E. C. "Causality in Samson Agonistes." Modern Language Notes 37 (1922): 333–38.

Krouse, Michael F. Milton's Samson and the Christian Tradition. New Jersey: Princeton UP, 1949.

Timberlake, P. W. "Milton and Euripides." The Parrot Presentation Volume. New Jersey: Princeton UP, 1935.

Tupper, J. W. "The Dramatic Structure of Samson Agonistes." PMLA 35 (1920): 121–36.

Whiting, George Wesley. Milton and This Pendant World. Austin, TX: U of Texas P, 1958.

Woodhouse, A.S.P. "Tragic Effect in Samson Agonistes." Rpt. Milton: Modern Essays in Criticism. Ed. A. E. Barker. New York: Oxford, 1965. 447–66.

EXERCISE

1. Think of three topics for "opinion" papers on general subjects that interest you. A good way to discover such topics is to think of subjects you wish you knew more about. State each topic as a question. Write out a brief summary of your opinion. Then write a critical research paper by investigating and documenting all the empirical assumptions implicit in your opinion. To what extent did the research end up influencing your opinion or the arguments you used to support it?

2. Think of three topics for long critical papers (2000–10,000 words) dealing with intellectual problems in your area of special interest or specialization. Could you write these papers without doing research? To what extent could each involve a significant research component? What type of research might be involved? How much would it improve the quality and validity of the paper?

3. Obtain a professional style guide, preferably one you are likely to use. Examine it. Compare and contrast it with other style guides, perhaps those obtained by other members of your writing class or group. Try to suggest functional explanations for the requirements of your style guide.

4. List the most important standard bibliographic sources and databases in your field of special interest or specialization. Locate each in a library, and make sure you know how to use it.

5. Compile a *selected* and *annotated* bibliography on a topic of interest to you and of use to others. "Selected" means you should list only those sources you consider most useful. "Annotated" means you should write one or several sentences telling what can be found in each source. Distribute this bibliography to some people who might find it useful.

Index

Correction Symbols ──────────────────────

Ab	Incorrect or inappropriate abbreviation	*Fn*	Inappropriate footnote form
agr	Faulty agreement, either between subject and verb or between pronoun and antecedent	*Format*	Inappropriate format
		Frag	Nonfunctional sentence fragment
Amb	Ambiguous; can be read more than one way	*Gr*	Grammatical error
apos	Misuse or absence of apostrophe	*Id*	Faulty idiom
		Ital	Italics (underlining) needed or misused
awk	Hard to read because awkwardly constructed	*lc*	Use lower case letters
Bib	Inappropriate bibliographical form	*Log*	Faulty logic
		num	Error in use or form of numbers
Cap	Error in capitalization	*¶*	Start new paragraph
Choppy	Choppy style caused by excessively short sentences or repetitive sentence structures	*no ¶*	Do not start new paragraph
		Pass	Ineffective use of passive voice
Coh	Passage hard to understand because it lacks transitions or other coherency cues	*Pn*	Punctuation error
		Q	Error in use or format of quotation
CS	Comma splice	*Red*	Excessive redundancy (substantive)
D	Inappropriate diction	*Ref*	Faulty pronoun reference
Dev	Inadequate development		
Det	Inadequate detail	*Rep*	Excessive repetition (of words or phrases)
DM	Dangling modifier	*R-O*	Run-on sentence
Emph	Inappropriate emphasis or lack of clear emphasis	*Source?*	Source of this concept or quotation should be indicated

Correction Symbols (cont.) _____

Sp	Misspelling
Tense	Error in verb tense
Shift	Inappropriate or inaccurate shift in verb tense
Title	Inadequate or ineffective title
Trans	Inadequate or faulty transition
Trite	Trite concept or word choice
Unity	Passage hard to understand because unity among concepts is not clear
Usage	Error in usage
Vague	Passage hard to understand because vague

Wo	Inappropriate or ineffective word order
Wordy	Excessive verbiage
WW	Word choice does not seem to reflect meaning
?	Reader cannot understand (perhaps because illegible)
//ism	Faulty parallelism
∽	Transpose (tr.)
#	Insert space
⌣	Delete space